The Coptic Chris

This book offers a comprehensive introduction to the heritage of Coptic Christians. The contributors combine academic expertise with intimate and practical knowledge of the Coptic Orthodox Church and Coptic heritage. The chapters explore historical, cultural, literary, and material aspects, including:

- the history of Christianity in Egypt, from the pre-Christian era to the modern day
- Coptic religious culture: theology, monasticism, spirituality, liturgy, and music
- the Coptic language, linguistic expressions of the Coptic heritage, and literary production in Greek, Coptic, and Arabic
- the material culture and artistic expression of the Copts: from icons, mosaics, and frescos to manuscript illuminations, woodwork, and textiles.

Students will find *The Coptic Christian Heritage* an invaluable introduction, while scholars will find its breadth provides a helpful context for specialized research.

Lois M. Farag is Associate Professor of Early Church History at Luther Seminary in St. Paul, Minnesota, USA. Her books include *St. Cyril of Alexandria, A New Testament Exegete* (Gorgias Press, 2007) and *Balance of the Heart: Desert Spirituality for Twenty-First-Century Christians* (Cascade Books, 2012).

The Coptic Christian Heritage

History, Faith, and Culture

Edited by
Lois M. Farag

Routledge
Taylor & Francis Group
LONDON AND NEW YORK

First published in 2014
by Routledge
2 Park Square, Milton Park, Abingdon, Oxon OX14 4RN

and by Routledge
711 Third Avenue, New York, NY 10017

Routledge is an imprint of the Taylor & Francis Group, an informa business

British Library Cataloguing in Publication Data
A catalogue record for this book is available from the British Library

Library of Congress Cataloging in Publication Data
The Coptic Christian heritage : history, faith, and culture / edited by
Lois M. Farag.
pages cm
Includes index.
1. Coptic Church--History. I. Farag, Lois M., editor of compilation.
BX133.3.C67 2013
281'.72--dc23
2013015796

ISBN 978-0-415-78102-2 (hbk)
ISBN 978-0-415-78103-9 (pbk)
ISBN 978-1-315-88389-2 (ebk)

Typeset in Bembo
by Taylor & Francis Books

MIX
Paper from responsible sources
FSC® C013056

Printed and bound in Great Britain by
TJ International Ltd, Padstow, Cornwall

To the Coptic people
who created, developed, and preserved a heritage that survived against all odds,
and to a heritage that is an inspiration to many

Contents

Illustrations

Figures

Maps

Tables

Contributors

John Paul Abdelsayed is working towards a PhD in the History of Christianity from the University of Notre Dame.

Febe Armanios is Associate Professor of History at Middlebury College. Her research focuses on Coptic Christians in Ottoman and modern Egyptian history. Publications include *Coptic Christianity in Ottoman Egypt* (Oxford University Press, 2011).

Mariam F. Ayad is Associate Professor of Art History at the University of Memphis. She recently directed the Opening of the Mouth Epigraphic Project at the Tomb of Harwa in Luxor, Egypt. Publications include *God's Wife, God's Servant: The God's Wife of Amun* (Routledge, 2009).

Lois M. Farag is Associate Professor of Early Church History at Luther Seminary in St. Paul, Minnesota. Her books include *St. Cyril of Alexandria, A New Testament Exegete* (Gorgias Press, 2007) and *Balance of the Heart: Desert Spirituality for Twenty-First Century Christians* (Cascade Books, 2012).

Gawdat Gabra is Visiting Professor of Coptic Studies at Claremont Graduate University. He was the director of the Coptic Museum in Cairo (1985). He is the author of several books related to the literary and material culture of Christianity in Egypt, including *Coptic Monasteries: Egypt's Monastic Art and Architecture* and *Christian Egypt: Coptic Art and Monuments through Two Millennia* (both AUC Press, 2002).

Maged S. R. Hanna is Curator of the Coptic Orthodox Cultural Center, Coptic Orthodox Patriarchate, Abbassya, Cairo, Egypt.

Maged S. A. Mikhail is Associate Professor of History at California State University, Fullerton. His publications include *The Holy Workshop of Virtue: The Life of John the Little by Zacharias of Sakha* with Tim Vivian (Liturgical Press, 2010).

Samuel Moawad is a Coptologist based at the Institute for New Testament Textual Research at the University of Münster, Germany. Publications include *Untersuchungen zum Panegyrikos auf Makarios von Tkōou und zu seiner Überlieferung* (Sprachen und Kulturen des Christlichen Orients 18), Wiesbaden: Reichert, 2010.

Carolyn M. Ramzy is working towards a PhD in Ethnomusicology at the University of Toronto. She completed a pre-doctoral fellowship with the American Research Center in Egypt and has curated a Library of Congress web project on Coptic Music.

Saad Michael Saad is Chair of the Coptic Studies Council at Claremont Graduate University and Managing Editor of the *Claremont Coptic Encyclopedia*.

Hany N. Takla teaches Coptic language at the University of California, Los Angeles. He is President of the St. Shenouda the Archimandrite Coptic Society and Director of the St. Shenouda Center for Coptic Studies.

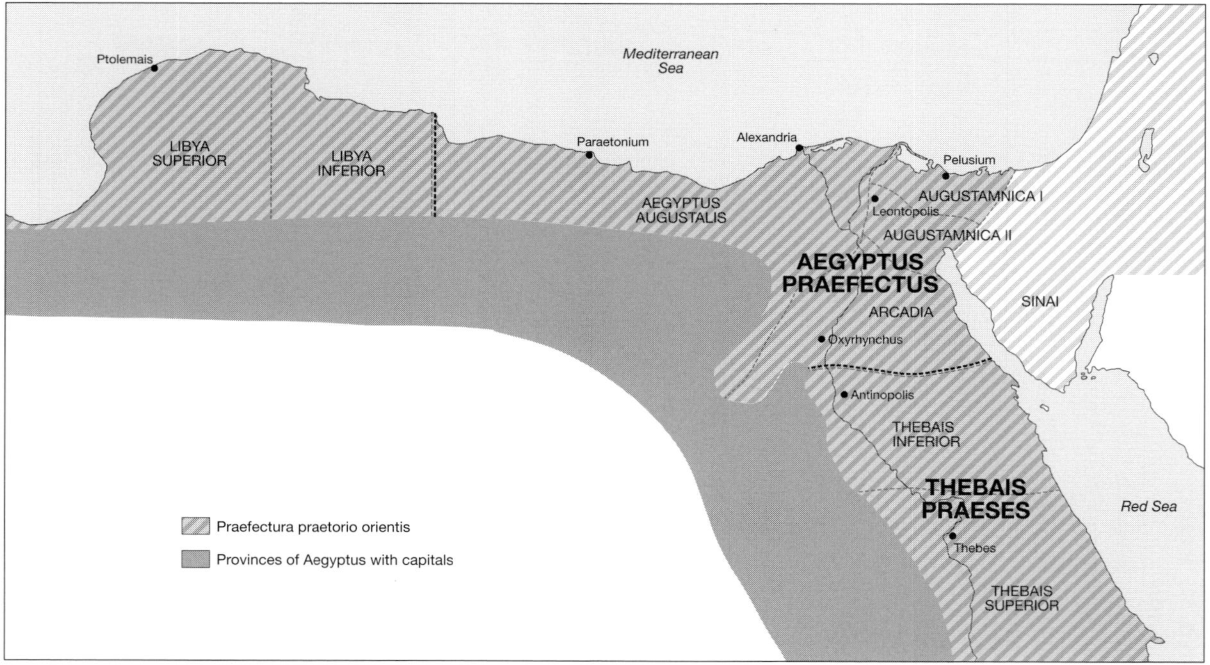

Map 1 The Roman Provinces of Fourth- and Sixth-Century Egypt

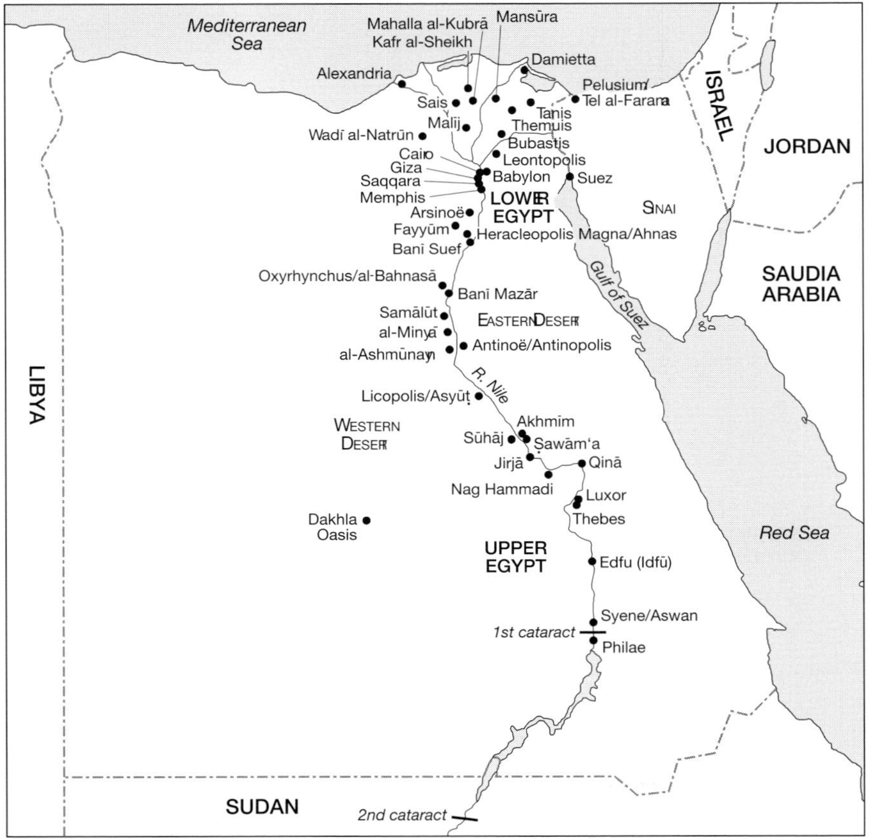

Map 2 General Map of Egypt

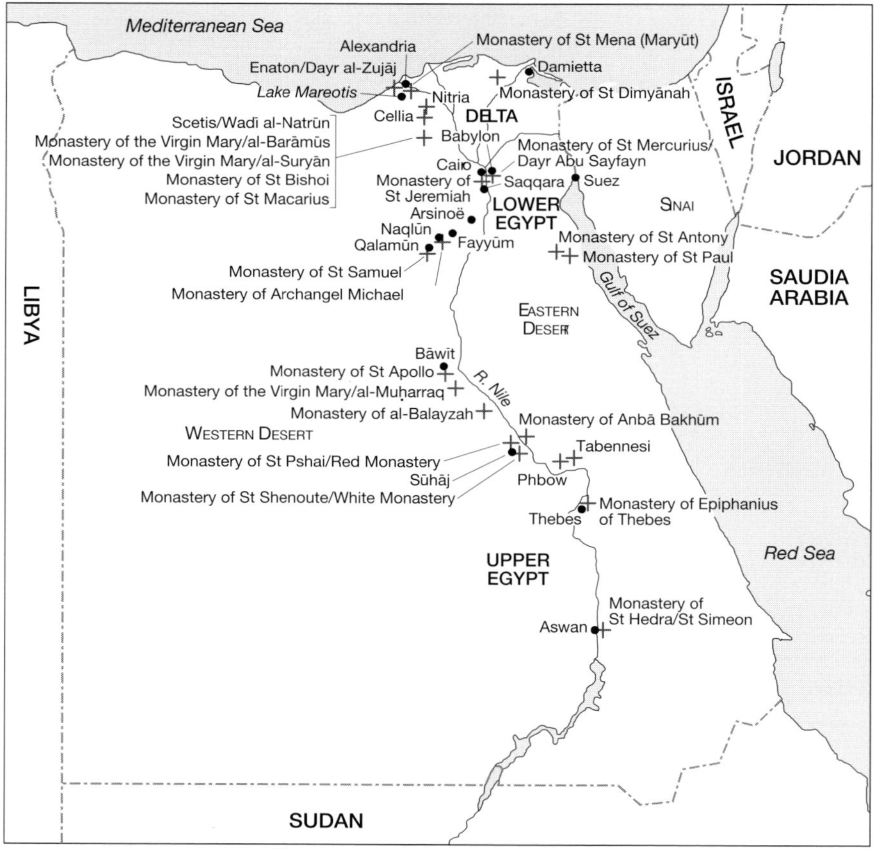

Map 3 Monastic Sites in Egypt

Introduction

Lois M. Farag

This book is the story of the Copts, the ancient dwellers of the Nile Valley, who accepted Christianity in the middle of the first century. It is an introduction to the story of 2,000 years of Christianity in Egypt. It is also the story of the Coptic Christian Heritage. This project began a few years ago and some of the contributors submitted their chapters before the political uprising of January 25, 2011. It was decided that the chapter on modern Egypt would not proceed beyond that date since events are still unfolding and history is still in the making even as this introduction is being written. The project is very timely, for it is important to introduce the heritage of the largest Christian community in the Middle East. The aim of the book is to introduce the reader to Christianity in Egypt in a comprehensive and systematic fashion. The goal is to provide a pedagogical tool for professors who would like to introduce the subject into their classrooms.

Before moving to a general overview of the book's organization and rationale, it is important to clarify the meaning of some frequently used terms: "Coptic," "the Coptic Orthodox Church," and the titles of the leader of the Coptic Church. The inhabitants of the Nile valley contemplated their landscape and observed the rich dark silt of the river covering their fields and called their country "Kēme," meaning "the black land," because of the silt's color. The Kēme people built the pyramids and the monumental heritage and culture that most children learn about at school. The Hebrew-speaking people called the land of Kēme "Misraim," the dual declension of Misr, the Semitic name of Kēme, which reflects the unified upper and lower kingdoms of Egypt. In the fourth century BC Kēme was colonized by the Greeks. When the Greeks arrived at the shores of Kēme they called it Aigyptios based on the name of the temple of *Het-ka-Ptah*, which they encountered when they first arrived. The port of Rakoti was renamed Alexandria after Alexander the Great. From the Greek Aigyptios is derived the English name Egypt, as well as the name of the country in the Latin and Romance languages. When the Arab tribes, who are Semitic, invaded Egypt in the seventh century, they heard the Greek name Aigyptios being used, but they called the land "Mīsr," from the singular form of its Semitic name, and the inhabitants of Kēme they called Miṣriyyīn. As their numbers increased, the Arabs began distinguishing between the two ethnic groups now living in the land, who were both now called Miṣriyyīn. Thus, they called the original inhabitants of the land "q-b-ṭ," derived from the Greek Aigyptios when you drop the vowels and Greek nominative ending following Arabic script. When the British and French colonized Kēme, they westernized the Arabic "q-b-ṭ" to "Copt." This is a very simplified explanation of a very complex term. In sum, the land of the Nile valley has been called Kēme, Misraim, Egypt, and Mīsr, and the inhabitants of the valley were accordingly called Egyptians, Copts, and Miṣriyyīn.

That is not the end of the story. These designations carry religious and political connotations that are reflected in the academic milieu. Some Biblical scholars translate the descendants of Ham in Genesis 10:6 as Egypt (example: New Revised Standard Version) based on the Greco-Roman nomenclature, while other Biblical scholars preferred to transliterate the same Hebrew name as Misraim (example: New American Standard Bible). The field of Early Christian Studies, or Patristics, reserves the term Egypt for the pre-Chalcedonian Greco-Roman period, and the term Coptic for the post-Chalcedonian period, thus dividing the heritage of the Church of Alexandria based on ecclesial politics. Some scholars even claim the literary output of the Greco-Roman era for the European heritage, thus excluding the Copts from their rightful heritage. Since the eighth century, Copts use the term "Coptic" to refer to their ethnicity and refer to their religion as Christianity, while their Muslim counterparts use the terms Coptic and Christian as synonyms, since all Copts are Christians. Thus in modern Arabic usage, the term does not discriminate between the people and their religion, so the term Coptic now carries a religious nuance. The term "Coptic" carries further nuances that scholars have not agreed on and is too complex to cover in the introduction.

The Coptic Orthodox Church is the Church of Alexandria or the Egyptian Orthodox Church. Churches in ancient times were called according to the capital of the province of the bishop's jurisdiction. The bishop of the diocese of Alexandria is the most senior bishop in all of Egypt and therefore the bishop or pope of the whole church. Because of ecclesial divisions from the fifth century, western literature has labeled the Coptic Orthodox Church with the derogative name Monophysite, referring to a theology refuted by the Coptic Orthodox Church. Some writers are overcoming such appellations by using terms such as Miaphysite, referring to the one nature of the Incarnate Son, or non-Chalcedonian, referring to the Coptic Orthodox Church's rejection of the decisions and theology of the Council of Chalcedon held in 451, as opposed to the western churches, which accept two natures in Christ and are therefore Diaphysite and Chalcedonian. The latter are also called Melkites, that is, those who are affiliated to the emperor's faith (from the Semitic "MLK," king). The significance of all these terms will unfold throughout the book.

Five main titles are given to the head of the Coptic Orthodox Church. The first is the title of "bishop," which was given to the heads of all early churches. But the bishop of Alexandria, whose jurisdiction extended to Egypt, Libya, Pentapolis (present day western Libya), Nubia and later Ethiopia, acquired further titles. The title "pope" was given to the bishop of Alexandria around AD 250, before its normative use in Rome. Dionysius of Alexandria (247–64) refers to his predecessor Heraclas (230–46) by the title "pope" and Eusebius of Caesarea uses the same title of Heraclas (Eusebius, *Hist. eccl.* 7.7.4). Alexander I (312–26) is addressed as "pope" by both his successor Athanasius and Arius (*Defense against the Arians*, 71; Arius' *Letter to Alexander of Alexandria*) (Abdelsayed 2012). The title "archbishop" and its simpler form "bishop" were used of Peter I of Alexandria (300–11) and his successor Alexander I (Vivian 1988: 70, 71, 78, 88, 185, 193). Archbishop was probably used by the early fourth century and was consistently used by the middle of the fourth century. The title "high priest" was used by both pagan and Jewish religious leaders. It is no surprise that Christians adopted the title since it is mentioned in the Old Testament and high priest is a particular image of Christ in the Epistles to the Hebrews (Abdelsayed 2012). The title "patriarch" began to appear officially in Coptic writings by the middle of the seventh century. It is not clear if this reflects the influence of the Syrian Orthodox Church or the Byzantine, or both together. By the end of the tenth century, Coptic–Arabic literature used this title heavily and sometimes almost exclusively (Abdelsayed 2012).

This brief synopsis of the various titles given to the head of the Coptic Orthodox Church not only conveys the development of these titles but should alert the reader that some titles were emphasized more than others at different eras. This is reflected in the chapters of this book, where the contributors use the titles most used in the era under discussion and in the literary sources they refer to. I would like to add that new titles did not make the previous ones obsolete; these official titles are consistently used in the consecration rites and liturgical prayers. Finally, to eliminate confusion for the reader, the head of the Coptic Orthodox Church holds the titles of Pope, Patriarch, Archbishop, High Priest, and Bishop.

The perspective of this book is not limited to the Greek and Latin sources and does not align with the Chalcedonian historical and theological perspective. This is a fresh approach to a tradition marginalized for centuries and which has been often written about from a colonialist point of view. With this approach we want to set a new scholarly trajectory for the study of the Coptic heritage. The field of "World Christianity" has already started to remedy the colonialist approach by seeing Christianity as a "world" religion rather than a western religion; Christianity in the west is no longer considered the standard or lens against which or through which all the Christians of the world are measured or seen. The hope is that a post-colonial approach will be applied to all studies of Christianity in Egypt. Undoubtedly, the dismantling of Orientalism and Euro-centric views will take some time because all current scholars were trained with this mindset, from which it will take them time to disentangle themselves.

This book surveys many topics if not whole fields of scholarship. Putting a whole field into a chapter of a few pages is a challenge and can never give the topic its full deserts. In addition, some topics, such as archaeology, architecture, modern contributions to art and literature, politics, and socioeconomic topics, were not included because of space constraints. Though each chapter can be read independently, they are also interconnected. Theology, for example, is better understood if read within its historical context. The same applies to other topics. There will inevitably be overlapping because all chapters address the same heritage. This is an introduction that will give the reader an overview of the Coptic heritage. Hopefully, it will encourage the reader to delve more deeply into the topics included. The selected bibliography should help the reader to further this endeavor.

The book is divided into four sections: history, and religious, literary, and material culture. The historical section embeds the whole story in its historical context. It is perplexing to the reader to find one people producing literature in so many languages if one does not follow the historical background that brought about the linguistic shift. Since the book focuses on the Christian heritage, we limited the pre-Christian history to one chapter. It was important to include this very swift introduction to pre-Christian Egypt to remind the reader of the routes of this heritage. Ayad did the impossible job of summarizing millennia in a short chapter. What she faced was a challenge to all contributors, how to introduce a whole field of scholarship in a few pages. Important aspects of the heritage had to be passed over to keep the size and scope at an introductory level. Farag writes about the early Christian era, which covers the introduction of Christianity to Egypt and the formative years that shaped Church theology, monastic tradition, ecclesial structure, and the Coptic ethos. The reader will observe that historical divisions follow political change. Thus, the early Islamic era does not mean the end of Christianity in Egypt, but rather that Christianity interacts with a different political system, which impacts the people as well as the church. Mikhail and Armanios write most eloquently about two eras, the early Islamic and the Ottoman. They are experts in a field that very few know about and the depth of their research and knowledge is illuminating. Hanna writes about the pre-modern era by highlighting the rise of the political–religious rhetoric that sets the stage for all events of our modern era. Saad writes about the modern era, introducing his personal experience to supplement aspects that have not yet been documented in a history still in the making. The January 2011 uprising and political rhetoric in present day Egyptian media are understood better within the historical context of the pre-modern and modern eras.

The section on religious culture has chapters on theology, monasticism, and spirituality written by Farag. The three topics are interconnected and thus written by one contributor. Monasticism has had a great influence on the Coptic spiritual heritage, and theology is the thread of which monasticism and spirituality are woven. There are very few studies about Coptic liturgy or music. The Coptic Orthodox Church is liturgical and in his chapter Abdelsayed sums up many aspects of the liturgical practices that set the rhythm of Coptic life. Ramzy writes about Christian Coptic music, both liturgical and popular. She includes in her chapter some of her research on the rare collection of Rāghib Muftāh in the Library of Congress.

Material culture is divided between the literary and the artistic. Under the section on literary culture we will be referring specifically to Christian literature, aligning with the book's theme. The inclusion of non-religious Coptic literature is beyond the scope of this introductory text. When we specify "Coptic" literary production we are not referring to language but to content, and in the case of this book we are referring to the content of the Coptic heritage as expressed in its various languages, that is, Greek, Coptic, and Arabic. Manuscript evidence indicates strong fluidity of the language and clean-cut divisions, such as between Roman Egypt and Coptic Egypt, raise more problems and are not helpful. Thus when we discuss Greek writings or Arabic writings, the composers are not ethnically Greek or Arab but Copts who are expressing their intellectual heritage in various tongues dictated by political conditions. During the early Christian era, writers understood Christianity as global rather than limited to one of the Roman provinces. The New Testament was written in Greek to ensure the global dissemination of the message, but this should not lead us to perceive of Christ or his disciples as being Greeks rather than Hebrews. The distinctiveness of the content overrode the language of expression since the message was in fulfillment of the Hebrew prophets' proclamation of the coming of a Messiah rather than an addition to the Greek pantheon of gods. English is the present language of information dissemination, but there are more English speakers than native English speakers; and how many of these can claim to be ethnically English? Coptic writers disseminated their message in both Greek and Coptic, and later in Arabic. When Copts used Arabic as a language of communication, distinctive terms were introduced into the language to express specific Christian ideas. An Arabic text is distinctively Christian based on the content and the specific use of the language.

In this section a chapter introducing the reader to the Coptic language will be followed by chapters on the Coptic Christian literary production expressed in Greek, Coptic, and Arabic. Takla introduces the Coptic language, explaining the many stages of its development. Takla's knowledge of Coptic manuscripts is demonstrated in his chapter on Coptic literature. Farag contributed the chapter on the Christian literary heritage written by Copts in Greek, highlighting the characteristics of the literary products and showing how representative they are of Egyptian Christian thought. Moawad writes about the Coptic Christian literature written in Arabic, revealing how prolific the Arabic Coptic Christian heritage has been. Finally, Gabra rounds out the discussion of material culture with a description of Coptic art in its many forms—icons, wood carvings, metal works, and many others—accompanied by exquisite illustrations.

I would like to thank each of the contributors for their enthusiastic participation in this project; all felt the need for such a book in the academy. I would also like to thank the Association of Theological Schools for its support of this project through the Collaborative Grant. This book can be used in courses on religion, the history of Christianity, comparative religion, Middle Eastern studies, missions, ecumenism, Coptic studies, Orthodox studies or Eastern Christianity. The book will be of interest to journalists and politicians, and any other interested readers who are closely following the events unfolding in the Middle East.

Bibliography

Abdelsayed, J. P. (2012) "Assessing the Date of Provenance of Rite of the Consecration of the Patriarch of Alexandria," paper presented at the Tenth International Congress of Coptic Studies, Rome, September 2012.

Vivian, T. (1988) *St. Peter of Alexandria: Bishop and Martyr*, Philadelphia: Fortress Press.

Part I

Coptic Christian History

1 The Pre-Christian Period

Changing Times and Cultural Endurance

Mariam F. Ayad

Egypt's ancient civilization was already over 3,000 years old when Christianity was first preached in Alexandria. Some have suggested that Egypt's cultural heritage contributed to the rather rapid spread of Christianity among its inhabitants. In this essay, we attempt to outline some of ancient Egypt's religious beliefs and cultural practices, placing them in their broader historical context and sociopolitical milieu.

Egypt's Geography and People

Egypt's geography has defined its boundaries since time immemorial. Located in the Northeastern corner of the African continent, Egypt is bordered to the North and the East by the Mediterranean and Red Seas, respectively (see Map 2). Additionally, two series of mountain ranges further define Egypt's Eastern and Western borders. Within the Eastern and Western mountain ranges lies a stretch of narrow, flat land, known as the Valley. Dissecting this narrow valley is the river Nile flowing from the heights of Lake Victoria in Uganda, through the Sudan, and into Egypt before reaching the Mediterranean in the North.

The Nile's origins in the African highlands impacted the Egyptian mindset. Thus, *ta-resy*, or "Upper Egypt," denoted the South from whence the Nile flowed, while *ta-mehou*, or "Lower Egypt," referred to the Delta in the Egyptian North. Reflecting this southward orientation are the Egyptian words for East and West. In Egyptian, *Imentet* denoted both the West and the right-hand side, while *Iabty* was both the East and the left-hand side.

An Egyptian Highway

In ancient times, the Nile formed the major "highway" of Egypt, facilitating the transport of goods and people from North to South and linking Egypt's longitudinal thousand miles from the Mediterranean to Aswan. Flowing from the African heartland in the South, the strong river current carried ships and boats northward. The north wind blowing from the Mediterranean propelled those same ships and boats southward. In fact, Egypt's earliest temples were portable shrines that were placed on boats and travelled upstream and downstream stopping at various villages and towns.

Along its course, the Nile created a lush green oasis in Egypt. In ancient times, the annual Nile inundation (flood) brought water and rich soil from the African heartland. Over the years, this rich mud alluvium deposited in the North, along the Mediterranean coast, creating the flat, fertile Egyptian Delta. Two main branches of the Nile bordered the Delta on its Eastern and Western sides, while to the North the Mediterranean Sea hemmed the base of its inverted triangle, at whose vertex lay Egypt's ancient capital, Memphis, a few miles to the South of Cairo.

In ancient times, seven branches of the Nile flowed through the Delta and irrigated its lands, making it one of the most fertile parts of Egypt. In several ways, Herodotus' famous statement, "Egypt is the Gift of the Nile," is not far off the mark. For if it were not for the Nile, the Egyptian landscape would have been very similar to the dry desert landscape characteristic of the rest of the North African Mediterranean coast just to the West of the Egyptian Delta and Nile Valley.

The Earliest Inhabitants

Along its banks, communities of hunters and gathers were able to find easy access to a variety of food sources: the fish in the river, the berries sprouting wild along the riverbanks, and small game to hunt for protein. These earliest cultures soon learned to cultivate the land and domesticate animals, moving from a subsistence economy to the relative ease of village life in ever-expanding settlements. The cultures that flourished on these sites are known as "Pre-dynastic," as they predate the unification of Egypt into one country, the establishment of a centralized government, and the emergence of successive ruling houses, or dynasties.

The Egyptian Calendar

The annual flood created a certain annual rhythm that evolved into a regular agricultural cycle. The Nile's annual flood defined the seasons for the Egyptians and gave rise to the Egyptian calendar (which remained in use in Coptic times, and continues to be used in Egypt today for agricultural purposes). The Egyptians divided their civil, or solar, calendar into three seasons, each comprising four months of thirty days each. Five epagomenal days completed the 365-day calendar. Literally meaning "above the year," these five days comprised the shortest month of the year, and were considered magically charged.

The Egyptian New Year coincided with the first day of the first month of *Akhet*. Literally meaning "horizon," *Akhet* was the flood season, when the entire land was covered with water. As the water receded, Egyptians sowed their seeds and waited for them to sprout. The sprouting season coincided with the winter months. Its Egyptian name, *Peret*, literally means the "coming forth" and reflects their understanding of how vegetation grew out of dry seeds buried deep in the soil. The last season of the year, *Shemou*, was the harvest season.

Egyptian Mythology and Worldview

Just as the annual flood affected the Egyptian conception of seasons and inspired the calendar, so also did Egypt's particular geographic nature affect much of its mythology.

Duality

The Valley and the Delta were considered as two parts forming a whole. This duality is most evident in the title most commonly held by Egyptian rulers—*nswt bity*, or "King of Upper and Lower Egypt" (literally, "He of the Sedge and the Bee"). The sedge and the bee were emblematic of the Valley and the Delta, respectively. Likewise, the sharp contrast between the red, barren desert sand and the dark, fertile mud of the Nile Valley and Delta formed another duality in the Egyptian mind: the "Red Land," *Deshert* in Egyptian—from which we get the English "desert"—and the "Black Land," or *Kemet*, in Egyptian, which later developed into *Keme*, Egypt's Coptic name (Černý 1976: 58).

To an ancient Egyptian, the barren desert not only contrasted sharply with the productive fertile "Black Land," but it was also a dangerous place, not only inhabited by wild beasts, but it was also where Chaos reigned supreme.

Isfet *and* Maat

Chaos, or *Isfet* as it was known in the Egyptian language, resided in the desert mountain ranges and beyond, and formed a direct threat to *Maat*. The forces of *Isfet* had to be constantly combated in order for *Maat* to prevail. Personified as a woman, who often appeared in the iconographic record as a feather, or equally frequently, as a woman with a single feather attached to her head, or sometimes only as a feather, it was the king's duty to maintain *Maat* (Hornung 1996: 74–75, 213–16). Victory in battle was the king's way of subduing the forces of Chaos/*Isfet* and bringing about *Maat*. *Maat* was the food on which the Egyptian gods survived—and it was the king's solemn responsibility to present *Maat* to them, either in the form of a military victory or as a votive statue.

Maat and Egyptian History

The constant tension between *Isfet* and *Maat* was a central theme of Egyptian culture, both on a national level as well as on a personal one. Nationally, the space between the two extremes defined, to the Egyptian mind, periods of stability and instability. Thus, periods of political stability and national unity were times when *Maat* prevailed, when rulers had successfully fulfilled their traditional role in expelling/subduing Egypt's enemies, an act that represented the ultimate defeat of the forces of chaos. By contrast, periods marked by the disintegration or fragmentation of centralized government were times when *Maat* was eclipsed by the greater forces of *Isfet*. In Egyptian literature such periods are portrayed as being plagued by civil war, disunity, drought, or famine. Historians and Egyptologists have come to call periods of prosperity "Kingdoms," while dubbing periods of civil unrest or foreign invasion/domination "Intermediate Periods."

The earliest Kingdom was the Old Kingdom (c. 2686–2181 BC) comprising the third to the sixth dynasties (Kuhrt 1995: 124, 135–60). The idea of dividing Egypt's long history into discrete dynasties dates back to the second century BC, when the Egyptian priest-turned-historian Manetho wrote a history of Egypt for Ptolemy II (Redford 1986: 297–317). In his account, Manetho organized Egypt's rulers into thirty dynasties. While in some cases Manetho's dynasties make sense, in other cases Manetho lumped together unrelated rulers and his divisions seem random.

The Old Kingdom was the age of the pyramid-builders, the establishment and expansion of centralized government under the rule of a king-god. The Old Kingdom witnessed the emergence of the king's full titulary, comprised of five titles; and the development of Pyramid Texts, the earliest genre of funerary literature whose purpose was to aid the deceased king achieve/attain an afterlife. The period also witnessed the initial administrative organization of Egypt into forty-two districts (*nomes*). The Old Kingdom also saw the earliest Egyptian expeditions into Nubia.

The First Intermediate Period (c. 2180–2040 BC) followed soon after the long reign of King Pepi II (Kuhrt 1995: 124, 158–60). His reign caused stagnation in the Egyptian administration, which led to the rise in the power of the local rulers (*nomarchs*), or rulers of the Egyptian *nome*, the smallest administrative unit, who eventually ceased to be royal appointees. Instead, their positions became hereditary. This situation, combined with a series of low Niles, which caused drought and a subsequent famine, led to the fragmentation of the state. A group of compositions, known collectively as "pessimistic literature," paint a very grim picture of the conditions prevalent during the First Intermediate Period.

The Middle Kingdom (c. 2040–1730 BC) comprises the latter half of the Theban eleventh dynasty and the twelfth dynasty (ibid. 124, 161–73). This period is known for its great literary works, such as the stories of the Eloquent Peasant, Sinuhe, and the Shipwrecked Sailor. It also witnessed the emergence of the Theban god Amun, who was to become the most prominent Egyptian national deity in later periods. The Middle Kingdom also witnessed the expansion of funerary literature, which became more widely available to members of the Egyptian elite, who chose to inscribe its spells and utterances on their coffins—hence, the term Coffin Texts.

The Second Intermediate Period (c. 1730–1550 BC) was another time of weakened central power compounded by the infiltration of groups of western Asiatic tribes into the Nile Delta (ibid. 124, 173–82). Collectively known as the

Hyksos, the Hellenized version of their Egyptian name *heqaw khasout* (literally, "rulers of foreign lands"), these groups appear in Manetho's account of Egyptian history as dynasties XIV–XV. In the Egyptian artistic repertoire they assume traditional modes of representation, although their names seem foreign. Although there has been some effort to link these groups to the Biblical narrative of the Hebrew sojourn in Egypt, the links seem tenuous at best. At the same time, a line of native rulers continued to reside in Thebes (Manetho's dynasty XVII). It was the last rulers of the Theban Seventeenth Dynasty, Sekenenre and Kamose, who initiated the effort to expel the Hyksos from Egypt. Ahmose, brother of Kamose, was able to drive the Hyksos out of the Egyptian Delta, and chased them across the Sinai and Gaza. Ahmose is credited with the founding of the Eighteenth Dynasty and restoring order to Egypt. As such, he is also considered the founder of Egypt's New Kingdom.

The New Kingdom (c. 1550–1069 BC) was the Age of Empire, when Egypt expanded South and Northeast (ibid. 124, 185–224). The Thutmoside rulers launched several expeditions into Nubia and managed to expand Egypt's southern border to the Second Cataract and, on occasion, pushed it as far South as the Fourth Cataract. It was also during the New Kingdom that Queen Hatshepsut (c. 1503–1482 BC) sent a mercantile expedition down the Red Sea to the land of Punt, which was probably located near the African horn (ibid. 186). The New Kingdom was an age of religious innovation. During the short reign of Akhenaton (c. 1353–1335 BC), Egypt's national deity became the solar disk, known in Egyptian as the Aten. It was the only time in Egyptian history that the state actively prevented the worship of other gods. The New Kingdom was the age of international diplomacy and international power struggles. The Egyptians and Hittites signed the earliest recorded peace treaty (ibid. 207). The New Kingdom was the age of the great temples and the great victories.

The First Millennium BC

The start of the first millennium BC witnessed a much-weakened Egypt. Gone were the days of the grand pyramids, lavish temples, and empire builders. A series of short-lived reigns, marked by internal turmoil, corruption, and economic decline marred the end of Egypt's Twentieth Dynasty. For instance, during the reign of Ramses IX (c. 1127–1108 BC), royal tombs were violated. When the tomb robbers were eventually caught and tried, the investigation revealed extensive corruption and neglect that extended to the highest level of the administration. Economic decline is also evident under the reign of Ramses X (c. 1108–1104 BC), whose administration failed to deliver the wages of the workmen and artisans responsible for excavating and decorating the royal tombs on time. Papyri from the workmen's settlement at Deir el-Medina detail the workers' resentment and discontent and their subsequent strike (Kitchen 1995: 243–48).

At the same time, the king's influence and power declined vis-à-vis the powers of his senior administrators, especially the vizier, his second in command. Effective power shifted to the South, where the Viceroy of Kush, Nubia's main administrator, and the High Priest of Amun at Karnak acquired progressively increasing power. As a sign of their increasing influence, holders of these two positions ceased to be royal appointees. Instead, their positions became hereditary. Inevitably, these powerful and ambitious individuals vied for power. During the last reign of the Twentieth Dynasty, a military conflict erupted between the High Priest of Amun and the Viceroy of Kush, who now controlled a sizeable portion of Egypt's military forces. Shortly afterwards, another High Priest of Amun, Herihor, effectively became the ruler of Upper Egypt, having combined military powers with his earlier religious responsibilities (ibid. 248–54). In Lower Egypt, Ramses XI abdicated all effective power to his vizier, Smendes. When an emissary was sent to Lebanon to purchase wood for the sacred barque of Amnu, it was Smendes, not the king, who supplied him with the requisite documents (ibid. 254–57).

Egypt During the Libyan Period

The rulers of the Twenty-first Dynasty (1069–945 BC), which marks the beginning of the so-called Third Intermediate Period, were of Libyan origin and so were the rulers of the dynasties that followed. By the beginning of the Twenty-third Dynasty, the stability that had characterized earlier periods of Egyptian history was long gone. The most characteristic aspect of this period is the total disintegration of central authority. Under the Libyans, Egypt was now divided into rival fiefdoms, with several competing dynasts ruling at the same time, each claiming royal authority, while in reality their influence may have extended only a few miles beyond their residence. Multiple dynasts ruling at Tanis, Leontopolis, Bubastis, and Sais, along with several other "lesser" chiefs, competed for control over the Egyptian Delta (O'Connor 1983: 238–41). This state of affairs was probably a result of the Libyans' tribal heritage (Ritner 2009: 327–40),which allowed them to rule alongside one another in "a loose confederation reinforced by family alliances" (Leahy 1985: 59).

The Nubians in Egypt

While this fragmentation may have fitted the feudalistic heritage of the Libyans, it represented a sharp break from the Egyptian ideal of how the country should be ruled. In c. 730 BC, Nubians marched northward proclaiming their intention to restore order to the land. They portrayed themselves as devout followers of the god Amun, their actions motivated only by a desire to restore *Maat*, or centralized government to Egypt.

The Nubian victory was recorded on a stone slab, known as the "Great Triumphal Stela." The stela details the siege of Memphis, its eventual fall, and the subsequent submission of the various Libyan dynasts to the Nubian king's authority (Kuhrt 1995: 629–31). Without appointing a deputy governor, the Nubian invader, Piye, returned to Nubia shortly after his victory and remained there until his death in c. 716 BC (ibid. 631). Soon, the rulers of the western Delta city of Sais revolted again. As a result, the Nubians had to re-conquer Egypt (Kitchen 1995: 378–80). While, initially, the Nubian rulers were satisfied to return to their homeland after their Egyptian excursions, which they often timed to coincide with Egyptian religious celebrations,[1] eventually they moved their residence to Memphis (ibid. 380–81). The move to Memphis was possibly intended to quench the expansionist efforts of the Delta rulers.[2] The Nubians also became increasingly interested in meddling in Near Eastern military conflicts and sent their armies several times to western Asia.

Possibly prompted by the expansionist ambitions of Egypt's Nubian rulers, the Assyrian armies of Esarhaddon invaded Egypt, reaching Memphis in 671 BC (ibid. 391–93). While the incumbent Nubian ruler seems to have survived this first invasion, a second invasion drove him all the way back to Nubia (ibid. 393). His successor's short-lived reign did not restore Nubian hegemony over Egypt. The Assyrians allied themselves with a Delta ruler and re-invaded Egypt in 663/64 BC. They succeeded in capturing Memphis, and installed Psametik I, a Delta ruler, as King of Egypt (Kuhrt 1995: 634–38). Eventually, Psametik I marshaled his troops South, bringing Middle Egypt under his control, and chased the last Nubian ruler, Tanwetamani into Nubia (Kitchen 1995: 394–98). Tanwetamani's flight to Nubia ended Kushite rule in Egypt, although the Kingdom continued to flourish in Nubia until the third century AD (Kuhrt 1995: 632; Welsby 1996).

Egypt under Saite Rule

Descended from the Twenty-fourth dynasty rulers whom the Nubians encountered during their northward expansion, the Twenty-sixth dynasty rulers are designated Saite, after their city of origin: Sais, in the western Delta. The dynasty officially commenced with the coronation of Psametik I (664–610 BC) at Memphis. While Psametik initially ruled as a vassal-king, loyal to the Assyrians, having forged an alliance with the Assyrian king Assurbanipal, he eventually asserted his independence. Similarly, his initial tolerance of officials who had served under the Nubians soon evaporated and he gradually began appointing his own "Delta men" in key positions in Upper Egypt (Kitchen 1995: 400–4). Abroad, Psametik extended Egypt's influence into the Levant and sent military expeditions into Nubia. Much like Old Kingdom rulers, Psametik I had to call on his district leaders (*nomarchs*) to gather troops for his expeditions, both against the Nubians to the South, and also against the recurring Libyan incursions from the West (Lloyd 1983: 282).

Foreign Mercenaries

Increasingly though Psametik began to rely on foreign mercenaries, particularly Carian and Ionian troops, to shore up his power—a policy that was faithfully followed by his successors. Although the unreliability of mercenary soldiers became evident early on, a strong belief that their military prowess was much superior to what was available locally kept them employed. The foreign contingents, however, were never integrated into the Egyptian army: Egyptian and Greek soldiers served under different commanders (ibid. 284–85). This division eventually led to trouble. During the reign of Apries (589–570 BC), growing resentment over the king's preferential treatment of the foreign contingents of his army, particularly the Greeks, led to turmoil. After the failure of a poorly executed expansionist campaign into Cyrene in 571 BC failed, the Egyptian troops, who had suffered massive losses, revolted against Apries. In the ensuing conflict, Apries relied primarily on his Greek navy to fend off the angry Egyptians. In the midst of the resulting conflict, a popular army general proclaimed himself king in Sais. The rapidly succeeding events of this period included an attempt on Apries' part to regain the Egyptian throne, but the Egyptian troops rallied around the Egyptian general, Amasis, and crowned him King of Egypt. One of Apries' attempts to regain the throne involved taking refuge in the Babylonian court and persuading Nebuchadnezzar to invade Egypt in order to reinstate him. If successful, the Babylonian court stood to gain enormous power and prestige in the region. Having formed an alliance with the king of Cyrene, Amasis was able to fend off the invading Babylonian troops. In the course of battle, Apries was killed (ibid. 285–86). Amasis' long reign (570–526 BC) was characterized by considerable pragmatism and foresight. He instituted several judicial reforms. Greek mercenaries were relocated from their base at Pelusium, along Egypt's Eastern border, to Memphis—a move that kept them closer to home, and consequently, more controllable. Amasis also established several long-term Mediterranean alliances, and conquered Cyprus. During Amasis' reign, Demotic, a highly cursive script, became widely used in Egypt (Allen 2010: 7).

The Persian invasion of 525 BC ended this last period of Egyptian national rule. Although the Egyptians revolted and the Persians were expelled some eighty years later, the last few dynasties were short-lived. In 343 BC, the Persians re-conquered Egypt. But this time, their rule was short-lived. Ten years later, in 332 BC, Alexander the Great captured Egypt as he swept though the Near East (Lloyd 1983: 286–87).

The Egyptian Pantheon and Triads

Possibly because of its long history, pre-Christian Egypt had a very complicated pantheon that encompassed a wide range of gods. A deity could manifest himself/herself in multiple ways: anthropomorphically (in complete human form, e.g. Osiris); zoomorphically (in complete animal form, such as Anubis, the jackal god or Hathor, the cow goddess); or as an animal-headed human (e.g. jackal-headed Anubis, cow-headed Hathor, etc.) (Hornung 1996: 100–28). Additionally, Egyptian gods were organized into family groupings comprising father, mother, and child, e.g. Phat, Sekhmet, and Nefertum at Memphis and Amun, Mut, and Khonsu at Thebes (Silverman 1991: 41). In fact, triads were the structural element of the ancient Egyptians' religion (Velde 1971: 80–88). This organizational scheme highlighted their reverence for family life and the value they placed on the reproductive aspects of family formation.

Genesis in Egypt

These triads were not always present in the various Egyptian accounts of how the world came into being. For instance, according to the Heliopolitan creation myth, the creator god Atum managed to set creation in motion when out of his issuance he engendered the first divine couple: Shu (male = air) and Tefnut (female = moisture). These, in turn, produced Geb (male = earth) and Nut (female = sky), whose progeny included the two rivals Osiris and Seth and the two sisters/mourners, Isis and Nephthys. Osiris, Isis, and their son Horus constitute the only triad in this myth. Similarly, the Akhmimic account imagined the creator god, Khnum, as the potter at his wheel. The Memphite cosmogony featured the god Ptah thinking and willing creation into being by the utterance of his mouth. While Thought and Utterance became personified deities in their own right, the Memphite cosmogony is the only Egyptian account that portrays creation *ex nihilo*.[3] There is no way of telling whether these myths were held in belief simultaneously, were regional, or evolved over time. But their sheer number is reflective of the Egyptians' comfort with plurality, and, more importantly, their religious tolerance.

Syncretism

In addition to patron deities of childbirth, harvest, and the like, the Egyptians also had local deities, whose influence was limited to a particular village or town, as well as national deities such as Amun, Osiris, and Ptah. These national deities could manifest themselves in different forms at different locales, e.g. the Nubian Amun of Napata was quite distinct from Amun-em-ope of the Luxor temple in Thebes. In other cases, individual deities could merge forming a new entity in a process known as syncretism. For example, two different forms of the sun god could merge to form a third, e.g. Re-Atum. The new, syncretic deity could share some features with the original deities or have totally different attributes (Hornung 1996: 91–99). This constant process of convergence (syncretism) may help explain how solar deities such as Amun-Re and Re-Atum became associated, during the New Kingdom and later, with certain Osirian attributes at nighttime, a time when the sun "died" before being re-born/resurrected again in the morning.[4]

Solar Religion

The Egyptians' recognition of the sun's role in making vegetation grow is evident in the many solar deities that were included in the Egyptian Pantheon. Re came to represent the sun at its highest at noontime. At sunrise, the gentle morning sun was associated with dung beetles emerging from the ground with the first light. Accordingly, the god Khepri, of the early morning sun, is often depicted as a beetle-headed god. At sunset he took the form of the aged god Atum, or the "Complete One" (ibid. 66–67). The Egyptians invented a special form of the sun at nighttime: Ram-headed Amun.

Osirian Religion

Agriculture also played a fundamental role in shaping Egyptian religious and funerary beliefs. Witnessing dry, shriveled seeds buried deep within the soil sprout and come to life after weeks of inactivity and apparent death may have given rise to the longest surviving Egyptian myth: The Myth of Osiris.[5] According to Plutarch's reconstruction of the story, it starts with Osiris as ruler of Egypt and brother–husband of Isis. Osiris is then tricked and murdered by his own brother, the god Seth, who was simultaneously envious of his brother and eager to claim the throne of Egypt for himself. Further, Seth cuts up Osiris' body and scatters the pieces all over Egypt. Isis, the loyal, mourning wife, travels throughout Egypt in search of her slain husband's organs. She manages to put his body together and revives him just long enough to conceive their son Horus. She then hides Horus in the marshes to protect him from his evil uncle. Once Horus grows up, he tries to reclaim his father's throne by bringing his case before a Divine Tribunal.[6] After many years at court, the struggle is settled in favor of Horus, who then becomes the "King of the Living." The Egyptians believed that the ruling king was the earthly embodiment of the god Horus, while the deceased king came to be identified with the god Osiris, at once the "king of the dead" and the "dead king."

Although the Myth of Osiris may have been partly rooted in the need to establish the right of royal succession as passing from father to son, rather than from one brother to the other, the myth played a central role in Egyptian funerary beliefs. It was only through a complete identification with Osiris that the deceased had any hope of resurrection.

The Judgment of the Dead

The vignette represented next to Chapter 125 of the *Book of the Dead* typically shows the deceased being led by the falcon-headed god Horus towards the god Osiris, the King of the Dead, who is represented at the far right of the scene seated on his throne and attended by his two sisters, Isis and Nephthys.[7] In the center of the scene is a pair of scales, attended by the jackal-headed god Anubis. On the left is the deceased's heart being weighed against the feather of *Maat*/Truth. If the heart contained any falsehood, the Egyptians believed, it would weigh the scales down, and waiting next to Anubis is a composite monster—part lion, part crocodile—eager to devour the deceased's heart if it proved heavier than the feather of *Maat*.

Maat and Personal Piety

On a personal level, *Maat* was central in the Egyptian value system. Egyptian funerary texts reveal that the Egyptians were very concerned with maintaining *Maat* in their daily lives. Nowhere is this more clearly seen than in tomb-autobiographies (Lichtheim 1992: 103–44). Inscribed near the tomb's entrance, these personal statements declared the deceased's impeccable moral conduct during his/her lifetime. Typically, the deceased used those statements to recount their performance of righteous acts of kindness and social solidarity, while denying committing any evil deeds. A Sixth Dynasty autobiography, for example, reads: "I gave bread to the hungry, clothing to the naked. I brought the boatless to land ... I was one who spoke fairly and repeated what was liked, I never spoke evilly against any man to his superior, for I wished to stand well with the great god" (Lichtheim 1973–78: 24). In time, the phraseology of these statements became standardized, even formulaic. Rather than reflecting an individual's actual acts of piety, the autobiographies reflect a certain moral code to which an Egyptian aspired. A similar morality also appears in the Egyptian *Book of the Dead*. Known to the Egyptians as the "Book of Going Forth by Day," the main purpose of this New Kingdom composition was to aid the deceased in achieving an afterlife. Written on papyrus, and often tucked within the deceased's mummy wrappings, this composition contained a collection of magical spells, hymns, and prayers, arranged into discrete "chapters." Chapter BD 125, variously referred to as "the Negative Confession" or the "Declaration of Innocence," contains similar declarations to those found in Old Kingdom tomb autobiographies and then some. For instance, "I did not kill; I did not cause to kill; I did not utter falsehood; I did not commit adultery; I did not take what was not mine; I did not take from the temple offerings; I did not pollute the Nile" (Faulkner 1972: 29–32; Hornung 1996: 181) become standard phrases of that chapter.

A Sense of National Identity

Through much of its history, Egypt had the same borders. Six cataracts (rock outcroppings) intercept the course of the Nile in the area between Aswan and Khartoum. Because these rock outcroppings hindered the ability to sail down the Nile, they formed a natural boundary marker for Egypt's southern border—and over the 3,000 years of Egypt's Pharaonic history, Egypt's southern boundary shifted back and forth between the First Cataract (at Aswan) and the Second Cataract (at Buhen in Nubia).

Because it was so tightly shielded from its neighbors, to an Egyptian, Egypt was the center of the world. On the other side of its natural boundaries lay Chaos. Outside its boundaries, Egyptian gods were no longer efficacious. An Egyptian's dearest desire was to return "home" to be buried in the vicinity of his or her local god.[8]

The mountain ranges, the cataracts, and the seas defined Egypt's borders and gave it a certain geographic integrity. These geographic features also contributed to Egypt's relative stability as they protected the country against the dangers of foreign invasions or the encroachment of foreign groups. Because the inhabitants of Egypt occupied the same plot of land for thousands of years, there arose among the Egyptians a particular sense of attachment to the land, a sort of national identity that predated the rise of modern nationalistic movements (noted also by Marsot 1985: 7). This strong sense of "national" identity contributed to the formation and continuation of a distinctly Egyptian culture. Egypt's Libyan, Nubian, Persian, and Macedonian rulers all understood this unique sense of identity and place. They all became traditional "Egyptian" rulers when they governed the country. So also, I would argue, when Christianity came to Egypt, it became distinctly Egyptian, or "Coptic."

Timeline

All dates BC era

4000–3500	Pre-dynastic (Nagada I)
3500–3200	Pre-dynastic (Nagada II)
3200–3100	Pre-dynastic (Nagada III)
3100–2686	Early Dynastic
2686–2180	Old Kingdom
2180–2040	First Intermediate Period
2040–1730	Middle Kingdom
1730–1550	Second Intermediate Period
1550–1069	New Kingdom
1069–664	Third Intermediate Period
664–525	The Saite Period
525–404	First Persian Period
404–343	Late Dynastic Period
343–332	Second Persian Period
332–305	Macedonian Period
305–30	Ptolemaic Period

Notes

1 Piye's two campaigns, for example, which he launched in his fourth and twenty-eighth regnal years (c. 744 BC and 728 BC, respectively), coincided with the *Opet*-festival on both occasions and with the Beautiful Valley on the second. On both occasions, Piye presented Amun-Re with many gifts. By paying homage to Amun, Piye undoubtedly strengthened his ties with the Theban elite and promoted his image as a pious supporter of the religious festivities taking place at the time.

2 The Saite ruler Bakenrenef's attempts to expand his sphere of influence.

3 For a complete account of the various Egyptian cosmogonies, see Lesko 1991: 90–96.

4 This idea is most clearly seen in the so-called books of the sky, namely the Book of Nut, the Book of the Day, and the Book of Night. For an overview of the content and organization of these compositions, see Hornung, 1999: 112–35. See also, Silverman 1991: 46.

5 A good analysis of the myth is found in Assmann 2001: 123–47.

6 For the story of the "Contendings of Horus and Seth," see Lichtheim 1973–78 (vol. II): 214–23.
7 As seen, for example, in the Eighteenth Dynasty funerary papyrus of Hunefer, currently in the British Museum, EA 9901/3. For the figure, see Faulkner 1985: 34–35.
8 A prime example of this belief is found in the Story of Sinuhe. See Lichtheim 1973–78: 222–33 for the text in translation.

Selected Bibliography

Allen, J. P. (2010) *Middle Egyptian: An Introduction to the Language and Culture of Hieroglyphs*, Cambridge: Cambridge University Press.

Assmann, J. (2001) *The Search for God in Ancient Egypt*, trans. D. Lorton, Ithaca: Cornell University Press.

Černý, J. (1976) *Coptic Etymological Dictionary*, Cambridge: Cambridge University Press.

Faulkner, R. O. (1972) *The Ancient Egyptian Book of the Dead*, London: Trustees of the British Museum.

——(1985) *The Egyptian Book of the Dead*, London: The British Museum.

Hornung, E. (1996) *Conceptions of God in Ancient Egypt: The One and the Many*, trans. J. Baines, Ithaca: Cornell University Press.

——(1999) *The Ancient Egyptian Books of the Afterlife*, trans. D. Lorton, Ithaca: Cornell University Press.

Kempt, B. J. (1991) *Ancient Egypt: Anatomy of a Civilization*, London: Routledge.

Kitchen, K. A. (1995) *The Third Intermediate Period in Egypt (1100–650 BC)*, Warminster: Aris & Phillips.

Kuhrt, A. (1995) *The Ancient Near East c. 3000–330 BC*, London: Routledge.

Leahy, A. (1985) "The Libyan Period in Egypt: An Essay in Interpretation," *Libyan Studies*, 16: 51–65.

Lesko, L. H. (1991) "Ancient Egyptian Cosmogonies and Cosmology," in B. E. Shafer (ed.) *Religion in Ancient Egypt: Gods, Myths, and Personal Practice*, London: Routledge.

Lichtheim, M. (1973–78) *Ancient Egyptian Literature*, 3 vols, Berkeley and Los Angeles: University of California Press.

——(1992) *Maat in Egyptian Autobiographies and Related Studies*, Orbis Biblicus et Orientalis 120, Freiburg: Universitätsverlag.

Lloyd, Alan B. (1983) "The Late Period," in B. G. Trigger et al., *Ancient Egypt: A Social History*, Cambridge: Cambridge University Press, pp. 279–348.

Malek, J. and Baines, J. (2000) *Cultural Atlas of Ancient Egypt*, London: Checkmark Books.

Manley, B. (1996) *The Penguin Historical Atlas of Ancient Egypt*, London: Penguin.

Marsot, A. L. Al-S. (1985) *A Short History of Modern Egypt*, new ed., Cambridge: Cambridge University Press.

Myliwiec, K. (2000) *The Twilight of Ancient Egypt: First Millennium BCE*, trans. D. Lorton, Ithaca: Cornell University Press.

O'Connor, D. (1983) "New Kingdom and Third Intermediate Period, 1552–1664 BC," in B. G. Trigger et al., *Ancient Egypt: A Social History*, Cambridge: Cambridge University Press.

Redford, Donald B. (1986) *Pharaonic King-lists, Annals and Day-books: A Contribution to the Study of the Egyptian Sense of History*, Mississauga, ON: Benben Publishing.

——(1993) *Egypt, Canaan, and Israel in Ancient Times*, Cairo: American University in Cairo Press.

Ritner, R. K. (2009) "Fragmentation and Re-Integration in the Third Intermediate Period," in *The Libyan Period in Egypt: Historical and Cultural Studies into the 21st–24th*

Dynasties: Proceedings of a Conference at Leiden University, 25–27 October 2007, Leiden: NINO.

Shafer, B. E. (ed.) (1991) *Religion in Ancient Egypt: Gods, Myths, and Personal Practice*, London: Routledge.

Silverman, D. P. (1991) "Divinity, Deity in Ancient Egypt," in Byron E. Shafer (ed.) *Religion in Ancient Egypt: Gods, Myths, and Personal Practice*, London: Routledge.

Trigger, B., Kemp, B. J., O'Connor, D. and Lloyd, A. B. (1983) *Ancient Egypt: A Social History*, Cambridge: University of Cambridge Press.

Velde, H. te (1971) "Some Remarks on the Structure of Egyptian Divine Triads," *Journal of Egyptian Archaeology*, 57: 80–88.

Welsby, D. A. (1996) *The Kingdom of Kush: The Napatan and Meroitic Empire*, Princeton: Markus Wiener.

2 The Early Christian Period (42–642)

The Spread and Defense of the Christian Faith under Roman Rule

Lois M. Farag

The Holy Family visited Egypt (Matt 2:13–21) and there were Egyptians at Pentecost (Acts 2:10), but the Church of Alexandria began with Mark the Evangelist preaching on the streets of Alexandria and establishing a church leadership, ordaining Anianus as the first bishop of Alexandria together with three presbyters and seven deacons (Callahan 1992: 62–68). The earliest reference to this tradition is in Eusebius of Caesarea's *Ecclesiastical History* (Eusebius, *Hist. eccl.* 2.16); he also lists, without any details, the names of eleven bishops who succeeded Mark, ending with Demetrius (r. 189–231) (ibid. 2.24; 3.14, 21; 4.1, 4–5, 11, 19; 5.9, 22). When Mark the Evangelist arrived in Alexandria, Egypt had been under Roman rule since 31 BC. This chapter will set the stage by describing the political, social, and economic context within which Christianity emerged in Egypt together with earliest evidence of church structure and organization. This will be followed by an examination of the Coptic Orthodox Church's relations with the Roman state under both pagan and Christianized emperors. The chapter will end with the demise of the Roman Empire in Egypt marked by the Arab conquest in 641.

Politics, Society, and Economy Under Roman Rule

Naphtali Lewis begins his book on life in Egypt under the Romans in this way: "'History rewards the victors', says an oft-quoted truism. The standard history of Rome and its empire is a familiar story of military successes and governmental decisions. The voice of the subjugated and the governed is rarely heard, and then it is usually filtered to us through the writings of Romans" (Lewis 1999: 1). Fortunately, papyri tell the story of the day-to-day concerns of Egyptians under Roman rule.

Egypt was of utmost importance for the Roman Empire as the bread basket of the empire. It provided Rome with its dole or *nonna* of grain. Later, when Constantinople became the capital of the Eastern Empire, Egypt provided grain to the new capital. It also supplied food to the troops fighting the Persians on the eastern frontier. For this reason the agricultural production of Egypt was closely monitored; its stability was the stability of the empire. Egypt did not use slave labor for agriculture. The Romans took a census every fourteen years, and many Egyptians in Alexandria had to return to their villages for the census. Those who remained in Alexandria had to get special permission to do so. The census enabled the Romans to maintain an iron grip on the collection of poll taxes from every Egyptian. Romans and Greeks were exempted from the endless list of taxes gathered from Egyptian farmers and workers. At the beginning of the Roman rule it is estimated that there were eight million Egyptians (ibid. 110, 116, 121, 159, 165, 169, 171, 173). Egypt in the eyes of the Romans and Greeks was a land of inexhaustible productivity.

Egyptians saw all their fertile land pass first to the Roman elite and court members and gradually to the emperor. The land was administered by Roman officials who leased the land to the highest bidder. This loss of land along with heavy taxation and discrimination against Egyptians for the benefit of Roman elites led to a serious revolt in AD 152, which lasted for a year. When the grain and food supply to Rome was interrupted, Emperor Antoninus Pius had to personally intervene. In AD 172–73 there was another uprising in Boukolia in the Nile Delta led by a pagan priest. During his visit to Alexandria in AD 215, Emperor Caracalla, for unknown reasons, ordered a horrific massacre of thousands of unarmed civilians throughout the city. Discontent was also expressed in anti-Roman papyri (ibid. 74, 205; Scarre 1995: 143–44). It was within this climate of political, social, and economic frustration that Christianity was spreading throughout Egypt.

The Spread of Christianity and Church Organization

The ecclesial structure followed the Roman administrative structure of Egypt. The Pharaonic administrative structure divided Egypt into thirty administrative districts, which the Greeks called *nomoi*, each with a capital city. Capital cities did not gain the status of Greek cities before the third century AD. "Given the fact that most cities in the Nile Valley were nome capitals back to Pharaonic times, we cannot expect them to have become Graeco-Roman cities right away" (van Ninnen 2007: 210). Roman administration hardly shifted the boundaries of these nomes and the capital city at its center became the metropolis. A group of nomes formed a province. By the time of Diocletian (AD 284–305) Egypt was divided into provinces, each with its capital; the number of these provinces fluctuated from two (Aegyptus praefectus and Thebais praeses) in the mid-fourth century, to six (Aegyptus Augustalis, Augustamnica I and II, Arcadia, Thebais inferior and superior) and then four (Aegyptus, Augustamnica, Arcadia, and Thebais) in the seventh century. The diocese of Egypt consisted of these provinces as well as Libya Superior (Pentapolis) and Libya Inferior (Libya Sicca) (see Map 1). Each province had a governor who was subject to the *praefectus Augustalis* (prefect), who was responsible for the whole diocese and was appointed by the emperor as his personal representative. The Roman prefect resided in Alexandria. Once per year he would travel around Egypt with some of his associates, solving administrative and judicial problems, and listening to and settling people's grievances (Lewis 1999: 19, 36; van Ninnen 2007: 207–25; Palme 2007: 245–46; Scarre 1995: 101).

Like the Roman governors, bishops of nomes resided in the metropolis. The bishop of Alexandria would visit the metropolitan bishops in the diocese of Egypt, whose boundaries followed those of the Roman diocese. Demetrius of Alexandria is the first bishop whose pastoral activity we know something about. He initiated the tradition of sending a Festal Letter to all the Egyptian nomes under his jurisdiction, which was continued by his successors for many centuries. Pope Dionysius (r. 247–64) visited Arsinoe to resolve a controversy led by Nepos, who called for millenarianism based on the Book of Revelation (Eusebius, *Hist. eccl.* 7.24), which indicates that by the middle of the third century the Pope of Alexandria had jurisdiction over all the Egyptian nomes.

Demetrius ordained three bishops in the Egyptian *chora* or villages. His successor, Pope Heraclas (r. 231–47), consecrated twenty bishops. By 324 there were fifty-seven bishops (Wipszycka 2007: 331–32). Socrates in his *Ecclesiastical History* mentions that Pope Alexander (r. 312–26) convened about a hundred bishops from his Dioceses of Egypt and Libya to discuss the Arian doctrine (Socrates, *Hist. eccl.* 1.6). His successor, Pope Athanasius (r. 326–73), together with ninety bishops from Egypt and Libya, wrote a synodical letter *To the Bishops of Africa* (Roman Africa is present day Mauritania, Western Sahara, Morocco, Algeria, and Tunisia). By the mid-fourth century, then, the synod of the Diocese of Egypt consisted of all of Egypt's and Libya's ninety bishops, and all were under the jurisdiction of the bishop of Alexandria. Canon 6 of the Council of Nicaea (325) affirmed that Egypt, Libya, and Pentapolis belonged to one jurisdiction following an ancient custom.

The spread of Christianity throughout Egypt did not mean the total elimination of ancient Egyptian religion. In Alexandria there were clashes between the Christian and pagan populations. This was triggered by laws issued by Emperor Theodosius (r. 379–95) against any non-Christian religious gatherings. Based on these laws, many temples throughout the empire were destroyed, including the famous Serapeum in Alexandria. Not all of Egypt, however, shared the Alexandrian experience; in other places pagans and Christians lived side by side. The majority of the population of the southern frontier island of Philae worshiped Isis, the goddess of the temple of Philae. Philae would not become a Christian island until Emperor Justinian, following an aggressive anti-pagan campaign, closed the Philae Temple in 535–37.

The story of the ordination of the second bishop on Philae gives us a glimpse of the custom of a bishop's ordination in fourth-century Egypt. According to Paphnutius, after the death of Macedonius the episcopal see of Philae was vacant for some time. The people met to discuss a successor. After three days of intense discussion they decided to choose a group of men whom they deemed fit for the position, and then cast lots. But the chief priest suggested that Mark, the disciple of bishop Macedonius, would be a suitable person. Most of those present accepted this suggestion. They travelled to Alexandria to meet Pope Athanasius and present Mark as the person chosen by the island for ordination. Athanasius ordained him bishop of Philae in the presence of the island's representative. Mark received a letter from Athanasius confirming his appointment.

When Mark returned to Philae, he read the letter in church to the public and celebrated the liturgy (Paphnutius 1993: 98–108).

This narrative illustrates the general structure of episcopal elections and consecrations. The clergy and laity of the vacant see would reach a unanimous decision on a candidate. Then delegates would present the candidate to the Pope of Alexandria. It was also possible for the people to present the pope with a choice between two rival candidates. Sometimes the pope chose a bishop for the nome on his own. Most candidates were monks, though in the early years laymen were possible (Wipszycka 2007: 337). Papyrological evidence informs us that bishops and clergy were literate, except maybe for the clergy of very small villages. The illiterate surely did not advance in the hierarchy (ibid. 342–43). Once ordained, the bishop was given a document from the Pope of Alexandria that was read in public informing the community of the legitimacy of his ordination and ecclesial authority over the nome. The process of choosing the bishop of Alexandria will be discussed further on.

Metropolitan bishops were responsible for choosing and ordaining the clergy within their nome. Clergy were responsible for the day to day activities within their local church as well as overseeing the local church's property. From this property revenue would be given to the bishop. Bishops were not allowed to sell any of the church's property but were to oversee the management of all of it. Because they were responsible for the entire budget, they were also responsible for the church's charities (ibid. 335).

Monasteries chose their own leader, who was in complete control of the management of the monastery, spiritually as well as financially. There was no reason for a bishop to interfere in monastic affairs except as an arbitrator. Monasteries were independent entities within the church (ibid. 341).

With the Christianization of the empire, Roman laws assigned bishops civic obligations and public service, since churches had become property owners. For example, they were to maintain public roads, city walls, and public buildings. The law permitted a bishop to be an arbitrator in a dispute, but only if the disputing parties agreed to his arbitration; the bishop had no official status to enforce his arbitration, however.

In Egypt, church-building was funded by private money. The state did not fund church-building as was done in other parts of the Roman Empire, which benefited from imperial building programs. Very few Egyptian temples were reused as churches. The architecture of ancient Egyptian churches has a distinctive Egyptian style that reflects indigenous traits and lacks the lavish elements of state sponsorship (van Ninnen 2007: 214; Farag 2012: 129).

The spread of Christianity throughout Egypt and the development of the church into a sophisticated structure inspired by the secular administrative model were attained through a long process of struggle between church and state.

The Church's Relations with the Pagan Roman Empire

When Mark the Evangelist proclaimed the Christian message in Alexandria, he was thrown in prison, tortured, and then dragged through the streets of

Alexandria to his death (Callahan 1992: 86–87, 96a). He was the first Christian martyr on Egyptian soil, but he would not be the last. Eusebius writes that the first persecution in Alexandria lasted four years (202–6) and was ordered by Emperor Severus (193–211). He dragged Christians from the province of Egypt in the north and Thebais in the south, that is, from all over Egypt, to be tortured to death in Alexandria (Eusebius, *Hist. eccl.* 6.1). Thus began a century of persecution and martyrdom for the sake of the Christian faith in Egypt.

The second major persecution was carried out by Emperor Decius (r. 249–51) around the time he issued an imperial edict for the citizens of the empire to offer sacrifices for the emperor; those who refused were to be tortured then executed. Eusebius asserts that persecution started a year before the decree was issued. He also describes the torture that the Christian writer Origen endured, as well as Bishop Dionysius' imprisonment and subsequent release by some Christians (ibid. 6.38–40). Eusebius gives an account of how Christians were pulled from their houses by their neighbors and asked to offer sacrifice to the emperor. When they refused, some were dragged in the streets, others beaten or tortured; some were imprisoned, others burned alive, and others recanted their faith fearing torture and death. Many Christian houses were looted and set on fire. Eusebius' detailed account informs us that the persecution did not discriminate between men and women, young or old, and it was not limited to Alexandria but spread throughout Egypt. Emperor Valerian (r. 253–60) issued two edicts, in 257 and 258, specifically targeting Christians, church hierarchy, and Christian senators. Bishop Dionysius was exiled during this persecution to Cephro in the Libyan desert. He described the courage of some Christians and asserts that the persecution affected all ages, genders, and social strata (ibid. 7.10–11).

Then comes what historians call "the Great Persecution," which occurred during Diocletian's reign (284–305). The persecution began with an order in 297/8 requiring all military and administrative personnel to offer sacrifice or leave their jobs. In 303 an edict was issued for the destruction of all churches and their books. In the same year, other edicts were issued for the imprisonment of all Christian clergy. A year later another edict ordered all Christians to offer sacrifice (Scarre 1995: 202). Eusebius writes that the number of those who suffered martyrdom in Egypt was in the "thousands" and that they died through gruesome tortures and killings (Eusebius, *Hist. eccl.* 8.7, 8, 10). The Diocletian era was so devastating to the Coptic Orthodox Church that they later renamed it "the era of the martyrs"; the *Annum Martyrum* of the liturgical calendar is counted from the ascension of Diocletian in 284. After Diocletian retired in 305, Galerius and Maximinus Daia continued the persecution. In 310 Maximinus, suffering from cancer, annulled the edicts of persecution on his death bed. Galerius died a few days later from an equally devastating disease. Six months later, Emperor Maximian rekindled the persecution, during which Pope Peter I was re-imprisoned and beheaded (ibid. 9.2, 6). Pope Peter I is known in Coptic history as the "Seal of the Martyrs."

Persecution did not prevent Egyptians from choosing the Christian faith preached by Mark the Evangelist. They chose Christianity under the penalty of death. They created new literary genres for the explication of their theology; they built churches, organized an ecclesial structure and its hierarchy, and saw their church leaders suffer with them for preserving the Christian faith and heritage. Ascetic and monastic practices also began to develop (see Chapter 8).

Religious persecution sprang from Roman ideology, which expected, if not demanded, the people to adopt the religion of the emperor as a sign of loyalty, both to the emperor and to the empire itself. By the third century, the emperor was considered a god as well as the political and military leader. Loyalty to the emperor who embodied these major state institutions became the symbol that united the empire. Not accepting the religion of the emperor would always be the cause of difficulties for the Copts, a theme that recurs throughout the history of Christianity in Egypt. Egyptians, however, hardly ever followed the emperor's faith. In tribal cultures, the tribe follows the leader and his faith, as happened with the Christianization of Europe. Egypt, however, was an agricultural, city-based culture in which Christianity spread through the personal conviction of one's faith. Following the faith of the emperor or tribal leader was not a cultural obligation.

The Church's Relation with the Christianized Roman Empire

The reign of Emperor Constantine (307–37) marked the beginning of a new era for the Roman Empire as well as for the history of Christianity. He shifted the seat of power to the eastern part of the empire by establishing a new capital in Constantinople, which became the center of government. By the 450s the western emperor had no power, even in Rome itself. The western empire with its capital Rome would face its demise in 476. These political shifts and the striving for power would affect many aspects of the history of Christianity in Egypt.

Constantine's Era and Athanasius

When Constantine became co-emperor, he issued the Edict of Milan, an edict of toleration of all religions which eventually ended the persecution. Constantine gradually began offering special preferences to Christianity and the clergy. He issued a law that exempted clergy from civil service, from collecting taxes, and from taxation (*CTh.* 16.2.1–2, 10). Churches could accept properties left in wills (ibid. 16.2.4). Bishops would not be summoned to secular courts but would be judged by a court of other bishops (ibid. 16.2.12); they had the right of jurisdiction according to Christian directives between Christian litigants (ibid. 1.27.1), among other privileges. The church had never had such privileges. At the same time, however, the state was gradually getting control of many aspects of the church and these privileges would become a bargaining chip to be withdrawn at the state's will.

The end of persecution set the church at peace with the state, but new internal challenges emerged. A certain priest by the name of Arius (d. 336) began preaching in the famous church of Baucalis in Alexandria. He became a popular preacher and gathered many admirers. But he propagated a theology that can be summed as the belief that Jesus Christ, the Son of God, is not divine. Such theology would jeopardize the Christian understanding of God as Trinity and salvation, in short, the essence of the Christian message. Pope Alexander of Alexandria (r. 312–26) convened a synod of Egyptian bishops at Alexandria and proceeded to excommunicate Arius. Meanwhile, Arius sought the support of bishop Eusebius of Nicomedia and the problem quickly extended beyond the Church of Alexandria. Bishops around the empire began to take sides and attempts at reconciliation failed. The debate extended beyond the church hierarchy as theological debates took place among the laity and began to galvanize public gatherings. Emperor Constantine, considering this theological debate a threat to the safety and unity of the empire, took matters into his own hands. He invited, or almost ordered, since he paid all travel expenses and accommodation to eliminate any excuse, all Christian bishops to meet in Nicaea, a city close to his new imperial residence in Constantinople. Bishops representing all the regions of the empire came; even those in the Persian Empire attended the council. The only exception was the Pope of Rome, who sent representatives to deliver his opinion in the debate; this precedent set the rule that the Pope of Rome never personally attended any ecumenical council before the separation of 1054. The council, through the influence of Athanasius of Alexandria, excommunicated Arius and issued a statement of faith that came to be known as the Nicene Creed.

This gathering in Nicea, which came to be known as the First Ecumenical Council (325), established other precedents in Christian history: An emperor, and only the emperor of the Roman Empire, had the right to call an ecumenical council, the gathering of all Christian bishops of the world to decide on theological and ecclesial matters. The Council of Nicaea was convened by state authority, not ecclesial. Another precedent was that, when the state approved of conciliar decisions, it enforced them by imperial might. Consequently, the bishops who refused to sign the statement of faith or the decrees of the Council of Nicaea were exiled from their episcopal sees by imperial orders based on the ecclesial decisions of the council. The Church of Alexandria and its bishops, Alexander of Alexandria and his successor Athanasius, who was then a deacon, were at the center of this debate and the theological stance of the Church of Alexandria was clearly expressed in the Nicene Creed. But when the emperor's stance towards Arianism changed, the bishops of Alexandria were exiled from their episcopal sees by military force.

The exiled Arian and Meletian bishops, members of a schismatic group within Egypt, lobbied against the Nicene bishops and eventually persuaded Emperor Constantine to exile Pope Athanasius. After the death of Constantine, his Arian son Constantius II (r. 337–61) and succeeding emperors, exiled Athanasius four more times. Athanasius (r. 326–73) spent half of his tenure in exile in defense of the Nicene theology. Athanasius was first exiled to Gaul (335–37) based on some false accusations. When he proved his innocence he returned, still keeping his position as Pope of Alexandria. Constantius II adopted a new policy; he sent the Arian Gregory, accompanied by a military force, to seize the episcopal see and replace Athanasius as bishop. Athanasius responded that this was against all Alexandrian church canons: Bishops are appointed after the laity and clergy agree on a person and request that he be their bishop. Bishops are not to be brought from outside the church or "from a distance" (Athanasius, *Circular Letter* 2). On another occasion Athanasius quotes a letter from Pope Julius of Rome in his defense, making the same case: Gregory was a stranger to the city of Alexandria, was not known to the laity, presbyters, or bishops there, was not baptized in that church, and was appointed in Antioch and installed by military force (Athanasius, *Defense Against the Arians* 30). Athanasius also quotes Hosius of Cordoba's letter to Constantius reprimanding the emperor for interfering in church affairs and ordering bishops to take church actions (Athanasius, *History of the Arians* 44).

Athanasius' response to the state's actions during the Arian controversy was crucial for the Church of Alexandria's relationship with the state. His policy is important because he was installed as bishop during the time of Constantine, the first emperor sympathetic to Christianity and the first to promulgate laws in favor of the church. It was a critical time in which the church was being shaped for a new era. Athanasius set the trajectory by making it clear that the bishops and laity would not allow the state to impose its decrees against church theology or canons, and the state was not to interfere by appointing its own candidates as bishops for the Church of Alexandria. Under the pagan empire, bishops and laity defended the faith with their blood against pagan oppression, which he himself had witnessed in his youth; after the empire became Christian, the bishops and laity would still defend orthodoxy with their own blood.

Athanasius was backed by the people. According to the historian Socrates, when Gregory arrived in Alexandria as the new Arian bishop, accompanied by 5,000 men, and besieged the church to apprehend Athanasius during the liturgical service, the people helped Athanasius to escape (Socrates, *Hist. eccl.* 2.11). Athanasius was now dispossessed of his episcopal see and all the church buildings came under the control of Gregory, who forbade non-Arians from attending church. Athanasius immediately began a program of building new churches for the faithful. Athanasius became the hero of the faith and the Coptic Church gave him the title "the Apostolic" for his defense of orthodoxy.

Athanasius' successor, Peter II (r. 373–80), was a pious figure who also faced exile for his defense of Nicene theology. When the Arian emperor Valens died, Emperor Theodosius (r. 379–95) ascended to the throne and Peter returned to Alexandria. Theodosius' tenure was characterized by full engagement in religious affairs, more than in his political or military responsibilities. Theodosius was pro-Nicene and a year after his ascension he issued an edict to the people of Constantinople to follow the faith of "Peter, Bishop of Alexandria, a man of apostolic sanctity; that is, according to the apostolic discipline and the evangelic doctrine, we shall believe in the single Deity of the Father, the Son, and the Holy Spirit, under the concept of equal majesty and of the Holy Trinity."

Only those who follow the faith of Peter II of Alexandria "shall embrace the name of Catholic Christians" (*CTh.* 16.2). Theodosius had inscribed in law Nicene theology, asserting the divinity of the Son. He also stated that the theology of Alexandria had become the standard of theological catholicity in the empire.

Theodosius embraced the Roman tenet that all subjects of the empire must follow the faith of the emperor. He issued edicts that forbade the offering of pagan sacrifice and non-Christians from assuming public positions, for "we believe that it is wrong that persons hostile to the Supernal Majesty and to the Roman laws should be considered the avengers of Our laws" (ibid. 16.7.5; 16.7.7; *NTh.* 3.2). His successive laws regarding pagan employment indicate that it took a long time for them to become effective. In 381, Emperor Theodosius issued a law that all churches seized by Arians were to be returned to orthodox bishops. That same year he called the Council of Constantinople to reaffirm Nicene theology and settle the more recent question of the divinity of the Holy Spirit. The affirmation of the Holy Spirit's divinity was added to the creed, which became the Niceno-Constantinopolitan creed. Canon Three of the council gave the bishop of Constantinople honor and privileges after the bishop of Rome, which Pope Leo of Rome would later challenge.

The Theodosian Era and Popes Theophilus, Cyril, and Dioscorus

Theodosius II (r. 408–50) was emperor during the tenure of three Coptic popes, Theophilus, Cyril of Alexandria, and Dioscorus. Theodosius' interest in theological issues, his policy of interfering in church affairs, and his relentless pursuit of heresy and paganism are the common threads that run through the events of the tenure of these three popes. Pope Theophilus (r. 385–412) was Athanasius' protégé. He took the opportunity of the pro-Nicene sentiments of Emperor Theodosius and launched a building program, building seven churches in Alexandria and renovating several other churches and monasteries beyond Alexandria. It was during his tenure that the Serapeum in Alexandria was demolished. Theophilus came to be regarded as a wise and respected arbitrator on three occasions: in the Meletian schism in Antioch regarding two orthodox bishops' claim to the see, in a dispute at Bostra regarding a succession disagreement, and in mediation in Palestine, where the authority of John of Jerusalem was undermined in his own diocese (Russell 2007: 11–17). Theophilus, however, became entangled in a controversy in the Nitrian desert that resulted in four monks, known as the Tall Brothers, fleeing to Constantinople. On their arrival, John Chrysostom, the bishop of Constantinople, was careful not to receive them on an official basis, hoping he could negotiate peace with their bishop Theophilus. The latter considered John Chrysostom's mediation interference in the internal affairs of the Church of Alexandria, especially because there were accusations against Chrysostom for interfering in the affairs of the Church of Ephesus. Events escalated and the Tall Brothers presented their petition to the emperor. Theophilus was summoned to Constantinople. The table was turned, however, and it was John Chrysostom who was put on trial, being accused, among other things, of squandering church funds. Chrysostom's justifiable though fiery and relentless rhetoric against the conduct of members of the imperial court, including the empress, as well as his public condemnation of the extravagant lifestyle of his own clergy, made him many enemies on the panel of judges presided over by Theophilus. He was deposed in absentia, having refused four summations to appear before the synod. Chrysostom's sympathizers have tarnished Theophilus' reputation in historical records. This episode with Chrysostom has overshadowed Theophilus' respected and gifted arbitration, knowledge of canonical law and theological acumen, and the role of the Coptic Church as an ecumenical negotiator.

Theophilus' successor, Cyril of Alexandria (r. 412–44), became entangled into the Nestorian controversy. Nestorius, the bishop of Constantinople, preached that the Virgin Mary was to be called *Christotokos* (Bearer of Christ) and not *Theotokos* (Bearer of God) based on his theological understanding that the Virgin Mary did not bear the Son of God, but the human Jesus who after birth was in conjunction with the divinity through his will. The implication of such a doctrine was that there were two persons in Jesus Christ, one divine and one human, loosely conjoined by will. Cyril expressed the unity as a unity of natures, which after the union became one nature in the one person of Christ. The unity of natures was without confusion, change, mixture, or the absorption of the human nature by the divine. Events escalated to a public exchange of letters. Cyril sent three letters to Nestorius, in the third requesting Nestorius to publicly anathematize twelve significant theological points. These included acknowledging the term "Theotokos" and the necessity of speaking about "union" rather than "conjunction" (Cyril, *Third Letter to Nestorius*). Unknown to Cyril, Emperor Theodosius had observed the escalation of the controversy and called for a council to convene in Ephesus (431). The council was polarized among two factions, pro-Nestorian and pro-Cyrillian. Cyril, as the most senior bishop, presided over the council, though an imperial representative was present to oversee the proceedings. The emperor closely monitored the council. After delays and interruptions, Nestorius was eventually deposed as bishop of Constantinople and returned to his monastery. Alexandrian theology had again triumphed as the yardstick of orthodoxy and Cyril's writings became an indispensable theological reference.

Theological debates did not abate with a conciliar decision. The debate regarding the nature of the person of Christ and how to understand the unity continued. Eutychius, an archimandrite of a monastery in Constantinople, was in correspondence with Pope Leo of Rome regarding the renewed activity of Nestorius' followers. Pope Leo responded on June 1, 448, to his "dearly-beloved son, Eutychius," thanking him for the update (Leo, *Letter 20*). When Eutychius was condemned for his controversial theology about the single divine nature of Christ incarnate by a local synod presided at by Bishop Flavian of Constantinople, he appealed to Leo. But Flavian also sought Leo's support, informing him of the defrocking of Eutychius. Flavian wanted the matter to be handled locally, and Leo's support would have finalized the matter. Leo, however, escalated the matter and the emperor called the Council of Ephesus II, which was presided at by Dioscorus of Alexandria (r. 444–58). In response, Leo started a campaign, writing a letter to Flavian (*Letter 28*, also known as the Tome of Leo), expressing his official theological stance towards the two-nature Christology, a letter to Emperor Theodosius, two letters to Empress Pulcheria in which he excuses himself from the council but urges her to interfere in the Eutychian controversy, a letter to the Council at Ephesus, and two to other dignitaries in Constantinople (*Letters 29–35*). The pope sent another letter to the emperor to dissuade him from convening the council in Ephesus (*Letter 37*). In Letter 38 he gives instructions to Flavian to accept Eutychius if he accepts the true faith. Leo was informed that his Letter 28 was not read in the council and that Eutychius had accepted the faith of Nicaea and was thus reinstated. Leo did not feel Ephesus II had followed his instructions, since Letter 28 was not read, and he dismissed the council as "The Robber's Council" (*Letter 95*). He then started another campaign to persuade the emperor to convene another council, reminding Emperor Theodosius that a single faith strengthens the empire (*Letter 69*). At this point in the correspondence, Emperor Theodosius died.

The Council of Chalcedon (451) and its Aftermath

The new Emperor Marcian and his wife Empress Pulcheria became great supporters of Leo and for good reason. Attila the Hun had already invaded Gaul and was on the outskirts of Rome. The new emperor needed all possible support to rescue the declining western part of his empire. Leo of Rome intensified his campaign for a new council in Italy. Marcian, however, decided the council would meet in Chalcedon under his watchful eye. Leo excused himself for not attending the council due to the dire political situation facing Rome and because there was no precedent for the bishop of Rome to attend a council. He was promised that his delegates would preside (*Letter 93*). Pope Dioscorus arrived at the Council of Chalcedon in 451 to find that the bishops who had been excommunicated by Cyril of Alexandria at the Council of Ephesus (431) were present and that the council was to accept the Tome of Leo, with which Dioscorus could not comply. Knowing that the situation was not in his favor, he refused to attend the meetings. He was summoned three times and then deposed by the council, not for theological reasons, but because he refused to submit to the summoning.

Leo received a letter from the Council of Chalcedon, dated November 451, informing him of the excommunication of Eutychius, but also informing him of Canon 28, which ratified Canon Three of the Council of Constantinople and gave the Church of Constantinople precedence by placing it second after Rome. The letter made it clear that, since the bishops of the East had accepted the Tome, Leo had to accept the primacy of Constantinople, reminding him of the support he received from Emperor Marcian (*Letter 98*). The Council of Chalcedon met to seal a political agreement between Marcian and Leo at a time when the emperor was losing his grip of the western empire. Leo attempted to annul Canon 28 (*Letters 104–7*) but was unsuccessful. As late as February 453, Leo had not confirmed the acts of the Council of Chalcedon because he would not accept Canon 28 (*Letter 110*). In further correspondence with Maximus, the Chalcedonian bishop of Antioch, he reiterated that he did not accept Canon 28 and still considered Antioch in third place after Rome and Alexandria thus placing Constantinople fourth (*Letter 119*). He signed his approval of the council in 454 (*Letter 132*). It is interesting to note that Alexandria and Antioch opposed the council regarding the orthodoxy of the faith, while Leo's objections were about ecclesial precedence.

Leo urged Empress Eudocia to pressure Dioscorus to accept Chalcedon (*Letter 123*). When Dioscorus died, Leo wrote to Julian of Jerusalem expressing his relief at Dioscorus' death (*Letter 140*). The events of Chalcedon were met with riots all over Egypt. Military force was used to suppress the monks, which Leo welcomed. When Leo received news that the Alexandrians considered him Nestorian, he ordered Proterius, the Chalcedonian bishop of Alexandria, to read his Tome in Alexandria to convince the people otherwise (*Letter 129*). When the non-Chalcedonian Timothy II was elected bishop of Alexandria, Pope Leo sent a letter to Emperor Leo (457–74) demanding that Timothy be deposed, arguing that the emperor was given secular rule and the guardianship of the church to eliminate heretics who weakened the empire (*Letter 156*). Emperor Leo exiled Pope Timothy to Gangra and sent another Timothy, accompanied by military force, to seize the episcopacy of Alexandria (*Letter 158, 165*). In 458 Emperor Leo I received a petition from the people of Alexandria, the dignitaries, and the guild of ship owners demanding the return of Pope Timothy II to his see. They threatened to stop the grain supply to Constantinople, especially since Alexandria itself was suffering from a grain shortage. There was discontent in Alexandria (Farag 2012: 126).

Pope Leo's behavior can be understood within its political context. The Germanic tribes had invaded Britain, Gaul, Spain, and Roman Africa. With the loss of the latter, Rome was unable to feed itself for lack of grain. Marcian observed the rapid decline of the western empire and accepted Leo's proposal in a frantic attempt to secure the last bastion of Roman allegiance. Marcian also wanted to strengthen the eastern empire, in view of the demise of the west, by asserting the political, as well as the religious, position of the eastern capital of Constantinople through Canon 28. Pope Leo considered this move a weakening of the western political center. His sense of urgency to establish Rome's absolute primacy is explicable within this political climate. The western empire fell in 476, though the actual "fall" started decades earlier. In addition, the eastern provinces of the empire, Syria and Palestine, were under continuous Persian attack and their loyalty was essential to secure the eastern frontiers. Attempts to achieve doctrinal unity by imperial decree created a permanently divided church.

The exile of Pope Dioscorus by the Council of Chalcedon and the appointment of Proterius, enforced by imperial order and military force, led to great violence in Alexandria. The memory of Athanasius' struggle for orthodoxy against Arian emperors was evoked. For the Church of Alexandria, the theological orthodoxy of Dioscorus was founded on the unchallenged orthodoxy of both Athanasius and Cyril. The legitimacy of Dioscorus' appointment followed the guidelines affirmed by Athanasius. For the Egyptians, Proterius was theologically and canonically illegitimate. The same argument would apply to all the imperially appointed bishops that followed.

Attempts at Unity

Emperor Zeno's reign (474–91) was interrupted by an insurrection by Basiliscus, who summoned Pope Timothy from exile. Timothy persuaded Basiliscus to send a circular to anathematize the Tome of Leo and Chalcedon's decisions (Evagrius, *Hist. eccl.* 3.4). According to Evagrius, 500 bishops signed the circular. Accacius, bishop of Constantinople, however, believed that nullifying Chalcedon would diminish the status of Constantinople; Basiliscus issued a counter circular to annul the first. Emperor Zeno regained power, and issued a document of unity, the *Henotikon*, written by Accacius. The *Henotikon* reiterated the condemnation of Nestorius and Eutychius, affirmed the twelve anathemas of Cyril of Alexandria, and excluded the Chalcedonian definition of faith (ibid. 3.12). Pope Felix of Rome refused the *Henotikon* and excommunicated bishop Accacius. The Accacian Schism was settled in 519 when Emperor Justin I satisfied the west by rejecting the *Henotikon* and affirming Accacius' excommunication.

Emperor Justinian (r. 527–65) was a strict enforcer of Chalcedonianism. He was ruthless with those who did not follow his faith (Prokopios 2010: 13.7). Roman emperors were the enforcers of conciliar policies, but Justinian became the creator of new religious policies. Justinian, on his own prerogative, without any conciliar decision, deposed Pope Theodosius of Alexandria (r. 535–67), who refused to follow the emperor's faith. He also closed all pagan temples, even the Isis temple of Philae on the southern Egyptian frontier. This is when paganism in Egypt finally began to fade away. Justinian called the Second Council of Constantinople (553), but failed to unite the east.

Theological disputes divided churches and weakened the eastern empire during a time when major military battles were taking place against the Sassanids (Persians) and later the Arabs. Constantinople suffered a military setback when the Sassanids conquered Egypt in 618 for its rich grain products. Constantinople could not feed its inhabitants or sustain the military. This was the first military invasion of Egypt after the Romans conquered it in 30 BC. John, the Chalcedonian bishop of Alexandria, fled to his homeland of Cyprus. During the tenure of John, known as the Almsgiver, orthodox popes of Alexandria were forbidden to enter the city (Evetts 1948: 214). This is when orthodox popes began residing in monasteries and practicing their pastoral care through the monasteries. After a political deal between Emperor Heraclius and the Sassanid military leader residing in Alexandria, the empire seized Egypt back in 629. Heraclius needed to unite the east. The appointment of Cyrus, the Chalcedonian bishop of Alexandria, consolidated his administrative, fiscal, military, and religious power over Upper Egypt (Palme 2007: 265). He used this power to impose the Chalcedonian theology on the church of Egypt. In the time of both Justinian and Heraclius, monks who did not adhere to Chalcedonianism were kicked out of their monasteries, which caused the devastation of many institutions.

After the Sassanid wars, Emperor Heraclius and Bishop Sergius of Constantinople attempted to unite the east through the doctrine of *Monoenergism*, which proposes that the activities (*energeia*) of the humanity and the divinity within the person of Christ are one and cannot be separated. *Monoenergism* was an attempt to convince the non-Chalcedonians, including Egypt, to accept the Council of Chalcedon. In 630, Cyrus, the appointed Chalcedonian bishop of Alexandria, began preaching *Monoenergism*. Sophronius, bishop of Jerusalem, started a vigorous campaign against *Monoenergism*. Pope Honorius I of Rome, accepted the doctrine of *Monoenergism* in 635, but Sophronius continued his opposition and soon acceptance of *Monoenergism* began to fade. Sergius and Heraclius abandoned the project. In 638, Sergius modified his doctrine with *Monothelitism*, which teaches that while Christ has two natures, he has one will (*thelema*). In the meanwhile, the successors of Pope Honorius, Popes Severinus and John IV of Rome rejected *Monothelitism* and the Chalcedonian churches were divided. At the Council of Constantinople (681), however, Rome and Constantinople agreed on a two-nature, two-will theology and anathematized the one-nature theology of the Church of Alexandria. Egypt, together with the rest of Mesopotamia, by now conquered by the Arabs, was not worth any compromise anymore. Besides, the council could not enforce decisions on churches beyond its political control. All these theological negotiations, the *Henotikon*, *Monoenergism*, and *Monothelitism*, consolidated the Rome–Constantinople political and religious front but created a wider rift with the Church of Alexandria.

In 641, the Arabs conquered Egypt. Roman armies defended Egypt and when they withdrew the Egyptians were defenseless. At first, the Egyptians thought they would leave, as the Sassanids had. Though some later historical accounts suggest that Egyptians helped the Arabs conquer Egypt, such suggestions defy logic. The Egyptians saw the Sassanids come and leave; it would be political suicide to help the emerging nomadic Arabs against two major empires, the Byzantine and the Persian. In addition, there was no religious or ethnic affiliation between the Egyptians and the Arabs. Egyptians did not help the Sassanids, so why would they help the Arabs? Why replace one conqueror with another? Moreover, neither the Egyptians nor Pope Benjamin, the bishop of Alexandria at the time, had the political power to negotiate a treaty with the Arabs.

The story of the first seven centuries of Christianity in Egypt is the story of great struggle for, witness to, defense of, and sacrifice for the faith. It is the formative period, when Christianity spread throughout Egypt and began to take the form that decided the shape and character of the Egyptian church through the centuries. Though the political climate was often adversarial, the church was able to develop its great theological, literary, monastic, and Christian heritage. It is a period marked by an extraordinary defense of the faith at all costs, which shaped the Egyptian Christian character.

Timeline

42	Mark the Evangelist preaches in Alexandria and founds its church
189–231	Demetrius, eleventh bishop in succession of Mark
202–6	First persecution in Alexandria under Emperor Severus
303	Diocletian persecution, "the Great Persecution"
311	Martyrdom of Pope Peter I, "the Seal of Martyrs"
313	The Edict of Milan for the toleration of religion, including Christianity
325	The Council of Nicaea
326–73	Athanasius "the Apostolic," Pope of the Church of Alexandria
381	The Council of Constantinople
408–50	Emperor Theodosius II
412–44	Pope Cyril of Alexandria, "the Pillar of Faith"
431	Council of Ephesus I
444–58	Dioscorus I of Alexandria, deposed by the Council of Chalcedon
450–51	Council of Chalcedon
458–80	Pope Timothy II, deposed
474–91	Emperor Zeno
482	*Henotikon*, document of unity
484–519	Accacian Schism
541	The Bubonic plague kills 20 to 50 percent of the population
610–41	Emperor Heraclius, collapse of the empire's eastern provinces, including Egypt
618–29	Sassanid Conquest, strengthened from Egyptian income tax and grain
640–41	Arab Conquest

Selected Bibliography

All short references are to primary sources available in many print editions as well as on the web.

Athanasius of Alexandria, *Circular Letter*.

——*Defense Against the Arians*.

——*History of the Arians*.

Bagnall, R. S. (1993) *Egypt in Late Antiquity*, Princeton: Princeton University Press.

Callahan, A. D. (1992) "The 'Acts of Saint Mark': An Introduction and Commentary," unpublished dissertation, Harvard University.

CTh. (1952) *The Theodosian Code*, ed. and trans. C. Pharr, New Jersey: Princeton University Press.

Cyril of Alexandria *Three Letters to Nestorius.*
Eusebius *Ecclesiastical History* (*Historia ecclesiastica* [*Hist. eccl.*]).
Evagrius Scholasticus *Ecclesiastical History* (*Historia ecclesiastica* [*Hist. eccl.*]).
Evetts, B. (ed.) (1948) *History of the Patriarchs of the Coptic Church of Alexandria II, Peter I to Benjamin I* (661), Patrologia Orientalis, tome 1, fasc. 4, Paris: Librairie de Paris.
Farag, L. (2012) "Roman Citizens without Roman Privileges: The Church of Alexandria and Roman Law," in M. Ayad (ed.) *Coptic Culture: Past, Present and Future*, Oxford: Oxbow.
John of Nikiu (1916) *Chronicle*, trans. R. H. Charles, London: Williams and Norgate.
Kiss, Z. (2007) "Alexandria in the Fourth to the Seventh Centuries," in R. S. Bagnall (ed.) *Egypt in the Byzantine World, 300–700*, New York: Cambridge University Press.
Leo of Rome *Letters.*
Lewis, N. (1999) *Life in Egypt under Roman Rule*, 2nd edn, Oakville, CT: The American Society of Papyrologists.
Orlandi, T. (1999) "The Coptic Ecclesiastical History: A Survey," in J. Goehring and J. Timbie (eds) *The World of Early Egyptian Christianity*, Washington, D.C.: The Catholic University of America Press.
Palme, B. (2007) "The Imperial Presence: Government and Army," in R. S. Bagnall (ed.) *Egypt in the Byzantine World, 300–700*, New York: Cambridge University Press.
Paphnutius (1993) *Histories of the Monks of Upper Egypt and the Life of Onnophrius by Paphnutius*, trans. T. Vivian, Kalamazoo, MI: Cistercian Publications.
Price, R. and Gaddis, M. (trans.) (2007) *The Acts of the Council of Chalcedon*, 3 vols, Liverpool: Liverpool University Press.
Prokopios (2010) *The Secret History*, trans. and ed. A. Kaldellis, Indianapolis: Hackett.
Russell, N. (2007) *Theophilus of Alexandria*, London: Routledge.
Scarre, C. (1995) *Chronicle of the Roman Emperors*, New York: Thames and Hudson.
Socrates *Ecclesiastical History* (*Historia ecclesiastica* [*Hist. eccl.*]).
Sozomen *Ecclesiastical History* (*Historia ecclesiastica* [*Hist. eccl.*]).
Theodoret *Ecclesiastical History* (*Historia ecclesiastica* [*Hist. eccl.*]).
van Ninnen, P. (2007) "The Other Cities in Later Roman Egypt," in R. S. Bagnall (ed.) *Egypt in the Byzantine World, 300–700*, New York: Cambridge University Press.
Wipszycka, E. (2007) "The Institutional Church," in R. S. Bagnall (ed.) *Egypt in the Byzantine World, 300–700*, New York: Cambridge University Press.

3 The Early Islamic Period (641–1517)

From the Arab Conquest through Mamlūk Rule

Maged S. A. Mikhail

The status of the Coptic Orthodox Church and community under Islamic rule fluctuated erratically due to several factors, such as the tenor of interpersonal relations among governing authorities and Coptic lay and clerical elites, regional politics, and caliphal relations with Byzantines and Crusaders. This inexorably complicates any attempt to succinctly summarize the history of the confession. Still, while assessing the standing of the community at any juncture is predicated upon a multitude of factors, the overall trajectory is obvious enough. From the seventh through the early sixteenth centuries, the Copts experienced radical demographic demise, lost a large percentage of their religious endowments (*awqāf*), and succumbed to a host of progressively stringent legal regulations. The harshest of these laws, the *dhull* (Debasement) Regulations—a restrictive body of laws, including clothing and riding regulations, that were often accompanied by a purging of non-Muslims (*dhimmīs*) from the administration—were not strictly enforced beyond limited periods ranging from a few months to a few years (Cohen 1994: ch. 4), but the frequency of their imposition increased under the Ayyūbids (1171–1250) and they were reissued at nearly every decade during the fifteenth century under the Mamlūks. Sobering as they are, these facts should not cloud another equally significant narrative of perseverance, adaptation, innovation, and the Copts' contribution to Egyptian society and culture.

Early Islamic Rule (641–61)

The Arab conquest of Egypt (completed by 642) prompted a sharp political break from Byzantine rule, but cultural continuity eclipsed the new political order on nearly every front. Scholars have forwarded various narratives for the conquest and the supposed attitude of the Copts toward the early Arab regime. Much of that literature has to be read with credulity, however. Many of the details of the conquest, which seem so vivid in ninth-century narratives, prove problematic upon closer examination, and while sectarian attitudes are easily discernible in later texts, seventh-century sources depict a variety of responses, many of which fail to conform to the tidy depictions of later authors (cf. Butler 1998; Hoyland 1997). Some Egyptians—Copts and Melkites—did collaborate with the

Arabs, though the earliest sources emphasize that the aid rendered was under duress (John of Nikiou, *Chronicle*: 120.30–31; cf. 121.5). Others fought against them, while others still simply came to terms with the advancing forces, safeguarding their lives and properties. Reliance on later sources is particularly striking in the normative literature's depiction of Patriarch Benjamin as an Arab ally who facilitated their conquest of the province (Fraser 1991). Minimally, the patriarch had been in virtual exile in Upper Egypt since 631 and only returned to Alexandria in 644 (well after the Arabs had conquered Egypt); he was in no position to aid or hinder the advancement of Arab armies. In the earliest post-conquest decades, most Egyptians seem to have viewed the Arabs as transitory occupiers, much like the Sassanids who years earlier dominated the province for a decade (619–29). It was not until the late seventh century that Egyptians began to perceive the Arabs as a permanent presence (Kaegi 1969).

Almost immediately after the conquest, secular elites (both Coptic and Melkite) demonstrated the important roles they would play under Islamic rule. The actions of the Coptic *dux* Shenoute of the Thebaid well reflect the new dynamic. Integrated into the nascent Islamic administration by joining the conquering general 'Amr ibn al-'Āṣ's personal entourage, Shenoute used his influence to negotiate for the return of Patriarch Benjamin from exile, and used his personal funds to restore the Church of St. Mark in Alexandria. Many elites functioned along similar lines, facilitating interactions among representatives of their respective religious communities and government elites, while patronizing and actively protecting their coreligionists and their assets in word and deed.

The early Arab administration mimicked the infrastructure of the former Byzantine bureaucracy, but it exhibited a penchant for centralization and tighter oversight (Sijpesteijn 2007). It even employed many of the same personnel; hence, the post-conquest administration remained largely staffed by Greek-speaking pro-Chalcedonians (Melkites). The initial dominance of pro-Chalcedonians, coupled with the early Arab government's indifference to confessional issues, allowed some Melkites to conduct an unofficial campaign of discrimination and harassment against the Copts by sequestering churches and increasing taxes, particularly on Coptic clergy. In general, the early Islamic government showed little interest in sectarian squabbles; the various sects of Christians and Jews were functionally lumped together as the People of the Book (*Ahl al-kitāb*, or People of the Pact (of Protection), *Ahl al-dhimmā*) and that sufficed (Bosworth 1982: I.37–51). Overwhelmingly, the nascent administration aimed to secure the Arabs' hold on the province and to tax it effectively. The Copts did enjoy some liberties during those early decades but, contrary to much of the extant scholarship on the issue, which assumes a close working relationship between the ecclesiastical hierarchy and early Islamic government, the liberties enjoyed were due to the lifting of Byzantine prohibitions rather than the granting of privileges by the Arab Muslim government.

One of the immediate repercussions of the conquest appears to have been a shift in religious affiliation. There is evidence to suggest that the Melkite community had gained converts throughout the first four decades of the seventh century—in part due to the saintly actions of the pro-Chalcedonian Patriarch John the Almsgiver (611–19), and subsequently on account of the strong-arm tactics of Cyrus (631–41), the prefect–patriarch appointed by the Emperor Heraclius. Nearly all significant conversions during the first century of Islamic rule, however, were by individuals and schismatic confessions who joined the Coptic hierarchy. Conversion to Islam throughout this period—though attested—was marginal (Mikhail forthcoming: ch. 4).

Umayyad Dynasty (661–750)

This status quo radically changed during the pivotal gubernatorial tenure of ʻAbd al-ʻAzīz ibn Marwān (685–705), whose most trusted secretaries, Athanasius the Syrian and Isaac the Egyptian, were anti-Chalcedonians who recruited many of their coreligionists to serve in the bureaucracy. ʻAbd al-ʻAzīz took a keen and, at that juncture, novel interest in the affairs of the Coptic community and hierarchy; he was the first Arab official to intervene in patriarchal elections, setting a precedent for governmental oversight and approval of patriarchal nominees that has lasted until the modern period. It was at that juncture that the abuses dealt by pro-Chalcedonian elites in the early decades of Arab rule were redressed, and the Copts began to be treated with deference—albeit for a short duration. The community also benefited from the personal relationship that developed between the governor and Patriarch Isaac (690–92), not to be confused with the above-mentioned secretary.

In the twilight of his career, ʻAbd al-ʻAzīz implemented an Arabizing edict issued by his brother, the Caliph ʻAbd al-Malik (685–705). Since the conquest, the Egyptian bureaucracy had maintained records primarily in Greek—though Coptic and Arabic documents also played a role—but in 705 ʻAbd al-Malik mandated that henceforth all records and correspondences must be kept in Arabic. By providing an impetus for Christian elites to learn Arabic, this edict set the language on a new trajectory. No longer limited to the Arab community and new converts to Islam, Arabic progressively morphed into the language of elites, social mobility and, later, under the ʻAbbasids, the language of literature and Egyptian Christianity.

In the early decades of the eighth century, a land survey coincided with the beginning of individual tax assessment, especially of the *jizya* (a poll tax demanded of non-Muslim males). Both developments translated into de facto tax hikes, which triggered the initial wave of the ill-designated "Coptic Revolts." Commencing in the second half of Umayyad rule and continuing intermittently into the early ninth century, many of these uprisings were localized disturbances, while a few, such as those that coincided with the *fitna* (811–13), the civil war between the sons of the Caliph Harūn al-Rashīd, al-Amīn, and al-Ma'mūn, were on an entirely different scale. Often romanticized and misconstrued, all of these "Coptic" revolts were incited by tax policies, and while the early revolts involved primarily Egyptians—those who were directly affected by tax increases—under early ʿAbbasid rule, Arab Muslims, who had become increasingly targeted for taxation, participated in these uprisings and even incited several of them (Morimoto 1981: 145–72).

The governorship of Qurra ibn Sharīk (709–14), which coincided with the early career of Patriarch Alexander II (704–29), proved significant on several fronts. Documentary sources present Qurra as a fair-minded and able governor, though his depiction in Christian (and Islamic) narrative sources is much less flattering. This was due in part to Qurra's dogged pursuit of taxes and, especially for the Christians, his appropriation of precious building materials, in particular marble, from churches.[1] Qurra's tenure also witnessed the first tensions pertaining to the building and upkeep of ecclesiastical properties and the first state-sponsored discriminatory edicts targeting the Copts, which were soon superseded in their severity by the short-lived policies of the Caliph ʿUmar II (717–20). A few years later, the minister of finance (*Ṣāḥib al-kharāj*), ʿUbayd Allāh ibn al-Ḥabḥāb (724–34), inaugurated the first official wave of Arab immigration to Egypt, which culminated with the novel act of settling the Arabs as farmers—rather than soldiers—in the heart of the Delta. These new settlers facilitated the spread of the Arabic language and provided a socio-religious network for early converts to Islam.

At mid-century, the Umayyads found themselves unable to resist an ʿAbbasid revolution that swept east to west within a few years. By 750, the ʿAbbasids firmly controlled the caliphate and had executed the last Umayyad caliph, Marwān II, in Upper Egypt. Chaotic on every front, the transition was particularly harsh on Patriarch Michael I. At one point, Marwān II had attempted to ransom the patriarch, but then opted to keep him as a hostage.

ʿAbbasid Rule (750–1258)[2]

The ʿAbbasids ushered in new, more equitable policies toward converts to Islam, who, aside from a few exceptional periods under the Umayyads, still had to pay the *jizya*. Many Muslims had long condemned this policy, which was reversed in the twilight of Umayyad rule and then permanently revoked by the new regime. This policy-shift prompted the first waves of mass conversion to Islam in Egypt; still, the above-mentioned pattern of intra-Christian conversions, from various sects to the demographically dominant Coptic confession, persisted through the ninth century (Mikhail forthcoming: ch. 4). Along with their new fiscal policies, ʿAbbasid scholars were the first to pose an intellectual challenge to Christianity (and Judaism). In Syria, the response was swift (see Griffith 2008: ch. 4). The earliest Arabic apology for the Christian faith dates within a few years of 750—a prelude to a massive body of literature that articulated and defended the Christian faith in Arabic. Over the next few decades, the Syrians also inaugurated a thorough translation project of the Christian scriptures into Arabic. The response in Egypt, however, lagged until the mid-tenth century. Once they began to compose in Arabic, however, the Copts drafted more Arabic Christian texts than nearly all their Christian neighbors combined (ibid. 136, cf. 92).

By and large, early 'Abbasid rule in Egypt proved fairly tolerant and stable. Many of the social disruptions documented in the first fifty years of their Caliphate stemmed from tax increases or land-surveys; hence, the persistence of the so-called "Coptic Revolts." At the end of the eighth century, the tenure of Patriarch John IV (776–99) appears to have been especially prosperous. Buttressed by favorable inter-communal relations, the patriarch inaugurated an ambitious building program that, in turn, called for the procurement and translation of relics to the new structures. (The relics of saints Macarius the Great and John the Little made their way to Wādī al-Naṭrūn (Scetis) during this period.) Nonetheless, throughout this period conversion to Islam persisted, and original composition in the Coptic language reached an all-time low.

The ninth century commenced with the demolition of churches. Harūn al-Rashīd had decreed that only the churches and synagogues that pre-existed the conquests may stand, but all those built under Arab rule had to be destroyed. Earlier, the ownership of ecclesiastical structures had come into question (especially in Jerusalem and Syria) but the tensions and policies relating to the construction and renovation of churches were somewhat novel. The early Islamic government did not restrict such projects; even the above-mentioned contentious incident in Egypt—during the tenure of Qurra ibn Sharīk—was likely a pretext for an intra-Muslim (Qaysī-Yamanī) dispute. Under the late Umayyads, officials had to be bribed, but building activities persisted and, as mentioned above, a sprawling building program commenced during the last decades of the eighth century. Still, al-Rashīd's edict set a precedent and, while it was only observed for a brief span, it led to the demolition of several churches, which the Christians were later allowed to rebuild. This pattern of demolition and reconstruction of churches punctuates Coptic historical annals.

At mid-century, the caliphate of al-Mutawakkil (847–61) brought about the first extended period of turmoil. He had prided himself on restoring orthodox Islam, a task he accomplished by ending the *miḥnā* (Inquisition) inaugurated earlier by the Caliph al-Ma'mūn (in 830) who sought to impose the doctrine of the created Qur'ān. Al-Mutawakkil further asserted his religious credentials by cracking down on the Sabians of Ḥaran, a largely Pagan population, and the *Zanadiqa* (Manicheans) of Persia, both of whom had hitherto been legally grouped with Christians and Jews under the umbrella of *Ahl al-dhimmā*. Al-Mutawakkil then shifted his attention to Christians and Jews. He ordered the destruction of churches, purged Christians from the bureaucracy, tried to force notables to convert to Islam, and imposed the full range of *dhull* regulations. These harsh policies did not abate until shortly before the caliph's death.

In the latter half of the ninth century, Aḥmad ibn Ṭūlūn (d. 884) succeeded in forging an autonomous ruling dynasty in Egypt. Ṭūlūnid rule (868–905) proved difficult for the church, though the community appears to have fared better. Copts still retained prestigious positions, but personal interactions between Ibn Ṭūlūn and Patriarch Michael III were strained; the governor often demanded exorbitant sums from the patriarch. Tradition maintains that Ibn Ṭūlūn employed a Copt, Ibn Kātib al-Farghānī, as the chief architect for a

Nilometer and the famous mosque that carries Aḥmad's name. While the originality of the design has been exaggerated (Behrens-Abouseif 1989: 50–56), the employment of the same architect for the two structures is likely. Ibn Ṭūlūn was succeeded by his son Khumārawayh, who demonstrated greater leniency in his interactions with the Coptic hierarchy than his father. Subsequent political events, the 'Abbasid reconquest of the province in 905, and the rule of the Ikhshīdids (935–69), are largely overshadowed in Christian sources that focus on internal problems: simony, the rising tide of conversion to Islam, and problems in the kingdom of Ethiopia, which received its highest ranking cleric, a metropolitan bishop, from Egypt until the early modern era.

Fāṭimids (969–1171)

Political chaos during the last years of Ikhshīdid rule, exacerbated by a series of low Nile inundations, facilitated the Fāṭimid conquest of Egypt in 969. General Jawhar took the province in the name of the Shi'ī Fāṭimids, who had already controlled the rest of North Africa for decades and would soon extend their rule into Syria. Immediately, Jawhar founded a new capital, al-Qāhira (Cairo: "The Victorious (City)"), and the al-Azhar Mosque, which became a prominent center for the propagation of Shi'ī Islam. Later, under the Ayyūbids, it developed into the leading center of learning among Sunnī Muslims. A few years after the conquest, in 973, the Fāṭimid imām (or caliph) al-Mu'izz (953–75) relocated from Mahdiyya (in modern day Tunisia) to his new capital accompanied, we are told, by a caravan of a thousand stumbling camels who had difficulty walking on account of the tremendous weight of gold each was carrying. Fāṭimid gold, Egypt's production of flax and sugarcane (two important cash crops), control over North Africa and Syria, and hegemony over the Red Sea trade rendered early Fāṭimid rule in Egypt an economically prosperous and politically peaceful period. ('Abbasid caliphs had lost much of their power by that point and they—along with the whole of Iraq—were subject to the political rule of the Shi'ī Buyids.)

Early Fāṭimid rule (969–96) proved significant for the Copts on several fronts. As Shi'īs in a predominantly Sunnī province, the dynasty exercised great restraint and balance in political and religious affairs. Many Coptic Christians served in the administration and, for the most part, Coptic patriarchs enjoyed an amicable relationship with ruling elites, including the imāms. At that time of constant secular and ecclesiastical interactions between Egypt and Syria, the Copts chose a pious Syrian merchant as their patriarch, Afraham (Abraham) ibn Zur'ah (975–78). (The Copts have had four patriarchs of Syrian descent.) He and the erudite Bishop of Ashmūnīn, Sawīrus ibn al-Muqaffa', would become the best-known Christian figures of this period.

Bishop Sawīrus was a theologian and an apologist of refined learning who wrote exclusively in Arabic (Griffith 1996), inaugurating a new genre: Coptic Arabic literature, a designation that encompasses Arabic Christian texts translated or authored by Copts.[3] In addition to original composition, the bishop's career dovetailed with the initial stages of two largely concurrent multi-generational translation programs and a shift in the use and perception of the Greek language. One project focused on translating Coptic (and some Greek) literature into Arabic (Rubenson 1996; Richter 2009), while a parallel program sought to translate Sahidic Coptic liturgical and literary texts into the Bohairic dialect. As for the Greek language, through the ninth century the Coptic hierarchy still issued official decrees in Greek, and fluency in that language was intentionally cultivated among its elites, but the language would lose its prestige among the Copts roughly around the tenth century. Still, the liturgical use of the Greek language survived among Coptic churches in Alexandria at least until the fourteenth century (Mikhail forthcoming: ch. 5).

While Patriarch Afraham inaugurated significant reforms against simony and concubinage,[4] and Bishop Sawīrus gained renown as a noted theologian and apologist, both attained popularity in large measure due to their involvement in one of the most famous miracles in Coptic history—the moving of al-Muqaṭṭam Mountain. Situated within the tenure of the Fāṭimid imām al-ʿAzīz (975–96), the account reflects the intercommunal polemics rampant among the three monotheistic faiths. The narrative begins in one of the *majālis* of the imām, gatherings in which the leading representatives of the three faith-communities civilly discussed religion (Lazarus-Yafeh *et al.*, 1999). At one such *majlis*, Bishop Sawīrus purportedly defeated his Jewish opponent, who later retaliated by informing the caliph that the Christian scriptures claim that if anyone has the faith of a mustard seed, they could move a mountain (Matt. 17:20; Mk. 11:23). Al-ʿAzīz then summoned the patriarch and informed him that unless he could prove the veracity of that verse, the Christians would be persecuted. After a three-day reprieve, in which the patriarch and the faithful observed a fast, Patriarch Afraham had a vision in which the Virgin Mary assured him that a devout one-eyed tanner would move the mountain. This three-day fast has been appended to the Fast of the Nativity and is annually observed by the Copts. The patriarch sought out the tanner and discovered the details of his pious life. Later that day, all three factions (Jews, Muslims, and Christians) convened at the base of al-Muqaṭṭam. As the Christians prayed, the tanner (named "Simon" in later sources) stood behind the patriarch with the congregation, and when the faithful cried out *kyrie eleison*, "Lord have mercy," the mountain moved. As a result, the account relays that the Christians were spared and allowed to rebuild several prominent churches. At its core, this account aims to prove the integrity of the Christian Scriptures, the alleged adulteration of which is a persistent theme in Islamic polemics (Mikhail forthcoming: ch. 11).

The tolerant rule of the early Fāṭimids ended with the reign of al-Ḥākim bi Amr Allāh (996–1021), whose erratic behavior and extreme policies have continued to live on in Coptic communal memories. At the dawn of the eleventh century, al-Ḥākim purged his bureaucracy of all Christians, forced some to convert to Islam, reissued the *dhull* regulations and eventually ordered the closure of all churches—an edict that was enforced for nearly three years. (Forty years later, a similar edict would be issued by the wazīr al-Yāzūrī.) Al-Ḥākim also incited the destruction of churches in Egypt, Syria, and Jerusalem. Most prominently, he attacked the Church of the Holy Sepulcher, *Kanīsat al-qiyāmā* (the Church of the Resurrection), which he dubbed *Kanīsat al-qumāma* (Church of the Rubbish Heap), an epithet that lingered in Islamic (Arabic and Persian) literature into the early modern period. It was after this oppressive reign that the renaming of the Coptic calendar gained wide acceptance. In the aftermath of the Arab conquest, the *Era of Diocletian*, a hitherto marginal solar calendrical system (year 1 = CE 284), attained prominence among Egyptians. It was first dubbed the *Era of the Martyrs* in Nubia, a designation that is first attested in Egypt in the late eighth century. By the third quarter of the ninth century, at the end of al-Mutawakkil's oppressive caliphate, the new label began to find its way into literary texts and inscriptions, but it would not completely displace the *Era of Diocletian* until the eleventh century (see Bagnall and Worp 2004 for the earliest documentary evidence).

In the aftermath of al-Ḥākim's persecution, the Copts rebuilt their churches and would later attain a reprieve from socio-religious discrimination in large part due to the influence of the Armenian *amīr al-juyūsh* (military wazīr) Bard al-Jamālī, who became the *de facto* arbitrator of power in Egypt from 1074 until his death in 1094, when he was succeeded by his son al-Afḍal Shahnshah. At mid-century, Patriarch Christodoulos (1046–77) inaugurated a second phase in the Coptic-to-Arabic translation program. Evidence for widespread Arabization among the Copts is commonplace during this period. Still, through the eleventh century, the process remained uneven, particularly in rural districts. Another of Patriarch Christodoulos' reforms—which may actually date to one of his predecessors, Patriarch Zacharias (1004–32)—ended the celebration of the Reserved Sacrament (or the Presanctified Gifts), which had been observed by the see of Alexandria at least since the fourth century (Taft 2000: 85).[5]

It is of note that the normative version of the so-called Covenant or Pact of 'Umar (*al-shūrat* or *al-'uhda al-'Umariyya*), likely dates to this period (Miller 2000). The "Pact" stands as the most important document for the legal status and treatment of *dhimmīs* in the caliphate. Typically attributed to 'Umar ibn al-Khaṭṭāb (636) or Caliph 'Umar II (717–20), the document certainly retains some early clauses, reflecting a seventh- or eighth-century context, but many of the stipulations, such as those focused on buildings, clothing, and even hairstyles, reflect a much later sociopolitical environment. By and large, the clauses of the Pact become increasingly complex and more encompassing the later the version of the text one reads.

Prompted by Bard al-Jamālī, Patriarch Cyril II (1078–92) officially relocated the seat of the Coptic patriarch to Cairo, where it has remained ever since. Rather than an event, however, this transfer is better contextualized as a decisive step in a lengthy process. Throughout Late Antiquity, Alexandria served as the nexus of political and ecclesiastical power; Arab rule, however, created a spatial schism in that respect. Fusṭāṭ, and later, Cairo, were simply too distant to allow for regular interactions among Coptic patriarchs and governing authorities. Hence, beginning in the eighth century, Coptic patriarchs often resided in proximity to the apex of the Delta. Patriarch Cyril's relocation was not altogether unexpected, though it still aroused local tensions since Fusṭāṭ–Cairo had its own bishop. The issue soon came to a head during the patriarchates of Michael IV (1092–1102) and Macarius II (1102–28), who met with stiff resistance from local civil and ecclesiastical elites who demanded to have their own bishop and objected to the proposition that the patriarch would control two dioceses (Alexandria and Fusṭāṭ–Cairo). The issue lingered until Patriarch Gabriel ibn Turayk (1131–45) simply refused to appoint a new bishop to the diocese. Best known for his *nomocanon*, Ibn Turayk also limited the number of liturgies prayed by the Copts (nearly a dozen) to the three that have been retained until today: the Alexandrian Basil, the Alexandrian Gregory, and that of St. Cyril I (the Liturgy of St. Mark).[6]

In general, popular sentiments towards the Copts took a turn for the worse after al-Ḥākim's rule, and would further deteriorate with the arrival of the crusaders. Throughout the twelfth and thirteenth centuries, the Copts provided the government with a vulnerable population, easily exploited to fund anti-crusading expeditions. Meanwhile, perceiving the Copts as a potential fifth column that might aid the cross-bearing crusaders, many Muslims began to distrust them, and, with officials often turning a blind eye, street mobs came to vent their frustration with crusader victories by attacking Coptic churches and establishments. The Copts certainly did not fare better with the crusaders, who perceived them as "heretics" whose blood was no more sacred than that of Muslims. Coptic–Muslim interactions reached a low point during the crusader era (Perlmann 1940–42).

Ayyūbids (1171–1250)

Ayyūbid rule is perhaps one of the most difficult to assess in Coptic history, witnessing major peaks and valleys (see Werthmuler 2010). On the one hand, during this period Coptic patronage seems to have reached an all-time high for both the restoration of ecclesiastical properties and the inauguration of major iconographic programs, such as those witnessed in the monasteries of St. Antony and St. Paul (Bolman 2002; Lyster 2008). The Ayyūbids are fondly remembered in Islamic historiography. Salāḥ al-Dīn (Saladin), the founder of the dynasty (1171), restored Sunnī rule to Egypt and mounted effective resistance to the crusaders at a time when the Near East had devolved into a jigsaw puzzle of jurisdictions and factional strife. Salāḥ al-Dīn carefully controlled his image as a pious Muslim and defender of Islam in order to consolidate his rule and galvanize resistance against the crusaders. In pursuit of that goal, however, he purged Christians and Jews from the administration and reissued the *dhull* regulations. Eventually, the harshness of his regime abated after the Arabs' victory at the Battle of Ḥaṭṭīn and the subsequent recapture of Jerusalem in 1187.

On another front, Ayyūbid rule proved to be one of the lowest points for the Coptic hierarchy. Cyril III Ibn Laqlaq had actively sought out the patriarchate since 1216 and finally achieved his goal in 1235 through several bribes to Muslim officials. A noted author and scribe, Cyril abused his office by unabashedly practicing simony on an unprecedented scale. Still, there is a silver lining of sorts to his tenure. As Orthodox Christians, the Copts uphold the belief that ultimate authority in the church does not reside with any one bishop (even the patriarch) but with the synod of bishops. To address Cyril's abuses, an ecclesiastical council convened and passed several reforms that effectively limited his authority. This was a rather bleak period for the hierarchy, but one that provides a pragmatic example of orthodox ecclesiology. One of these reforms led to the appointment of the noted monk, priest, and scholar Bulūs al-Būshī as Bishop of Miṣr to oversee the activities of the patriarch. After Cyril's death in 1243, the patriarchal office remained vacant for seven years.

Mamlūks (1250–1517)

In 1250 a regiment of Kipchak Mamlūks (military slaves),[7] who had been the elite corps of the last Ayyūbid ruler, al-Ṣāliḥ Ayyūb, gained control of Egypt at a pivotal juncture. As part of the Seventh Crusade, Louis IX of France had captured Damietta and was preparing to march on the rest of the Delta.[8] The Baḥrī ("river") Mamlūks, so named on account of the proximity of their barracks to the Nile, stopped his offensive, and used the victory to bolster their political hold over the province. Even more serious, however, were the Mongols, who had destabilized all of Asia. The caliphate suffered during the initial wave of the Mongol conquests under Genghis Khan, but it was devastated by the second assault led by the Great Khan's grandson, Hülegü, who sacked Baghdad and killed the last caliph in 1258. Two years later, the Mamlūks dealt the Mongols their first major defeat at the Battle of 'Ayn Jālūt (1260), a prominent victory that enabled the Mamlūks to consolidate their rule over Egypt and propelled them to the forefront of the Islamic world as the ideological successors to the caliphate; a perception they actively cultivated through word and deed. Over the next fifty years, they would bring the crusader presence in the Near East to an end and check the advancement of the Mongol Īlkhāns, eventually signing a treaty with them in 1322.

In many ways, the Baḥrī Mamlūks followed through with Ayyūbid religious policies but, as first generation converts anxious to prove their piety, they followed them with greater rigor—an attitude made more rigid by the Mongol invasion. Many Muslims, wondering how God could have allowed such mass slaughter at the hands of pagans, interpreted the Mongol invasions as divine chastisement prompted by the acceptance of un-Islamic innovations (*bida'*)—such as those associated with the Sūfīs—and dealing too leniently with the People of the Book, who are commonly referenced as *kuffār*, "infidels," in the literature of that period. These sentiments emerged in the writings of various Arab Muslim authors, most notably *Shaykh al-Islam* (the Elder of Islam), the noted theologian and jurist Ibn Taymiyya (d. 1328), who articulated these sentiments into a legal bulwark that proved more restrictive to non-Muslims than any previous code.

In his day, Ibn Taymiyya was a polarizing figure who met resistance due to his rather conservative views, but there is no denying his long-term impact on Islamic thought and jurisprudence. The new hard line, though often mitigated through interpersonal relations with ruling authorities, as well as bribes and fees, may be observed on several fronts (Gottheil 1908, 1912, 1921; Perlmann 1958, cf. 1975). In regard to places of worship, even the right to repair existing structures, which is explicit in ninth-century texts, was abrogated; Christians had to seek permission to repair even the most ancient of their churches and governors were under no compulsion to grant such requests. According to Ibn Taymiyya, even if a governor chose to destroy all the churches of Egypt, he would still be acting within his legal rights (O'Keeffe 1996). The fact that such a drastic act never occurred, however, betrays the moderate attitudes that typically prevailed among Egyptian officials and jurists despite the increasingly rigid letter of the law.

Baḥrī rule marks the twilight of Coptic Arabic literature and a spike in conversion to Islam (Little 1976). Authors such as the encyclopedist Ibn al-Rāhib (c. 1210–90), Abū al-Barakāt ibn Kabar (d. 1324), and al-Makīn "the Younger" (d. c. 1300) continued to write a staggering volume of texts on a wide array of subjects, but they would have few successors. By the fifteenth century, the volume of Coptic Arabic literature abated; older texts continued to be copied, but original composition and the two translation programs discussed above nearly came to a halt. Arguably, the most important fifteenth century text is *al-Tartīb al-ṭaqsī* [*The Ritual Order* or *Ordo*] of Patriarch Gabriel V (d. 1427) which, together with *al-Jawharah al-nafīsah* [*The Precious Pearl*] of Ibn Sabbā' (fl. early fourteenth century), has exercised the greatest influences on the shape of Coptic liturgical celebrations until this day (Mistriḥ 1966; Abdallah 1962).

In 1354 popular riots targeted several churches in Cairo, including the church housing the relics of the Martyr John of Senhut, which were annually dipped into the Nile for a blessing during a three-day festival. The feast was observed by Christians and Muslims alike in what resembles a modern Egyptian *mawlid* (or *mūlid*).[9] On the heels of these riots, the government seized 25,000 acres of Coptic religious endowments (*awqāf*), a crippling economic loss for the community.

Over the course of the 1380s the Baḥrī Mamlūks were overcome by their own Circassian Mamlūks, who were recruited from the Caucasus. Initially housed in a tower (*burj*) in the citadel, these Burjī Mamlūks ruled until the Ottoman conquest of Egypt (1517). Their reign began well enough. Patriarch Matthew I (d. 1408) enjoyed an amicable relationship with the founder of that dynasty, the Sultan Barqūq, but this would prove exceptional. Burjī Mamlūk rule was one of the worst in Egyptian history. Seemingly everything that could go awry did: the plague hit every single decade, the economy contracted, and political transitions were volatile and often accompanied by riots. These factors affected all Egyptians, but such events often sparked outbursts of mob violence that specifically targeted the Copts, their homes, churches, and monasteries.

While this "long century" of Burjī rule was crucial for the fate of the community, it remains one of the worst documented and studied in Coptic history.

Still, several developments may be highlighted. The first is the persistence of conversion to Islam on all levels. Coptic lay elites continued to play a prominent role, and while the Mamlūk regime still employed many Christians, significantly, the most powerful and renowned officials of this era were families of Coptic converts to Islam: the Banū al-Haysam, Banū Kātib Jakam, and Banū al-Jī'ān (Garcin 1998: 307; el-Leithy 2005).[10]

This was also a new age of martyrdom, though most instances involved Christians who, after converting to Islam, had a change of heart and returned to the Christian faith. In that situation, many (re-)converted privately and relocated to other districts or to monasteries (MacCoull 2000), but some publicly proclaimed their renewed Christian faith and were executed. Such individuals are documented throughout Islamic rule, though there seems to have been a surge at the beginning of the fifteenth century when forty-nine individuals were martyred (Swanson 2010: ch. 8 and App. I).[11] Similar acts of martyrdom are documented down to the very end of the period surveyed—Ṣalīb was martyred in 1512 (Armanios and Ergene 2006; cf. Zaborowski 2005). At the dawning of the Ottoman conquest, the Copts had lived nearly 900 years under Islamic political rule and social hegemony. As farmers, merchants, scribes, artisans, and officials, they remained firmly interwoven into Egypt's sociocultural fabric, but arguably, as a community, their greatest achievement was "simply" surviving the fifteenth century. Typically, mere survival is hardly worthy of note and logically every generation owes its very existence to its predecessors; still, all subsequent accomplishments of the Copts, whether under Ottoman rule or in the modern era, owe something to the tenacity of the generations that persevered during that demoralizing century, perhaps more than any other.

Timeline

622–61	Patriarchate of Benjamin I
641	Arab Conquest of Egypt
661–750	Umayyad Dynasty
685–705	Governorship of 'Abd al-'Azīz ibn Marwān
704–29	Patriarchate of Alexander II
717–20	Caliphate of 'Umar II: first anti-*dhimmī* legislation
743–61	Patriarchate of Michael I
750–1258	'Abbasid Dynasty
847–61	Caliphate of al-Mutawakkil
868–905	Ṭūlūnid rule of Egypt
905–35	'Abbasids regain control of Egypt
935–69	Ikhshīdid rule of Egypt
950–1000	Career of Bishop Sawīrus ibn al-Muqaffa'
969–1171	Fāṭimid Rule
996–1021	Imāmate of al-Ḥākim bi Amr Allāh
1046–77	Patriarchate of Christodoulos
1084	Official relocation of patriarch to Cairo

1131–45	Patriarchate of Gabriel ibn Turayk
1163–70	Crusaders repeatedly target Egypt
1171–1250	Ayyūbid rule
1218	Crusaders attack Damietta (Dumyāṭ)
1235–43	Patriarchate of Cyril III Ibn Laqlaq
1249	King Louis IX takes over Damietta
1250	Rise of the Mamlūk Sultanate
1250–1390	Baḥrī (Turkoman) line
1290	Death of Abū Shākir ibn al-Rāhib
1354	Confiscation of 25,000 acres of Coptic religious endowments
1365	Crusaders sack Alexandria
1390–1517	Burjī (Circassians) line
1409–27	Patriarchate of Gabriel V
1517	Ottoman conquest of Egypt

Notes

1 A Byzantine export lacking in Islamic lands, marble was often confiscated from churches and reused in mosques and palaces.

2 The ʿAbbasids directly controlled Egypt in 750–868 and 905–35, and they legitimized the rule of the Ṭūlūnids, Ikhshīdids, and Ayyūbids.

3 The first Egyptian Christian to write exclusively in Arabic was Eutychius (Saʿīd ibn Baṭrīq), the Pro-Chalcedonian Patriarch of Alexandria (d. 940).

4 Simony, the buying and selling of ecclesiastical offices, had several causes, but in one respect the practice mimicked the means by which governmental posts were secured at the time. Concubinage came about as affluent Copts sought to emulate the trappings of prestige and luxury they observed among their Muslim counterparts.

5 The alleged patristic evidence denouncing the practice is pseudonymous and late. This reform was likely prompted by abuses that crept in during the few preceding centuries.

6 The Byzantine liturgies of Saints Basil and Gregory differ significantly from the Alexandrian/Coptic rite.

7 Baḥrī Mamlūks were recruited from the Kipchak Steppe in modern Russia. Mamlūk (lit. "the one owned") designated "slave" soldiers, a staple of Islamic armies from the 830s through the nineteenth century. Mamlūks entered the caliphate as slaves. Once purchased, however, they were converted to Islam and freed, but remained in the service of their former owner, the *ustadh mamlūk*.

8 Crusaders attacked Egypt on five occasions from 1163 through 1170, and again in 1219–21, 1249, 1270, and 1365.

9 Patriarch Gabriel II (1131–45) had failed to bring this aspect of the Feast of the Martyr (*ʿīd al-shahīd*) to an end.

10 Coptic converts were always part of the administration: e.g. Ibn Mammātī, the author of the famous *Kitāb qawānīn al-dawāwīn*. Still, their prevalence during Mamlūk rule is striking.

11 Swanson (2010: chs. 7–9) discusses several leading religious figures of that period.

Selected Bibliography

Abdallah, A. (ed. and trans.) (1962) *L'ordinamento liturgico di Gabriele V, 88° Patriarca Copto (1409–1427)*, Cairo: Edizioni del Centro Francescano di Studi orientali cristiani.

Armanios, F. and Ergene, B. (2006) "A Christian Martyr under Mamlūk Justice: The Trials of Ṣalīb (d. 1512) according to Coptic and Muslim Sources," *Muslim World*, 96(1): 115–44.

Bagnall, R. S. and Worp, K. A. (2004) *Chronological Systems of Byzantine Egypt*, 2nd edn, Leiden: E.J. Brill.

Behrens-Abouseif, D. (1989) *Islamic Architecture in Cairo: An Introduction*, Leiden: E.J. Brill.

Bolman, E. S. (ed.) (2002) *Monastic Visions: Wall Paintings in the Monastery of St. Antony at the Red Sea*, New Haven: Yale University Press.

Bosworth, C. E. (1982) "The Concept of *Dhimma* in Early Islam," in B. Braude and B. Lewis (eds) *Christians and Jews in the Ottoman Empire: The Functioning of a Plural Society*, 2 vols, New York: Holmes & Meier.

Butler, A. J. (1998) *The Arab Conquest of Egypt and the Last Thirty Years of the Roman Dominion*, 2nd edn, P. M. Fraser (ed.), Oxford: Clarendon Press.

Cohen, M. R. (1994) *Under Crescent and Cross*, Princeton: Princeton University Press.

Den Heijer, J. (1989) *Mawhub ibn Mansur ibn Mufarriǧ et l'historiographie Copto-Arabe: Étude sur la composition de l'Histoire des Patriarches d'Alexandrie*, Louvain: Peeters.

——(1996) "Coptic Historiography in the Fāṭimid, Ayyūbid, and Early Mamlūk Periods," *Medieval Encounters*, 2(1): 67–98.

Fraser, P. M. (1991) "Arab Conquest of Egypt," in A. S. Atiya (ed.) *The Coptic Encyclopedia*, 8 vols, New York: Macmillan.

Garcin, J.-C. (1998) "The Regime of the Circassian Mamlūks," in C. F. Petry (ed.) *The Cambridge History of Egypt*, vol. 1, *Islamic Egypt 641–1517*, Cambridge: Cambridge University Press.

Gottheil, R. J. H. (1908) "Dhimmis and Moslems in Egypt," in R. F. Harper, F. Brown and G. F. Moore (eds) *Old Testament and Semitic Studies in Memory of William Rainey Harper*, vol. 2(1–3), Chicago: University of Chicago Press.

——(1912) "A Fetwa on the Appointment of Dhimmis to Office," *Zeitschrift für Assyriologie*, 26: 203–14.

——(1921) "An Answer to the Dhimmis," *Journal of the American Oriental Society*, 41: 383–457.

Griffith, S. H. (1996) "Kitāb Misbāh al-'Aql of Severus Ibn al-Muqaffa': A Profile of the Christian Creed in Arabic in Tenth Century Egypt," *Medieval Encounters*, 2(1): 15–42.

——(2008) *Church in the Shadow of the Mosque: Christians and Muslims in the World of Islam*, Princeton: Princeton University Press.

Hoyland, R. G. (1997) *Seeing Islam as Others Saw It: A Survey and Evaluation of Christian, Jewish and Zoroastrian Writings on Early Islam*, Princeton: Darwin Press.

John of Nikiou (1919; 1981) *The Chronicle of John (c. 690 AD) Coptic Bishop of Nikiu*, R. H. Charles (trans.), Amsterdam: APA-Philo Press.

Kaegi, W. E. (1969) "Initial Byzantine Reactions to the Arab Conquest," *Church History*, 38(2): 139–49.

Lapidus, I. M. (1972) "The Conversion of Egypt to Islam," *Israel Oriental Studies*, 2: 248–62.

Lazarus-Yafeh, H., Cohen, M. R., Somekh, S., and Griffith, S. H. (eds) (1999) *The Majlis: Interreligious Encounters in Medieval Islam*, Wiesbaden: Harrassowitz.

el-Leithy, T. (2005) "Coptic Culture and Conversion in Medieval Cairo, 1293–1524 A. D.," Ph.D. Diss., Princeton University.

Little, D. P. (1976) "Coptic Conversion to Islam under the Baḥrī Mamlūks, 692–755/1293–1354," *Bulletin of the School of Oriental and Asian Studies*, 39(3): 552–69.

Lyster, W. (ed.) (2008) *The Cave Church of Paul the Hermit at the Monastery of St. Paul in Egypt*, New Haven: Yale University Press.

MacCoull, L. S. B. (2000) "The Rite of the Jar: Apostasy and Reconciliation in the Medieval Coptic Orthodox Church," in D. Wolfthal (ed.) *Peace and Negotiation: Strategies for Coexistence in the Middle Ages and the Renaissance*, Turnhout: Brepols.

Mikhail, M. S. A. (2010) "An Orientation to the Sources and Study of Early Islamic Egypt (641–868)," *History Compass*, 8(8): 929–50.

——(forthcoming) *From Byzantine to Islamic Egypt: Religion, Politics, and Identity after the Arab Conquest*, London: I.B. Tauris.

Miller, D. E. (2000) "From Catalogue to Codes to Canon: the Rise of the Petition to 'Umar Among Legal Traditions Governing Non-Muslims in Medieval Islamicate Societies," Ph.D. diss., University of Missouri-Kansas City.

Mistriḥ, V. P. (ed. and trans.) (1966) *Pretiosa Margarita de scientiis ecclesiasticis/al-Jawharah al-nafīsah fī 'ulūm al-kanīsah*, by Yuḥannā ibn Abī Zakariyya ibn Sabbā', Cairo: Edizioni del Centro Francescano di Studi orientali cristiani.

Morimoto, K. (1981) *The Fiscal Administration of Egypt in the Early Islamic Period*, Kyoto: Dohosha.

O'Keeffe, B. (1996) "Aḥmad ibn Taymiyya, Mas'alat al-kanā'is (the Question of the Churches)," *Islamochristiana*, 22: 53–78.

Perlmann, M. (1940–42) "Notes on Anti-Christian Propaganda in the Mamlūk Empire," *Bulletin of the School of Oriental and African Studies*, 9(4): 843–61.

——(1958) "Asnawi's Tract against Christian Officials," in S. Lowinger and J. Somogyi (eds) *Ignace Goldziher Memorial Volume*, vol. 2, Jerusalem: Rubin Mass.

——(ed. and trans.) (1975) *Shaykh Damanhuri on the Churches of Cairo, 1739*, Berkeley: University of California Press.

Petry, C. F. (ed.) (1998) *The Cambridge History of Egypt*, vol. 1, *Islamic Egypt 641–1517*, Cambridge: Cambridge University Press.

Richter, T. S. (2009) "Greek, Coptic, and the 'Language of the Hijra': the Rise and Decline of the Coptic Language in Late Antique and Medieval Egypt," in H. M. Cotton *et al.* (eds) *From Hellenism to Islam: Cultural and Linguistic Change in the Roman Near East*, Cambridge: Cambridge University Press.

Rubenson, S. (1996) "Translating the Tradition: Some Remarks on the Arabization of the Patristic Heritage in Egypt," *Medieval Encounters*, 2(1): 4–14.

Sidarus, A. (1978) "Coptic Lexicography in the Middle Age: The Coptic Arabic Scalae," in R. McL. Wilson (ed.) *The Future of Coptic Studies*, Leiden: E.J. Brill.

——(2001) "Medieval Coptic Grammars in Arabic: The Coptic Muqaddimāt," *Journal of Coptic Studies*, 3: 63–79.

Sijpesteijn, P. M. (2007) "New Rule over Old Structures: Egypt after the Muslim Conquest," in H. Crawford (ed.) *Regime Change in the Ancient Near East and Egypt*, Oxford: Oxford University Press.

Swanson, M. N. (2010) *The Coptic Papacy in Islamic Egypt 641–1517*, Cairo: American University at Cairo Press.

Taft, R. F. (2000) "The Frequency of the Celebration of the Eucharist throughout History," in M. E. Johnson (ed.) *Between Memory and Hope: Readings on the Liturgical Year*, Collegeville: Liturgical Press.

Werthmuler, K. J. (2010) *Coptic Identity and Ayyubid Politics in Egypt, 1218–1250*, Cairo: American University at Cairo Press.

Zaborowski, J. R. (ed. and trans.) (2005) *The Coptic Martyrdom of John of Phanijōit: Assimilation and Conversion to Islam in Thirteenth-Century Egypt*, Leiden: E.J. Brill.

4 The Ottoman Period (1517–1798)

Beyond Persecution or Tolerance

Febe Armanios

In exploring Coptic life under Ottoman rule (1517–1798), scholars face enduring misperceptions about an epoch traditionally seen as persecutory towards Egypt's Christians. To begin, the limited sources available about Copts can exacerbate and reinforce the idea that they were deeply marginalized within Ottoman Egyptian society. Aside from scattered mentions in known Egyptian chronicles, there are minimal references to Copts in Muslim literary or legal sources. Copts were primarily governed by local power holders—religious scholars (*'ulamā'*), military households, or their own communal leaders—and they scarcely provoked the interest of Ottoman sultans, their deputies, and seemingly later historians.

The difficulty in escaping past paradigms is also amplified by the tendency to investigate the Coptic experience as separate from that of other Christians. Parallels between Copts, Anatolian, Levantine, or Balkan Christians have usually been overlooked, and the idea that Copts experienced a unique type of marginalization and suffering has persisted. It is indeed tempting to study Copts as if they lived in isolation. On the whole, Coptic lay elites (many known as *arākhina* or *archons*) were employed within Egypt's bureaucratic and military establishment. In contrast, other non-Muslims in most Ottoman territories had access to diverse economic opportunities through the capitulations system, an arrangement in which European businessmen and consular representatives transferred trading privileges commonly to Catholics, Greek Orthodox, Armenians, and Jews who in turn served as translators or commercial agents. The latter paid reduced tariffs compared to native Muslim or non-Muslim merchants (Armanios 2011: 19–21).

Because they were mostly concentrated in Egypt, Copts were limited in their participation within these arrangements or in international trade. Unlike non-Muslims who were connected to networks of coreligionists throughout the Mediterranean basin, few Copts if any worked within the commercial sector (Raymond 1973–74 [1999]: Vol. II, 456). Also, many clergy and laity appear to have shunned economic, political, or social connections with Europeans, especially with the French who had come to represent the Catholic Church, an ideological rival to the Coptic establishment during the Ottoman period. As the traveler Carsten Niebuhr noted in 1762, "The Copts have an insurmountable aversion to the Roman Church" (1792 [1978]: Vol. I, 104).

Upon closer examination, however, one finds important parallels between Copts and other Ottoman non-Muslims. For instance the rise of those lay elites, the archons, mirrored developments taking place among the Greek elites of Istanbul (the Phanariots) and the Armenian elites (the *amīras*). Coptic neo-martyrdom texts from this era share a great deal with Bulgarian and Greek correlates (Armanios and Ergene 2006: 116, 129–34; Armanios 2011: 45–57). Coptic-authored narratives show how pilgrimage to Jerusalem allowed Copts to participate in a common ritual with other Ottoman Christians. Clerical sermons in the late eighteenth century reveal the effects of the Coptic encounter with European missionaries in Egypt, and how it forced Copts to redefine their identity and communal boundaries (Armanios 2011: 91–115, 117–45). In all, a strong cultural interchange and, occasionally, competition endured between Copts and other Christians in the Ottoman world.

The prolific output of Coptic-authored manuscripts during this period challenges the seemingly immutable perception of Coptic existence as dark, barren, and even tragic, and indicates that there was a vibrant and enduring Coptic religious life, supported by wealthy patrons or endowed by important monastic establishments. Hundreds of manuscripts were copied or written by monks, priests, or lay scribes between the sixteenth and eighteenth centuries. Unfortunately, most of these sources have been either inaccessible to researchers or neglected within existing scholarship. Available documents can be read in tandem with European traveler and missionary accounts which offer rich, if at times biased, accounts of Coptic life.

Finally, it is worth noting that some historians have undervalued the role of religion and of religious identity within the study of Coptic history (Guirguis 2005: 211). Too often, modern history-writing has privileged nationalist discourses that seek to find commonality and even homogeneity among all Egyptians. Partially for this reason, Coptic perspectives were long neglected, because they were deemed as adding little to a corpus of information primarily built on the experience of the majority of (Muslim) Egyptians. For the Ottoman period, however, it is important to (re)consider the place of religion in the articulation of a specific Coptic identity. Religious traditions, practices, and theological beliefs, as documented by Coptic writers, capture the ways in which they differentiated themselves from other communities. As they faced economic, political, or ideological threats, particularly from Roman Catholic missionaries and newly converted Coptic Catholics in the eighteenth century, Coptic Orthodox religious leaders called for a moral renewal, for a revival of the Coptic faith, one that would keep believers on the "correct" path. While seemingly rigid on the surface, these developments show that Copts were adaptable, flexible, and open towards new forms of religious articulation, especially during periods of crisis (Armanios 2011: 6–11).

Background on Ottoman Egypt

The Ottoman conquest in 1517 must have been traumatic for all Egyptians. Unseating the Mamlūk sultans and ending their domination of the Eastern

Mediterranean was swift but, when the shock dissipated, many must have realized that their land, center of a powerful empire for over two centuries under the Fatimids (909–1171) and nearly three under the Mamlūks (1250–1517), had fallen in stature. Egypt was now absorbed into the folds of a grand but distant empire and relegated to a provincial status, one of thirty provinces under Ottoman control. Cairo, the historically vibrant capital, was at least momentarily no more "Mother of the World," "*Umm al-Dunya*," as its inhabitants had come to call it. This state is well-captured in the biting words of Muṣṭafa 'Alī, an Istanbullite Ottoman official who traveled to Cairo decades after the conquest in 1599:

> If a city by the name of Cairo
> Is given the title of Mother of the World,
> The husband of that whore is all done in,
> Honesty and chastity she has lost completely.
> Though her city and river are regarded
> The one as the world, the other as all that exists in it
> Considering her present inhabitants
> She is a desert filled with serpents and scorpions.
>
> (1975: 26–27)

During the conquest, thousands were killed, a calamity which shattered Egyptian morale, as did the Ottoman practice of forced exile or *sürgün* (İnalcık 1969–70: 235): manuscripts, buildings, and people were carted away to Istanbul (Winter 1992: 10). Leading Copts were among those taken to the new capital, prized for their skills in woodwork, metallurgy, and finance. Their exile must have been a painful development for the entire community (Armanios 2011: 16).

Still the Ottoman period was one of modest recovery for Copts and despite restrictions long enshrined in Islamic legal codes and traditions, community leaders were able to spearhead important artistic, literary, and cultural projects. Copts were also emboldened to challenge Islamic prohibitions against non-Muslim religious expression by celebrating feasts and festivals in public spaces and seemingly with the approval of local authorities. It is likely that the Copts' confidence in upholding their traditions was related to the fact that they were more numerous and usually more powerful than Egypt's other non-Muslims (Winter 1992: 220). From the sixteenth to the eighteenth centuries, Copts constituted roughly 4 to 8 percent of the total population (Armanios 2011: 19).

In Ottoman Egypt, the political administration of non-Muslims fell mostly to local power holders. On rare occasions and in serious times of crisis, the Ottoman Porte was informed about intersectarian squabbles, but there is no indication that these necessitated frequent interventions from the sultanate. Initially, after the conquest, the Ottomans employed Egyptian *'ulamā'* to collect the traditional taxes (*jizya* or *jawālī*) from non-Muslims (Winter 1992: 116, note 43). Over time, this duty was transferred to the military officers who were consolidating their power during the seventeenth and eighteenth centuries.

Egypt quickly became the Ottomans' most valuable province, since it bordered strategic sea routes and was located close to Islam's holiest cities, Mecca and Medina. In controlling Egypt, moreover, the Ottomans were able to secure vital trade and military routes, competing with Europeans for naval dominance of the Mediterranean and Red Seas (Crecelius 1981: 14). For sultans and local notables, opportunities for making money were plentiful; political and economic developments in the seventeenth and eighteenth centuries, as related to landholding, tax-farming, and trade, opened prospects for ambitious, well-connected elites under whose patronage many Copts would become dependent. Although Ottoman rulers attempted to stabilize Egypt's political system in order to facilitate their collection of taxes, conflicts between various factions and individuals vying for a share in the lucrative taxation structure created frequent volatility and chaos. The advancement of Coptic archons became intertwined with the rising and falling fortunes of their ambitious patrons. At times, as in the case of the renowned archon Ibrāhīm al-Jawharī (d. 1795), paralleling their benefactors' success, archons amassed great wealth and political clout; at others, their patrons' downfall led to a fateful demise (Armanios 2008: 65–66; 2011: 30–31).

The decades following the conquest also ushered in a general spiritual outpouring as seen by the popularity of Sufism and of religious festivals or *mawālid*. The regular outbreaks of plague, famine, and civil strife triggered a public expression of piety among all Egyptians, both in urban and rural centers. Indeed, early modern Egypt saw the noticeable articulation of popular religion as one way of dealing with death, starvation, and everyday struggles (Staffa 1977: 36; Winter 1992: 130). In the late sixteenth and seventeenth centuries, Ottoman rulers were also shifting their focus from conquest to building a powerful Sunni Muslim Empire (Hathaway 1998: 35). While stylizing themselves as supreme Sunni leaders, Ottoman sultans patronized religious customs such as the annual pilgrimage or *ḥajj* to Mecca; indeed, its funding, organization, staffing, and execution became vital to the Porte's agenda (Crecelius 1981: 14; Hathaway 1998: 36). In times of crisis, the patronage of popular festivals, pilgrimages, religious infrastructure, and Sufi orders worked to strengthen Ottoman rule in provincial territories. As will be noted, Coptic community leaders in Egypt would also finance the construction and repair of religious sites, support religious manuscript reproduction, and fund religious festivals as a way of maintaining their standing, and perhaps even to protect their financial assets from theft and frequent bedouin incursions (Armanios 2011: 26–31; Staffa 1977: 321–23).

Social Divisions within the Coptic Community

For Copts, the Ottoman conquest created apprehension and opportunity. While Copts were liberated from their oft-repressive Mamlūk overlords, they also lost their direct political and economic connections to the central administration in Cairo. Ottoman sultans seemed to know or care little about this parochial minority; their centuries-old familiarity with Greek, Armenian, and

Balkan Christians overshadowed interest in and knowledge of smaller Christian groups in the newly-conquered Arab territories. In any case, so long as the annual tribute was paid, Istanbul was often "more concerned with Yemen and the Hijaz than with Egypt" (Winter 1992: 18).

Traditionally, Copts had lived in rural areas and following the conquest a majority continued to be farmers and craftsmen. In villages and towns, Copts were least established in the merchant classes, but some worked as winemakers and wine-sellers, whose shops were closed during periods of strict religious enforcement (Raymond 1973–74 [1999]: Vol. II, 456; Winter 1998: 208). As the French traveler Claude Étienne Savary noted in 1785, Coptic farmers in the Fayyum region cultivated "the olive and the vine their forefathers planted, still gather excellent grapes, of which they make the most agreeable white wine" (1786: Vol. I, 424). Most Copts, like their Muslim correlates, earned meager incomes, and many lived and died in utter poverty. On the whole, ordinary men and women came to depend on their richer brethren for protection, donations, and support (Armanios 2011: 32–34).

In the Ottoman period, Copts formed significant communities in Egypt's major cities, in Cairo, Alexandria, Asyūt, and Jirja, among others. Indeed, during the seventeenth century, they were well-represented in a number of urban sectors, as noted by the Coptic–Catholic writer Yūsuf Abudacnus, serving as:

> [s]ecretaries to the principal Turks, Chancellors, Quastors, Procurators Regalium muncrum, Commissioners of tithes and Customs, etc. so that they have in their hands the whole Great Sultan's Revenue proceeding out of this country. Others of them are Arithmeticians, or Geometricians, to meet and measure out of the Ground, and to cast up the money yearly going out of Egypt. The Commons amongst them are either Artificers or Servants: Artificers are of the following professions, goldsmiths, jewelers, shoe-makers, smiths, tailors, masons, engravers, carpenters.
>
> (1675 [1692]:30)

Some Copts, it seems, coped with the changing Ottoman milieu by finding different ways of making ends meet, specifically by seeking employment within Egypt's expanding financial and military bureaucracy. These men likely began their careers by attending Coptic communal schools, institutions that were similar to Muslim *kuttāb*. Coptic *kuttāb* taught religion, writing, and mathematics in efforts to prepare the best and brightest for those lucrative posts. Abudacnus affirms that the Coptic education emphasized:

> [r]eligion and good manners [and Coptic children] learn[ed] to read and write in Arabic and Coptic tongues. Boys also are wont in these schools to commit to memory the psaltery, and St. Paul's Epistles; they learn for the most part Geometry and Arithmetic, because these two studies are very useful and necessary upon the account of the overflowing of the Nile.
>
> (1675 [1692]: 30)

Having acquired basic skills in reading, religion, and mathematics, a student's education would be later supplemented by direct mentoring and training into specific professions. Gradually, the most talented made their way into Egypt's administrative and fiscal bureaucracy. These elites would protect their community's hegemony over certain posts, guarding their social, economic, and political interests against perceived (and real) competition from other non-Muslims (Armanios 2011: 27–28).

In Ottoman Egypt, literate Copts worked regularly as *mubāshirīn* or agents, who often kept registers on revenues and expenditures in a special Copto-Arabic script that "made it incomprehensible to all but those especially initiated into the secrets of its formation and use" (Shaw 1962: 341). *Mubāshirīn* also served as financial representatives for wealthy patrons, handling business transactions and various administrative affairs. Copts constituted an important part of the *muḥāsiba* or accounting department of the Egyptian treasury (ibid. 202, 345), and Coptic *kuttāb* (clerks or scribes) staffed multiple parts of the Egyptian administrative structure, conducting cadastral surveys and filling various ranks of the Egyptian treasury (Armanios 2008). The Copts' extensive experience was also essential in tasks in the annual measurement of the Nile, and as the German traveler Johann Michael Vansleb noted in the seventeenth century, in dating weather patterns and religious festivals:

> [Copts] are esteemed because of the computation of the time; for the Mahometans in all their actions, either private or public, never make use of their own computation, but of that of the Copties, as the justest and the best for the business: For example, they say not, that the Rains fall such and such a day of their month, but such a day of the month of the Copties. They reckon Easter, called Camsins [Khamasin], not after their Beiram, but according to the Easter of the Copties: so that they govern all their actions, and all their public affairs, not according to their own, but according to the Copties Calendar.
>
> (1678: 20; also Evliya Çelebi 2008: 77, 170)

Because of their trustworthiness, their knowledge, and their experience, Coptic elites rose to influential posts and became close to local political and military households. Within their community, archons formed a vital conduit between ordinary Copts, who were mostly marginalized from the political system, and the center of power. Indeed, the entire community became sensitive to the wavering fortunes of these archons as they quickly became the most vocal and powerful champions of Coptic issues (Armanios 2011: 26–31).

Archons also collaborated with the clergy and helped develop a community that was vibrant and active. The eighteenth century, in particular, became a period of religious and cultural renewal marked by an increased interest in church and monastic renovations, artistic development—especially the creation of icons and illuminated manuscripts—the revival of traditional rites such as pilgrimages, and the development of religious shrines (Armanios 2008). During his travels, Carsten Niebuhr recounted an anecdote, involving the known Coptic scribe and artist Ibrāhīm al-Nāsikh (ca. 1755), which reveals the depth of this cultural effervescence and the cautiousness with which Copts protected their manuscripts from European travelers:

> [There was] a Copt named Ibrāhīm Ennasch [al-Nāsikh], a man of learning and polished manners, whose employment was in copying the books of the liturgy; by which he earned at the rate of half-a-crown in three days. My friend saw, in the hands of this Egyptian, a dictionary of a great many genuine old Coptic words, with their explanations in Arabic. He was also informed by Ibrāhīm Ennasch, that there still are, in several convents in Upper Egypt, a good number of Coptic books; but his informer knew nothing of their nature or contents. The clergy conceal these books with great care, for fear, as they say, lest the Catholics carry them off, and, after falsifying their contents, print them in Europe. Thus they have hitherto remained unknown. If those ecclesiastics could be persuaded that we are not all of the same party as the Pope, and were at the same time gratified with something to alleviate their extreme poverty, copies of the books in this hidden literary treasure might surely be obtained.
>
> (1792 [1978]: Vol. I, 106)

Aside from guarding valuable manuscripts from potentially extortionist European travelers, what was the clergy's status and role within the community? In the Ottoman period, patriarchs were commonly chosen by elite (lay and clerical) members of their community, and their selection was generally approved by local Ottoman governors (*pāshas*) and notables. In the seventeenth century, for instance, Abudacnus reported that "[The Coptic Patriarch] takes his power from the Vice Roy or *Bacha*, who commands in Egypt in place of the Emperor" (1675 [1692]: 4). Ceremonially, Abudacnus reveals the significance of this process: after the patriarch was selected by the bishops and the most elite laymen "he is brought to the Bacha or Vice-Roy for that time in Egypt, by whom he is constituted Patriarch of the [Copts], and from whom he receives a Grant of his first petition; which is, that he may govern the church, according to the institutions of the Ancestors" (ibid. 6). Coptic annals of this period relate how the selection of several patriarchs was mostly based on political negotiations within the community (Khater and Khs-Burmester 1970: 278, 290, 292). Commonly, the most powerful archons with some consultation from the bishops selected a monk from a particular monastery, usually St. Antony or St. Paul on the Red Sea, or Al-Barāmus in Wādī al-Naṭrūn, and through this candidate, they would exert a great deal of authority over church and communal administration (Armanios 2008: 67–72).

In general, the Ottoman period witnessed some decline in clerical leadership. In the seventeenth and eighteenth centuries, archons who were closely linked to military and civilian elites invested their rising fortunes into various forms of religious patronage, often challenging or even supplanting the patriarch's political and religious authority. Patronage of the arts, architecture, or literature helped maintain a sense of Coptic collectiveness and identity (ibid.). Bringing greater visibility to their patrons, these investments also strengthened the archons and their extended households within the community and in broader Egyptian society. This influence can be seen in the figure of Nayrūz Abu Nawwār (Nayrūz Nawwār Ghaṭṭās, d. 1760) who served as a *mubāshir* for the leader of the Jalfī household 'Alī Kethūda 'Azbān al-Jalfī from 1730 to 1737, and then was employed by the powerful military leader Radwān Kethūda 'Azbān al-Jalfī until 1740 (Guirguis 1999: 54, note 24; Hathaway 1997: 56, 86). Perhaps his proximity to these notable political figures made Nayrūz the ideal advocate for his community during a crisis in 1734 involving the *jawālī* taxes (Shaw 1962: 151), upon which many impoverished Copts were arrested due to their failure to pay. At the same time, Nayrūz was also named a superintendent or administrator (*nāẓir*) over several Coptic churches and monasteries and spent a great deal of his personal income on their maintenance (Armanios 2008: 68; Guirguis 1999: 54, note 24).

The burgeoning influence of the laity over the clergy can be seen especially in the disputes over the practice of polygamy, akin to Muslim practice. During the reign of Patriarch Murqus V (1602–13), Copts in the Nile Delta region demanded the right to freely practice polygamy and solicited the help of the bishop of Damietta, who declared that polygamy conformed with biblical teachings. Murqus V, however, openly forbade polygamy and excommunicated the bishop in punishment for siding with the dissenters. A group of influential archons, supporters of the bishop, then conspired against the patriarch: they petitioned the Ottoman governor, who ordered the patriarch to be beaten and then imprisoned. The Bishop of Damietta and his supporters then convinced another monk to become the standing patriarch, and this "new" patriarch announced that Copts could practice divorce and polygamy as they wished. Soon after, however, the Coptic elites of Cairo and Upper Egypt rebelled—seemingly in a regional dispute against the archons of Damietta—and convinced the Ottoman governor to restore Murqus V to his rightful place (Armanios 2011: 44–45; Buri 1931: 244–47; Nakhla 1954 [2001]: Vol. IV, 62–63).

Faced with growing lay authority, clergymen throughout the Ottoman period feared the further erosion of their positions and utilized their spiritual authority to elicit loyalty from their flocks. At times, they closely collaborated with the archons in reviving important religious rites. By the mid-eighteenth century, however, and in dealing with perceived immoralities particularly among the elites—including drinking alcohol or coffee, concubinage, and intermarriage or fraternizing with Catholics—clergymen began to respond more forcefully. Wealthy archons were essential for protecting the community and for financing revivalist projects, but for motivated clerical leaders, the laity would have to be purified from any immoralities appropriated from their Muslim patrons or, perhaps more dangerously, from Catholic missionaries.

Religious Life in the Ottoman Period

The Coptic religion during the Ottoman period was diverse, rich, and noticeably shaped by the Copts' encounters with other religious communities. Efforts by church and communal leaders to preserve and conduct traditional religious institutions and rites were quite prominent in this era. Copts had active churches in most urban centers and modest parishes in rural areas (Vansleb 1678: 76, 141–48). The community regularly assembled there for liturgical prayers but also to celebrate religious feasts and weddings. Religious ceremonies included men and women, and were lively occasions for the entire community. For the seventeenth century, Vansleb provides a colorful and unique depiction of a Coptic wedding ceremony held inside one of those churches:

> [A]fter morning-prayer, the friends and parents led first the bridegroom, and next the bride, from their houses to the Church, with several lighted tapers before them, and singing through the streets hymns in the Copties language, and striking with little wooden hammers against some sticks of Ebony wood, which is their music. When they were come to the Church, they led the bridegroom into the inner chancel, where usually the prayers are said, and brought the bride to the place of the women. Then the priests and the people began in the Chancel their prayers mingled with hymns, which lasted very long.
>
> (1678: 203–5)

The desire for fellowship and spiritual comfort motivated men and women to participate in such lively (if lengthy) services, but within poorer communities, Copts also sought charity and spiritual comfort from their churches. The abysmal state of some rural parishes was frequently noted by travelers. While visiting the town of Zifta in the Nile Delta in the eighteenth century, for instance, Carsten Niebuhr wrote that the town:

> [had] a church belonging to the Copts, the congregation of which consists of three hundred families. Those good people asked me to see their church: it is ill-built, dirty, and hung with cobwebs. During the public worship, they stand, leaning on their staves. Their churches are adorned with bad paintings. I saw one in which Jesus Christ, and the Blessed Virgin, with several of the Saints, appeared mounted proudly on horseback.
>
> (1792 [1978]: Vol. I, 46)

Historically, the interior, private space of the church—with its distinctive rituals and iconography—was important since under Islamic rule, Copts and other non-Muslims faced many, if inconsistently enforced, restrictions on their public religious life. They were generally prohibited from building new or repairing old houses of worship. Limitations also extended to the ringing of church bells, ritual processions, and the display of crosses, banners, or icons (Armanios 2011:

17). However, in Ottoman Egypt, as seen from Vansleb's description of a wedding ceremony, the Coptic community continued to challenge these provisions. Some decades later, Niebuhr similarly described these occasions as related to important Coptic festivals:

> The Copts have their feasts, as well as the Mahometans, and contribute, by their ceremonies, to the general amusement. These festivals are sometimes celebrated by night. The streets are then illuminated by the blaze of resinous wood in a chaffing dish, held up on a long pole. They use also another more luminous flambeau, which is a machine constituting of diverse pieces of light wood, to which are hung a number of small lamps, and the whole carried on a pole, as the former. When these festivals are celebrated by day, the people divert themselves upon swings, and with other similar amusements.
>
> (1792 [1978]: Vol. I, 125–26)

Legal codes restricting the public display of non-Muslim religious life were thus subject to the arbitrary interpretation of regional and local rulers. In contrast to the relative openness with which Copts practiced some of their religious rituals, the Ottoman traveler Evliya Çelebi noted in the seventeenth century that Janissary soldiers arbitrarily taxed any Copt who passed in front of Cairo's Sufi lodges in what he characterized as "a location of injustice" (2008: 168).

Even with legal–official restrictions in place, the Coptic leadership would spearhead a visible religious resurgence. Supporting a multiplicity of potent religious practices helped preserve communal cohesiveness. Both clergy and laity understood that a strong and vibrant community, with defined traditions, rituals, and boundaries, could reinforce their own authority and create stronger allegiances between the masses and their communal patrons. Lay and clerical leaders, to this end, used creative tactics in dealing with external threats, especially during the height of Catholic missionary activities in the eighteenth century. They supported a prolific manuscript production of hagiographies, miracle narratives, and sermons; this attempt to codify the history and beliefs of the community shows resilience in dealing with developing challenges to dogma, political leadership, and religious life (Armanios 2011: 148–49).

Coptic manuscripts from the Ottoman period reveal the community's notable attention to martyrdom: promoting narratives of sacrifice on behalf of one's religion rallied the community during times of duress. After the Mamlūk period, during which many boisterous Coptic festivals had become suppressed, Copts patronized martyr shrines, specifically outside of Cairo, as a way of preserving traditional religious rites. Religious shrines, such as that of fourth-century St. Dimyānah in the Nile Delta town of Bilqās, fostered closer relationships between Coptic saints–intercessors and devotees. In the seventeenth and eighteenth centuries, Dimyānah's annual springtime festival attracted Coptic and Muslim pilgrims, bedouins, and local Ottoman political and military leaders—the latter brought regiments to serve as security guards. Food, drinks, entertainment, and the miraculous apparitions of Coptic saints connected different communities in a shared carnivalesque experience (Armanios 2011: 65–90).

At the same time, there was also increased interest in intercommunal and intra-Christian rituals. The pilgrimage to Jerusalem during the Great Lent and Easter, for instance, allowed some Copts to join with Greeks, Armenians, Syrians, and Ethiopians in one of Christendom's holiest cities. To make the annual pilgrimage in the eighteenth century, Coptic communal leaders frequently risked their lives and properties. They negotiated with Muslim religious leaders, Ottoman governors, and Janissaries, as well as bedouins, receiving special permissions to ensure the success of the pilgrimage. On certain years, these negotiations failed and Copts were attacked or prevented from traveling to the Holy Land. In general, however, the pilgrimage to Jerusalem became a more elaborate ceremony throughout the Ottoman era. As some Copts became wealthier, they could afford to travel with greater pomp and circumstance, and they could use their valuable political connections to guarantee the success of their long journey (ibid. 91–115).

Muslim official involvement in numerous facets of Coptic religious life was noticeable in the Ottoman period, challenging common notions that non-Muslim communities living under Islamic governance were mostly insular and reluctant to engage Muslims in their internal communal affairs. Aside from seeking the protection of soldiery at festivals and of soliciting legal permits to make their annual pilgrimage to Jerusalem, Coptic communal leaders and clergymen approached Ottoman governors and Muslim magistrates about arbitrating community practices such as the right to practice polygamy, as seen earlier, or the limitation of Catholic missionary encroachment on Copts. During the eighteenth century, for instance, in the Upper Egyptian town of Akhmīm, tensions erupted between Coptic Orthodox and Catholic missionaries over the recruitment of Coptic boys to be educated in Rome (Rufayla 1898 [2000]: 269). Coptic families accused European missionaries of kidnapping their children and allegedly filed their complaints in Islamic courts (Frazee 1983: 219). Copts, especially men, regularly filed their requests for divorce in Islamic courts, which were far more lenient in granting these permits than the Coptic Church (Milād 1983; El Nahal 1979).

Internally, Coptic writers and copyists engaged both the official religious dialogue sponsored by the clergy and also its recipients on the popular level. For example, as her festival became highly popular during the seventeenth and eighteenth centuries, Dimyānah's Arabic hagiography was copied multiple times by Coptic scribes and distributed among churches and to individual patrons all over Egypt. The focus on familiar Egyptian locales in Dimyānah's life narrative likely made her story accessible to a wide array of audiences. Ascetic values in her legend—such as gender segregation, virtue, purity, dutifulness, and obedience—were commonly upheld for women in Ottoman Egyptian society and would have resonated with readers or listeners of this story (Armanios 2011: 86–89).

Likewise, connections between religious writings and popular belief can be seen within clerical sermons of the late eighteenth century. Coptic clergymen authored dozens of homilies directly addressing their own parishes. Rather than relying on ancient sermons by established church fathers, they wrote new sermons in colloquial Egyptian Arabic, addressing topics such as pride, avarice, polygamy, drunkenness, lewd behavior and blatant disobedience of church rituals. Indeed it would be in this period that clergymen would use the pulpit to characterize a specific Coptic identity and to distinguish a pure Coptic morality from the perceived vices of others (ibid. 117–45).

Renewal, Reform, and Orthodoxy in the Eighteenth Century

The struggles over who had the right to define the boundaries of and lead the Coptic Orthodox community—clergy or laity—began to intensify in the early eighteenth century and were spawned by new external threats. At a time when Catholic missionary activism increased, particularly in Upper Egypt, clergymen launched a religious reform program and began to reinforce their leadership position. In this process, they offered increasingly refined expressions of an Orthodox identity, using terminology that has continued to be echoed until today.

At first, Catholic missionaries—active since the late seventeenth century—had won only a small number of converts in Egypt, but they had become noticeably aggressive in their tactics, demanding, for instance, that Coptic converts burn their manuscripts and mocking traditional Coptic Orthodox customs (Hamilton 2006: 87). European Catholic merchants, moreover, favored the new Syrian Catholic immigrants to Egypt, who fled persecution in their native lands in the early eighteenth century. The Syrian Catholics were active in trade and gradually replaced Jews as customs officials at the Mediterranean and Red Sea ports. They attained these important and lucrative positions, in part, because of their close alliance with the French, whose interest in importing Egyptian grain increased during this period. In the early to mid-eighteenth century, the French had "fostered a commercial revival and encouraged growth of a new and increasingly non-Egyptian class directing an export-oriented economy" (Gran 1979 [1998]: xiv). They rewarded those Syrian Orthodox who adopted Roman Catholicism with capitulations agreements in exchange for loyalty and allegiance. Gradually, competition intensified among all clients of Egypt's political and military leaders who sought to prove their loyalty to local patrons, as did tensions between non-Muslim communities who came to vie over "the same sources of income: the production and sale of alcoholic beverages; commerce in jewels, gold, silver and other goods; money-changing, moneylending and government fiscal service" (Winter 1992: 221).

Despite the successful conversion of a few Coptic Orthodox to Catholicism in the eighteenth century, of laity and even some prominent clergymen, most Coptic archons were committed to ensuring that their community persisted as Egypt's most dominant Christian sect and that they, instead of new Coptic Catholic converts or Syrian Catholics, would be recognized and favored by local political and military leaders. As the traveler Charles Sigisbert Sonnini wrote in the eighteenth century:

> Being numerous, as they [Copts] constitute the true Egyptian race, and powerful, as they enjoy the confidence of the great, whose affairs they superintend, these aborigines, so different from their ancestors, take, in their turn, advantage of their influence, to represent all the Franks as at once a dangerous and despicable set of men.
>
> (1800: 631)

By taking this "anti-Frankish" stance, many archons showed their fidelity to their Muslim employers and proved that they were resilient against external pressures. Europeans were frequently blamed for corrupting the moral fabric of Islamic society, particularly by spreading habits such as smoking and drinking (Grehan 2006: 1362). By maintaining their faith and even at times persecuting the Catholics, Coptic archons outwardly showed their loyalty to local power-holders (Armanios 2008: 64–67).

On the other hand, using church pulpits to encourage a moral revival, Coptic Orthodox clerical leaders warned fellow believers against converting to Catholicism and adopting the much-hated "Frankish" identity, as they called it. Public oration was one of the most effective means to shape popular opinion in the early modern Middle East. Missionaries had quickly learned local dialects and converted native preachers to Catholicism; subsequently, their sermons grew more effective (Heyberger 1994: 355). Moreover, missionaries viewed Coptic Orthodox clergymen with noticeable disdain. In 1719, the French Catholic priest Claude Sicard reported that the new Coptic patriarch was "strong with ignorance and imbued in heresy. In the past, I had many meetings with him in our Cairo house, but in vain. I do not know if his new dignity will make him change feelings. He does not yet have sanctity" (Sicard 1982: Vol. I, 59).

As they "counter-preached" against Catholics, Coptic clergymen—especially Patriarch Yu'annis XVIII (r. 1769–96) and Bishop Yusāb of Jirja and Akhmīm (r. 1791–1826)—reminded fellow believers that the Coptic identity was made up of two parts: faith (*imān*) and race or nation (*jins*). These parts were inseparable and both would be lost if Copts adopted a "foreign" religion. Clergymen blamed "Franks" for creating intra-communal dissent and for promoting heterodox practices which weakened authentic Coptic traditions. By clearly defining what it meant to be a Coptic "Orthodox" in contrast to a "Catholic" and a "Frank" and by outlining what behaviors, social mores, habits, and values defined Coptic-ness the clergy rallied Copts to renew their faith under their leadership (Armanios 2011: 117–45).

The religious renewal that had been mostly sponsored by the archons since the late seventeenth century had focused on the arts, rebuilding, architecture, iconography, manuscript production, and religious rites. Through preaching, clergymen led their own renewal, a moral one, as they sought to standardize church traditions on marriage, confession, fasting, and prayer, and to revamp the priesthood, ultimately to inaugurate a reform program unique to their area of expertise.

By the late eighteenth century, tensions between laity and clergy, and between Coptic Orthodox and Catholics—in the context of religious life—regularly played out in the pulpits. Clergymen cautioned that greed, self-indulgence, immoral games, and excessive celebrations involving "adulterous" women were introduced by an "outside" culture whose vices had infiltrated the Coptic community, a community that should be pure, steadfast in its faith, and disciplined in its practice. While they may have lacked the archons' financial and political clout, Coptic clergymen used preaching and the pulpit, a traditionally clerical domain, to express their moralizing ideals. This sort of rhetoric was not necessarily innovative in and of itself: similar patterns, partly a consequence of increased contact with Europeans, could be seen among other Christians and among Muslims in the early modern Middle East (ibid. 132–33). What emerges as prominent among Copts in Egypt during the Ottoman period, however, is a seemingly urgent call to define the community's moral and religious boundaries, both by the clergy through preaching and standardization of the faith, and by archons through multiple acts of religious patronage (Armanios 2008: 67–70; 2011: 117–45).

Conclusions

Generally, historians of the Copts have regarded the nineteenth century, specifically the Muḥammad 'Alī period (1805–48), as the first glimpse of recovery for Copts since Egypt had fallen under Islamic control in 641. In reality, the presumed "decline" of Coptic life prior to the nineteenth century is due more to the absence of a critical and investigative gaze at Coptic Christian history in the early modern period than to a communal stagnation or external persecution. Through an understanding of the rising fortunes of Coptic archons, it is easy to see why the Ottoman period witnessed a gradual transformation and at times weakening of the clerical leadership. Within the community, those few archons who attained eminent positions in the political and economic power structure became respected and admired by their less fortunate coreligionists. The communal revival which began to manifest in the late seventeenth and eighteenth centuries allowed the archons, at times in collaboration with clergy, to augment their political position within the community.

The most successful Coptic leaders could support a Christian community that had gradually, over centuries, shifted from being the dominant cultural and demographic force in Egypt to a small minority (Armanios 2011: 15–18). In the seventeenth and early eighteenth centuries, archons and clergy helped spawn a visible cultural awakening. But from their positions of power and through delicate negotiations with local Muslim rulers, archons became the most prominent protectors of Coptic interests. For their part, the clergy utilized religious rhetoric and writings to rouse the spirit of the masses. They refused to submit to what can be easily called the "age of the archons." As they faced the reality of growing lay authority, clergymen relied upon their religious prowess to elicit loyalty from their flocks. They directed their voices to the masses and worked to create a more cohesive, unified, and defined Coptic Orthodox identity, one which became most clearly articulated by the end of the eighteenth century and which would resonate into the modern period.

Timeline

1517	Ottoman Conquest of Egypt by Sultan Selīm I (1512–20)
1524	the Ottomans issue the *Qanūn-nāme* (legal code) to govern Egypt; Coptic Patriarch Yu'annis XIII dies (r. 1484–1524)
1609	a major rebellion erupts against Ottoman rule, led by the cavalry (*sipāhī*) corps
1660	outbreak of civil conflict between the Fiqārī and Qāsimī factions
1676	Coptic Patriarch Murqus VI dies (r. 1646–76)
1697	the Franciscans found a mission in Upper Egypt, Nubia, and Ethiopia; the Jesuits establish a center in Cairo
1709	the Copts make a successful pilgrimage to Jerusalem
1711	civil war erupts within the Janissary military ranks
1718	the notable Coptic archon Jirjis Abu Manṣūr al-Ṭūkhī dies of the plague, as does Coptic Patriarch Yu'annis XVI (r. 1676–1718)
1734	a Coptic protest erupts in Cairo against the institution of new taxes
1748	the Copts fail in their attempts to make a pilgrimage to Jerusalem
1768	Coptic Patriarch Murqus VIII dies (r. 1745–68)
1770	the Coptic archon Rizqallah al-Badawī, 'Alī Bey al-Kabīr's trusted advisor, dies
1772	'Alī Bey al-Kabīr is defeated and unseated from power as virtual sovereign of Ottoman Egypt (r. 1760–72)
1775	the co-rulers Ibrāhīm Bey and Murād Bey ascend to power
1791	Anba (Bishop) Yusāb "al-Abbaḥ" (the Eloquent) is named bishop over Akhmīm and Jirja
1795	the leading Coptic archon Ibrāhīm al-Jawharī dies
1796	Coptic Patriarch Yu'annis XIII dies (r. 1769–96)
1798	Napoleonic invasion of Egypt.

Selected Bibliography

Abudacnus, Y. (1675; 2nd edn 1692) *The True History of the Jacobites, of Ægypt, Lybia, Nubia, &c.*, trans. E. Sadleir, London: R. Baldwin.

Armanios, F. (2008) "Patriarchs, Archons and the Eighteenth-Century Resurgence of the Coptic Community," in W. Lyster (ed.) *The Cave Church of Paul the Hermit*, New Haven, CT: Yale University Press/The American Research Center in Egypt.

——(2011) *Coptic Christianity in Ottoman Egypt*, New York: Oxford University Press.

Armanios, F. and Ergene, B. (2006) "A Christian Martyr under Mamluk Justice: The Trials of Salib (d. 1512) according to Coptic and Muslim Sources," *Muslim World*, 96(1): 115–44.

Buri, V. (1931) "L'Unione della chiesa Copta con Roma sotto Clemente VIII," *Orientalia Christiana*, 23(72): 105–264.

Crecelius, D. (1981) *The Roots of Modern Egypt: A Study of the Regimes of 'Ali Bey Al-Kabir and Muhammad Bey Abu Al-Dhahab, 1760–1775*, Chicago: Bibliotheca Islamica.

El Nahal, G. H. (1979) *The Judicial Administration of Ottoman Egypt in the Seventeenth Century*, Chicago: Bibliotheca Islamica.

Evliya Çelebi (2008) *Seyahatname*, Volume 10, S. A. Kahraman, Y. Dağlı, and R. Dankoff (eds), Istanbul: Yapı Kredi Kültür Sanat Yayıncılık.

Frazee, C. (1983) *Catholics and Sultans: The Church and the Ottoman Empire 1453–1923*, London: Cambridge University Press.

Gran, P. (1979; 2nd edn 1998) *Islamic Roots of Capitalism: Egypt, 1760–1840*, Syracuse, NY: Syracuse University Press.

Grehan, J. (2006) "Smoking and 'Early Modern' Sociability: The Great Tobacco Debate in the Ottoman Middle East (Seventeenth to Eighteenth Centuries)," *The American Historical Review*, 111(5): 1353–54.

Guirguis, M. (1999) "Idārat al-azamāt fī tarīkh al-qibṭ: namūdhaj min al-qarn al-thāmin 'ashr," *Annales Islamologiques*, 33: 45–59.

——(2005) "The Coptic Community in the Ottoman Period," in N. Hanna and R. Abbas (eds) *Society and Economy in Egypt and the Eastern Mediterranean, 1600–1900; Essays in Honor of André Raymond*, Cairo: American University in Cairo Press.

Hamilton, A. (2006) *The Copts and the West 1439–1822: The European Discovery of the Egyptian Church*, Oxford: Oxford University Press.

Hathaway, J. (1997) *The Politics of Households in Ottoman Egypt*, Cambridge: Cambridge University Press.

——(1998) "Egypt in the Seventeenth Century," in M. W. Daly (ed.) *The Cambridge History of Egypt, Volume 2, Modern Egypt, from 1517 to the End of the Twentieth Century*, Cambridge: Cambridge University Press.

Heyberger, B. (1994) *Les Chrétiens du Proche-Orient au temps de la réforme Catholique (Syrie, Liban, Palestine, XVIIe-XVIIIe siècles)*, Rome: École Française de Rome.

İnalcık, H. (1969–70) "The Policy of Mehmed II toward the Greek Population of Istanbul and the Byzantine Buildings of the City," *Dumbarton Oaks Papers*, 23: 229–49.

Khater, A. K. and Khs-Burmester, O. H. E. (trans.) (1970) *History of the Patriarchs of the Egyptian Church, Known as the History of the Holy Church* [*HPEC*], vol. 3, part 3: *Cyril II–Cyril V (1235–1894 AD)*, Cairo: Société d'Archéologie Copte/Institut Français d'Archéologie Orientale du Caire.

Milād, S. (ed.) (1983) *Wathā'iq ahl al-dhimma fi'l 'asr al-'uthmānī wa ahammiyatuha al-tarīkhiyya*, Cairo: Dār al-Thaqāfa lil-Nashr wa'l-Tawzī'.

Muṣṭafa 'Alī (1975) *Mustafa 'Ali's Description of Cairo of 1599*, ed. and trans. A. Tietze, Vienna: Verlag der Österreichischen Akademie der Wissenschaften.

Nakhla, K. S. (1954; 2nd edn 2001) *Silsilat tārīkh al-bābawāt baṭārikat al-kursī al-iskandarī*, 5 vols, Wādī al-Naṭrūn, Egypt: Maṭba'at Dayr al-Sayyida al-'Adhrā', Dayr al-Suryān.

Niebuhr, C. (1792; reprint edn 1978) *Travels through Arabia and Other Countries in the East*, 2 vols, trans. R. Heron, Beirut: Librairie du Liban.

Raymond, A. (1973–74; 2nd edn 1999) *Artisans et commerçants au Caire au XVIIIe siècle*, 2 vols, Cairo: Institut Français d'Archéologie Orientale.

Rufayla, Y. N. (1898; 2nd edn 2000) *Kitāb tārīkh al-umma al-qibṭiyya*, Cairo: Metropol.
Savary, C. E. (1786) *Letters on Egypt*, trans. Anon., London: G. G. J. and J. Robinson.
Shaw, S. (1962) *The Financial and Administrative Organization and Development of Ottoman Egypt, 1517–1798*, Princeton: Princeton University Press.
Sicard, C. (1982) *Œuvres*, 3 vols, M. Martin (ed.), Cairo: Institut Français d'Archéologie Orientale du Caire.
Sonnini, C. S. (1800) *Travels in Upper and Lower Egypt undertaken by Order of the Old Government of France*, London: J. Debrett.
Staffa, S. J. (1977) *Conquest and Fusion: The Social Evolution of Cairo A.D. 642–1850*, Leiden: Brill.
Vansleb, J. M. (1678) *The Present State of Egypt; or a New Relation of a Late Voyage into that Kingdom Performed in the Years 1672 and 1673*, trans. M. D., London: John Starkey.
Winter, M. (1992) *Egyptian Society under Ottoman Rule, 1517–1798*, New York: Routledge.
——(1998) "Ottoman Egypt, 1525–1609," in M. W. Daly (ed.) *The Cambridge History of Egypt, Volume 2, Modern Egypt, from 1517 to the End of the Twentieth Century*, Cambridge: Cambridge University Press.

5 The Pre-Modern Period (1798–1952)

The Age of Citizenship and Reform

Maged S. R. Hanna[1]

Introduction

Many historians characterize the period that begins with the 1798 French occupation and ends with the July 1952 Revolution as the era that launched Egypt, and parts of the Middle East under French occupation, into a modern renaissance and openness to the West. Such sweeping statements, however, should be made more cautiously. The multi-ethnic, multi-religious, and multicultural structure of the Ottoman Empire, and the good status of the Coptic Orthodox community in the eighteenth century in particular, ultimately culminated in a vibrant and engaged Coptic community at the beginning of the nineteenth century. This enabled the Coptic community to play a prominent and important role in nineteenth- and twentieth-century Egypt. The fact that the Copts were marginalized, and their access to most jobs restricted—because their jobs were confined to administrative and financial positions—led some scholars to suggest that their role was limited to paying taxes and the *jizyah* (a head tax paid by non-Muslims to Muslim rulers) without crediting them with their distinctive and effective role as nation builders.

In addition, the secular trend that permeated Egyptian society and its religious institutions by the end of the eighteenth century, which also affected the Copts as an integral part of Egyptian society, strengthened the leadership of influential Coptic lay members—the Archons—who supervised religious institutions and their activities, which culminated in a genuine renaissance that affected Coptic lives. This led to an increasing role in ecclesial work for the laity during the nineteenth century, which was one of the factors that led to the establishment of the *Majlis al-Milli* or Coptic Community Council in 1874. Though this secular council faced many confrontations and a struggle for power between it and the Holy Synod, especially in the first half of the twentieth century during the tenure of Pope Cyril V, it persisted and was engaged in many of the delicate ecclesial events in this era (Carter 1986: 28–42).

The chapter will present the history of the Copts in this era through the themes of the French occupation (1798–1801), the reign of Muḥammad 'Alī and his dynasty (1805–1952), and the political, religious, and socioeconomic role of Copts before and during the 1952 revolution.

The French Occupation (1798–1801)

The Copts in the Eyes of the French Expedition

The French expedition organized by Napoleon Bonaparte published the results of its research during its three-year stay in Egypt in the *Description de l'Egypte*. The book describes the leading and primary figure of the Copts as a religious and secular leader, a pontiff or "patriarch," with unlimited power, except for what established norms and the will of the rulers dictate. He arbitrates among his people, though his decision is not final since disputing parties—with their mutual agreement—can seek the arbitration of a Muslim judge, who usually agrees with the patriarchal rule (Al-Shāīb 1992). The patriarch does not rule on crimes, except for minor ones, which require a reforming rule rather than punishment. When a Copt is accused of, for example, theft from a Muslim, the latter seeks the ruling of the patriarch; but if the Muslim is the accused, the Copt seeks the rule of a Muslim judge or seeks justice from the city ruler. Major crimes such as murder are not within the jurisdiction of the patriarch, but rather the city police, who chase and punish the culprit. Sometimes however, the culprit bribes the judge and escapes judgment (ibid.).

The *Description* describes the method by which the Copts choose their patriarchs. The patriarchs are chosen from the Monastery of St. Antony.[2] Bishops and high-ranking priests joined by Coptic archons, totaling about forty to fifty persons, convene to choose a successor by voting; the monk who receives the highest votes is installed as patriarch. Bishops and metropolitans form the second rank of the Coptic church. The revenue of these bishops comes from diocesan donations. The main income of the patriarch, the small amount of 10,000 *Bwṭāqa* or *Khurda*, is generated from charitable trusts, though an additional, and sometimes substantial, income can be generated through irregular donations. Alexandria is the official, historical patriarchal residence, but the patriarch now resides in Cairo to manage church affairs and defend his rights before the Muslim powers. Priests also have status within Coptic society, though they are ignorant and poor. Their church canons permit their marriage, which should take place before their ordination. They can marry only once. When one of the priests dies the archons of his church nominate a successor to the metropolitan, who ordains him immediately. All churches are owned by the clerical body and expenses are paid through donations (ibid.).

Copts trust their clergy blindly. The priests have great influence over them and manipulate such honor for their own profit. They are as ignorant as the people. Very few of them are educated or capable of reading church books, which are the only books still using the Coptic language. Though the clergy are honored, the Coptic man does not permit his wife to be unveiled before a priest or even the patriarch, except by special permission from the husband (ibid.).

Such was the report of the scholars of the French expedition regarding eighteenth-century Copts and their religious leader, the patriarch. The French expedition provided important information about the judicial system of that era, the means of electing a patriarch and his income, the relationship of the people with their clergy and other details about Coptic society. The report did not take into consideration the insurmountable pressures imposed on the Coptic community both before and after the French expedition, which in 1805 led to the burning of the patriarchal residence in Ḥārit al-Rūm, forcing the patriarch to move his residence to the al-Azbakīa quarter. They also did not record the repercussions of the French expedition after its departure. The Copts were accused of high treason for collaborating with their French coreligionists, since both the French and Copts are Christians.

The Political Position of the Copts after the French Occupation and the Role of General Ya'qūb Hannā

When the French left, most leaders did not think beyond Egypt returning under Ottoman rule. One Egyptian, however, was thinking of an Egypt independent from all foreign control. He was the Coptic General Ya'qūb Hannā, who in August 1801 presented the project for the emancipation of Egypt for the first time in its history. According to some documents of the British foreign ministry, General Ya'qūb saw that the French occupation "was not an ill-fated period that should be abolished for the return of Ottoman rule, but a new beginning for Egypt and the Egyptians since the French occupation severed the ties with the Ottomans and weakened the power of the Memluks" (Ghobrial 1932: 15). It should be noted that Ya'qūb aimed to fight the Mamlūks in Upper Egypt and thus sided with the French to achieve his goal. The French eventually promoted him to the rank of general for his military role. Politically shrewd, he realized that, with the French departure, it was an opportune time for Egypt's independence; all the ingredients for independence were within reach. He took a Coptic delegation on one of the French ships, leaving after the French military had left Egypt, to call for Egypt's independence among European leaders. In August 1801, however, he died onboard the ship before reaching the southern shores of France. This ended the delegation's mission and the project of independence was abandoned (Sūrīal 1984: 95).

Some historians have presented Ya'qūb as a traitor and a French agent, suggesting that he fled Egypt with the French because he knew that if he stayed he would be executed for treason. But those who research Egyptian history recognize that General Ya'qūb's intent was to make Egyptian independence an "international" case. General Ya'qūb was traveling to Europe to negotiate his project of independence with Britain and to assure Britain that Egypt's independence would not affect its commercial interests in the African continent. He anticipated that if Britain attempted to invade Egypt, the French, who still had an interest in Egypt, would stop them. Ya'qūb thought that this was the best time for independence, but if Britain did not back the project it was doomed to failure. General Ya'qūb was a pioneer in demanding Egyptian sovereignty, working towards its realization, and planting the idea of independence in the Egyptian mind.

The Reign of Muḥammad ʿAlī and his Dynasty (1805–1952)

Political Aspects: The Coptic Political Role

The Era of Muḥammad ʿAlī (1805–48)

Muḥammad ʿAlī inaugurated the modern Egyptian state. This era is characterized by the modernization of agricultural methods, the building of factories, the rebuilding and modernization of the army, and the establishment of a sophisticated governmental administration. Muḥammad ʿAlī introduced, for the first time, compulsory military service for all Egyptians. He sent hundreds of Egyptians to study modern science in Europe, particularly to France. The Copts, however, did not benefit from most of these social advancements. For example, after Muḥammad ʿAlī issued the 1822 edict for obligatory conscription, thus creating the first Egyptian (i.e., not Ottoman) army, 376,000 soldiers had been drafted by 1839, but there was not a single Coptic soldier. In addition, the hundreds of fellowships for studying abroad for military, medical, architectural, agricultural, and veterinary studies did not include a single Copt. The Copts were still confined to their role in the financial administration, collecting taxes and recording income tax. But with the expansion of the governmental administration, the Copts held many government positions. Still, the majority of Copts were poor farmers. Nevertheless, the stage set by this era made possible an important role for Copts and a vital Coptic participation in politics.

The era of Khedive Saʿīd (1854–63) and Khedive Ismāʿīl (1863–82), of the Muḥammad ʿAlī dynasty, was characterized by what might be called "citizen rights." In 1855 Saʿīd abolished the *jizyah* tax for the first time since the Arabs conquered Egypt in the seventh century and in 1857 drafted Copts into the Egyptian army, which was previously forbidden. Ismāʿīl depended more on Egyptians within the bureaucracy of his administration. When he promulgated the law for the first judicial court in Egypt, the regulation against appointing Christians was not listed. For the first time, a Coptic judge was appointed to the court. In 1866 and 1870, the first Coptic members of the chamber were appointed. He also gave the title "Pasha" for the first time to a Copt, to Buṭrus Ghāli, who also became the first Coptic prime minister in the history of Egypt. In 1880, he issued a law for military conscription which stated that all Egyptians were to be drafted into the army regardless of religion. He extended education to all, regardless of religion; many Copts enrolled in his schools and some were eligible for fellowships to study in Europe. In general, the modernization efforts started by Muḥammad ʿAlī created a sense of Egyptian citizenship, which created a new relationship between Muslims and Christians and also enabled Copts to become prominent in the public sphere.

This period was followed by the ʿUrābī revolution (1881–82), which raised the slogan of "Egypt for the Egyptians." Two Copts were appointed to the House of Representatives or Representative Council (*Majlis al-Nūwāb*), which was formed during the revolution. ʿAbd-allāh al-Nadīm, an Islamist intellectual, preached about national unity between Christians and Muslims. In spite of all this, the Copts did not play any role in the 'Urābī revolution. Though it was supported by the populace, it was primarily a military coup led by high-ranking Egyptian military officers. Since there were still hardly any Copts in the army or the highest military echelons, they did not participate in the coup. On the other hand, though 'Urābī and his companions fought for issues of interest to all Egyptians, regarding the army, foreign debt, relationships with European countries, the powers of the Khedive (the ruler of Egypt), and the judicial structure, the revolution used Islamic vocabulary and ideas, particularly those of Jamāl al-Dīn al-Afghānī, an Islamic political activist. This Islamist rhetoric did not attract the Copts.

The British Occupation (1882)

The relationship between Christians and Muslims and the status of Copts worsened during the early period of the British occupation. Contrary to expectations, the British adopted a discriminatory policy against the Copts, especially regarding public appointments. Lord Cromer (1841–1917), the British agent and consul-general, was careful not to hire Copts in an attempt to appease the Muslim majority, especially because the Copts did not support the British occupation, fearing similar reprisals from the Muslims to what they had experienced during the French occupation (Carter 1986: 58–60). Cromer depended primarily on Christians from Mesopotamia.

During this period Musṭafā Kamil led the National Party (*al-Ḥizb al-Waṭanī*), using Islamic rhetoric and calling for Ottoman rule as a means of emancipation from the British occupation. Nevertheless, the party included two Copts, Murquṣ Ḥannā and Wīṣā Wāṣif. The party was associated with two famous Islamic figures, Shīkh 'Ali Yussif and Shīkh 'Abd al-'Azīz Jāwīsh, who enthusiastically promoted the idea of an Islamic University, which created a gap between the Copts and the party. After the death of Musṭafā Kamil, things became worse. When Muḥammad Farīd took over the leadership in 1908, he objected to the appointment of Buṭrus Ghāli as prime minister, losing what little support the party had from the Copts. The decade of 1908–18 was characterized by the retreat of the national movement, the public escalation of religious tension, and the general deterioration of the relations between Christians and Muslims. This was exemplified in the press in a war between the Islamic papers of *al-Liwā'* and *al-Mū'id* and the Coptic papers of *Miṣr* and *al-Waṭan* (ibid. 43–50). In addition, there was disagreement on contentious issues, such as the Coptic right to equal employment and to teach Christianity in schools, and the Islamic record in Egypt since the time of 'Umar ibn al-'Aṣ. The assassination of the Coptic Prime Minster Buṭrus Ghāli in 1911 by a man connected to the National Party escalated the tension (ibid. 12).

The Coptic Congress of Asyūṭ

Metropolitan Macarius of Asyūṭ (1897–1944) called for a Coptic Congress and invited some of the leading Coptic figures, such as Tawfīk Dws, Murquṣ

Ḥannā, and Akhnūkh Fānūs, to meet in Asyūṭ on March 5–8, 1911, to discuss the antagonistic and deteriorating relationship with the Muslims.[3] One thousand people attended this congress, a large number for a town in Upper Egypt. These were some of their demands:

- Sunday as an official holiday for Copts
- Employment based only on merit and equality between Christians and Muslims in high-ranking leadership positions
- Christian religion to be taught in schools to Coptic students
- Establishment of a system that guaranteed Coptic representation in the judicial councils (the first time the principle of quota representation was demanded)
- That the government allocate money to fund Coptic schools from the land tax, of which the Copts paid 16 percent.

These demands aroused the fear of the Muslims. In April 1911 they organized a counter Islamic congress, called the Egyptian Congress, which met in ʻAin Shams and was led by Ryād Pasha, a former prime minister. Five thousand people attended. These were their decisions:

- Political rights are not to be divided among the nation's religious groups
- Friday is the only official holiday and Islam is the religion of the state
- Employment is based on merit and the government has to make sure that the Copts do not receive more than their proportion in society
- No change to the voting law to guarantee Coptic representation on judicial councils.

In short, the Islamic congress refused most of the Coptic demands. These meetings represent the tension between the Christians and Muslims during this period. Nevertheless, it was an occasion on which, for the first time, the issue of Coptic rights became a point of debate and the full citizenship of Copts was asserted (ibid. 13–14).

One would expect that ethnic and religious tensions would fade with modernization. To understand why they didn't we need to understand the process of modernization in Egypt. Modernization took place within the larger vision of Muḥammad ʻAlī of creating a powerful nation able to defend itself and expand its territory. For this aim, he wanted a strong, modernly equipped military based on modern western science and technological advancements. Modernization took place from the top down for the support of a powerful dictatorial state motivated by territorial expansion. Modernization was not a long-term plan for the modernization of the state, but a short-term plan with a specific goal. It is no surprise that the main interest was in science and technology. There were no fellowships for linguistics, philosophy, or humanities in Muḥammad ʻAlī's educational programs and the modernization project was not interested in art, new ideas, or other aspects of a civilized society. The natural outcome was that the modernization copied from France in science and technology was not accompanied by principles of democracy, equality, or secularization. Technology was introduced within an underdeveloped and immature political and cultural milieu that resisted any accompanying cultural or social modernization. And because this change was taking place while Egypt was occupied by western powers, resisting modernization was viewed as resisting occupation and western hegemony over the country.

The 1919 Revolution

Some consider 1919–52 the golden age of "national unity" or religious harmony in Egypt. Though it was not as rosy as some paint it, it was one of the best eras for Christian and Muslim relations. The 1919 revolution was the springboard for Copts to engage in national movements. It recognized that religious antagonism had reached a level that could lead to disastrous results that would definitely hamper the nationalist movement, especially since Britain claimed it was staying in Egypt to preserve and protect Coptic rights (ibid. 73). Sa'ad Zaghlūl, as a leader in the 1919 revolution and founder of the Wafd Party, recognized the importance of including the Copts in the national movement since both Copts and Muslims shared the common aspiration of independence. The Wafd Party (Delegation Party) was a nationalist political party that sought the departure of the British and developed the 1923 Constitution that would govern the country after the departure of the British. The writings of this period exhibit an exceptional spirit of unity. Copts participated in the revolution, and all Egyptians carried slogans such as "Religion is for God and the country is for all," "Nationalism is our religion," or "Let the Crescent live with the Cross." Priests spoke in mosques and sheikhs (Muslim clerics) in churches, and the celebration of the Coptic New Year (Naīrūz) was considered a national celebration. Copts were politically well represented in the Wafd Party.

During the drafting of the 1923 constitution, the notion of a Coptic quota in judicial courts was dismissed on the grounds that such policies affirm discrimination. It was conjectured that the religious harmony accompanying the 1919 revolution would evolve into a total disregard for the role of religion in politics. The Muftī, however, the highest ranking Islamic official of religious law in the country, insisted that the constitution must declare that Islam is the religion of the state. This was met with opposition from the *al-Waṭan* newspaper because it created discrimination. All the Wafd Party nominees for judicial elections were elected without discriminating between Christians and Muslims and equally no discrimination was observed in the 1925 or 1926 elections. The 1920s was a decade where religious discrimination in Egyptian politics was minimal. As Table 5.1 shows, Coptic representation in parliament was fairly consistent in that decade. The average Coptic representation from 1924–50 was 6.13 percent. It was 7.47 percent in the 1920s but dropped off considerably in the 1930s to 2.66 percent, briefly reviving in the early 1940s to 10.23 percent.

Table 5.1 Coptic Representation in the Parliament from 1924 to 1952 (adapted from Carter 1986: 143)

Year	*Total number of parliament representatives*	*Number of Coptic parliament representatives*	*Percentage of Coptic representation*
1924	214	16	7.48
1925	214	15	7.00
1926	214	12	5.60
1929	235	23	9.79
1931	150	4	2.66
1936	232	20	8.62
1938	264	6	2.27
1942	264	27	10.23
1945	264	12	4.55
1950	319	10	3.13

The spirit of non-discrimination did not last. This chapter cannot go into details in this matter but a few examples regarding Coptic participation in Egyptian politics will suffice. The 1919 revolution failed in its main goal, independence from the British. The long years of negotiations that followed, which ended in the 1936 treaty, weakened the majority Wafd Party. On the other hand, the Wafd Party in general and Sa'ad Zaghlūl in particular were worried that the revolution would lead to social demands, so the socialist party and workers' unions were abolished. In addition, the Wafd Party did not present any social or agricultural reforms, employees' protections, etc., which were issues that the Wafd Party had campaigned for to gain the popular trust. People were angry about social conditions resulting from poverty, unemployment, inflation, and other grievances. But the party was scared that this would lead to a mass social movement. The Wafd Party limited the revolution to demanding independence through negotiations without any further vision towards social reforms, which could have solved the problem of anti-Coptic discrimination and eliminated social discontent.

During the 1930s and 1940s, the Wafd Party rallied around the slogan of democracy, which entailed drafting a constitution, parliamentary elections, and the creation of new political parties. None of these goals, however, impacted people's lives. Though there was great support for the party, people soon realized there was no actual change, especially since the king opposed any change by repeatedly dissolving the cabinet and trying to prevent the reelection of the Wafd Party by rigging the vote. Thus, the main political aims of independence and democracy were not achieved. Though Copts were elected to the parliament as members of the Wafd Party, they were forbidden from particular positions, such as the Ministry of Justice, Ministry of Culture, and Ministry of the Interior, and discrimination persisted in the military, the police force, and especially in promotions to high positions. In addition, no Copts were appointed as university presidents or deans. All Wafd Party cabinets kept al-Khaṭṭ al-Hamayūnī law, which prohibited any renovation or building of churches without the permission of the Ottoman sultan, which after the fall of the Ottomans became the Egyptian king's prerogative. Moreover, the Wafd Party did not oppose Muḥammad al-'Azabī's ten conditions, issued in 1934, which curtailed all attempts to build a church. The political parties of the 1930s and 1940s, *al-Aḥrār al-Dustūriīn* and the *Sa'adī* parties, began using the Coptic presence in politics as their rallying cry against the Wafd Party, accusing it of favoring the Copts at the expense of Muslims' interests. They also protested against the high percentage of Coptic employees in the Ministry of Finance. With the growing rise of Islamist parties, such as the Muslim Brotherhood and the *Maṣr al-Fatāh*, and their increasing engagement in politics, the Islamic rhetoric became more violent, which led to an increase in ethnic and religious tension that culminated in many attacks on the Copts. At the same time King Fārūq, who with the help of Sheikh al-Marāghī of Al-Azhar, a high-ranking Islamic authority in Egypt, wanted to become an Islamic caliph and reestablish the Islamic Caliphate, used this rhetoric to his benefit (ibid. 91–92). In the 1938 elections, the *al-Aḥrār al-Dustūriīn* party accused Makram Ebeid, the Wafd Party secretary, of being anti-Islamic and favoring the Copts at the expense of the Muslims. He left the Wafd Party and joined with the king's and minority parties, which affected any political support the Copts could have. In the 1940s many of the Coptic youth found a place in the communist party, though it was a weak party and did not address any of the Coptic concerns. The anti-Coptic sentiment escalated with the Muslim Brotherhood's rhetoric and attacks on churches in Cairo. In March 1949 they burnt a church in Zaqāzīq, in the Delta, and called for the boycotting of all Coptic businesses and services (ibid. 275).

The 1952 Revolution

The organization of the Free Officers that led to the 1952 military coup had only one Copt in a leading position. As mentioned before, the Coptic presence in the military and police force was minimal, though the Naserist era would create more sectarian divisions in the society. Jamāl 'Abd al-Nāṣir, the president of Egypt, adopted the rhetoric of Arab nationalism, which revolved around Islamic religious identity, and for the first time adopted a quota policy for Copts. 'Abd al-Nāṣir did not address sectarian tension. Instead he ignored it completely, thus giving the impression it did not exist. This was connected with the nature of the Naserist project. 'Abd al-Nāṣir was suspicious of local capitalists and the United States, which eventually led him to cooperate with the Soviet Union and nationalize all private property, eliminating local capitalism. The state took the leading role in all development projects. For the Naserist project to succeed, it adopted the banners of independence from occupation, Arab unity, and cooperation with third world countries. 'Abd al-Nāṣir based his success on a broad populist base, promising social justice. The socialist agenda he adopted provided, regardless of religious affiliation, free education and free health care, and promised employment for all college graduates. This policy facilitated the social advancement of the poor. In addition, his constant preoccupation with Israel allowed sectarianism to recede into the background.

This does not mean there was no discrimination. The nature of the Naserist project made the state the major player, while the people played the role of recipients. All political opposition was eliminated for the sake of protecting the Naserist project. Raising issues of minority rights or discrimination was forbidden, since sectarian struggle would lead to the instability of the political system. Under this system, no Copt held any leading position, there was a meager parliamentary representation, representation in ministries receded, and very few study fellowships abroad were granted to Copts. ʻAbd al-Nāṣir did not end the restrictions on church building, but preserved al-Khaṭṭ al-Hamayūnī law and the conditions of Muḥammad al-ʻAzabī. ʻAbd al-Nāṣir addressed Coptic issues as follows: He would grant the pope a couple of church building permits every now and then, and the pope chose which churches were to be built. He, unofficially, put a quota of 5 percent on Coptic positions in the military and police force. When no Copts won seats in the parliamentary elections of 1964 and 1968, ʻAbd al-Nāṣir appointed a certain number of Copts to the parliament, thus securing Coptic gratitude. This policy made the church the official representative of Coptic concerns, a political role. Church permits and Coptic appointments were considered grants to the church. With the nationalization program of ʻAbd al-Nāṣir seizing most of the Copts' properties, and the retreating rights of the Copts, many middle-class and trained Coptic professionals began emigrating. The Arab nationalism program promoted by ʻAbd al-Nāṣir, with its emphasis on Islamic identity, fostered a cautionary attitude towards the Copts, who could not be part of this identity.

The Religious Aspect: The Role of Coptic Popes

The tenure of Pope Peter VII (1809–52), known as al-Jāwlī, coincided with the rule of Muḥammad ʻAlī.[4] The Treaty of Kuchuk Kainrji (1774) marked the end of the Russo-Turkish war (1768–74) and gave Russia the right to protect Christians in Ottoman territories. Russia used this right to successfully instigate the Greeks, Arabs, and Bulgarians to revolt against the Ottomans (al-Najār 1953: 148). The Russians used this treaty to approach Pope Peter VII to accept the protection of the Russian czar. Pope Peter VII responded to the Russian envoy with a question, "Does your Czar live forever?" When the envoy responded in the negative, Pope Peter replied "You live under the protection of a Czar who dies, but we live under the protection of the Almighty God and he is our only protector" (Tādrus 1911: 50). Pope Peter is credited with not accepting the protection of a foreign nation.

Pope Cyril IV (1854–61) is known as the "Father of Reform" and for solving the problems with Ethiopia.[5] He is most famous for his educational reform, in which he established schools for both boys and girls, a revolutionary move for the time. He also imported a printing press from Europe to print school books and ecclesiastical books. He forbade forced marriages or the marriage of underage girls. He formed a register of Coptic endowments. He made pastoral visits in Egypt and Ethiopia. During the rule of Khedive Muḥammad Saʿīd, Theodore, Emperor of Ethiopia, attacked the southern border of Egypt and looted and imprisoned some people of the south. Rather than responding with another military attack, Khedive Saʿīd opted for peace and asked Pope Cyril IV to represent Egypt in truce negotiations; religiously, the Ethiopian church was under the jurisdiction of the Coptic pope. The latter accepted the task. On his arrival in Ethiopia, he presented gifts on behalf of Khedive Saʿīd. He successfully concluded a truce between Egypt and Ethiopia. At the end of the negotiations Pope Cyril requested that the Protestant English missionaries be made to leave Ethiopia to preserve the orthodoxy of Ethiopia (Shārūbīm 1900: 120). Theodore of Ethiopia started implementing the policy, which angered the British and suggested to Saʿīd that depending on Pope Cyril to gain a truce with Ethiopia was not dignified. It would be better to mobilize troops at the Egyptian borders (ʿSkārūs 1913: 161). This in turn suggested to Theodore of Ethiopia that Cyril was sent to distract him while the Egyptian military mobilized on the Sudanese border (Shārūbīm 1900: 121). By that time, Saʿīd had arrived in the Sudanese capital, Khartoum, which solidified the rumors spread by the British. Theodore immediately imprisoned Pope Cyril and would have killed him had it not been for the queen's intervention (ʿSkārūs 1913: 163). When Theodore learned that the rumors were without merit, he released Cyril from prison. Cyril sent a letter to Saʿīd dispelling the rumors, which convinced Saʿīd to withdraw his army. Cyril returned to Egypt accompanied by an Ethiopian envoy with a letter of peace (Rīāḍ 1961: 42).

Pope Cyril V (1874–1927) was contemporary with Khedive Ismāʿīl (1863–79) and four more rulers: Khedive Tawfīq (1879–92), Khedive ʿAbbās II (1892–1914), Sultan Ḥussīn Kamil (1914–17), and King Fu'ād I (1917–36). Pope Cyril V is the longest serving pope in the history of the Coptic church (52 years).[6] He was pope during the ʿUrābī revolution, the British occupation, the 1919 revolution, and a period of tension between Christians and Muslims. He sided with ʿUrābī against the British. When ʿUrābī wanted to continue fighting the British after the fall of Alexandria, Khedive Tawfīq removed him from his position as Minister of Defense. The National Society opposed this decision and issued a resolution on July 17, 1882, to continue fighting the British, forcing Tawfīq to reinstate ʿUrābī as Minister of Defense. Pope Cyril V participated in signing this resolution. When the British occupied Egypt, he was determined not to let the Coptic church be under British protection. He sided with Saʿad Zaghlūl's 1919 revolution for independence from the British. His tenure came at a critical juncture in Coptic–Muslim relations. He built churches, renovated monasteries, and built schools for boys and girls. He helped in the founding of the Coptic Museum by Murqus Simaykah in 1908.

The tenure of Pope Cyril V coincided with the formation of the *Majlis al-Milli*, the lay Coptic Community Council, which was the beginning of a long power struggle between the laity and the clergy. One of the main issues of the struggle was over control of monastic endowments and their revenue. By the early twentieth century revenue from monastic endowments was huge, but the monks were living in a deplorable state and the Coptic community reaped no benefits from it. Abbots as well as bishops opposed any lay control over the endowments' revenue. The Coptic press, however, relentlessly criticized the clergy and sided with the *Majlis al-Milli*, which campaigned for reform. In 1927 the *Majlis al-Milli*, led by Sūrīal Jirjis Sūrīal, succeeded in getting parliament to pass a law that would empower them to supervise Coptic endowments and oversee the finances of schools, churches, societies, and monasteries. It also addressed issues of personal status and control of the Coptic press (Carter 1986: 30). This unprecedented, sweeping power was secured for the laity during a period of a power vacuum in the church due to the senility of Pope Cyril V.

The *Majlis al-Milli*, with the help of the British, succeeded in securing the election to the papacy of John XIX (r. 1928–42), who promised the *Majlis al-Milli* the reform they sought. This dismayed the Holy Synod which in 1937, with the support of the government, regained control over the endowments (ibid. 34). In 1944, the *Majlis al-Milli* was again heavily involved in the nomination of Macarius III to the papacy (r. 1944–45); he also promised reform. Once in power, Macarius sought a government decree for full control over secular and financial church affairs, but he died before the decree was issued (ibid. 36). This was followed by the election of Yusab II (r. 1946–56) who promised the *Majlis al-Milli* supervision over the endowments, but once he was installed he took control of the *Majlis al-Milli* by a government decree (ibid. 37). This continuous struggle for power gave an opportunity for both the government and the British to interfere in church affairs. The *Majlis al-Milli* was consumed with the power struggle and achieved little success in the financial reform it campaigned for, while losing its prestige among the Copts. The *Majlis al-Milli* was successful, however, in limiting government control over education in Coptic schools and personal status jurisdiction and constantly fought discrimination against the Copts.

The Social and Economic Aspect and the Role of Coptic Laity and Religious Institutions

The secularization process that characterized this era was accompanied by the rise of Coptic archons and families who played a leading role in the political as well as the economic, social, and educational aspects of Egyptian society. This had great impact on the Copts. The most famous Coptic philanthropists are Ibrāhīm al-Jawharī and his brother Jirjis. Their endowments for churches and monasteries were massive and their philanthropy toward families and individuals, regardless of religion, earned them a name in Coptic history.

Coptic laity formed many social organizations, which worked side by side with and supported the religious organization. A group of Coptic laity formed the Coptic Philanthropic Society in 1880. Prominent Islamic figures, such as

Sheikh Muḥammad 'Abdu, Sheikh Muḥammad al-Najār, Sheikh 'Abdallāh Nadīm, and others, attended the inauguration ceremony. The Coptic Philanthropic Society founded the Mashghal al-Buṭrusī to prepare young women with skills to earn their living. They founded the Coptic Hospital in 1911 in the Fajjālla quarter; it moved to its present location on Ramses Street in 1926. They also built many Coptic schools for boys and girls, an industrial school in the Būlāq quarter, and, finally, a girls' college.

This revival was not limited to the main cities of Cairo and Alexandria but extended to other cities as well as small towns and villages. For example, the laity built the Great Coptic School in 1893 (Manqarīus 1895: no. 13: 102–3), followed by a school for girls in Qinā (in southern Egypt), which opened on Monday October 14, 1895 (ibid. no. 21: 167–68). In the same year they opened schools in Manṣūra (in the Delta), one for girls and another for boys, in Banī Mazār, Kafr al-Sheikh, Zaqazīq, and other places (ibid. no. 6: 47–48). Metropolitan Mitā'ūs of Jirjā and 'Akhmīm opened a school in 'Akhmīm at his own expense (ibid. no. 9: 72). Hegumenos Peter of the Monastery of al-Muḥarraqin Upper Egypt opened a school beside the monastery (Manqarīus 1896: no. 31: 248). When the school in the village of Milīj in Minūfiah province was closed because of high tuition costs, Metropolitan Yū'anis of Biḥīra and Minūfiah personally financed the re-opening of the school (Manqarīus 1895: no. 31: 248).

The developments of the nineteenth century led to the rise of a class of Coptic merchants and landowners, which was accompanied by a noticeable increase in Coptic children attending Egyptian and foreign missionary schools. This in turn led to the increase of the Coptic middle class. The Copts, who were 7 percent of the population in the nineteenth century, still played the major role in managing Egypt's state finances. They held 20 percent of total state capital, 45 percent of government employment, and 40 percent of government salaries (Sūrīal 1984: 63–92). Though the accuracy of these statistics might be questioned, they show the rise of the merchant class and landowners, and of the middle class of educated Copts who eventually took up the cause of Coptic rights, demanding equal employment to Muslims, asking for equal days off, and demanding that Christian religion be taught in schools. This does not mean that the majority of Copts were rich, but rather that the rise of this class raised the case of Coptic equality.

The Educational Aspect and the Role of Foreign Missions: Catholic and Protestant

In 1622, the Catholic Church founded the Sacred Congregation for the Propagation of the Faith with the mission of targeting non-Catholic Christians, particularly in the Middle East. In 1632, a group of medically well-trained Franciscan monks arrived in Jirjā and established a medical clinic. At first they were viewed with great suspicion but after healing the province's ruler and members of his family, their missionary success began to rise. They focused on converting poor Christian peasants to Catholicism to form the early nucleus of the Catholic Church in Egypt. Their number remained always very small in comparison to the Protestant missionaries that would arrive later in Egypt. After educating the first generation of Coptic students in Rome under the supervision of the Sacred Congregation for the Propagation of the Faith, they targeted their missionary work on Cairo. Some of the famous students of the school were Rūfāīl al-Ṭūkhī, Ṣāliḥ Yusṭus al-Marāghī, and Rūksī Qudsī al-Ṣabāgh (Metzler 1961: 36–62). They targeted every high-ranking Coptic cleric who had a problem with the Coptic Orthodox Church, in addition to priests and monks.

In 1854 John Hogg of the Presbyterian Church arrived in Egypt and built a church in the 'Azbakiya district of Cairo. The Presbyterians intensified their missionary activity in the southern city of Asyūṭ, where two prominent families converted to the Protestant faith, the families of Khayāṭ and Wīṣā. When a few Presbyterian converts burnt and destroyed icons of a church in Asyūṭ violence erupted (Sūrīal 1984: 143–51). This violence prompted Pope Demetrius II to visit Upper Egypt, accompanied by one of the most famous preachers of the day, Philotheos Ibrāhīm Bughdādī.

During the time of British colonization, missionary activities in Egypt gained their greatest advantage, especially under the supervision of Lord Cromer (1841–1917), who reinforced all foreign missionary activities in Egypt and Sudan by providing full privileges and access that natives could not have. Protestant activities in Egypt alerted the Orthodox Church to the need for a more comprehensive theological educational program to educate its clergy. A Coptic seminary was opened on November 29, 1893. One of its graduates was Habīb Jirjis, who reinvigorated the Coptic Church with his reform ideas and established the "Sunday School" movement to revive religious education among young Copts. Other seminaries followed. Pope Cyril V opened a seminary for monks in Cairo on December 4, 1896 (Manqarīus 1896: no. 31: 303). He appointed as headmaster Bishop Sīdārus, who later became the instructor of all monks in Egypt. Another seminary was formed in the patriarchal residence of Alexandria; in 1928 it moved to Hilwān, Cairo. Other seminaries followed in the rest of Egypt (Manqarīus 1897: no. 27:112–13, and 1896: no. 31: 263).

This era was transformative for both Egypt and the Coptic church. The dreams of territorial expansion of Muḥammad 'Alī and colonization by the French and British facilitated exposure to western science and technology, though they did not lead to the full understanding of a democratic secular society. Secularization was opposed by Muslim religious leaders and was accompanied by the rise of strong Islamist movements, most notably the Muslim Brotherhood in 1928. Secularization influenced the Coptic church as well. The *Majlis al-Milli* was established with some resistance, but it gave more power to the laity in the church. Colonization encouraged and strengthened missionary activities in Egypt, which created awareness in the Coptic church of the important educational and social work that needed to be addressed in the church. These developments along with secularization helped in the revival of the Coptic Orthodox Church.

Timeline

1798	Napoleon Bonaparte invades and occupies Egypt
1801	Napoleon leaves Egypt, repelled by the British and Turks
1805–1952	Muḥammad ʻAlī's dynasty
1809–52	Pope Peter VII
1854–61	Pope Cyril IV, "the Father of Reform"
1859–69	Suez Canal built
1874	Establishment of the *Majlis al-Milli* or Coptic Community Council
1874–1927	Pope Cyril V
1881–82	ʻUrābī revolution
1882	British invade and occupy Egypt
1911	Coptic Congress of Asyūṭ
1922	Fūʻad becomes king of Egypt
1928	Muslim Brotherhood founded by Hassan al-Banna
1936	Fārūq succeeds his father as king of Egypt
1948	War with the new state of Israel
1948	Egyptian government dissolves the Muslim Brotherhood
1952	Military coup by the Free Officers, 1952 Revolution

Notes

1 Translated by Lois M. Farag.

2 That was the practice during the period of the French expedition. The Coptic patriarch was and is still chosen from the monks from any of the Coptic monasteries, though the monks of the Monastery of St. Antony have the largest share of nominations to the patriarchate throughout history.

3 Metropolitan Macarius of Asyūṭ was born in Maḥala al-Kubrā, Lower Egypt. He was a monk of St. Bishoi Monastery and left the monastery for personal reasons. Pope Cyril V ordained him priest and then metropolitan of Asyūṭ in October 1897. He achieved a lot for his diocese, which led to his election to the papacy in February 1944 with the name of Macarius III. He clashed with the *Majlis al-Milli* and sought seclusion at the Monastery of St. Paul in 1945. He died on August 31 of the same year without achieving much for the church.

4 Pope Peter VII was born in the village of al-Jāwlī, Asiyūṭ. He joined the Monastery of St. Antony and was tonsured with the name Manqarīws. Pope Mark VIII wished to ordain him metropolitan of Ethiopia but he refused. He was ordained general metropolitan with the name of Theophilus and succeeded Mark after his death as Pope Peter VII in 1809. He lived a simple and pious life and died in 1852.

5 Pope Cyril IV was born in Ṣawām'a of Sūhāj and joined the Monastery of St. Antony at a young age. He soon became the hegumenos of the monastery in 1840. He was ordained a general metropolitan in 1853 to oversee the church because Khedive Saʻīd would not approve his ordination as pope. He oversaw church matters for fourteen months and then was elevated to the papacy on June 4, 1854, where he led the church in an era of reform, especially in educational matters, in a very short time. He was called the "Father of Reform" because of his extraordinary achievements.

6 Pope Cyril V was born in Banī Suef and joined the Monastery of the Virgin Mary commonly known as al-Suryān. His family, who did not agree to him joining the monastery, pulled him out and took him back to their village. He left his family again and joined the Monastery of the Virgin Mary commonly known as al-Barāmūs and was

tonsured with the name of John. He was a copyist and then became hegumenos of the monastery. On November 1874 he was elected to be Pope Cyril V.

Selected Bibliography

Al-Najār, Ḥ. (1953) *al-Sīāsa wa al-'astrātījīah fi al-sharq al-awsṭ*, vol. 1, Cairo: no publisher.

Al-Shāīb, Z. (trans.) (1992) *Description of Egypt by the Scholars of the French Expedition*, Cairo: The Trust of Cultural Development.

Carter, B.L. (1986) *The Copts in Egyptian Politics 1918–1952*, Cairo: The American University in Cairo Press. [Recommended reading]

Ghobrial, S. (1932) *General Ya'qūb wa al-fāris lāskārīs wa mashrūa' istiqlāl miṣr 1801*, Cairo: al-Ma'ārif Press.

Guirguis, M. (2008) *An Armenian Artist in Ottoman Egypt*, Cairo: The American University in Cairo Press.

Manqarīus, Y. (1895) *Magalat al-Ḥaq*, nos. 6, 9, 13, 21, 31, Cairo: no publisher.

——(1896) *Magalat al-Ḥaq*, no. 31, Cairo: no publisher.

——(1897) *Magalat al-Ḥaq*, no. 27, Cairo: no publisher.

Metzler, J. (1961) "Das Apostolische vikariat der Kopten unter Massimo Giuaid (1821–31)," in *Euntes Docete*, no. 14, Roma: Paideia Editrice.

——(1968) *The Pontifical Missionary Library: De Propaganda Fide*, Roma: Pont. Univ. Urbaniana de propaganda fide.

Rīāḍ, Z. (1961) *al-dhikrā al-m'awīa l'ābī al-'iṣlāḥ al-bābā kyrilus al-rābi'* (1861–1961), Cairo: no publisher.

Shārūbīm, M. (1900) *al-Kāfi fi tarīkh Maṣr al-qadīm wa al-ḥadīth*, Cairo: no publisher.

'Skārūs, T. (1913) *Nawābīgh al-'aqbāṭ wa mashāhīrīhīm fi al-qarn al-tāsī' 'shīr*, vol. 2, Cairo: no publisher.

Sūrīal, R. (1984) *al-mujtama' al-qibṭy fi miṣr fi al-qarn 19*, Cairo: Mktabat al-Maḥaba.

Tādrus, R. (1911) *Al-'aqbāṭ fi al-qarn al-'ishrīn*, vol. 1, Cairo: Jarīdat Miṣr.

Valognes, J-P. (1994) *Vie et mort des chrétiens d'Orient: des origins à nos jours*, Paris: Fayard.

Wakin, E. (2000) *A Lonely Minority: The Modern Story of Egypt's Copts*, New York: Morrow.

6 The Modern Period (1952–2011)

An Era of Trials, Tribulations, and Triumphs

Saad Michael Saad

The history of contemporary Egypt is most starkly marked by two revolutions: the army revolution in 1952 and the populist revolution in 2011. Throughout the nearly 2,000 years of Christianity in Egypt, both the ecclesiastical hierarchy and the Coptic people have often been subject to forces of discrimination and persecution by both Christian and non-Christian governments. Modern history is no exception. Copts are, however, much more than an oppressed Christian minority. As this volume illustrates, they are inheritors and preservers of an ancient civilization, builders of a modern nation, and defenders of Christian orthodoxy. The popes of this era—Pope Yusab II (1946–56), Pope Kyrillos VI (1959–71), and Pope Shenouda III (1971–2012)—played a significant role in recent Coptic history, as have the activities and faith of the Coptic people, the modernization of Egypt, the rapid expansion of the Coptic diaspora, and the spread of globalization and ecumenism.

This chapter seeks to describe and analyze the flow of crucial events in Coptic history from Pope Yusab's election in 1946 up to the present day, noting especially the internal and external challenges in the 1950s, relief and progress in the 1960s, relations between church and state under Pope Shenouda III, the achievements made despite hardships over the past four decades, and the role of the Copts in the 2011 revolution. Within this historical context, certain topics are addressed including the problematic personal status law, the evolution of Ethiopian–Coptic ecumenical progress in and outside Egypt, and the development of the Coptic world and Coptic media. Other topics germane to this era, such as spirituality, monasticism, liturgical and linguistic revivalism, theological developments, music, and art, are covered in their respective chapters.

Pope Yusab's Patriarchate: A Decade of Internal and External Challenges—and Achievements

The 1952 Egyptian Revolution changed the course of history in Egypt and the Middle East, and the subsequent political, social, and economic reengineering of the country affected the Copts and their church in serious ways. Despite these challenges, the Copts adapted to the new reality and survived, even flourished, in certain fields. Having acted as nation-builders in an open society following western models of democracy under the Muhammad Ali dynasty, the Copts continued their contribution to the socialist system that President Gamal Abdel Nasser (1952–70) gradually introduced. They even embraced socialism theologically.[1]

At the outset, the army revolution was welcomed by Copts and Muslims alike. It promised socioeconomic reform, put an end to the British occupation that began in 1882, and restored law and order using a disciplined army. But soon the Copts began to realize that their status was compromised in many areas of Egyptian life. Socialism and dictatorship took their toll on all Egyptians, but the Coptic share was far greater in certain areas such as sociopolitical structures, wealth redistribution, and the 1955 personal status law.

As the revolution banned all political parties, the Copts who enjoyed prominence in politics were forced to abandon their political careers. Coptic representation in parliament and in upper government dropped dramatically (Wakin 1963: 43–47; Heikal 1983: 154–55). The government curtailed the functions of most non-governmental organizations including the Coptic Community Councils,[2] benevolent societies, cultural centers, hospitals, and schools. These Coptic organizations formed an important safety net against discrimination, and their diminishment threatened Coptic social well-being, culture, self-identity, and self-determination.

When land reform was applied, wealthy Coptic landowners, along with all Egyptians, were forced to give up their land to the state without compensation. But when the government conducted redistribution of landownership among poor farmers, hardly any Copts could be traced on the receiver's list. This is the constant historical Coptic problem: share the pain but not the gain. The discrimination went further: the government insisted that monasteries, dioceses, and other Coptic institutions fall under the same land reform ceiling as individual citizens (100 feddans per family), although the revenue of institutions' lands went to hundreds if not thousands of beneficiaries (Wakin 1963: 150–51). Islamic institutions did not suffer the same land reform restriction because such property was administrated by the Ministry of (Islamic) Endowment.

The Coptic Orthodox Church was in no position to meet this array of new political and social challenges. In 1946, an electoral body composed of clergy and laity elected the metropolitan of Jirjā to become Patriarch Yusab II (M. Shoucri, "Yusab II," in Atiya 1991: 2363–64). Because of his deteriorating health, the patriarch increasingly allowed his personal servant to influence important church decisions such as selections for the episcopate. The result was corruption. In September 1955 Yusab was relieved of his duties and a council of three metropolitans was elected to administer the church's affairs (Atiya 1968: 114–15; van Doorn-Harder 2011: 71, 90, 99). One of the three was Metropolitan Mikhail of Asyuṭ, who has been described as a "towering figure" for revival in his diocese, fighting discrimination, and promoting ecumenism, even to the present day (Watson 2000: 103).

In the same week, exploiting the absence of the patriarch, the government issued a new personal status law, which transferred judicial powers on personal status (marriage, divorce, and custody of children) from the Coptic Community Councils to the state judiciary system. The new law has several provisions destructive to the integrity and self-determination of the Christian family. Most prominently, if a spouse converts to Islam, the Muslim party gains nearly all legal rights. The Christian party cannot inherit from the Muslim party, nor receive custody of children in case of separation or divorce, nor receive income (alimony). Children under eighteen years of age are automatically counted as Muslims and cannot easily convert or return to the Christian faith until they reach eighteen, and even then only stand a slim chance of success in court.[3] Even worse, if the husband converts to Islam, he may apply for a court order against his wife for Bāīt al-Ta'ah (home of obedience), legally forcing her to live with him and accept rules to which she did not agree at the time of their Christian marriage, such as polygamy. Strong Coptic protests against the new law, from its initial decree to the present, have been consistently diffused by promises of change from the government (Wakin 1963: 99–102; van Doorn-Harder 2011: 113–14, 185).

Despite such "disputes without and fears within" (2 Corinthians 7:5 NRSV), important milestones were achieved. Due in large part to the resilience of Copts with reforming and progressive attitudes, new parishes and churches were built around the country, translation of patristic literature increased, the Coptic Seminary expanded its campus and curriculum, and the Sunday School movement continued to expand and provide services. In due course, this revival provided leaders who rose to key positions in the Coptic Seminary, parishes, episcopacy, and even the papacy. In 1954, the Institute of Coptic Studies was established and continues to this day to teach, research, and promote aspects of Coptic civilization and church heritage (Atiya 1968: 118; Hasan 2003: 88).[4] It especially succeeded in reviving ancient Coptic art and conserving the treasures of liturgical hymns.

Pope Yusab died on November 14, 1956, while the nation was struggling with the outcome of the Suez War, and it took time for the Coptic church to recover. It was wounded, bruised, and divided. The patriarchal election law was updated by the Holy Synod and decreed by President Nasser on November 3, 1957. Because the law was so fiercely opposed by the Community Councils and the Sunday School movement, the new patriarch was not elected until 18 months after the decree (M. Shoucri, "Patriarchal Election," in Atiya 1991: 1911–12; Meinardus 1970: 128–41; Watson 2000: 47).

The 1960s: Relief and Progress Under Pope Kyrillos' Liturgical Spirituality

For at least the ninth time in their history, the Copts used a hybrid of election and casting of lots to determine the next patriarch (Saad and Saad 2001). First, a nominating committee narrowed down clerical nominees and, on the basis of the highest of ecclesial endorsements, selected seven candidates. Then, an electoral body of about 500 individuals, drawn from both clergy and laity, ranked the candidates through voting. The top three entered into a "sanctuary casting of lot." After a divine liturgy on Sunday, April 19, 1959, a five-year-old child picked the folded paper that stated "Abouna Mina el-Baramousy." The new patriarch was enthroned on May 10, 1959, and took the name Kyrillos (Cyril) VI (M. Shoucri, "Cyril VI," in Atiya 1991: 679–81; Meinardus 1999: 79).

Pope Kyrillos succeeded in uniting the church by leading a genuinely pious life. He staunchly encouraged both liturgical and monastic revival, which included public, daily celebration of the Eucharist at sunrise and vespers at sunset, and the building of the church's ninth monastery, the Monastery of St. Menas at Maryūt (Meinardus 1999: 79). He made himself completely accessible. He acted from strength and used his authority with wisdom and rigor. The pope's spiritual aura and practices gave the Copts a new hope and impetus for progress and also won him the admiration and cooperation of national and world leaders, both political and religious.

The unity of the church under Pope Kyrillos was a strong factor in improving the social, political, and religious standing of the Copts in the 1960s, which in turn facilitated cultural activities and church achievements. In addition, factors external to the church resulted in further improvements. For example, the adoption of socialism increased opportunities for Copts to be hired and promoted fairly in many government and public sector organizations. Nasser's international goals and image were better served by fair treatment of the Coptic minority. His dispute with the Muslim Brotherhood prompted a move away from their Islamist extremism and toward openness to pluralism. As a result of these internal and external factors, positive signs of integration and goodwill were increasingly manifest in many areas of society, and cases of discrimination or violence were acknowledged and addressed. For instance, unlike under Sadat and later Mubarak, the ridiculing of Christianity and Christians in the media and classroom was punished, as were attacks against Copts and churches. The church enjoyed friendly relations with al-Azhar and it was popularly known that the patriarch's wishes were respected by the government (Heikal 1983: 157).

Despite lukewarm relations with Nasser in the first years after his 1959 enthronement, Pope Kyrillos developed an intimate relationship with the president, who sincerely believed in the holiness of the patriarch. The friendship resulted in many gains for the church and the Copts. Probably the most visible, both physically and figuratively, was the construction of the new St. Mark's Cathedral in Cairo with moral, legal and financial sponsorship by the government under Nasser's personal direction. In 1965, Nasser even laid the foundation stone of what became one of the largest cathedrals in the world (Heikal 1983: 158).

The apparitions of the Holy Virgin Mary on the roof of St. Mary Church in Zaitūn, Cairo, which began on April 2, 1968, were significant to both the Copts and the nation. The exuberance continued with the inauguration of the new

St. Mark Cathedral in Cairo on June 25, 1968, which was attended by Nasser, Emperor Haile Selassie of Ethiopia, patriarchs, cardinals, and diplomats from around the world. The night before, the church received relics of St. Mark from Venice as a gift from the Vatican. It was a celebration befitting the nineteenth centennial of the martyrdom of the founder of the Coptic Orthodox Church (van Doorn-Harder 2011: 111, 124).

Pope Shenouda's Charisma and Relations with the Nation and the World

Pope Kyrillos passed away on March 9, 1971. The nation and the church mourned. He was a spiritual icon for both. In order to elect a new pope, the 1957 patriarchal election law was applied for the second time. The new patriarch, Pope Shenouda III, was enthroned in an international event on November 14, 1971, broadcast live on national television (ibid. 155–58).

During his first year in office, Shenouda gained the admiration of most sectors of Egyptian society. He was a man with many talents and diverse experience, both secular and religious: desert hermit, spiritual leader, poet, scholar of Christianity and Islam, revolutionary, charismatic speaker, and embodiment of Coptic identity who worked for national unity. He masterfully crossed barriers of race and religion and reached out with goodwill and hospitality to all. His publicized program was versatile and, for a time, it seemed as though the situation of the Copts in Egypt was transitioning from good in the 1960s to better in the 1970s.

On the national front, the possibilities for Coptic participation and action were also unprecedented. During 1972, the patriarch was invited to write a weekly column in *al-Gumhūrīa*, the third largest daily newspaper in Egypt. At the outbreak of the October 1973 war with Israel, Shenouda astonished all sides by volunteering his service as a former army reservist. Such a gesture, though it did not materialize, was greatly welcomed to raise morale. His presence and speeches were solicited by the state on various national occasions, and his contributions were meaningful and significant.

As the patriarch of the largest Christian church in the Middle East, Shenouda's visits overseas were of great religious and political significance. He became the first Coptic pope in over 1,500 years to visit the Patriarch of Constantinople (1972) and the Pope of Rome (1973), as well as the first ever to visit the Patriarch of Moscow (1972) and the Archbishop of Canterbury (1979). He worked toward the goal of ecumenical unity with other orthodox churches and participated in dialogues with Catholic and Protestant churches. During his visits abroad, he was welcomed by many presidents, from Assad of Syria (1972) to Jimmy Carter (1977) and George H. W. Bush (1989) at the White House (Abdelsayyed 1981). Even then Colonel Gaddafi, the strong advocate for an Islamic state, invited Shenouda to address a political convention in Libya in 1972 (Abdelsayyed 1976).

Tumult and Triumph from 1972 to 1985

In the early years Anwar Sadat and Shenouda seemed to cooperate and even admire each other,[5] but three major issues problematized relations to the point of no return: (1) how to overcome discrimination and violence against the Copts, (2) the extent of applying Islamic law to the Coptic minority, and (3) the exploitation of Copts in the normalization of relations with Israel.

The 1970s were an intensely dynamic decade for Egypt. Sadat, who became president in October 1970, embarked on a new strategy for Egypt: to gradually replace Nasser's Arab nationalistic, secular, and socialist system with an Egyptian nationalistic, Islamist, and capitalist one. A thriving Coptic church with a talented patriarch was both an asset and a liability for the new strategy.[6] The nation also struggled because of an impasse with Israel, which had occupied Sinai since the 1967 war. A blend of Westernization and Islamization must have seemed a good strategy for Sadat. For this reason and to combat his Nasserist opponents, Sadat allowed the religio-political organization, the Muslim Brotherhood, to resume its activities in Egypt after Nasser had banned it in 1954 (Heikal 1983: 116–27).

As byproducts of Islamization began to emerge, Coptic representation in government fell noticeably and precipitously. For the first time since their inception in 1886, the parliamentary elections of 1976 did not produce any Coptic members. Similar declines, also the result of increased Islamization, were observable even at entry-level positions in many key fields such as the armed forces, the police, the judicial system, the diplomatic corps, and academia.

Beginning with the destruction of a church in al-Khanka in 1972 (ibid. 162), acts of violence against Copts and churches escalated in frequency and magnitude of harm. Textbooks and the media frequently ridiculed Christianity and stereotyped the Copts. Sermons in mosques routinely damned the Copts along with Jews and Americans. Discrimination was—and still is—openly or covertly practiced in many aspects of life. Since 1972, in a period called the "era of the martyrs" (Watson 2000: 142–50), more than fifty major cases of violence against Coptic communities, as well as prevalent discrimination, have been extensively reported in the media and by scholars and commentators (Thomas and Youssef 2006; also see Minorities at Risk Project 2004).[7] The Copts, however, have persisted, survived, and even thrived despite challenges to their lives and civilization.

In 1980, a new Egyptian constitution made Islamic Shari'a the primary source of legislation. The patriarch voiced his opposition to the next imminent step: total application of Islamic law on all citizens in all aspects of life (Hasan 2003: 108).[8] Shenouda also opposed Sadat in his move to make Copts the prototype for the normalization of relations with Israel while the peace treaty, signed on March 26, 1979, was being negotiated. The proposed first step toward normalization was for the Copts to pilgrimage to Jerusalem, since this had been closed to them since the Six Day War. Shenouda's fears were based on a historical record in which even the perception of an association with foreigners, not to mention a former enemy, was perennially a motivation for, or a pretext to justify, acts of violence against Christian minorities in the Middle East (Heikal 1983: 219–21). After Foreign Minister Ismail Fahmi resigned in protest against Sadat's intention to visit Israel in 1977, Sadat appointed a Copt, Boutros Boutros Ghali, to serve as Minister of State for Foreign Affairs and accompany him to Israel and later negotiations.

In June 1981, a serious attack on the Copts in Zawya el-Hamra, a district of Cairo, resulted in hundreds of Copts being murdered and injured. The government was passive during and after the slaughter. Copts in America protested against Sadat during his August 1981 visit to the White House (ibid. 222–31; Scott 2010: 73). The atmosphere became volatile and Islamists continued their campaign against the Copts and Sadat's peace with Israel. Sadat apparently perceived that a government attack on the Copts would punish the uncooperative patriarch and camouflage his own simultaneous attack on the Islamists. On September 5, 1981, he placed the patriarch under house arrest in St. Bishoi Monastery and ordered the imprisonment of eight bishops, approximately 160 priests, 1,500 Coptic activists, 5,000 Muslim clergy and fundamentalists, and 200 prominent politicians (Heikal 1983: 227–41). On October 6, 1981, a group of Islamists assassinated Sadat while he was on a viewing stand celebrating the anniversary of the 1973 war. The Copts had a sense of divine providence,[9] the Islamists rejoiced in a mission accomplished, and the enemies of the peace treaty celebrated throughout the Arab world.

President Hosni Mubarak inherited the complicated legacy of Sadat: its great achievements and its costly mistakes. In response to the Coptic–Muslim crisis, Mubarak was slow to release Coptic prisoners and even slower to return the bishops and Pope Shenouda to their sees. International pressure was evaded for years on the pretext that the imprisoned and exiled were safer due to Islamist threats and the possibility of communal unrest.[10] Eventually, the patriarch acquiesced to a number of unjust conditions for his release, including regular trips to the monastery and a requirement to vacate Cairo on Fridays, the Muslim holy day (Watson 2000: 116).

After 1,213 days under house arrest, Pope Shenouda's first public appearance was the midnight Christmas liturgy at Cairo Cathedral on January 7, 1985. His relations with the state, al-Azhar, society, and the world went from good to excellent in the years after his release. He has been tireless in cementing national unity and has received several international awards for this role. The last was the 2011 Augsburg Peace Prize, awarded in Germany every three years to an individual who has contributed significantly to the cause of peaceful coexistence between different faith communities.

National and International Achievements Despite Hardships

Although it has been a difficult era, the Copts have persisted and occasionally made monumental achievements in numerous fields. They have used their creativity in private enterprises, promoted Coptic art and music, defended their religion and church, revived ancient monasteries, and struggled and often succeeded in building churches, hospitals, schools, orphanages, and media outlets. In 2003, in a surprising but welcome move, President Mubarak even declared Coptic Christmas (January 7) a national holiday. On the pastoral and ecclesiastical fronts, especially over the past four decades, dioceses, monasteries, and seminaries have witnessed unprecedented growth because of the vision and energy of Pope Shenouda both inside and outside Egypt. It is remarkable that during his papacy the number of dioceses has increased from some twenty-five to one hundred—the majority of which were created by dividing existing dioceses in response to local ministerial needs—and monasteries have increased from a mere dozen to at least sixty and counting (van Doorn-Harder 2011: 174; Chaillot 2009).

Many modern sons of the pharaohs have become influential, some within Egypt and others internationally. The list includes the aforementioned Boutros Ghali, who became the United Nations Secretary-General (1992–96). It also includes others recognized in this chapter, as well as many cabinet and parliament members in Egypt, Naguib Sawiris, a billionaire who in 2011 founded the Free Egyptians Party, Sir Magdi Yacoub, the first surgeon to perform a heart transplant in the United Kingdom, Dina Habib Powell, the former White House Personnel Director, and a host of world-class professionals in almost every field.

Under Pope Shenouda, the Sunday School movement, benevolent societies, religious educational institutions, and Community Councils continued to provide the laity with vehicles for revival, self-expression, education, and internal reform. At the same time, however, the decision-making process within the church, as well as the church's interface with society and politics, has increasingly become influenced and in many cases dominated by the clergy (Watson 2000: 47; Hasan 2003: 233–34, 243; van Doorn-Harder 2011: 156, 175–76, 187–88). Copts, especially those in Community Councils, government positions, civil society leadership, and media therefore often find themselves walking a tightrope, caught between the authoritarianism and brutality of the state, the threat of attack by Islamists, and the conservatism of the central administration of their own church. Tensions between the laity and the clergy have occasionally revealed themselves in spiritual and daily matters as well, such as Pope Shenouda's ban on pilgrimages to Jerusalem, which remains in effect to this day (Hasan 2003: 109; Watson 2000: 131). More recently, since the 2011 revolution, lay members have protested and demonstrated against the government. For the sake of peace and safety, the patriarchate usually discourages such acts.

Copts, both lay and clergy, have founded and utilized media outlets inside and outside Egypt as a means to represent Coptic identity and integrate it with modern Egyptian culture and international ideals. As such, Coptic media broadcasts church services, defends human rights, promotes civil society, and nourishes a cooperative attitude toward Islam and Muslims. It boosts the self-consciousness of the Copts, affords them opportunities to actively express their positions on social and political matters, and appeals to the soul of the Egyptian nation and Islamic conscience.

The Sunday newspaper *Watani*, under its editor-in-chief Youssef Sidhom, is the pinnacle of Coptic expression and nationalist progressive journalism. *Watani* was established by Antoun Sidhom in 1958, closed by Sadat in 1981, and re-opened in 1984 after a court battle. In 2001 *Watani International* was founded with additional Arabic and English pages under Magdi Khalil and Samia Sidhom, respectively. Two Coptic television channels were launched in Egypt in 2007 and are broadcast to most of the world via satellite: Aghapy TV, founded and directed by Bishop Botros, and CTV (Coptic TV) founded and guided by the benevolent Copt Sarwat Bassily.[11] In 2010, the Coptic Diocese of Los Angeles under Bishop Serapion founded the LogosTV satellite channel. There is even a station for young Copts in the Diaspora, the Christian Youth Channel.

From Daughter to Sister Church: The Evolution of Ethiopian–Coptic Relations

Although Christianity may have reached Ethiopia in Apostolic times, the hierarchical structure was not formalized until the time of St. Athanasius in the fourth century. Since then the Coptic pope ordained the bishop of Addis Ababa and oversaw the administration of the Ethiopian Church. In later centuries, the Copts, being under siege themselves, appreciated the dignity and strategic dimension of having the Ethiopian church as a daughter church. Meanwhile, Egypt's rulers had a vested interest in keeping Ethiopia in the Coptic ecclesiastical fold in order to leverage political pressure on Ethiopia.

With the 1942 liberation of Ethiopia from the Italian occupation and the spirit of independence that swept Africa in the 1950s, Ethiopians sought a higher degree of ecclesiastical independence. In 1951, for the first time in the history of the Ethiopian church, an Ethiopian rather than Egyptian Copt was ordained as Metropolitan of Addis Ababa. Soon after the 1959 enthronement of Pope Kyrillos VI, the two churches came to an agreement by which Metropolitan Basilios of Addis Ababa was elevated to Patriarch-Catholicus in a solemn liturgy at Cairo Cathedral attended by Emperor Haile Selassie on 28 June 1959. The Pope of Alexandria was to remain "the supreme spiritual head of the Church of Ethiopia" (Partrick 1996: 164; Meinardus 1999: 134). However, upon the death of both Kyrillos and Basilios in 1971, the Ethiopians pushed for complete independence, and on May 9, 1971, Patriarch Theophilos was enthroned in Addis Ababa. Coptic Metropolitan Antonious led a delegation that participated in the inauguration.[12]

Both Pope Kyrillos, in 1960 and 1965, and Pope Shenouda, in 1973, were invited to Ethiopia and received an imperial welcome. However, the Ethiopian communist revolution in 1974 devastated the Ethiopian church, not to mention its relation to the mother (now sister) church. Soon after the communist retreat in 1991, warm relations between the two churches were restored and formulated in a protocol approved in 1994.

Ecumenical Progress Within Egypt and Without

In contrast to its relative isolation from the world since the Arab invasion in AD 641, the Coptic Church emerged as more ecumenically conscious in the twentieth century. It joined the World Council of Churches (WCC) in its earliest days, becoming a full member at the WCC General Assembly in Evanston, Illinois in 1954. The Copts participated in many activities of the WCC and in 1989 Pope Shenouda was elected to its eight-person Presidency Council. When the need emerged to establish ecumenical forums based on regional interests and concerns, the Coptic Church was involved as well. The All Africa Conference of Churches (AACC), for example, was formed in 1963 in response to the need to address joint challenges facing Christians in the newly liberated African continent, and more recently has addressed the HIV/AIDS pandemic. Similarly, the Middle East Council of Churches was formed in 1974 to address joint political and social challenges facing Middle Eastern Christians.

Unity Strengthened among the Non-Chalcedonian Orthodox

With the emergence of the worldwide ecumenical movement in the twentieth century, the five non-Chalcedonian (Oriental) Churches felt a need for a closer fellowship in order to distinguish their joint identity and meet the demands of ecumenism as one group. These churches are the Coptic, Syriac, Armenian, Ethiopian, and Malankara (Indian) Orthodox Churches. Emperor Haile Selassie hosted the first of such conferences in Addis Ababa in January 1965. In that event, the prelates of the five churches, which had not formally met since the Council of Chalcedon in AD 451, gathered to discuss the role of their churches in the modern world, cooperation on matters of church education and evangelism, relations with other Christian churches, and issues related to peace and justice (Atiya 1991: 1845–46). Since then, the churches have maintained cordial relations, holding joint liturgies, participating in sacramental exchanges, and coordinating positions when addressing relations with the Eastern Orthodox and the Catholic churches.

Bridges between the Chalcedonian and Non-Chalcedonian Churches

Working from a modern understanding of the political environment that caused the rift between the churches at Chalcedon, the non-Chalcedonian and Chalcedonian Orthodox families of churches have renewed cordial theological relations over the past sixty years. Frequent visits among the leadership have promoted an atmosphere conducive to understanding one another's theological positions. One such ecumenical result came in 1987 in the form of a joint statement on Christology signed by both sides at St. Bishoi Monastery in Egypt (Chaillot and Belopopsky 1998: 36). In 2001, the Coptic and Greek Patriarchs of Alexandria took an additional step toward reconciliation by allowing mixed families to be mutually accepted for communion in either church.[13]

Warming of Relations between Coptic and Catholic Churches

A strong bridge with the Vatican was built in 1968 when, as mentioned earlier, the Vatican gifted a portion of the relics of St. Mark venerated in Venice to the new St. Mark's Cathedral in Cairo. Pope Paul VI invited Pope Shenouda to the Vatican—the first visit of a Coptic prelate in over 1,500 years—where they held theological and pastoral exchanges that resulted in a historic Common Declaration issued May 10, 1973. On this occasion, the Vatican also gifted a portion of the relics of St. Athanasius, the twentieth Coptic Orthodox Pope, to his successor Pope Shenouda, the 117th Coptic Pope, along with marble flooring for the new Cairo Cathedral. Pope Shenouda developed a cordial relationship with the Coptic Catholic Church and in February 2000 received in his office the venerated Catholic Pope John Paul II.

Development of the Coptic World

In modern times, waves of Coptic immigration have been motivated by a variety of factors: the revolution and land reform in the 1950s, socialism and wars in the 1960s, and the continued rise of Islamization and violence against Copts since the 1970s. In response to the first wave of Coptic immigration, Pope Kyrillos VI ordained Bishop Samuel in 1962 for Social and Ecumenical Services including pastoral care of the Copts in Europe, America, and Australia. Exponential growth, however, came with the stronger immigration movement in the 1970s. As a result, and because of Pope Shenouda's personal involvement, the Coptic church in the Diaspora has blossomed into seventeen dioceses, several hundred parishes, some dozen monasteries, twelve seminaries, and numerous benevolent, educational, and media organizations. The United States is home to the largest number of Copts outside Egypt (Saad 2013, 2010; Guirguis and van Doorn-Harder 2011: 179–82, 1997: 255–72; Atiya 1991: 1620–24).

Following the Coptic legacy of missionary work, Pope Shenouda ordained Bishop Antonious Markos in 1976 for missionary work in Africa, and ordained Bishop Paul in 1995 for the region of Eastern and Central Africa. Their efforts have been successful in establishing sixty-five churches, three monasteries, and many medical centers and schools. Many Copts, including second-generation immigrants, travel from one continent to another to work as volunteers in these and other missionary centers (Watson 2000: 72–92).

As the Copts spread across the world, they have carried with them rich traditions of art, architecture, literature, language, spirituality, and music. These treasures are preserved and propagated by immigrants and second-generation Copts in a number of settings, including homes, churches, community centers, films, and social media outlets, not to mention in universities through specialized programs of Coptic studies. Due to these developments, the world is discovering more aspects of Coptic civilization (Saad 2013, 2010).

Copts, the 2011 Revolution, and the Precarious Future of Egypt

The revolution that began in Cairo's Tahrir Square on January 25, 2011, and led to the end of the Mubarak era on February 11, 2011, opened a new chapter for women, Copts, and other minorities in Egypt, one which at present, however, does not seem promising. Copts participated in the protests from the beginning and arguably even inspired the revolution itself.[14] As a result, there was an initial surge of nationalistic unity between Copts and Muslims, sparking hope for a true democracy in which women and minorities could enjoy basic human rights.

New challenges, however, quickly and ferociously emerged, especially for two groups. Female protesters are exposed to public humiliation by state forces, including virginity tests, sexual assault, and beatings. Unfortunately daily life has become increasingly difficult for the Copts as well, with thirteen major attacks on groups, communities, churches, and monasteries in 2011 alone. The worst of these occurred on October 9, 2011, when three army tanks plowed down unsuspecting Coptic demonstrators in front of the Egyptian Television Network building on Maspero Street. The tanks and subsequent shooting killed twenty-seven people—all Copts—and injured hundreds more. The attacks continued for twelve hours in the neighborhood, and even took place against the injured and their families at the Coptic Hospital. In defiance and triumph over evil, 70,000 people attended a twelve-hour special religious vigil held on November 11, 2011, at St. Simeon the Tanner Monastery in Mukattam, just outside Cairo. The Copts on that night, as always, took seriously the call to "Love your enemies and pray for those who persecute you" (Matthew 5:44 NRSV). Many Muslims participated in the demonstration and vigil in solidarity with the Copts.

Copts and progressive Muslims have demonstrated their commitment to a civil society by creating political parties such as the Free Egyptians Party which led the liberal Egyptian Bloc coalition in the 2011 parliamentary elections. However, the election results only served to confirm the plight of women, Muslim liberals, and minorities. Only eight women and six Copts (including one Coptic woman) from all parties won seats in the 498-member People's Assembly. A total of thirty-four from the Egyptian Bloc were elected, including nineteen Free Egyptians, while the Islamists won more than 72 percent. Though disenfranchised, Copts, as well as liberal and secularist Muslims, continue to present a significant moral and electoral force in preserving democracy and guarding Egyptian national identity. Their goal is to ensure that Egypt does not succumb to Islamist forces that might transform the nation into a theocracy. It remains to be seen, however, whether the Copts will feel empowered and continue to contribute to their society in the new political environment that emerges, or whether they will be silenced by intimidation and threats of violence, in response to which many have already resorted to emigration (Lagnado 2011).

Conclusion

Modern Coptic history is an important lens through which to situate and understand the broader history of Egypt from Nasser's revolution in 1952 to the people's revolution in 2011. The productivity and resilience of Copts during those sixty years stand as a counterpoint to the declining pluralism in education, media, and politics in the Egyptian society. Coptic history has clearly been shaped by national politics, but it is also true that the Copts, by holding fast to ideals including freedom of worship, human rights, women's rights, and nation building, have in turn constructively and creatively influenced contemporary Egyptian history and civilization.

It is also the case that Coptic identity has, in no small part, been shaped by the personalities and leadership principles of the patriarchs during this era, all of whom have been politically engaged for the sake of their flock. To an increasing degree these patriarchs have had to maintain cordial relations with the state and reconciliatory tones in the society, while simultaneously sympathizing with the injustices toward Copts. At the most basic level, however, the daily function of the clergy of the church has in large part been to help the Copts navigate between their personal, community, religious and social identities.

If the 2011 revolution has demonstrated the latent energy of Egyptians to fight injustice, it is not surprising that the increasing and disturbing levels of intolerance against religious minorities, women, and liberalism have been countered by a deepened Coptic spiritual life, resolve to fight for and defend human rights, and improved ecumenical outreach. The revolution also strengthened traditional alliances between the Copts, women's rights advocates, and progressive Muslims—all fighting together for a genuinely democratic and civil society. These realities in Egypt and in the expanding Diaspora have ushered in a new era in the history of the Copts, marked in equal measure by tribulation and struggle, agony and anticipation, resilience and revival, challenge and opportunity.

Timeline

1946	Pope Yusab II enthroned
1952	Nasser leads an army revolution that removes King Farouk
1953	Egypt becomes a republic
1955	Pope Yusab II removed from office, dies the following year
1959	Pope Kyrillos VI enthroned
1967	Egypt is defeated in the Six Day War
1968	St. Mary apparitions in Zaytun, St. Mark relics returned to Egypt, new Cairo Cathedral dedicated
1970	President Nasser dies and President Sadat becomes president

1971	Pope Kyrillos VI dies and Pope Shenouda III enthroned
1972	Burning of a church in al-Khanka, the first of fifty major violent acts against Coptic communities in the next forty years
1973	Egypt begins war to liberate Sinai from Israeli occupation
1980	New Egyptian constitution makes Islamic Shari'a the primary source of legislation
1981	Massacre in Zawya el-Hamra by Islamists; eighteen Copts killed, hundreds injured
1981	President Sadat exiles Pope Shenouda III and imprisons about 1,700 Copts
1981	President Sadat assassinated by Islamists in retaliation for peace with Israel
1981	Hosni Mubarak becomes president, in office for next thirty years
1985	Pope Shenouda returns to Cairo under unjust conditions
1997	Massacre at church in Abu Qurqas by Islamists; ten Copts killed
2000	Massacre in el-Kosheh by Islamists on New Year's Day; twenty-one Copts killed, thirty-three injured
2009	Six Copts killed as congregation leaves church in Nag Hammadi after Christmas liturgy (January 7)
2010	Copts demonstrate against injustice and violence, and many are injured or killed by Islamists and security forces
2010	Bomb on New Year's Eve (December 31) kills twenty-one Copts while leaving an Alexandria church
2011	President Mubarak resigns (February 11) and is sentenced (June 2, 2012) to life in prison as an accomplice in the killing of unarmed demonstrators
2011	Naguib Sawiris, a Copt, establishes the Free Egyptians Party (April 3) which wins 4 percent of parliament seats
2012	Pope Shenouda III dies (March 17)
2012	Pope Tawadros II enthroned (November 18)

Notes

1 Socialism was often praised in the Christmas and Easter messages of Pope Kyrillos VI (Partrick 1996: 165). Coptic authors did similarly.

2 Community Councils (*Majlis Milli*) were introduced by a government–church agreement in 1874 to formalize the participation of laity in the administration of a number of church functions, such as finances, education, and jurisdiction over personal status issues. Each diocese has a Community Council elected by members of the church, and there is a General Community Council chaired by the pope in Cairo (A. A. Bestawros, "Community Council, Coptic," in Atiya 1991: 580–82).

3 Specific recent court cases are included in United States Department of State 2008: 1820.

4 The Institute and church at large benefited from two groups: firstly, from highly qualified academicians such as Aziz Atiya (history), Sami Gabra (archeology), Murad Kamil (Semitic languages), Zaher Riyad (African studies), Ragheb Moftah (music), Habib Gorgy (art), Isaac Fanous (iconography), Iris Elmasri (history), Sulayman Nasim (education), and Gawdat Gabra (Coptology); and secondly, from Habib Jirjis' disciples at the

seminary, such as Nazeer Gayed (later Pope Shenouda, theology), Wahib Attalla (later Bishop Gregorious, theology), Saad Aziz (later Bishop Samuel, sociology), and Fr. Salib Suriel (canon law).

5 For example, despite tensions between the two men in their home country, Heikal (1983: 161–65) writes "[President] Carter told Shenouda that he has heard a lot about him from President Sadat, who had spoken very highly of him."

6 Coptic presence in the armed forces was greatly encouraged during Nasser's time. This led to high visibility for the Copts during the 1973 war. For example, General Fouad Aziz Ghali, a Copt, led the Second Army to victory in breaking the legendary Barlev Wall.

7 For more details and analysis of those acts of violence, one may conduct an internet search for articles by the following prolific scholars and intellectuals: Saad Eddin Ibrahim, Tarek Heggy, Alaa Al Aswany, and Sayyed al-Qimni, who are Muslims; and Youssef Sidhom, Adel Guindy, and Magdi Khalil, who are Copts.

8 Arguably, the efforts of Copts prevented the total application of Shari'a law in Egypt, which is historically significant and deserves further investigation by scholars (Hasan 2003: 103–22).

9 On the other hand, some Copts actually took issue with Shenouda's opposition to Sadat's moves and felt that the patriarch's house arrest was a tolerable price for communal peace (Medina 1981; Heikal 1983: 238; Watson 2000: 102–3).

10 Over the next thirty years Mubarak worked under yet another pretext of even-handedness that in reality traded persecution of the Copts for peace with the Islamists. Such a strategy was indirectly rebuked by President Barack Obama in his speech at Cairo University on June 4, 2009: "Among some Muslims, there is a disturbing tendency to measure one's own faith by the rejection of another's. The richness of religious diversity must be upheld—whether it is for Maronites in Lebanon or the Copts in Egypt." See Obama (2009).

11 Sarwat Bassily has also led and financed many charitable, cultural, and educational projects. For example, he generously initiated endowments for chairs in Coptic Studies at the American University in Cairo and Claremont Graduate University in California. He served as a member of parliament and deputy head of the General Community Council for several terms.

12 Relations between the churches were already strained by the disputed ownership of Dayr al-Sultan, a monastery adjacent to the Church of the Holy Sepulcher in Jerusalem (Archbishop Basilios, "Dayr al-Sultan," in Atiya 1991: 872–75).

13 "Pastoral Agreement Regarding the Sacrament of Matrimony Between the Patriarchate of Alexandria and the Coptic Church in 2001 by Shenouda III and Petros VII," accessed on December 28, 2012, www.orthodoxunity.org/state05.html

14 It has been conjectured that the massive Coptic protests in Egypt and worldwide against the bombing of an Alexandrian church on New Year's Eve, less than a month before the revolution, played a formative role in the general protests that soon followed.

Selected Bibliography

Abdelsayyed, G. (1976) "Islam and State in Mediterranean Africa," *Africa Report*, March–April, 21(2): 42–45.

——(1981) "A Coptic Pope in North America: A Historical Analysis," *Coptologia*, 1: 56–64.

Atiya, A. S. (1968) *History of Eastern Christianity*, London: Methuen.

——(ed.) (1991) *The Coptic Encyclopedia*, New York: Macmillan.

Chaillot, C. (2009) "The Life and Situation of the Coptic Orthodox Church Today," *Studies in World Christianity*, 15(3): 199–216.

Chaillot, C. and Belopopsky, A. (eds) (1998) *Towards Unity: The Theological Dialogue between the Orthodox Church and the Oriental Orthodox Churches*, Paris: Inter-Orthodox Dialogue.

Gabra, G. (2009) *The A to Z of the Coptic Church*, Lanham: Scarecrow Press.

Guirguis, M. and van Doorn-Harder, N. (2011) *The Emergence of the Modern Coptic Papacy: The Egyptian Church and Its Leadership from the Ottoman Period to the Present*, Cairo: American University in Cairo Press, 53–188.

Hasan, S. S. (2003) *Christians versus Muslims in Modern Egypt: The Century-Long Struggle for Coptic Equality*, Oxford: Oxford University Press.

Heikal, M. H. (1983) *Autumn of Fury: The Assassination of Sadat*, New York: Random House.

Lagnado, L. (2011) "Egypt's Embattled Christians Seek Room in America," *The Wall Street Journal*, 24 Dec 2011.

Medina, S. C. (1981) "Egypt's Copts in Crisis," *Time Magazine*, 28 September, 118(13): 58.

Meinardus, O. F. A. (1970) *Christian Egypt Faith and Life*, Cairo: American University in Cairo Press.

——(1999) *Two Thousand Years of Coptic Christianity*, Cairo: American University in Cairo Press.

——(2006) *Christians in Egypt*, Cairo: American University in Cairo Press.

Minorities at Risk Project (2004) *Chronology for Copts in Egypt*, Online. www.unhcr.org/refworld/docid/469f38841c.html (accessed December 28, 2012).

Obama, B. (2009) "Remarks by the President on a New Beginning" White House Press Office. Online. www.whitehouse.gov/the-press-office/remarks-president-cairo-university-6-04-09 (accessed December 28, 2012).

Partrick, T. H. (1996) *Traditional Egyptian Christianity*, Greensboro: Fisher Park Press.

Saad, S. M. (2010) "The Contemporary Life of the Coptic Orthodox Church in the United States," *Studies in World Christianity*, 16(3): 207–25.

——(2013) "Coptic Civilization in the Diaspora," in G. Gabra (ed.) *Coptic Civilization*, Cairo: American University in Cairo Press.

Saad, S. M. and Saad, N. M. (2001) "Electing Coptic Patriarchs: A Diversity of Traditions," *Bulletin of St. Shenouda the Archimandrite Coptic Society*, 6: 20–32.

Scott, R. M. (2010) *The Challenge of Political Islam: Non-Muslims and the Egyptian State*, Stanford: Stanford University Press.

Thomas, M. and Youssef, A. A. (eds) (2006) *Copts in Egypt: A Christian Minority Under Siege. Papers Presented at the First International Coptic Symposium, Zurich, September 23–25, 2004*, Goettingen: Vandenhoeck & Ruprecht.

United States Department of State (2008) *Country Reports on Human Rights Practices for 2007.*

van Doorn-Harder, N. and Vogt, K. (eds) (1997) *Between Desert and City: The Coptic Orthodox Church Today*, Oslo: Institute for Comparative Research in Human Culture.

Wakin, E. (1963) *A Lonely Minority: The Modern Story of Egypt's Copts*, New York: William Morrow.

Watson, J. H. (2000) *Among The Copts*, Brighton: Sussex Academic Press.

Part II

Coptic Religious Culture

7 Theology

Defending Orthodoxy

Lois M. Farag

Coptic Orthodox theology is complex and has been expressed over the span of almost two millennia in at least three languages, Greek, Coptic, and Arabic. This makes any endeavor to encapsulate "Coptic Orthodox Theology" a difficult task. Coptic theology has its firm foundation in the Church fathers, particularly those of Alexandria. It is not influenced by the theology of Antioch but has good knowledge of the Cappadocians. Latin theology, such as that of Augustine, is unfamiliar to Alexandrian theological thought. From its inception in the early centuries of Christianity, Coptic theology developed certain characteristics that made it distinctive and certain principles and theological frameworks that have guided the theological discussion ever since. This theological synopsis presents these principles and frameworks within a historical perspective, paying special attention to the founding fathers of Coptic theology, Cyril and Athanasius. It will focus on primary texts with the intention of hearing the theologians in their own words.

Patristic and Biblically Based Coptic Theology

Biblically based theology means a theology that presents its argument by drawing on Biblical texts, using language and vocabulary quoted directly from or alluding to Scripture. The Biblical character of Alexandrian patristic theology distinguishes it from the systematic theology that emerged from the medieval scholastic tradition, which presents arguments based on philosophical reasoning and theories. Most theologians of the early church in Egypt wrote extensive Biblical commentaries and through their close attention to the Biblical text they formed their theology. A representative example of such practice would be Cyril of Alexandria (r. 412–44). He was well trained in rhetoric and applied rhetorical tools to the Biblical text, explaining difficult words, detecting grammatical problems, clarifying names of geographical places, explaining the historical context, etc. He would then immerse the reader into the deeper, spiritual, and theological meaning of the text, thus transforming the type into the truth of Christ. Typology, according to Cyril, means examining the deeper meaning of events or themes taken from Scripture to reveal their true meaning. As Paul found the crossing of the Red Sea to be a type of Baptism (1 Cor 10:2) and Melchizedek, a type of Christ (Heb 7), Cyril would, for example, interpret the healing of the blind man in John 9: 6–7 to be a type of the calling of the Gentiles; the creation of the new eye indicates that Christ is the creator of all things, and the washing in the pool carries a mystical connection to Baptism (Cyril 1885: 18–21). The interpretation according to type is deeply rooted in the Coptic tradition and is even incorporated in liturgical readings. For example, the Sixth Hour of Good Friday commemorates Christ hanging on the cross: At this hour the church reads Numbers 21 where Moses made a bronze serpent and set it on a pole; as those who looked at the bronze serpent lived, those who look at Christ hanging on the cross and believe will be granted eternal life. Neither Cyril nor Athanasius of Alexandria (r. 328–73), the founders of Coptic theology, used allegory in their Biblical interpretation. Theophilus of Alexandria (r. 385–412) also expressed caution towards using allegory, writing that it should be used "only in so far as it is not contrary to the truth, does not distort the factual record, follows the sense of sacred Scripture" (Russell 2007: 160).

Athanasius and Cyril together firmly established the principle that Biblical interpretation and, eventually, theology had to be carried out within a Trinitarian framework. When Arius denied the divinity of the Son so that, consequently, the Son was understood as an entity distinct from God the Father, Athanasius concluded that, if this were the case, we would not have a Trinity but a Quaternity (Athanasius, *Letter to Epictetus*). If the Son was divided while he was one with the Father, then there would not be three persons in the Trinity but four. While Athanasius is speaking about the Son, and explaining his nature, he is putting the entire discussion within the larger framework of the Trinity; we cannot understand the Son outside or apart from the Trinity.

Another principle of Biblical interpretation that shaped theological rhetoric was not dividing the voices of the Biblical narrative with respect to Christ. Athanasius attributes the problems of Arius to his method of reading the Gospel narrative. He argues that Arius mistakenly attended to the human characteristics of the Son without putting the Son's divinity within the same framework (Athanasius, *Contra Arianos* 3.41). The same problem faced Nestorius who could not reconcile the different depictions of Christ in the Gospel and concluded that two distinct persons or hypostases—a human hypostasis and a divine—became Christ. In his *Third Letter to Nestorius* Cyril gave an almost identical response to that of his predecessor Athanasius, anathematizing anyone who assigned some of the Gospel narrative to a man, apart from the Word, and other parts of the narrative to the Word alone.

Athanasius and Cyril were consistent in upholding these principles of Biblical interpretation and this consistency was maintained by succeeding Coptic theologians. Athanasius is called "The Apostolic" in the Coptic Church for his defense of the faith and laying the foundation of Coptic Orthodox theology, which was later elaborated by Cyril.

Salvation and the Incarnation

Athanasius of Alexandria, in his monumental work *On the Incarnation*, explains the necessity of the Incarnation for human salvation and why it was necessary that the Word, the Son of God, bring about salvation. God created the world through the Son (John 1:1–3). He created humans with the ability to choose between good and evil because he created them in the image of the Word and endowed them with reason. Humans transgressed the commandment, chose the material world over the contemplation of God, and came under the sentence of death and corruption (Athanasius 2008: 3). Now that humanity needed salvation and renewal, it was only God the Word and creator who could renew his creation (ibid. 1); he was to suffer and die on behalf of the humanity made in his image. But God does not die; God the Word is incorporeal, incorruptible, and immaterial (ibid. 7, 8). He had to become Incarnate to die on our behalf. We are the object of his Incarnation (ibid. 4). He took a body like ours and made it his very own. When he died on the cross, we died in him; he overcame death by his Resurrection and we rose with him. He conquered death and overturned the sentence of corruption from which humanity suffered (ibid. 8). Death no longer has hold over humanity. Because Christ conquered death by the Crucifixion and Resurrection, destroying death through the cross, when Christians die, they do not fear death, for it has no power over them anymore. Now Christians die without fear and by conquering the fear of death become witnesses to the Resurrection (ibid. 27). The Resurrection is the greatest proof of victory over death, proof that Christ is alive and active in the world (ibid. 30). The Word renewed his image within humanity so that through him humanity can once more come to know God the Father and be in his likeness (ibid. 12–14). Christ granted the renewal of creation. By his Resurrection, the giver of life has given life and incorruption to humanity, introduced virtue, immortality, and desire for heavenly things (ibid. 31).

Within this vision of salvation, both the divinity of the Son and his humanity are crucial. Athanasius concludes his treatise by writing:

> But for the searching and right understanding of the Scriptures there is need of a good life and a pure soul, and for Christian virtue to guide the mind to grasp, so far as human nature can, the truth concerning God the Word. One cannot possibly understand the teaching of the saints unless one has a pure mind and is trying to imitate their life. … Similarly, anyone who wishes to understand the mind of the sacred writers must first cleanse his own life, and approach the saints by copying their deeds.
>
> (ibid. 96)

Athanasius' concluding statement makes clear that this theological vision is not abstract theological speculation; the Incarnation and salvation are very much part of the Christian's journey because they have granted the Christian a renewed life. Salvation is a way of life, a *politeia*. It is the life of the saints, which leads to a pure soul that guides the mind to the "right understanding of Scripture." The Anaphoras (Eucharistic prayers) of the Coptic liturgies of St. Basil, St. Cyril, and St. Gregory all have a synopsis of the Incarnation and salvation, which shows the centrality of this theological theme. The understanding of the vivifying power of the Resurrection and the renewal of God's image within the person guides Coptic Christians in their ethical notions, conduct, and interactions with their neighbors and the world. Coptic theology and the reading of Scripture are interdependent and both inform the practice of spirituality, liturgy, and moral conduct.

The Trinity

Cyril of Alexandria explains that for someone to claim that he believes in God, this belief should be in God the Father, the Son, who became Incarnate, and the Holy Spirit (Cyril 1885: 232–33). Although Cyril clearly emphasizes each person of the Trinity, he repeatedly insists that this must entail recognizing the unity of the Trinity by affirming and speaking about the One God. Cyril, together with Athanasius, is upholding what the universal church has asserted in the Nicene Creed, which begins "I believe in God" and then describes each person of the Trinity. Cyril's oft-quoted Trinitarian formula, "All things are from the Father through the Son in the Holy Spirit," expresses the oneness of the Trinity's activity and the relationship between each person within the Trinity. Distinction is accompanied by unity in one and the same thought.

Severing the unity of the Trinity threatens the faith and Christian understanding of God. When Arius denied the divinity of the Son, Alexander of Alexandria (r. 312–26) understood this claim to jeopardize the Christian understanding of the Trinity, the Godhead, and the whole essence of our salvation. Decades later, the Macedonians denied the divinity of the Holy Spirit. In response to these two claims, which threatened the essence of the Trinity and the Christian faith, bishops of the universal church at the Council of Nicea (325) and the Council of Constantinople (381) set the tenets of Christian orthodoxy by issuing the Nicene Creed, by which those being baptized assert their orthodoxy during their baptismal rite. The synodical letter accompanying the Creed renounced as heretical "division of substance or of nature or of the Godhead, and ... introduction of some nature which was produced subsequently, or was created, or was of a different substance, into the uncreated and consubstantial and co-eternal Trinity" (Tanner 1990: 28). In addition, Canon 1 of the Council of Constantinople states that "the profession of faith of the holy fathers who gathered in Nicaea in Bithynia is not to be abrogated, but it is to remain in force" (ibid. 31). The Nicene Creed defined the Trinity and became the yardstick of orthodoxy. It was further established that nothing was to be added or deleted from the Creed. This gives a sense of finality to the definition of the faith.

Christology

Half a century later, Nestorius, the Bishop of Constantinople, advocated the idea of a unity according to will or good pleasure between two natures and two hypostases (the Greek word for person) within the person of Christ. He used the term "conjunction" rather than Cyril's preferred term "union" when speaking about the unity of natures within Christ. To the term Theotokos, birth giver of God, he preferred the use of Christotokos, birth giver of Christ, which implied that the Virgin Mary gave birth to Jesus, a separate human hypostasis, who came to be conjoined with the hypostasis of the Logos at the time of the Incarnation. This Nestorian vision implied that the unity is between two hypostases, one of the divine Logos and Son and the other of a human being. Two different hypostases or persons imply two sons and two activities. This division led Cyril to accuse Nestorius of asserting two sons and thus a quaternity rather than a trinity in the Godhead. In his *Third Letter to Nestorius*, Cyril of Alexandria issued twelve anathemas that encapsulated the main points of opposition to Nestorianism. Cyril insisted that the Virgin Mary be called "Theotokos" (Anathema 1). Furthermore, the expression of unity of the divinity and the humanity excludes any division of the hypostasis or the person of the One Christ (Anathema 3).

Cyril describes the Incarnation as the unity of the divine and the human natures in the "one nature of God the Word Incarnate." This oft-used formula represents Cyril's theological vision of the unity of the natures. Its repetition in several texts excludes different interpretations. In this unity, Cyril writes, the divine nature of the Word was not changed into something it never was, nor was the flesh transformed into the divine nature of the Word. There is one Son and "he has one nature even when he is considered as having assumed flesh endowed with a rational soul" (Cyril 1995: 77). Cyril adds that, in the case of Christ, the divinity and the humanity "came together in a mysterious and incomprehensible union without confusion or change. The manner of this union is entirely beyond conception." Cyril continues that this incomprehensible union in the one nature of the Word Incarnate occurred without confusion or mixture; if anyone thinks in another way they will "be offering us two sons and two Christs" (ibid. 77–79). Cyril speaks about the unity of natures according to the hypostasis and acknowledges the one Christ, one Son, one Lord and one nature of the Incarnate Son. In the *Letter to Eulogius* Cyril writes that when Nestorius speaks of "two natures" to signify the difference between the flesh and the Logos, he denies the unity. In his *Letter to Acacius*, bishop of Melitene, he asserts that the two natures are united, but after the union we cannot speak of two distinct natures but of the one nature of the Son. He explains that, based on this understanding of the one nature, we cannot attribute some gospel sayings to his humanity and others to the Word of God or God alone (Cyril 1987, Letters 1–50: 73–4; *Third Letter to Nestorius*, Anathema 4). Such a division of the sayings presupposes two persons or two hypostases of Christ. Cyril is very consistent and clear in his understanding of the oneness of Christ and the oneness of his nature, within which there is no confusion, change, mixture, or the absorption of the human nature by the divine. Cyril, like Athanasius, is consistent in applying the principle of not dividing the Gospel sayings between the human and divine natures lest we end up with two persons in Christ. Cyril's vision of the nature of Christ was agreed to at the Council of Ephesus (431). This theological articulation expresses clearly the Coptic Orthodox understanding of the nature of Christ and invalidates the (mis)label of "Monophysitism," of which the Coptic Church was often accused.

Less than two decades after the council, Eutyches (378–454), an archimandrite in Constantinople, while acknowledging the "one nature of Christ," defined this one nature as the divine nature only. In response to this assertion, Leo of Rome accused Eutyches of Apollinarianism. According to Leo, Apollinarius denied the existence of the soul, reason, and true flesh of the Incarnate Son, claiming this flesh was formed of divine substance (Leo, *Letter* 59.5). In his *Letter to Julian*, Leo asserts that Eutyches denied the reality of Christ's human flesh, saying he wore human flesh in appearance only (Leo, *Letter* 35.1). Based on this assessment Leo equated Eutychianism with Apollinarianism. In his *Letter to Flavian*, Bishop of Constantinople, Leo accuses anyone who does not acknowledge the two natures in the Incarnate Son of being both Eutychian and Apollinarian. This polemical rhetoric has been used from the time of Leo to the present day. Western Christian literature, whether scholarly or ecclesiastic, followed Leo's assessment and falsely accused the Coptic Orthodox Church of Apollinarianism and Eutychianism which is commonly referred to as "Monophysitism." The Coptic Orthodox Church acknowledges the one nature of God the Word Incarnate according to Athanasius' and Cyril's theology. Cyril explains the Incarnation as the Word becoming actual flesh and having flesh "as his own." The flesh, according to Cyril, is composed of a soul, a perishable and earthly flesh, and a spirit of life. This is not the vision expressed by either Eutyches or Apollinarius, or what came to be called Monophysite theology. The stark difference is clear. The Confession in the Coptic Orthodox liturgy clearly states, "He [the Son] made it [his humanity] one with his divinity without mingling, without confusion, and without alteration," which removes any suspicion of Monophysite theology.

Leo considered his letter to Flavian, known as the Tome of Leo, the most representative work of his theology, expressing the fullness and clarity of his confession of the Incarnation (Leo, *Letter* 93.2). In his letter to Julian, bishop of Cos, he says that the Tome is the full refutation of Eutychianism. To the monks of Palestine he writes that his Tome is "sufficiently explicit and stands in no need either of correction or explanation" (Leo, *Letter* 124.1). Leo's Tome was used to write the Definition of the Council of Chalcedon (451). Since Leo and the Chalcedonian churches consider the Tome the representative document of the two natures of Christology, both the Tome and the Definition deserve our special attention.

Leo writes in the Tome that "each form [Latin *forma*] performs what is proper to it in communion with the other, the Word achieving what is the Word's, while the body accomplishes what is the body's" (Price and Gaddis 2005: 19). Leo introduced the Latin term "forma" rather than the commonly used term "nature" to describe the elements of unity.[1] Eastern theologians used the term "form" primarily to express the divine kenosis, God emptying himself and taking human form, as in Phil 2:7, but not as an element of union. Further on in the Tome, Leo explains the raising of Lazarus in these terms: "It does not belong to the same nature to weep in an emotion of pity for a dead friend, and to raise that same friend from the dead with a word of power" (Bindley 1980: 227–28). Leo also wrote that after the Incarnation "the properties of both natures and substances were preserved and co-existed in one person" (ibid. 226). These quotes from Leo's letter clearly indicate that he used the terms form (*forma*), nature (*natura*), and substance (*substantia*) synonymously (ibid. 169–70). Leo no longer speaks about the "unity of natures," a foundational premise in Cyril's understanding of the Incarnation, but instead uses such terms as "form" and "substance" or "hypostasis" to describe the elements of unity. These statements from the Tome created a lot of confusion. It is interesting to observe that in the first quote the "form," whether human or divine, performs the activity, while in the second quote, as well as in the remainder of the Tome, it is the "nature" that is the subject of the activity. Leo understood nature to mean a concrete entity and equated it with hypostasis, which led him to the conclusion that each nature performs what is proper to itself.

It is crucial to compare the Tome's explanation of the raising of Lazarus with the explanation of the same miracle by Athanasius to recognize a different way to attribute the activity. According to Athanasius, when Christ summoned Lazarus out from the tomb, as human he gave forth his voice to raise Lazarus, and as divine he raised Lazarus from the dead. There is no separation between the human calling on Lazarus to arise and the divine raising of Lazarus from the dead; it is one and the same act. This is an excellent example of Athanasius' Biblical interpretation in which the divine and the human voices and activities are not separated but are considered to be one and the same activity. Other miracles are to be interpreted in the same way. Christ healed Peter's mother-in-law (Lk 4:38–41) when "he stretched his hand humanly, but stopped the illness divinely" (Athanasius, *Contra Arianos* III, 32). The flesh is not external to any of his actions but is his own (ibid.) for he was true God in the flesh and true flesh in the Word (ibid. 41).

Cyril develops the same vision, insisting that, after the Incarnation, the body and the Word are indivisible (Cyril 1874: 417). The body is not of the same nature as the Word but they came together to become one in union and in an incomprehensible agreement (ibid. 417). The body is not an instrument of the Word, nor is it obeying orders. Rather the body is united in complete agreement with the Word; as the Word is life giving, so is the body of Christ, as is shown in the Eucharistic mystery. Christ took the daughter of the chief of the synagogue "by the hand" and "called out, 'Child, get up!'" (Lk 8:54). In this miracle he gave life by the power of his command as God and again through the touch of his flesh to show that it was one intrinsic activity through both (ibid. 418–19). When Christ raised the widow's son of Nain he approached the dead son and "touched the bier" and "he said, 'young man, I say to you rise!'" (Lk 7:14). The activity of raising the widow's son included the power of the command and the touching of the bier (Cyril 1983: 155, 201). Cyril asserts that, as the body of Christ is life giving and raises the dead, those who partake of the Eucharistic mystery are partaking of the life-giving body of Christ and partaking of immortality. If the body carries out what is proper to the body, and is not united to the Son "as his own," then how can this flesh be a life-giving flesh? The unity as explained here is not only a physical inseparability and indivisibility, but it also includes a unity in activity. The oneness of the activity of the divine and human natures is not an intellectual exercise; it affects the understanding of the Eucharistic mystery, an intrinsic part of the life of the Church, and it affects the understanding of the Incarnate Son and salvation. It is clear that Athanasius' and Cyril's vision of Christ is irreconcilable with Nestorius' or Leo's vision, which included a duality of both nature and activity.

Timothy of Alexandria (457–77) found many difficulties in Leo's Tome. One of the difficulties is that, while Leo asserts that there is one person, he "subverts" the oneness of the person "by speaking of 'one' and 'another'. How, then, tell me, could 'one' have become 'one and another'? For 'one' and 'two' cannot be thought of as being the same, neither can the concept of unity be attributed to 'one and another'" (Ebied and Wickham 1985: 152). Another difficulty with Leo's statements quoted above lies in the firm principle that a nature cannot have an activity without a hypostasis; therefore, a nature cannot be assigned an activity. For a nature to carry out an activity, it has to be hypostasized. Timothy asserted in clearly spelled-out statements the underlying principle of differentiating between nature and hypostasis (Timothy Aelurus 1919: 228–29). The Definition of Chalcedon clearly states that Christ is "acknowledged in two natures … the property of both natures is preserved and comes together into a single person." But for Alexandrian theology and Aristotelian logic this means two hypostases. So when the Definition speaks of two natures, each doing what belongs to it, and a single person and a single hypostasis, there is a logical contradiction.

The three Alexandrian Coptic theologians, Athanasius, Cyril, and Timothy, insisted on the one nature of the Incarnate Word to guarantee the one hypostasis with, consequently, one activity, in that order. They also had a clear understanding of the difference between nature and hypostasis. Coptic theologians assert that the oneness of the activity is an indication of the oneness of the person or hypostasis. Both Athanasius and Cyril gave attention to the activity of the Trinity and the Incarnate Son. The activity of the Trinity is guided by the formula: all things are from the Father through the Son in the Holy Spirit. As the oneness of activity of the Trinity does not negate the difference and distinctiveness of each person so the oneness of the activity of the Son does not negate or obscure the difference of the natures.

Timothy, like his predecessor Dioscorus, was of the opinion that if the faith of the saints decays over time, then it is necessary to constantly change and update it, but if the faith of the saints is based on unshakable foundations, then we cannot change what is constant (ibid. 222, 242). It is worth mentioning that the proceedings of the first Council of Ephesus also state that

> It is not permitted to produce or write or compose any other creed except that the one which was defined by the holy fathers who were gathered together in the holy Spirit at Nicaea. Any who dare to compose or bring forth or produce another creed ... , if they are bishops or clerics they should be deprived of their respective charges and if they are laymen they are to be anathematized.
>
> (Tanner 1990: 65)

These proceedings, like Canon 1 of the Council of Constantinople previously mentioned, make clear that no amendments or additions to the Nicene Creed are permissible. Based on the theology just summarized and the canons of Ephesus I and Constantinople, the Coptic Orthodox Church did not accept the amendments of 451, which came to be called the Chalcedonian Definition. Similarly, for theological and the same canonical reasons, the addition to the Nicene Creed of the double procession of the Holy Spirit, that is the addition of the term "and the Son" after "the Holy Spirit ... who proceeds from the Father," was not accepted by the Coptic Orthodox Church.

Coptic Orthodox Theology in a New Diction

The Arab conquest of Egypt of 641 consigned the Copts to political and religious isolation from western Christianity, though not from the rest of the eastern Christians who came to share Arabic as a common language. The theological vocabulary and the whole heritage had to be translated from Greek and Coptic into Arabic. In this massive linguistic shift themes such as the oneness of the nature of Christ and the oneness of the Trinity and the Godhead were still discussed, but in addition the faith had to be defended against Islam. The composition of Biblical commentaries, characteristic of Alexandria, continued. Theologians like the tenth-century bishop Sawīrus ibn al-Muqaffa‘ were pioneers in writing theological treatises in the Arabic language and engaging in inter-religious dialogues with the Melkites, Jews, and Muslims (Ebied and Young 1975; Chébli 1909).

By the time of Sawīrus ibn al-Muqaffa‘, the key points of contention in the theological debates between Chalcedonians and non-Chalcedonians were more clearly understood, at least in the Christian East. It became clear that there was no agreement about the meaning or use of certain theological terms, such as hypostasis or person, nature, and essence, just to mention a few. We have already observed that by the sixth century the debate about the definition of terms was already heated. Later, however, it became important to define theological terms before delving into any theological topic. Arabic-speaking Christian scholars, whether Copts, Syrians, or Melkites, came to be well versed in Aristotelian logic thanks to Syrian monastics who translated the whole philosophical corpus from Greek and Syriac into Arabic. Coptic scholars defined all theological terms using Aristotelian logic as a common foundation shared by all Christians of the East, as well as educated Arabs who were introduced to philosophy. A major rhetorical shift thus emerged with the linguistic shift. Coptic writers would begin a treatise with a lengthy introduction defining terms before defending the oneness of the nature of Christ or the oneness of the Trinity. The use of this rhetorical tool can be traced up through the nineteenth century. But this does not mean that Scriptural arguments were abandoned; thus, fourteenth century Coptic scholars like Ibn Kabar and Ibn al-Makīn clarified the term hypostasis by referring to Hebrews 1:3, in which there is no division in the hypostasis of the Incarnate Son who purified us from our sins and who sat in glory on the right hand of the majesty (Samir 1971: 44; Ibn al-Makīn 1999: 256). Such arguments show these theologians' command of the Biblical text in both Greek and Coptic. Besides these features, most Coptic writers would include a chapter or more elucidating the Nicene Creed. Since following Chalcedon additions to the Nicene Creed were a point of contention, with the argument that the Nicene Creed contains all the tenets of the faith, elucidation of the Nicene Creed became normative for Coptic theology for the education of the Coptic laity and for the defense of the faith against the Chalcedonians (Samir 1971: 40–58; Chébli 1909: 143–61). Coptic scholars writing in Arabic preserved knowledge of patristic sources, which they often invoked. They were also well versed in Islamic thought and included refutations of Islam either within theological treatises or under separate titles. With colonization and later globalization, western churches began to rediscover the Christians of Egypt. There is great hope that ecumenical dialogue will eliminate centuries of misunderstanding, correct false accusations, overcome historical memory, and create more understanding between east and west in a world that is getting smaller with modernity.

Notes

1 It should be noted that Nestorius chose to speak about the union of "prosopa" (meaning persons), Cyril chose to speak about the union of "natures according to the hypostasis," while Leo speaks about the union of "formae" or "hypostases" (meaning persons).

2 Refer to the chapter on the Greek Literature of the Copts for more references.

Selected Bibliography

Athanasius of Alexandria, *Contra Arianos.*

——*Letter to Epictetus.*

——(2008) *On the Incarnation*, New York: St Vladimir Orthodox Theological Seminary [reference to section number]

Bindley, T. H. (1980) *The Oecumenical Documents of the Faith*, Westport, Connecticut: Greenwood Press.

Chébli, P. (1909) *Réfutation de Sa'īd Ibn-Batriq (Eutychius); Le Livre des Conciles*, Paris: Patrologia Orientalis, 3.

Cyril of Alexandria, *Third Letter to Nestorius*.
——(1874) *The Commentary on St. John*, vol. 1, trans. P. Pusey, Oxford: James Parker.
——(1885) *The Commentary on St. John*, vol. 2, trans. T. Randell, Oxford: James Parker.
——(1983) *Commentary on the Gospel of St. Luke*, trans. R. P. Smith, Astoria, NY: Studion Publishers.
——(1987) *Letters 1–50*, trans. J. I. McEnerney, Washington: Catholic University of America Press.
——(1987) *Letters 51–110*, trans. J. I. McEnerney, Washington: Catholic University of America Press.
——(1995) *On the Unity of Christ*, trans. J. A. McGuckin, New York: St Vladimir's Seminary Press.
Ebied, R. Y. and Young, M. J. L. (1975) *The Lamp of the Intellect of Severus ibn al-Muqaffa' Bishop of al-Ashmūnain*, Louvain: Corpus Scriptorum Christianorum Orientalium, 365–66, Scriptores arabici, 32–33.
Ebied, R. Y. and Wickham, L. R. (1985) "Timothy Aelurus: Against the Definition of the Council of Chalcedon," in C. Laga, J. A. Munitiz, and L. Van Rompay (eds) *After Chalcedon: Studies in Theology and Church History offered to Professor Albert Van Roey for His Seventieth Birthday*, Louvain: Orientalia Lovanienisia Analecta, 18.
Ibn al-Makīn (1999) *al-Mawsu'ā al-lahutiyya al-shahīra bī al-ḥāwī*, ed. A Monk from the Monastery of al-Muḥarraq, vol. 2, Cairo: Dār Nwbār.
Leo of Rome, *Letter to Flavian*, Letter 28. Also known as the Tome.
——*Letter to Julian Bishop of Cos*, Letter 35.
——*Letter to the Clergy and People of the City of Constantinople*, Letter 59.
——*Letter to the Synod of Chalcedon*, Letter 93.
——*Letter to the Monks of Palestine*, Letter 124.
Nau, M. F. (1903) "Histoire de Dioscore Patriarche d'Alexandrie, ecrit par son disciple Theopiste," *Journal Asiatique*, 10(1): 1–108 (Syriac), 241–310 (French).
Price, R. and Gaddis, M. (trans. and eds) (2005) *The Acts of the Council of Chalcedon*, 3 vols, Liverpool: Liverpool University Press.
Russell, N. (2007) *Theophilus of Alexandria*, London: Routledge.
Samir, S. K. (1971) *Miṣbāḥ al-ẓulmah fi 'īḍāḥ al-khidmah li-l-qiss Shams al-Riyāsa Abū al-Barakāt al-ma'rūf b-ibn Kabar*, Cairo: Maktabat al-Kārūz.
Tanner, N. P. (1990) *Decrees of the Ecumenical Councils*, vol. 1, Washington, D.C.: Georgetown University Press.
Timothy Aelurus (1919) *Extraits du Timothée Aelure XI-XVI*, ed. F. Nau, Paris: Patrologia Orientalis, 13.

8 Monasticism

Living Scripture and Theological Orthodoxy

Lois M. Farag

Monasticism is a response to Christ's call to "follow me" and "be perfect" (Luke 18:22, Matt 5:48). The Samaritan woman "left her water jar" and followed him; Andrew and Peter immediately left their nets and followed him; and the Virgin Mary and John followed him to the Cross, disregarding threats against their lives. Calls, when accepted, usually include sacrifice and renunciation. Monasticism is the story of the varying calls to follow Christ and to be perfect as the heavenly Father is perfect. Christ demonstrated his love for humanity by his Incarnation and the Cross; those who follow him reciprocate this love by renouncing everything for his sake. This chapter is the story of those who loved God more than themselves; it is the story of monasticism. It is a synopsis of the beginning of the monastic way of life, its development in Egypt to the present day, and its role in the life of the faithful and the church.

The Beginning of Monasticism

At first, Egyptian men and women who responded to the call to follow Christ lived a prayerful life in their family homes, rented lodgings, or lived on the outskirts of their towns. There is enough documentation in papyri of complaints, from either landlords or tenants, that indicate that the tenant was a monastic (Bagnall and Raffaella 2006: 200). A legal document from the fourth century informs us of a certain Ammonios, an *apotaktikos* (a renouncer), whose heirs disputed the inheritance. Another informs us of two sisters, Theodora and Tauris, *monachai apotaktikai* (female monastic renouncers), who leased the basement of their property (Goehring 1999: 20–26, 53–72). Athanasius' *Discourse on Virginity* is addressed to women living in their homes as monastics. Athanasius advises them to read Scripture, pray the psalms, and work to support themselves, and he calls this an "angelic" life. Such monastic renouncers who lived an ascetic life of prayer within towns or cities began to form an alternative lifestyle. All monastics were ascetics but not all ascetics were monastics.

A certain Antony (251–356) was contemplating his life after the death of his parents. He entered church one Sunday and heard the gospel reading from Matt 19:21: If you want to be perfect, sell your possessions for a treasure in heaven and "follow me." Antony considered this a personal message from God and sold most of his possessions. When he visited the church again he heard the gospel message from Matt 6:34: "Do not worry about tomorrow." He left the church, gave away the rest of his possessions, and entrusted his sister to a group of women living a life of prayer and contemplation similar to the *monachai apotaktikai* (female monastic renouncers). Antony first lived in front of his house, and then moved to the outskirts of his village to emulate the lifestyle of another monk living the life of solitude and renunciation. Antony started as an *apotaktikos*, a monk living in his house, then outside his village. But then he did something very different, he went to the desert and eventually became "the founder of monasticism," though there were many monastics before him. By the early fourth century, the term monastic (*monachos* for a male monastic or *monache* for a female monastic) described those living a solitary life regardless of location. With the development of various monastic lifestyles, the term began to be qualified in various ways: with *apotaktikos* to indicate one living in the city; anchorites or semi-anchorites for those living an eremitical lifestyle; cenobites for those living in community, usually close to towns or cities; with many other monastic variations in between.

Many heard of Antony and followed him into the desert. They sought his advice, whether spiritual or otherwise, thus redefining the role of the monastic as spiritual leader and guide. Not all who sought his advice returned to the city; some of the men were so influenced by his life and spirituality that they decided to live close to him and to constantly seek his counsel. The first monastic community with a father or monastic leader at its center emerged; it became the nucleus of the present day Monastery of St. Antony in the eastern Egyptian desert near the Red Sea. Another monastic community sprouted up near the grave of Paul the Hermit, whom Antony befriended and later buried. The Monastery of St. Paul has been closely connected to the Monastery of St. Antony, which is about thirty kilometers northwest of it. Two of Antony's disciples, St. Macarius and St. Amoun, were founders of monastic communities in the western desert of Egypt.

Abba Macarius (c. 300–c. 390), also known as Macarius the Spiritbearer, lived for some years as an anchorite on the outskirts of his village after his wife's death. He was falsely accused of impregnating a woman and when his innocence was proven he left the village for Scetis, in the northwestern desert of Egypt. Living as an anchorite in the desert, he fell victim to many thoughts and decided to seek counsel from Antony. During the second visit, Antony clothed Macarius with the monastic *schema* (or habit). Macarius remained with Antony as his disciple until Antony died; he buried him and returned to Scetis. People began gathering around Macarius; he offered them spiritual guidance and put them to work to support themselves. As the number of his disciples grew, Macarius built a church to serve the monks, who still preserved their solitary discipline. These disciples, while maintaining the solitary lifestyle, began to form their own monastic groups. By the time Macarius died at the age of ninety-five he had laid the monastic foundations of Scetis (Vivian 2004). Presently, there are four active monasteries in Scetis (present day Wadī al-Naṭrūn): the Monastery of al-Barāmūs, the Monastery of the Virgin Mary (commonly known as that of the Syrians), the Monastery of St. Bishoi, and the Monastery of St. Macarius.

Figure 8.1 The Monastery of St. Antony in the eastern desert [photograph by Lois M. Farag]

Figure 8.2 The Monastery of St. Paul in the eastern desert [photograph by Lois M. Farag]

Figure 8.3 The Monastery of the Virgin Mary (commonly known as al-Barāmūs), Wādī al-Naṭrūn [photograph by Lois M. Farag]

Figure 8.4 The Monastery of St. Bishoi, Wādī al-Naṭrūn [photograph by Lois M. Farag]

Figure 8.5 The Monastery of the Virgin Mary (commonly known as that of the Syrians), Wādī al-Naṭrūn [photograph by Lois M. Farag]

Figure 8.6 The Monastery of St. Mena, Maryūt [photograph by Lois M. Farag]

Figure 8.7 The Monastery of St. Mercurius for women in Old Cairo [photograph by Lois M. Farag]

Abba Amoun, another of Antony's disciples, went to the Mountain of Nitria in the western Egyptian desert, and lived there for twenty-two years. People began gathering around Abba Amoun and Nitrian monasticism was founded. Palladius, an early visitor to the Egyptian desert, claims the monks there had reached 5,000 in number (Palladius and Meyer 1964: 41–43; Russell 1980: 111). Though the accuracy of the number is debated, it indicates that Nitria was crowded with monks. Upon the advice of Abba Antony, Amoun decided to establish another monastic center at Kellia (or the Cells) to accommodate the growing number of monks. The new center was twelve miles away; it was close enough for the monks to benefit from the liturgical services of Nitria and far enough to preserve their solitary lifestyle.

In Upper Egypt, St. Pachomius (c. 292–346) and later St. Shenoute (348–466) organized the monastic lifestyle of the *Koinonia* (Greek for common life), or cenobitism, for those who did not have the physical or spiritual stamina to live in solitude. This lifestyle provides a spiritual milieu where seekers can achieve their spiritual aspirations without anxiety and receive spiritual support from other members of the community. After Pachomius built his first monastery at Tabennesi, in southern Egypt, his sister Mary joined him and built a monastery for women close to his (Veilleux 1980). The *Koinonia* model was successful during the lifetime of Pachomius and thousands joined his monasteries, of which there were nine for men and two for women. Abba Shenoute joined his uncle, Abba Pjol, who was a monk and archimandrite of what would become the White Monastery. After the death of his uncle in 385, Shenoute succeeded him and became archimandrite. He formed a federation of three monasteries that hosted about 2,200 men and 1,800 women monastics. This required some building projects, including a large church attended by monastics of both genders. The Shenoute federation followed the *Koinonia* model in a more strict fashion and with a different monastic philosophy. The Shenoute system offered the opportunity for monastics living in *Koinonia* to withdraw to the desert and live in seclusion without severing their ties to the monastery, thus remaining dependent on the monastery for support. This system preserved the eremitical ethos of Coptic monasticism, an ethos preserved to this day in the communal monastic tradition of twenty-first century Coptic monasticism. The Shenoute federation exhibited interest in social issues; for example, they would distribute bread to the villagers during famine, or secure the release of captives from invading Blemmyes (Bell 1989: 50, 68). The federation was also a literary center with a large library, for Shenoute himself was well versed in both Greek and Coptic.

This list of monastic figures and centers might give the impression that monasticism in Egypt was only in these centers. The thirteenth-century *Churches and Monasteries of Egypt* mentions 181 autonomous monasteries. The Coptic Encyclopedia, under "Dayr" (monastery) mentions 176 autonomous monasteries. Monasticism spread from the Monastery of the Enaton and the communities of Syncletica and Dimyānah on the Mediterranean, on the very northern edge of Egypt, to that of Abba Aaron near Aswan on the very southern border (see map 3). The Enaton monastic center (Dayr al-Zujāj) began around the end of the third century and was located near the ninth milestone west of Alexandria. It was a conglomeration of individual cells and monastic gatherings that surrounded the cell of a holy charismatic monastic; it played an important role during the Chalcedonian debate (Atiya 1991: 954–58). On the eastern side of the Mediterranean, a certain Dimyānah, daughter of Marcus, the governor of the district of Burullus near the modern city of Damietta, asked her father to build her a house where she could retire to read Scripture and pray. Her father consented and soon forty other women joined her. During the persecution of Emperor Diocletian (284–305), Marcus agreed to offer incense to the idols. Dimyānah urged him to acknowledge his Christian faith. When it was known that Marcus had recanted at his daughter's urging, Dimyānah was tortured and then executed. She was martyred with the other forty women who joined her. Her life is documented in the Coptic Synaxarium under 13 Ṭūbah. This is an example of a small monastic community funded by a rich patron, in this case Dimyānah's father. The women's monastic community of Saint Syncletica on the outskirts of Alexandria has a similar history. There we have information about the founder, but the history of the community vanishes into oblivion (Bongie and Schaffer 2001). Many other communities, especially for women, were formed through the patronage of wealthy Christians but disappeared, either because the funding dried up, because the charismatic founder died, or because persecution annihilated the monastic inhabitants. It is a pattern that would be repeated through history.

At the very southern border of Egypt, at Aswan, we hear about a certain Abba Aaron who after a life-threatening experience vowed to become a monk. When his life was spared, he went to Scetis. His parents were tracking him to sway his mind, so he went south and eventually arrived at the very southern Egyptian border at Aswan. People began to visit him and he cured their sick. Gradually, his fame spread and a new community was formed (Paphnutius 1993: 114–41). Numerous other communities emerged around charismatic, holy, and pious monastic figures whose fame led to the foundation of local monastic communities such as those at Asyūt, Naqlūn, Qalamūn, al-Ashmūnayn, Akhmīm, Dakhla Oasis, Fayyūm, Samālūt, and Saqqara, just to name a few.

The monastic way of life attracted thousands of Egyptian men and women. The *Historia Monachorum* describes the city of Oxyrhychus (present day al-Bahnasa) at the end of the fourth century as a city "full of monasteries"; the bishop of the city claimed there were 30,000 monastics, two-thirds of them women (Russell 1980: 67). Scholars debate the authenticity of such numbers, but they indicate that significant numbers of men and women were attracted to the monastic life. Antony became the quintessential model of monasticism, even for the *Koinonia* model. Many followed his example, living in crevices of the earth as anchorites, or in rooms in a village, or in isolated huts outside the village. When people perceived the saintly life of a monastic, word spread among neighboring cities and eventually followers settled around him and a new monastic community emerged. This was repeated all over Egypt. The forms of monastic living were as varied as the number of monastic gatherings that appeared. This was how monasticism started, developed, and spread throughout Egypt.

The Monastic *Politeia* or Way of Life

Athanasius describes Antony's *politeia* (way of life) as following an ascetic discipline, supporting himself through work to meet his basic necessities, giving away anything left over to those who were in need, praying unceasingly, and reading and memorizing Scripture (*Life of Antony* 3.5). He describes the daily rhythm of the monks gathered around Antony as follows:

> So there were in the mountains monastic dwellings like tents filled with heavenly choirs singing psalms, studying the Bible, fasting, praying, rejoicing in the hope of the things to come, working in order to give alms, having love for each other and being in harmony with one another.
> (*Life of Antony* 44.2)

The Life of Pachomius describes the monastic rule based on those "who went before us," that is, earlier tradition: to spend the night in prayer and reciting Scripture, to work to provide for the daily subsistence while giving the rest to the poor, to follow an ascetic discipline, fasting till evening, never eating oil or cooked meats or drinking wine. As to prayer, the rule gives a detailed description of the *synaxis* (prayers of the monastic gathering) and unceasing prayer (Veilleux 1980: 31). In addition, Pachomius "did not want any clerics in his monastery, for fear of jealousy and vainglory" (ibid. 47). The *Life of Shenoute* says that he lived as an anchorite, persevered in the recitation of Scripture, and practiced great asceticism, fasting for a week at a time and the whole of Great Lent, spending day and night in prayer, and sleeping only at daybreak (Bell 1989: 45–46).

Antony's monastic way of life represents the foundational pattern of monastic living in Egypt. It became the model to emulate whether one was an anchorite, a semi-anchorite, living a communal life, or in any other form of monastic life. From the various descriptions of diverse monastic settings common themes and daily rhythms emerge. Daily activities were divided among work, prayer, studying Scripture, singing psalms, fasting, giving alms, loving your neighbor as yourself, pursuing virtue, and striving for the heavenly kingdom. In the semi-anchoritic lifestyle, the monastic would spend Monday to Friday in solitude. The monk would wake up at dawn for morning prayers, and then start his daily work, mostly basket weaving, during which his heart and thoughts were engaged in memorizing and contemplating Biblical verses, and prayer. At three in the afternoon the monk would have his first meal. The monk then resumed his work and prayer till bedtime. On Saturdays and Sundays he attended the liturgy and partook of the Eucharist, after which the brothers would eat an agape meal together. Saturday night would be spent primarily in chanting psalms and prayer. The weekend gathering was an opportunity for monks to ask the elders for advice, exchange spiritual experiences, and check on each other. Thus, the Eucharistic gathering was at the center of the monastic structure; the whole week revolved around the Sabbath meeting, where the monks would get their spiritual needs met. At the end of the weekend, each monk would exchange his weekly work product for bread, water, utensils for basket weaving, and other supplies needed to sustain him during the following week.

The Pachomian communal system required all to pray, fast, follow ascetical practices, and work in large scale economic projects; hence, the monk was not to worry about or be responsible for selling his work product. For example, the monk would farm, or might work at the central bakery, which provided bread for the whole community, rather than worry about his personal bread portion. It has to be noted that such communal activity, such as baking or farming, was to be done in silence so that the monk could still be engaged in contemplation on his memorized Biblical passages and personal unceasing prayers. Eating the meal in community was also done in silence and conversation in general was controlled to escape the trap of unending gossip within communities. The solitary ethos, in spite of the *Koinonia*'s engagement in large scale economic enterprise, was still the prevailing monastic ideal. It should be noted that the Pachomian rule does not include the taking of vows. There are still no vows in the Coptic monastic rite, as is customary in the Latin rite of consecration; nevertheless, the monastic is still bound for life to live the monastic lifestyle.

When the Emperor Justinian (r. 527–65) and the Chalcedonian Church hierarchy attempted to force the Pachomian monks to adhere to the Chalcedonian faith many of them refused to succumb to their threats and left their monasteries. This eventually led to the destruction of the *Koinonia* monastic system (Goehring 1999: 139, 241–61 and Kuhn 1978). The Shenoute monastic model, which was very similar to that of Pachomius, lasted for less than 1,000 years. Smaller, independent monasteries survived, however. But the destruction of the Pachomian monasteries and the later demise of the Shenoute monasteries had implications for the Coptic monastic *politeia*, reinforcing the significance of the anchoritic and semi-anchoritic system within Coptic monasticism. By the ninth century, the anchorites of Scetis as well as those in the eastern desert had to retreat behind walls for protection from recurring tribal attacks. But this retreat behind walls should not be understood as an adoption of the communal system.

The Seventh to the Nineteenth Century

The ups and downs of monasticism reflected the ups and downs of the political and socioeconomic upheavals in Egypt. Prior to the fifth century, monasticism flourished in Egypt. Its fame resounded in the wider world and many came to see and learn from the wisdom of Coptic monastics. From the middle of the fifth century, after the Council of Chalcedon (451), the imperial hierarchy made every effort to subject the Coptic monastics to the new Chalcedonian position with the aim of subduing Egypt. The violent persecution that ensued led to the scattering of the monks, or their resistance unto death, and the end of the Pachomian system. But monastics were instrumental in preserving the Orthodox faith and protecting the lives of the Coptic patriarchs. By the middle of the seventh century the Arabs invaded Egypt and the dynamics of persecution changed. The following is a sample of pivotal events that marked the ups and downs in the history of monasticism for the following twelve centuries.

The Copts suffered greatly from natural as well as man-made disasters. The obligation of monastics to pay excessive tributes to Arab rulers was one of the earliest blows that affected monasticism in the eighth century. Under the Fatimid Caliph al-Hakim bi-'Amr Allah (r. 996–1020) most Coptic churches and monasteries were closed and many were destroyed. Later, the Crusaders' invasion of Egypt led to a backlash on the Copts (Lyster 2008: 46). Egypt suffered from the Black Death (1347) and the anti-Dhimmi measures of 1354, which were equally devastating (ibid. 49). These are examples of events that led to the decline of the Christian population in general and, consequently, the monastic population. In some cases they led to the emptying of some of the monasteries. For example, the Monastery of Anba Hidrā (known in the west as the Monastery of St. Simeon) in Aswan, which was built in the fifth century, was destroyed in the eighth century, rebuilt in the tenth century, and finally destroyed by the thirteenth century (Dāūd 2003: 184). The Monastery of St. Shenoute was in ruins by 1365, but was repopulated in 1995 (Dāūd 2006: 104). The story of Coptic monasticism is the story of the Coptic community's constant resurgence.

By the thirteenth century there was a revival in the Coptic community in which the Monastery of St. Antony took a leading role, demonstrated by artwork produced by the artist Theodore and his team, which has been preserved to the present day. This renewal was accompanied by a massive literary activity in manuscript production. By the fifteenth century the monastery was in decline. Some scholars suggest that this decline was caused by a massacre of monks in 1484, others think the Bedouin attacks were the cause. The sixteenth century witnessed the revival, reconstruction, and repopulation of the monastery. By the early nineteenth century, the Bedouins disrupted monastery caravans and the monks faced many hardships. To protect the monastery from the continuous attacks, the walls were extended to incorporate more land and the water spring (Bolman 2002: 173–75).

The Monastery of St. Paul shared in the thirteenth century revival but by the fifteenth century the monastery fell into ruins and the Bedouins looted most of its contents. In the eighteenth century the monastery was repopulated. The Cave Church was enlarged, a mill room was built, and the walls and the keep were repaired. The woodwork of the monastery churches was completed and endowments (*waqf*-statements) were allotted to the monastery through the generosity of Coptic archons. The library was rebuilt, which was accompanied by manuscript production. The renovations included the painting program of the Cave Church (Lyster 2008: 52–59, 241).

Scetis suffered about seven barbarian attacks from the fifth to the eleventh century and each one of them almost annihilated monasticism there. But then the monks would return and repopulate the monasteries again. By the fifteenth century Scetis was so weakened that it could not provide popes for the church as was customary. It was during that time that the Coptic church began to depend more on the eastern desert Monastery of St. Antony for its leaders (Bolman 2002: 174). Other monastic communities have provided leaders for the church. For example, during the fourteenth and fifteenth century the Monastery of al-Muḥarraq in Upper Egypt provided five popes, while one pope came from al-Qalamūn.

Monastic revival also has to be credited to influential Coptic lay members, known as archons. Without their social influence, financial support, and zeal for the Coptic church, hardly any of these revivals could have taken place. They contributed not only to monasteries but to churches, art, literature, and the general well-being of the Coptic community. In the case of monasteries, they helped in the building and renovation of the physical structure and the church paintings and woodwork; they financed the copying of manuscripts; and they granted endowments to the monasteries. The painting program of the Church of St. Antony (1232–33) was created by a team of Coptic artists lead by Theodore and was funded by thirty archons (ibid. 37). Some archons were interested in one venue or another, but the generosity towards the churches and monasteries of Egypt of one particular archon, Ibrahim al-Jawhari, has surpassed all others.

Coptic monasticism hosted foreigners from its very inception. Foreigners from all over the Roman Empire came to the Egyptian monasteries; we are indebted to many of their writings for our knowledge of the early history of monasticism. These visitors included such figures as John Cassian and Palladius. After the fifth century foreign residents were primarily non-Chalcedonians. The Monastery of St. Antony alone hosted Syrians, Ethiopians, and Armenians (ibid. 175–78). The presence of Syrian monks is well attested in Scetis and, in particular, in Dayr al-Suryān, but also in the Monastery of Epiphanius of Thebes (Winlock and Crum 1926: 140). Ethiopian monastics lived in many of the Coptic monasteries of both men and women. They considered the monasteries of Scetis and al-Muḥarraq, where the holy family resided for some time during their flight to Egypt, to be holy places. They also thought of Coptic monasteries as pilgrimage stops on their way to Jerusalem. Present oral tradition within Coptic monasteries still preserves their memory. Ethiopian monastics were engaged in an active literary program of copying and translating many manuscripts into Ge'ez. Some of the original Coptic manuscripts disappeared and are preserved only in translation.

The Role of Monasticism in the Coptic Orthodox Church

Monasticism is a spiritual force in Coptic society. From its inception it attracted thousands of Christians who aspired to live a life that would bring them closer to God. The faithful sought advice from monastics, not only in spiritual matters but in most matters of life, and returned to their homes transformed. The sayings of the early desert fathers and mothers, known as the *Apophthegmata Patrum* (Sayings of the Desert Fathers) or Paradise of the Fathers, were written down for future generations to benefit from their wisdom. These sayings are still a principal source of monastic wisdom in Coptic monasteries. The global fame of the desert fathers and mothers of Egypt has attracted foreigners from the fourth century to the present day. Recently, western scholars have shown an interest in the writings of the Coptic monks, whether from a literary or spiritual perspective, which has come to be known in western literature as "Desert Spirituality." As for the Coptic Church, monastic spirituality has influenced lay spirituality in many ways, including fasting, the centrality of Scripture, the use of the monastic prayers of the hours (*Agpeya*) as the daily prayers of the faithful, just to mention a few. In addition, many laypeople have monastics as their spiritual guides.

Historically, monasticism represented theological orthodoxy within the Coptic Orthodox Church, starting with Antony himself. When the Arians claimed that Antony held their views he left the desert for Alexandria and publicly denounced the Arian heresy (*Life of Antony* 69–70). When Athanasius was exiled for his strong stand against Arianism, he "retreated once more into the desert," indicating that monastics offered him refuge more than once (Socrates, *Hist. eccl.* 14). From the early years of monasticism, monastics were an important part of the theological dialogue. Cyril of Alexandria's first letter was addressed to the "fathers of monks and to those practicing the solitary life," who are described as "firm in the faith of God." Cyril thought the solitaries should be aware of and participate in the theological debate engulfing the Church. Shenoute made it clear that he was on the side of Cyril of Alexandria and against Nestorius.

When the Chalcedonian debate escalated, emperors and Chalcedonian ecclesiastical authorities made every attempt to control the monasteries, knowing well that by controlling the monastics' theological stance they could control the faith of the church. When Emperor Justinian (r. 527–65) attempted to force monks living in the Pachomian *Koinonia* to adhere to the Chalcedonian faith, many of them left their monasteries, following the head of the central monastery of Pbow, Abba Abraham, who refused to accept the Chalcedonian faith and succumb to the threat of the emperor (Goehring 1999: 241–61). Not only were monks dispersed from their monasteries, but as Stephen, the narrator of the life of Apollo, informs us, there were martyrs who witnessed to the non-Chalcedonian faith (Kuhn 1978: 26). Persecution, martyrdom, and the scattering of monks from their monasteries eventually led to the demise of the *Koinonia.* Emperor Heraclius (r. 610–34) assigned Cyrus, bishop of Phasis in the Caucasus, to be both patriarch and prefect in Alexandria, and thus exercise full control of the religious, military, and political forces of Egypt. *The Life of Samuel of Kalamun* (or Qalamūn) informs the readers that Cyrus pursued the fleeing Coptic Pope Benjamin through the monasteries of Scetis, torturing the monks to get information about Benjamin's whereabouts and forcing them to sign and accept the Chalcedonian faith. The *Life* explains this was "because it was on those elders [meaning the monks] that the entire country of Egypt depended" (Alcock 1983: 80); if they could sway the monastics the laity would follow. Samuel, a monk in Scetis, was flogged and tortured, losing an eye, while John, the priest of Scetis, fled. When Samuel fled to another monastic community in the Naqlūn, he was pursued and again tortured along with the monks of Naqlūn.

Monasteries became a theological battleground and the stronghold that preserved church orthodoxy. During the Chalcedonian persecution, monasteries became the patriarchal residence. Again, when for nine years Caliph al-Hakim bi-'Amr Allah (r. 996–1020) forbade Copts to celebrate the liturgy, the monasteries in the desert preserved the daily celebration of the liturgy. Monasteries also preserved the literary, artistic, and other aspects of the Coptic heritage. These examples demonstrate the pivotal role monastics and monasteries played in preserving the church, the Coptic Orthodox faith, and, I might even add, the Coptic ethos itself.

Coptic monasteries preserved the Coptic theological, literary, and spiritual heritage; they also provided the church with the ecclesiastical hierarchy. In the Coptic Orthodox Church, bishops and popes are selected from among the monastics. Monasticism provides the church with its leaders, and it is these leaders who influence the theology, spirituality, and formation of the next generation of laity and local leaders, i.e. priests, and the trajectory of the church in general. The last two popes of the Coptic church, Pope Cyril VI (r. 1959–71) and Pope Shenoute III (r. 1971–2012), were solitaries, which reflects the relationship the laity have even with the monastics living in solitude.

The Modern Era

Coptic monasticism is witnessing a revival, led by visionary leaders, which started in the late 1940s and early 1950s for men and in the early 1960s for women monastics. Monasteries have been renovated, rebuilt, modernized, and expanded to accommodate the growing number of monastics. Some ancient monasteries, such as the monasteries of St. Shenoute, have been repopulated. Coptic monasteries are not confined to Egypt anymore; with the more global Coptic presence, Coptic monasteries are now found in Europe, the United States, Australia, and Asia. Many of the men and women joining the monasteries are college graduates and are keen to rekindle the Coptic monastic and spiritual heritage. Monasteries are spiritual centers where the laity spend time for spiritual guidance and contemplation, and this has revived the spirituality of the whole Coptic church.

Modernization has impacted the monastic *politeia*. The traditional basket weaving and manuscript copying are obsolete industries and not self-sustaining. In addition, monasteries have acquired land around the ancient monastic sites to provide more security and protection from encroaching building projects. This has required farming the desert on a large scale and conforming to land reclamation laws; every effort has to be exerted to make such agricultural projects successful. Monastery rebuilding, renovations, and large scale projects such as farming require a large workforce, which necessitates the total participation of the whole monastic community. For all these practical reasons, Coptic monasteries have adopted a more communal *politeia*, while preserving the semi-anchoritic and anchoritic ethos of the Coptic tradition. Monastic *politeia* was also affected by modern highways that made desert monasteries very accessible to visitors; the era of traveling for days to reach the desert monasteries is gone. Scetis is ninety minutes' drive from Cairo, making it possible for some to attend the morning liturgy with the monks. The modern era has witnessed an unprecedented monastic revival on the spiritual as well as the physical level, and this was achieved within one monastic generation. The story of this revival is still in progress and it will surely leave its stamp on history.

Monasticism is a major component of the Coptic Orthodox heritage. It has had its ups and downs, reflecting the fate of the Coptic community, but it has never disappeared. Its capacity for constant renewal despite socioeconomic and political factors is the source of its strength and the strength of the Coptic heritage. Coptic monasticism has always produced visionaries who have preserved, sustained, enriched, and revived the Coptic heritage through the centuries. Monasticism is at the heart of Coptic Orthodoxy.

Selected Bibliography

Abu Salih the Armenian (2001) *The Churches and Monasteries of Egypt*, trans. B. T. A. Evetts, New Jersey, NJ: Gorgias Press.

Alcock, A. (1983) *The Life of Samuel of Kalamun by Isaac the Presbyter*, Warminster, England: Aris & Phillips.

Atiya, A. (1991) *The Coptic Encyclopedia*, s.v. "Dayr," New York: Macmillan.

Bagnall, R. and Raffaella, C. (2006) *Women's Letters from Ancient Egypt 300 BC–AD 800*, Ann Arbor: University of Michigan Press.

Bell, D. (trans.) (1989) *Besa, The Life of Shenoute*, Kalamazoo, MI: Cistercian Publications.

Bolman, E. (2002) *Monastic Visions, Wall Paintings in the Monastery of St. Antony at the Red Sea*, New Haven and London: Yale University Press.

Bongie, E. B. and Schaffer, M. (2001) *The Life & Regimen of the Blessed & Holy Syncletica*, Toronto: Peregrina.

Dāūd, N. K. (2003) *Tārīkh al-Masīḥīyya wa Āthārhā fi Aswān wa al-Nūba*, Cairo: Saint Mark Institute for Coptic History Studies.

——(2006) *Tārīkh al-Masīḥīyya wa al-Rahbana fi Ibrūshīyyati Sūhāj wa Akhmīm*, Cairo: Saint Mark Institute for Coptic History Studies.

Evelyn-White, H. G. and Hauser, W. (1973) *The Monasteries of the Wadi 'n Natrūn*. New York, Metropolitan Museum of Art, Egyptian Expedition, 1926-[33]. New York: Arno Press.

Farag, L. (2009) "Beyond their Gender: Contemporary Coptic Female Monasticism," *Journal of World Christianity*, 2(1): 111–44.

Gabra, G. (2002) *Coptic Monasteries, Egypt's Monastic Art and Architecture*, Cairo: The American University in Cairo Press.

Goehring, J. E. (1999) *Ascetics, Society, and the Desert*, PA: Trinity Press.

Harmless, W. (2004) *Desert Christians, An Introduction to the Literature of Early Monasticism*, New York: Oxford University Press.

Kuhn, K. H. (1978) *A Panegyric on Apollo Archimandrite of the Monastery of Isaac by Stephen Bishop of Heracleopolis Magna*, CSCO 395, Louvain: Secrétariat du CorpusSCO.

Lyster, W. (ed.) (2008) *The Cave Church of Paul the Hermit at the Monastery of St. Paul, Egypt*, New Haven and London: Yale University Press.

Palladius and Meyer, R. T. (1964) *Palladius: The Lausiac History*, New York: Paulist Press.

Paphnutius (1993) *Histories of the Monks of Upper Egypt and the Life of Onnophrius by Paphnutius*, trans. T. Vivian, Kalamazoo, MI: Cistercian Publications.

Rubenson, S. (ed.) (1995) *The Letters of St. Antony: Monasticism and the Making of a Saint*, Minneapolis: Fortress Press.

Russell, N. (trans.) (1980) *The Lives of the Desert Fathers: The Historia Monachorum in Aegypto*, Kalamazoo, MI: Cistercian Publications.

Socrates, *Ecclesiastical History* (*Historia ecclesiastica [Hist.eccl.]*).

Veilleux, A. (ed. and trans.) (1980) *Pachomian Koinonia, The Life of Saint Pachomius and His Disciples*, vol. 1, Kalamazoo, MI: Cistercian Publications.

Vivian, T. (ed.) (2004) *Saint Macarius, the Spiritbearer: Coptic Texts relating to Saint Macarius the Great*, New York: St. Vladimir Seminary Press.

Vivian, T. and Athanassakis, N. (trans.) (2003) *Athanasius of Alexandria, The Life of Antony: the Coptic Life and the Greek Life*, Kalamazoo, MI: Cistercian Publications.

Vivian, T. and Greer, R. (eds) (2004) *Four Desert Fathers: Pambo, Evagrius, Macarius of Egypt, and Macarius of Alexandria: Coptic Texts Relating to the Lausiac History of Palladius*, Crestwood, NY: St. Vladimir's Seminary Press.

Winlock, H. E. and Crum, W. E. (1926) *The Monastery of Epiphanius at Thebes*. New York: Arno Press.

9 Spirituality

In God's Presence

Lois M. Farag

Coptic Orthodox spirituality is liturgically centered, Biblically based, ascetically oriented, and culminates in a life of prayer and virtuous living. Liturgy and the liturgical calendar mark the rhythm of the Coptic life and unite the Coptic community around the world. Coptic spirituality is multifaceted, as the chapters of this book demonstrate, especially those on liturgy, monasticism, and music. The Eucharistic liturgy is the focal point that feeds and is fed by the spiritual life of the faithful. In preparation for the liturgy, a Copt reflects on his or her spiritual progress or lack thereof through prayer, meditating on Scripture, fasting, and confession. Other activities, such as church or community service, are also part of the spiritual life of the average Copt. Monastic spirituality is the spring that rejuvenates all these activities. The fruit of all these diverse spiritual activities is a life of Christian virtue. Virtue is the fruit of the Holy Spirit working in the Church and the life of the faithful. Coptic Orthodox spirituality stems from early Church traditions, which have been handed down from generation to generation and are manifested in present day practices. The constraints of this chapter require us to focus primarily on present day practices with limited references to their historical roots.

The liturgy and the liturgical calendar are at the heart of Coptic spirituality. The liturgical calendar sets the rhythm of Coptic life by fixing the dates for various fasts, feasts, and religious commemorations and prescribing the Eucharistic and seasonal hymns that accompany them. Attending church is not limited to the Sunday liturgy. All Coptic dioceses coordinate services so that within each vicinity there is a daily liturgy; even in small churches liturgy is held at least on Sundays, Wednesdays, and Fridays and for major liturgical commemorations. Pope Theophilus of Alexandria (r. 385–412) wrote: "Blessed are those who shall frequent the church daily, both morning and evening, and especially at the time of the receiving from the holy mysteries of the body and blood of the Lord Jesus Christ. For through these he shall become united to the angels in heaven, as he sees them face to face, and answers them mouth to mouth with their salutation of 'Alleluia'" (Russell 2007: 78). Cyril of Alexandria (r. 412–44), in his Second Sermon on Luke, also refers to the daily Eucharist. In the early thirteenth century, Buṭrus, bishop of Milīj, refuted the Melkites who accused the Copts of belittling the Eucharist by partaking of it daily (Samir

1971: 309) an indication that Copts were known for attending daily liturgies. Pope Cyril VI (r. 1959–71) is known to have celebrated the liturgy daily. Historically, there were periods when Copts were prevented from attending the liturgy, for example during the eleventh century, but presently Copts attempt to attend liturgy with vespers and matins as often as they can.

The liturgical day and services start the previous evening with the service of the evening Offering of Incense, followed in the morning by the morning Offering of Incense and the liturgy. After the evening offering the priest makes himself available to the faithful who want to repent and confess their sins in preparation for partaking of the Eucharistic mystery the following day; the priest is also available for confession most of the week. Confession helps the person to meditate on their conduct in preparation for repentance and spiritual progress. In most cases the priest acts as the spiritual director of the one who confesses. Others prefer to have a monastic for spiritual direction. Coptic spirituality has a monastic character which will be discussed further on.

Copts attending the liturgy refrain from all food and drink from midnight the night before. If it is a period of fasting, then they break the fast with food that does not contain any animal products, that is, a vegan diet. Fish is permitted during the fasts of Advent, the Apostles, and the Virgin Mary, though not during Great Lent or on Wednesdays and Fridays. A general overview of Coptic fasts would include these main markers: Before the Feast of the Nativity, i.e. Christmas, the Copts fast forty-three days; before the Feast of the Resurrection, fifty-five days. The Copts fast every Wednesday and Friday of the year except during the Easter season. They fast for fifteen days in August before the commemoration of the Assumption of the body of the Virgin Mary and a three-day Nineveh fast a fortnight before Great Lent. The fast before the feast of the Apostles Peter and Paul starts after Pentecost and lasts till the feast of the Apostles on July 12, so the length varies depending on the date of Pentecost. A simple tally would total an average of 240 days of fasting per year. That means Copts abstain from all animal products two-thirds of the year. Fasts include periods of abstinence from food determined after consultation with the spiritual director. This fasting regimen is currently observed by the laity, young and old, and is not limited to monastics or clerics. The liturgical calendar establishes the rhythm of family life since dietary constraints impact when Copts celebrate private events. There are no weddings during fasting days.

Fasting is preparation for receiving the gifts of the Spirit. Thus Copts fast from midnight before partaking of the Eucharist in preparation for receiving the gift of the remission of sins, the gift of life, immortality, and eternal life. They fast before the Feast of the Nativity to dwell on the mystery of the Incarnation and the role of the Virgin Mary in this mystery, and during Great Lent, before the Feast of the Resurrection, to meditate on Christ overcoming death and granting salvation and renewal of life to the faithful. Before all feasts of the Church, the Copts fast in preparation for and in contemplation of the mystery. Fasting fosters discipline, penance, renunciation, and attentiveness to the Spirit. When the Copts face persecution or hard times, the whole church fasts even on days when no fasting is prescribed by the calendar. The Copts believe God's promise that with fasting and prayer they can overcome all adversaries ("But this kind never comes out except by prayer and fasting," Matt 17:21). Coptic spirituality is ascetically oriented.

Prayer, and unceasing prayer, is at the center of Coptic spirituality and is often accompanied by fasting. The laity daily observe the *Horologion* or *Agpeya*, the prayer of the hours. The *Agpeya*, discussed in greater length in Chapter 10, is prayed twice, once in a communal form during the liturgy and once privately. As the liturgical calendar marks the rhythm of the year, the *Agpeya* marks the rhythm of the day. Throughout the day the *Agpeya* guides the faithful, through the selection of psalms and accompanying prayers, to contemplate on the Trinity, Christ's salvific act, the work of the Holy Spirit within their daily life, and the life of virtue and righteousness. The faithful start their day contemplating the Resurrection, newness of life, and the life of new beginnings; with the rising sun they meditate on Christ the true light and the light of the world. With these prayers the faithful offer thanksgiving and ask for guidance and blessings during the day. They are strengthened with the power of the Resurrection and salvation and brightness of God's light within humanity and within the world. At the third hour (9:00 AM) the faithful contemplate the Holy Spirit and its work in their lives and the life of the church. The themes of the following hours (from the sixth to compline) reflect on the Passion, the cross and burial; they become times of personal contemplation on the life of Christ and a daily journey contemplating human salvation. As the faithful contemplate the cross throughout the day, they are ready to contemplate Christ's burial, or their own small death of sleep, at the end of the day. As the day is winding down and darkness covers their surroundings, the faithful reflect on their day. Was it in accordance to God's commandments? Did they spend their day in purity and virtue? If this were the last day of their lives, would they be ready to meet the Lord, as the midnight prayer proposes? If not, it is time to offer contrition and repentance to the Lord. With these thoughts throughout the week, the Coptic Christian is in constant prayer and contemplation on God, salvation, and the life of virtue. When the faithful attend the liturgy the transition is seamless, it is one continuous prayer.

The faithful prepare for the liturgy through confession, fasting, prayer, and reading Scripture. Copts consider reading Scripture a spiritual activity closely connected to prayer; reading Scripture supports prayer and prayer enlightens the reader to understand the deeper meaning of Scripture. The amount of daily Scripture reading varies according to the spiritual level of the person. The faithful memorize Biblical verses for their contemplation during the day and parts of the psalms to have a life of inner prayer wherever they are. These varied exercises energize the prayer life of the faithful and engage the mind in spiritual thoughts throughout the day. The roots of the prayer life and the practices of Scripture reading and memorization are to be found in the Coptic monastic tradition and many laypeople observe them. In addition, weekly Bible studies, in which the whole community shares in reading Scripture and contemplating on it together, are held in churches during the week or after Saturday vespers. Summer "competitions" are held to encourage children and young people to read Scripture and plant within them the habit of having Scripture as their daily companion. Scripture becomes a personal as well as a communal fountain of life and the source of wisdom.

With these spiritual practices, the faithful approach church ready to be immersed in the liturgy. When the faithful enter the church they are in the house of God, they are in the presence of God, and they inwardly recite some psalm verses suitable for the occasion, such as: "Happy are those who live in your house, ever singing your praise" (Ps 84:4 NRSV), "Holiness befits your house, O LORD, forevermore" (Ps 93:5 NRSV), or "I, through the abundance of your steadfast love, will enter your house, I will bow down toward your holy temple in awe of you" (Ps 5:7 RSV). With these or similar verses, the faithful bow before the altar and give praise to God. The church is the house of God, the place where the angels and saints are offering praise to God, the place where heaven and earth meet. The faithful now stand in heaven giving praise to God, accompanying the heavenly realm in praise. The sanctuary is the Holy of Holies, the dwelling place of God Almighty, where the angels, martyrs, and saints are present sharing in the heavenly praise with the faithful. The church is not a place separated from the world, but the place where the faithful bring the world and their concerns before God. The chapter on the liturgy describes the topics of the litanies that offer supplications for the needs of the faithful who are sick, traveling, married, single, rich or poor, young or old; for the clergy, the country, creation, and the world; for protection against natural disasters, the church, and other supplications. After the faithful lift their hearts with all their concerns before God, they leave the church with their hearts filled with divine peace, filled with the Spirit, ready to face their worldly concerns. In the liturgy, the Copts present the world to God and bring God to the world.

The centrality of liturgy in the Coptic Orthodox life is revealed in the liturgical prayers. In the Coptic liturgy of St. Basil, during the Epiclesis (the prayer for the descent of the Holy Spirit), after the priest finishes making the sign of the cross over the Eucharistic bread and wine, he stretches his hands towards the Eucharist and says: "Our Lord, God, and Savior Jesus Christ, given for the remission of sins and eternal life to those who partake of Him." And he continues: "Make us all worthy, O our Master, to partake of Your Holies, unto the purification of our souls, our bodies, and our spirits, that we may become one body and one spirit, and may have a share and an inheritance with all the saints who have pleased You since the beginning." When the priest utters these prayers, the response of the faithful is "Lord have mercy," said three times. When the faithful partake of the Eucharist, their sins are remitted and they are granted eternal life; this sums up the aspiration of every Christian. The body and blood of Jesus Christ purifies the soul, body, and spirit of the faithful. This is the purity they strive for every day of the week, a purity that makes them one body and one spirit with all Christians and with all the saints who preceded them. This speaks to the essence of Coptic spirituality, and the striving of the faithful for the life of virtue and purity.

The Coptic liturgy also informs the laity about Church theology. The priest confesses the faith of the Church in the Trinity—"One is the Holy Father, one is the Holy Son, one is the Holy Spirit. Amen"—and in "The Body and the Blood of Emmanuel our God; this is true. Amen," which is followed by an audible "Amen" from the faithful. During the last confession, he acknowledges, followed by the faithful, that this is the life-giving flesh of the Incarnate Son, acknowledges the whole theme of the Incarnation and salvation, and speaks clearly about the union of natures: "He made It [humanity] one with His divinity without mingling, without confusion, and without alteration." The whole theme of the Incarnation, Crucifixion, and Resurrection is confirmed many times during the liturgy. The Coptic faithful become not only spiritual people during the liturgy, but also theologians. It is with this faith and with this spirituality that the faithful approach and partake of the Eucharist.

The laity are not bystanders or observers of the liturgy. The whole congregation, young and old, are active participants in the sung liturgy and participate in all liturgical responses. If there are no laity present, the priest cannot offer the liturgy. There is no "private mass" in the Coptic Orthodox Church, for the priest is there to serve the people in their service to God. Liturgical hymns, as in all Christian traditions, have always been a source of spiritual comfort to the faithful. They are the conduit that leads the faithful into the liturgy and transports them, for example, from the somber contemplation of Paschal Week to the joyous commemoration of the Feast of the Resurrection; the tunes carry the faithful subliminally from one liturgical season to another. The shared liturgical experience unites Copts wherever they are in the world and anchors them in one faith, one spirit, and one body of Christ. As for non-liturgical chants, choirs have become very popular, especially among the youth, and are a means of expressing their spirituality beyond the confines of the defined, standardized liturgical music. All churches have youth choirs, which represent the popular spirituality of the faithful.

Icons in the Coptic church are not merely for decoration but have liturgical and educational functions. They are placed on church walls in the order of the Biblical readings of the Procession of the Cross, which is celebrated three times a year. Icons of Biblical events are used in the liturgical processions that celebrate those events, as in the case of the Procession of the Resurrection, which has the icon of the Risen Lord at its center. Similarly, icons are used when commemorating the saints, especially the patron saint of the church. Icons on the Iconostasis are placed in an order followed in all Coptic churches. At the center over the altar door is the cross flanked by the Virgin Mary and John the Evangelist; below the cross is a large icon of the Eucharistic Supper flanked by icons of the twelve disciples arranged in a line with six on each side. To the right of the altar door are the icons of Christ enthroned and John the Baptist. To the left of the altar door are the icons of the Virgin Mary holding Christ and the Annunciation. If there is space available, other icons may also adorn the church. The church apse has the painting of Christ Pantocrator, or the Risen Christ, or other themes depicting the glorified Lord. When the faithful, during the liturgy, gaze at these icons they are reminded of the cloud of witnesses attending the liturgy and sharing their praise; they cannot but feel that the church is heaven on earth. On the other hand, icons serve as an educational tool, narrating to the faithful the story of salvation and the work of the Spirit in the church. An iconographer "writes" an icon and children, as well as adults, are taught to "read" the icon to learn the theological and spiritual message conveyed by the theme of each icon (Henein 2010). Copts do not "pray" to icons or saints; the Copts pray to God and ask the intercession of the saints. The Coptic church did not pass through a period of iconoclasm like the Byzantine churches. The lives of the saints serve as powerful models to emulate; they are the cloud of witnesses. The church teaches the faithful about the lives of the saints through the Synaxarium, a daily liturgical reading that narrates the lives of the saints of the day, and through icons.

The saints are neither distant figures, whose lives are merely read in liturgical readings or depicted in icons for aesthetic beauty, nor removed from the lives of the faithful; the saints are living with the faithful. Since 1968, the Virgin Mary has appeared four times above four different churches in Egypt. The Coptic Orthodox Synod has investigated and issued approval of these four apparitions. The Virgin Mary appeared to thousands of bystanders, Christians and Muslims alike. The apparitions appeared intermittently over periods spanning a few weeks to a few months. In all four apparitions, the Virgin Mary did

Figure 9.1 The nave and Iconostasis of St. Mena's Church at Riverside, California. Courtesy of John Paul Abdelsayed

Figure 9.2 The nave of St. Mary's Church, the Monastery of St. Mercurius for women, Cairo [photograph by Lois M. Farag]

Figure 9.3 St. Mena Church, Riverside, California. The shape of the church building is a combination of Noah's ark and the tabernacle [photograph by Lois M. Farag]

not leave messages with a person, or appoint a messenger to deliver a special message to the church's hierarchy; she appeared to the people to comfort them and strengthen their faith before difficult times. The first apparition was on April 2, 1968, over the Church of the Virgin Mary at Zaitūn, one of the Cairo suburbs. According to the April 2 entry in the Coptic Synaxarium, a Muslim Public Transportation Garage guard, 'Abd al-'Aziz 'Ali, "saw a luminous body" over the church dome and instantly began shouting, "light over the dome." Other garage workers, all Muslims, came and saw the light over the dome. When they approached the church, which was across the street, "they saw a young lady in white, kneeling by the cross at the top of the dome." The men began to shout out at the lady lest she fall off the smooth dome, thinking she was attempting suicide. The shouts attracted passersby, and slowly the crowd began seeing the lady in a bright light with an olive branch and white doves flying around her. This is when the bystanders began to realize that this was the Virgin Mary. They directed a flood light at the apparition to remove all doubt, but were surprised that the apparition was still there and the light became even brighter. They cut off all electricity from the area but the lady in bright light became even brighter and clearer and began moving around the dome. The crowds started shouting, "She is the Virgin … She is the Mother of Light …" This was the testimony of Christians and Muslims alike. By the end of the day thousands of Christians and Muslims came to the Church of the Virgin Mary at Zaitūn to witness the apparition. She appeared in Zaitūn to thousands of people for more than two years in different forms, and was seen even by skeptical Muslims. Hundreds testified to miracles occurring.

The second apparition began on March 25, 1986, at the Church of St. Dimyānah in Papadopolo, Shubrā, in Cairo. Shubrā is one of the most populated districts in Cairo. The Virgin Mary first appeared beside the church steeple, then on the dome, and then a bright light began spreading over the houses beside the church. Immediately crowds gathered to watch the miraculous apparition. She then appeared with a halo of light. Sometimes she spread her hands in blessing and greeting of the crowds; at other times she would appear with a lowered head indicating sadness. On other days, she appeared in different forms inside the altar during the Divine Liturgy (Victor and Al-Fāris 2011: 25–28). The third apparition began on August 17, 2000, at the Church of St. Mark in Asyūṭ, Upper Egypt, where she appeared, followed by a bevy of doves, above the domes of the church (ibid. 29–31). This apparition lasted for a few weeks. The fourth apparition began on December 10, 2009, in the Church of the Virgin Mary and Archangel Michael, in Al-Warāq, Giza. The first to witness the apparition was Said Aḥmad Muḥammad, the Muslim owner of a nearby café. He said that at 11:00 PM he and all those sitting at the café saw a very bright white light above the church dome, and the light began spreading until it was seen from miles away. Immediately, people followed the light in curiosity until they arrived at the church. Crowds began gathering. By 1:00 AM the Virgin appeared wearing white and moving between the two steeples. She then moved above the middle dome and the church cross began to rise above her crown. In the following days thousands gathered around the church and witnessed the Virgin Mary taking different positions on the church dome accompanied by light and doves (ibid. 33–36). Some videos of the last two apparitions are posted on YouTube.

All of the apparitions were accompanied by miracles, which have been recorded by the papal committee. The Virgin Mary did not leave any messages in any of the four apparitions. Such apparitions strengthen the faith of the Copts. The faithful would stand all night in front of the church where the apparition had happened and was expected. They would sing hymns and praises all night accompanied by personal devotions. After the apparition or the witness of a miracle, there would be a flow of hymns of joy and thanksgiving. Apparitions create unprecedented spiritual revivals in a matter of hours, a spiritual renewal that would take hundreds of spiritual leaders years to achieve.

The churches where the apparitions occurred became pilgrimage sites, but this is not unusual. Pilgrimage to Christian sites is a very common spiritual activity among Copts. There are many ancient Christian sites in Egypt, including ancient monasteries and ancient churches, to which pilgrimage is made, especially those visited by the Holy Family (Matt 2: 13–15). Families will spend the whole day at a site, starting by attending the liturgy, then spending the day in the spiritual exercises of reading Scripture, prayer, contemplation, and singing hymns. It is also common at some of these sites for Sunday School teachers to spend a day with their students, taking the opportunity to teach the children about the saints and church history. Monasteries are also a destination of pilgrimage; there individuals or groups will spend a day or more in contemplation and seeking spiritual guidance from monastics. Many Copts make retreats in monasteries. What they learn and experience from their monastic mentors during these retreats permeates to the rest of the Coptic community. Many Copts have monastic spiritual guides. Monasteries are the spiritual center of the Coptic church. Monastic spirituality emerged in the deserts of Egypt and became known in the west as "desert spirituality."

Coptic monastic spirituality is at the root of Coptic prayer life and spiritual exercises. For example, in the fourth-century monastic office each liturgical hour comprises twelve psalms accompanied by silent prayers and readings from the Old and New Testaments, with more readings from the Epistles and Gospels on Saturdays and Sundays (Taft 1993: 57–73). The present day *Agpeya* still preserves the twelve psalms, prayers, and a reading from the New Testament for each hour. The fourth-century monastic office developed to become the daily office of the laity. Not only the office, but the daily spiritual monastic practices became normative for Coptic spirituality. Some of these monastic practices have been preserved in the *Sayings of the Desert Fathers*. These sayings inform us of the monastic practice of reading Scripture daily, retaining Scriptural verses in memory and in the heart, using Scripture as a source of prayer and contemplation, and following Scriptural precepts as a guide to Christian conduct. The sayings also tell the reader that this is not that simple. The monastics acknowledge many difficulties that hinder the mind and heart from achieving the goal of unceasing prayer and analyze the reasons for such difficulties. In short, the sayings provide the reader detailed descriptions of difficulties faced when trying to achieve the goal of being in the constant presence of God. The advice they give is practical and relevant to any Christian regardless of one's station in life, whether lay or monastic, for they address the basic, shared human experience. Through these readings famous monastic figures such as St. Antony, St. Macarius, and St. Bishoi, among many others, became models for the Coptic laity (Farag 2012).

Copts are very active in church and social services. All church activities are sustained by voluntary work. Religious education of children and young people is carried out by men and women volunteers through Sunday School instruction, usually held after the liturgy. Serving the poor, "The Brothers of Christ," is part of all church services in both urban and rural areas. This service includes not only financial support, but also medical and educational support. It includes assistance in small projects, especially for women, to help them better support their families, and may extend to technical or even moral support. Most Copts give back to the church that gave birth to them in the baptismal font.

This is the spiritual fountain that is available to all Copts and each chooses to drink of this spiritual source as best fits their spiritual thirst. Unceasing prayer is the central theme of Coptic spirituality, punctuated by liturgies, *Agpeya* and individual prayers, reading Scripture, fasting, and examining one's life in order to live in accordance with Scripture. In short, it is to live a life of righteousness, virtue, and holiness. All these spiritual activities feed into the prayer life. Unceasing prayer is the seamless thread that unites these activities into one coherent Christian life. It bridges the gap between the public and the private to form a life of Christian holiness, a life of Coptic spirituality.

Selected Bibliography

Bell, D. (trans.) (1989) *Besa, the Life of Shenoute*, Kalamazoo, MI: CistercianPublications.

Bongie, E. B. and Schaffer, M. (2001) *The Life & Regimen of the Blessed & Holy Syncletica*, Toronto: Peregrina.

Budge, W. (ed. and trans.) (1984) *The Paradise of the Fathers: Being Histories of the Anchorites, Recluse Monks, Coenobites and Ascetic Fathers of the Deserts of Egypt between A.D. CCL and A.D. CCCC Circiter*, Seattle, WA: St. Nectarios Press.

Chryssavgis, J. and Penkett, P. (trans.) (2002) *Abba Isaiah of Scetis, Ascetic Discourses*, Kalamazoo, MI: Cistercian Publications.

Farag, L. (2009) "Worshiping in the Spirit: Pentecost – Theology, Liturgy, and Scripture," *Coptic Church Review: A Quarterly of Contemporary Patristic Studies*, 30(1): 22–32.

——(2012) *Balance of the Heart, Desert Spirituality for Twenty-First-Century Christians*, Eugene, OR: Cascade Books.

Henein, A. L. (2010) *Understanding the Icon of Saint Anthony the Great*, Los Angeles: Holy Virgin Mary Coptic Orthodox Church.

Mathew the Poor (2003) *Orthodox Prayer Life*, Crestwood, NY: St Vladimir's Seminary Press.

Mikhael, M. and Vivian, T. (eds) (2010) *The Holy Workshop of Virtue: The Life of John the Little*, Collegeville, MN: Liturgical Press.

Russell, N. (1981). *The Lives of the Desert Fathers: The Historia Monachorum in Aegypto*, London: Mowbray.
——(2007) *Theophilus of Alexandria*, London: Routledge.
Samir, S. K. (1971) Miṣbāḥ al-ẓulma fī 'īḍāḥ al-khidma li-l-qiss Shams al-Riyāsa Abū al-Barakāt al-ma'rūf b-ibn Kabar, Cairo: Maktabat al-Kārūz.
Swan, L. (2001) *The Forgotten Desert Mothers: Sayings, Lives, and Stories of Early Christian Women*, New York: Paulist Press.
Taft, R. (1993) *The Liturgy of the Hours in East and West*, Collegeville, MN: Liturgical Press.
Veilleux, A. (ed. and trans.) (1980–82) *Pachomian Koinonia*, 3 vols, Kalamazoo, MI: Cistercian Publications.
Victor, M. and Al-Fāris, R. (2011) *Magd Mar̄iam, ẓuhwrāt al-'dhrā' fy maṣr wa al-'ālm*, Cairo: Mw'sasat Waṭany li-l-ṭibā'a wa al-nashr.
Vivian, T. (1993) *Histories of the Monks of Upper Egypt: and, the Life of Onnophrius*, Kalamazoo, MI: Cistercian Publications.
——(2004) *Saint Macarius, the Spiritbearer: Coptic Texts Relating to Saint Macarius the Great*, Crestwood, NY: St. Vladimir's Seminary Press.
——(2008) *Witness to Holiness: Abba Daniel of Scetis*. Kalamazoo, MI: Cistercian Publications.
Vivian, T. and Athanassakis, A. (trans.) (2003) *Athanasius of Alexandria, The Life of Antony: the Coptic Life and the Greek Life*, Kalamazoo, MI: Cistercian Publications.
Vivian, T. and Greer, R. (eds) (2004) *Four Desert Fathers: Pambo, Evagrius, Macarius of Egypt, and Macarius of Alexandria: Coptic Texts Relating to the Lausiac History of Palladius*, Crestwood, NY: St. Vladimir's Seminary Press.
Ward, B. (1984) *The Sayings of the Desert Fathers: The Alphabetical Collection*, Kalamazoo, MI: Cistercian Publications.
——(1986) *The Wisdom of the Desert Fathers: Systematic Sayings from the Anonymous Series of the Apophthegmata Patrum*, Oxford: S.L.G. Press.
——(2003) *The Desert Fathers: Sayings of the Early Christian Monks*, London: Penguin.

10 Liturgy

Heaven on Earth

John Paul Abdelsayed

"Surely the Lord is in this place … How awesome is this place! This is none other than the house of God, and this is the gate of Heaven!" (Gen 28:16–17). Jacob's declaration at Bethel would also characterize the Orthodox understanding of the Church as not simply a type and figure of Heaven, but the actual substrate of that future transformation (Evdokimov 1965: 7). Such a heavenly paradigm is the foundation upon which the entire liturgical tradition of the Coptic Orthodox Church is established. This chapter only begins to describe the complexity, breadth of influence, and theological depth of the liturgical tradition of the Coptic Orthodox Church. This chapter is a synopsis of the liturgical life in the Coptic Orthodox Church.

The Liturgical Year

Calendar

Although the exact date of its origin is unknown, the Coptic calendar is based on the ancient Egyptian lunar calendar, which was replaced around 4236 BC by the more accurate solar calendar. The apparent incompatibilities between these calendars were resolved by another solar calendar with 365 days and three four-month seasons. The seasons were based on the regular flood of the Nile and the agricultural activities in Egypt: Akhit or Akhet, the season of inundation (flooding); Perit, Peret, or Proyet, the season for planting crops; and Shemu, Shenou, or Shomu, the season for harvesting (Kosack 2012: 2).

The Coptic calendar contains 12 months, each with 30 days. To these are added five intercalary days, often referred to as the "little Month" (*epagomenē*; Gr. *hai epagomenai*; *Arabic*: *al-shahr al-ṣaghīr*) or the "forgotten days" (*ayyām al-nasī*). In the Middle Ages, due to the great persecutions under Emperor Diocletian, the Copts set their New Year on Tout 1 (or September 11 on the Gregorian) and made AD 284, the year Diocletian was chosen emperor, the beginning of the era (Teres 2000: 215). The calendar was titled the Year or Era of the Martyrs, conventionally abbreviated as AM, for *anno martyrum*. On the year prior to the Gregorian leap year, one day is added to the last month (for a total of six days), yielding the Coptic leap year. The Coptic liturgical calendar,

Table 10.1 The Coptic Calendar and its Seasons

Ancient Season	*New Kingdom*	*Coptic (Sahidic)*	*Greek*	*Arabic (Transliteration)*	*Gregorian Equivalents*
Akhet	Dwhty	Thout	Thout	Tout	Sept. 11/12–Oct. 10/11
	Pa-n-ipat	Paopi	Phaophi	Babeh	Oct. 11/12–Nov. 10/11
	Hwt-hwr	Hathor	Athyr	Hatour	Nov. 11/12–Dec. 10/11
	Ka-hr-ka	Koiak	Choiak	Kiahk	Dec. 11/12–Jan. 8/9
Proyet	Ta-abt	Tobi	Tybi	Touba	Jan. 9/10–Feb. 7/8
	Pa-n-mxr	Meshir	Mechir	Amshir	Feb. 8/9–Mar. 9
	Pa-n-amn-htp	Paremhat	Phamenoth	Baramhat	Mar. 10–Apr. 8
	Pa-n-mnwt	Paremoude	Parmouthi	Baramouda	Apr. 9–May 8
Shomu	Pa-n-xnsw	Pashons	Pachon	Bashans	May 9–Jun. 7
	Pa-n-int	Paoni	Payni	Ba'ouna	Jun. 8–Jul. 7
	Ipip	Epip	Epiphi	Abib	Jul. 8–Aug. 6
	Msw-r'	Mesori	Mesore	Mesra	Aug. 7–Sept. 5
		Kouji Nabot		al-shahr al-ṣaghīr	Sept. 6–Sept. 10/11

which is distinct from the Julian and Gregorian calendars, is outlined in Table 10.1.

Liturgical Year

The liturgical calendar includes seven major and seven minor feasts of Christ. The major feasts are Annunciation (Paremhat 29, April 7), Nativity (Koiak 29, January 7), Theophany (Tobi 11, January 19), Sunday of the Palms, Resurrection, Ascension, and Pentecost. The minor feasts are Circumcision (Tobi 6, January 14; January 1 Julian), the Entrance of our Lord into the Temple (Meshir 8, February 15), the Flight to Egypt (Pachons 24, June 1), the Miracle at the Wedding of Cana (Tobi 13, January 12), Transfiguration (Mesori 13, August 19), Holy Thursday, and Thomas Sunday. Most of the major feasts follow a period of fasting. Fifty-five days of fasting precede the Feast of Resurrection and 43 days the Feast of Nativity. An additional day of preparation, called "Paramon," precedes the feasts of Theophany and Nativity. If the feast falls on a Sunday or Monday, the Paramon begins on a Friday, since strict abstinence is not allowed on Saturdays or Sundays. The Feast of Resurrection has no Paramon, since Bright Saturday is the only day in the year in which strict abstinence is allowed.

There are also seven commemorations for the Blessed Virgin throughout the year: the annunciation of her birth (Mesori 7, August 13), her nativity (Pachons 1, May 9), her presentation in the Temple (Koiak 3, December 12), her dormition (Tobi 21, January 29), the translation of her body (Mesori 16, August 22), her apparition in Zaitūn in 1968 (Paremhat 24, April 2), and her miraculous dissolution of the chains of St. Matthias the Apostle (Paoni 21, June 28). Many of these events, though not mentioned in Scripture, were adopted from ancient traditions associated with the *Protoevangelion of James*, some of which are also celebrated in Catholic and Orthodox Churches, although on different dates.

Each Coptic month contains three commemorations: the Annunciation, Nativity, and Resurrection of the Lord on the 29th (except for Meshir and Paremhat), the departure of the Holy Virgin Mary on the 21st, and Archangel Michael on the 12th.

The Coptic Orthodox Church also commemorates the Apostles Peter and Paul on Abib 5, July 12. This follows a fasting period that begins the day after the Feast of Pentecost. Two feasts of the Cross are observed: the discovery of the Holy Cross on Paremhat 10 (March 19), and the consecration of the Church of the Holy Resurrection in Jerusalem on Thout 17–19 (September 27–29).

The crown of the liturgical year in the Coptic Orthodox Church is the Holy Week of Pascha. The services were expanded during the early centuries, abbreviated during the time of Patriarch Gabriel II ibn Turayk (1131–45), and a few generations later expanded again by Bishop Peter of Bahnasā (Zannetti 2009: 137).

Lectionary

The Coptic *Katameros* (Lectionary) contains five volumes: the annual cycle for the Sunday Gospels; the Great Fast (Lent); the Holy Pascha Week; the Holy Fifty Days (from the Resurrection to Pentecost); and the daily readings. Each day contains nine scriptural readings: three psalms and three Gospel readings (i.e. for Vespers, Matins, and the Liturgy, i.e. the Eucharist), one selection from the Pauline Epistles, one from the Catholic Epistles, and a reading from the Book of Acts. This arrangement is at least as old as the twelfth century (ibid., 130). The Synaxarium, an extended daily biography of the saints, is read immediately following the selection from the Acts during the Divine Liturgy. The *Difnar*, a shorter and more doxological version of the saint's life, is read towards the end of the Midnight Psalmody.

The fixed Sunday readings (those not included in the period of the Great Fast through Pentecost) contain 40 Sundays, and are structured according to the work of the Holy Trinity: The Sundays of the first month are related to the love of God the Father. Those of the next six months concern the Grace of the Only-Begotten Son and His earthly ministry. And the Sundays of the last three months, which follow Pentecost, deal with the Communion and Gift of the Holy Spirit. Finally, the readings of the "Little Month" focus on the Second Coming of the Lord and the End of Times. The agricultural year was also taken into account in the lectionary cycle. For example, two Sundays of Hatour concern the Parable of the Sower, since this time of year corresponds to the period of sowing. The readings of the weekdays in ordinary time are generally arranged thematically according to the commemoration of the daily saint, with special readings selected for the commemoration of angels, apostles, martyrs, monastics, and patriarchs.

Liturgical Tones

Over 70 years ago, Oswald Burmester (1938: 141) remarked, "Coptic hymnography is a vast virgin forest, beyond whose confines no Coptic or liturgical scholar has as yet penetrated." Whether from complex acrostics to simple rhymes, or from didactic poetry to recurrent refrains, Coptic hymnography has yet to attract the scholarly attention it warrants. Coptic hymnody may well be the most ancient ecclesiastical music still in use today.

Coptic hymns are generally categorized into several tunes or tones of the year, with a distinct melody and rhythm for each liturgical season. *Sanawi* is used during the annual season, called "ordinary time" in the West, *Farāiḥy* during festal seasons, *Koiaki* during the Nativity Fast, *Sha'ānīnī* on the Sunday of Palms and Feasts of the Cross, and *Baskha* (or sorrowful tune), in the Holy Pascha Week and for funerals. Some tunes carry the names of towns, such as the *Singāry* tune, from the Northern Delta town; or the *Adrīby* tune, named after the town of Atribis in Upper Egypt (Malaty 1993: 355).

The praise of the Midnight Psalmody contains: (1) four canticles or odes, which alternate between two biblical canticles and two psalm selections (Ex 15:1–21, Ps 135 (136), Dan 3:1–67, and Ps 148–50); (2) the daily Psali, a metrical hymn of four lines praising the Lord Christ, that varies according to the day and liturgical season (O'Leary 1911: 51); (3) the daily *Theotokion*, a hymn dedicated to the Holy Virgin for each day of the week;[1] (4) a hymnological periphrastic "interpretation" (*ermenia*) (ibid. 56); and (5) a non-biblical text usually with unrhymed strophes of four lines called the Lobsh ("crown," consummation). Most probably, this was a later addition that summarized and bridged the *Theotokion* with the concluding prayer of the day. The praise of the Koiak Psalmody has additional praises of the Virgin Mary, the Trinity, and the Incarnation.

The Mysteries

Like other apostolic churches, the Coptic Orthodox Church upholds seven mysteries or divine graces of the Holy Spirit. These mysteries are holy Baptism, Chrismation, Eucharist, Repentance and Confession, Matrimony, Orders, and Unction of the Sick. While most Orthodox Churches have informally appropriated the Council of Trent's (1545–63) solemn definition of seven sacraments by the Roman Catholic Church, Orthodox understanding of these mysteries may differ. Some prefer to speak of more than seven mysteries, and include services such as the blessing of homes, the consecration of monastics, the great blessing of water, and the funeral service. Alternatively, others speak only of one mystery—the Divine Liturgy or the Eucharist—as *the* mystery of mysteries, to which all others are inextricably united. Traditionally, all other mysteries were conducted within the celebration of the Divine Liturgy, and were not considered finalized or "sealed" until the partaking of the Eucharist.

The Orthodox understanding of "mystery" is more expansive than the notion of "sacrament." In the West, *sacramentum* is "a sign of the sacred" which points beyond itself and causes what it signifies (Augustine, *De Doctrina*, 11), while the reality (*res, res tantum*) characterizes the spiritual effect of that sacrament (Aquinas, *Summa Theologica* III.73). The East explains both using the term "mystery" to characterize the heavenly realities and the divine grace of the Holy Spirit working in the mystery towards the sanctification and glorification of the soul. In Scripture, mystery signifies a heavenly revelation of the hidden wisdom of God, which is neither fully known nor unknown.[2]

The Mystery of Holy Baptism

Liturgical scholars often assert that the Coptic Liturgy of Baptism is one of the oldest living traditions in the history of the rite. Burmester (1954: 27) argued that the similarities between the Coptic and Greek rites suggest an origin before 451.

The baptismal rite contains three anointings using three separate oils. Following her absolution, the mother is anointed with regular or "simple" oil (from Bright Saturday, also called "Apocalypse oil"). After the renunciation of Satan, the candidate is anointed with the oil of exorcism, also referred to as the "oil of catechumens" or the "oil of gladness" (*Galilawen*, from the Greek *elaion agalliaseōs*). After baptism, the candidate is anointed with the Holy Chrism, oil consecrated by the pope and all the bishops of the Holy Synod. With these same three oils, the baptismal waters are blessed by means of several litanies, readings (Tit 2:11–38; 1 Jn 5:5–14, Acts 8:26–40, Ps 31:1, 2; Jn 3:1–21), and psalms (Ps 29:3, 4; 34:5, 11; 66:12; 55:7–10; 132:13).

The renunciation of Satan mentioned above is not simply a one-time event. As soldiers declare war against the enemy, the renunciation (*apotaxis*) was an act of declaration against all the spiritual enemies. This practice is understood as a daily and life-long spiritual struggle against sin, and dates to the fourth century, or earlier. After this renunciation, the candidate professes his or her allegiance (*syntaxis*) to the Holy Trinity and the Apostolic Church by turning to the East and reciting the Apostolic Creed. Each Divine Liturgy includes petitions for the confirmation of catechumens so they may proceed steadfast in the Orthodox doctrine and praxis.

At the conclusion of these prayers, the candidate is brought from the West to the baptismal font, where he or she is immersed three times, with the declaration, "I baptize you [name] in the Name of the Father, and of the Son, and of the Holy Spirit. Amen."

The Mystery of Chrismation

The Mystery of Chrismation (also called *Mayrūn*, from the Greek word for chrism, or "Seal of the Holy Spirit") immediately follows Baptism. Cyprian of Carthage, Cyril of Jerusalem, and Tertullian record this ancient practice. It confers the "seal of the gift of the Holy Spirit" and makes the newly baptized a "purified vessel of our Lord Jesus Christ." The candidate receives 36 signs of the cross in chrism, on the forehead, nostrils, mouth, ears, eyes, heart, back, arms, and legs. As in other Orthodox Churches, this mystery is administered by priests and is not exclusively an episcopal privilege.

After Chrismation, the candidates are clothed in white garments, since they have put on Christ and have become a new creation (cf. Gal 3:27; Rev 3:5, 18). They are crowned with crowns signifying the glory, honor, virtue, and righteousness received within the mystery. A *zinnar* (a girdle of red ribbon) is draped over the right shoulder to represent self-control and the Christian struggle through the blood of Christ. In the past, these garments were worn continuously for seven days, then removed and washed of any chrism on the eighth day. Today, the *zinnar* is removed after partaking of the Eucharist, the baptismal procession, and the final instructions.

The Divine Liturgy of the Eucharist

The Divine Liturgy of the Eucharist is understood in the Coptic Orthodox Church as the "mystery of mysteries," the great "mystery of godliness,"[3] or simply, "the great mystery." Its historic evolution in the Church of Alexandria would necessitate a voluminous treatise—which extends far beyond the scope of this brief chapter.

The obscure evolution of the anaphoral prayers is resolved during the middle ages by Canon 26 of Patriarch Gabriel II Ibn Turyak (1131–45), which authorized three anaphoras: those attributed to St. Basil of Caesarea, St. Gregory of Nazianzus, and St. Cyril of Alexandria (also known as the anaphora of St. Mark).[4] Prior to this, it is possible that several other anaphoral prayers were used in the Coptic Orthodox Church, as in the Ethiopian Rite.[5] According to medieval custom, the anaphora of St. Basil is typically celebrated in ordinary time, St. Gregory during the feasts of the Lord, and St. Cyril during the month of Koiak (during the Nativity Fast) and the Great Fast.

Three major medieval reforms took place during the fourteenth and fifteenth centuries, as represented in three monumental works: Yūḥannā ibn Abī Zakariyya ibn Sabbā''s Precious Jewel in Ecclesiastical Sciences (*al-Jawhara al-nafisa fi 'ulūm al-kanīsa*); Ibn Kabar's The Lamp of Darkness for the Explanation of the Service (*Miṣbāḥ al-ẓulma wa-iḍāḥ al-khidma*); and perhaps the most important, Patriarch Gabriel V's (1409–27) Ritual Order (*al-Tartīb al-ṭaqsī*), intended to regulate liturgical practice (Takla 1997–98).

The earliest known custom limited the celebration of the Eucharist to Sundays. Some regions included Saturday worship by the end of the fourth century, and daily liturgies by the fifth century (Regnault 1999: 126–38). Medieval canons restricted midnight liturgies to the feasts of Nativity, Epiphany, and Resurrection. These canons also forbade a priest from celebrating the liturgy more than once per day, or from using the same altar, liturgical vessels, or vestments on the same day (Malak 1982: 6–7).

The Eucharistic bread offered in the Divine Liturgy, called the *qurbān* or Lamb (*ḥamal*), is prepared with the utmost care. It is made from fine wheat

Figure 10.1 The Eucharistic bread. Courtesy of St. Mark Coptic Orthodox Church Boston

flour, water, and leaven, and baked in the church's oven, located in the room called "Bethlehem." It is baked on the day of the celebration of the Divine Liturgy while reciting the psalms. The Lamb is a circular loaf, with a large circular stamp containing the Greek inscription of the Trisagion, a cross of 13 squares, symbolizing Christ and the twelve Apostles, and five holes representing the wounds of the Crucified Lord. Typically, five loaves are offered during the Liturgy, representing the five sacrifices of the Old Testament. Any prime number (higher than one) of loaves may also be offered, symbolizing the unity and indivisibility of the Holy Trinity. Only one is chosen for the Offering (cf. 1 Cor 10:17), and the remaining loaves are distributed as a blessing to the faithful at the conclusion of the Divine Liturgy.

During the Offering of the Lamb, the loaves are offered to the celebrant in a basket, before the door of the altar, as he declares: "Here is the Lamb of God Who takes away the sin of the world!" (Jn 1:29). Then the celebrant selects the most pristine loaf, the spotless lamb (Ex 12:5), and examines the wine to make sure it is not spoiled. He cleans the Lamb with one of the altar veils, blesses it with the wine in the sign of the cross (along with the other loaves), and then "baptizes" the Lamb with water at the side of the altar. He wraps it in the cloth, and processes around the altar, followed by the altar servers carrying the cruets of wine and water and candles.

After the Thanksgiving Prayer at the altar, the Absolution of the Ministers is made outside the sanctuary, followed by the offering of incense throughout the church. Selections are read from the Pauline Epistles, the Catholic

Epistles, the Book of Acts, and the *Synaxarium*, a reading of the daily saint(s). The Trisagion, Litany of the Gospel, Psalm verse, and Gospel are then chanted. After the sermon, the three Great Litanies are prayed, followed by the reciting of the Creed and the Prayer of Reconciliation. The latter concludes with the lifting of the main altar veil (*prospherin*), and the apostolic kiss of peace. The anaphora proper, the Eucharistic Prayer, then begins, the most ancient part of the liturgy. It is here where Cyrillian liturgy differs from the two others in structure and content.

All anaphoras contain litanies for the needs of the congregants (the sick, the travelers, the departed, the offerings and presenters, the married, the rich, the penitents, the young and old); the clergy (patriarch, bishops, priests, deacons); the consecrated (monks, virgins, ascetics, readers, chanters, exorcists); the needy (the poor, widows, orphans, strangers, captives, unbelievers); the secular offices (the president, soldiers, leaders, government employees); the natural orders (air, rivers, soil, seeds, herbs, plants, vines, trees, cattle, islands, deserts); and for protection against natural disasters (famines, plagues, earthquakes, drowning, fire, captivity, war, and even heresy). In this way, the faithful offer continual prayer for the unity of the Church, peace throughout the world, and the prosperity of all God's people and creation.

During the Institution Narrative, the recitation in the anaphora of Christ's words at the Last Supper, the celebrant uses his right thumb to separate the Lamb into two sections, starting with the upper right corner of the *Spoutikon*,[6] the central square piece. He then partially breaks the upper and lower portions of the Lamb while reciting Christ's words to "take" and "eat" (1 Cor 11:24). The Lamb is slightly broken, but it is not fully separated until the introduction to the fraction. At that time, the leftward portion, two thirds of the whole, is separated from the rightward portion, which is placed above it in the form of a cross.

Figure 10.2 The Eucharistic bread during the fraction. Courtesy of St. Mark Coptic Orthodox Church Boston

During the fraction, the celebrant breaks the body into 12 pieces. Several fraction prayers can be said which are left to the discretion of the celebrant, unless the liturgical season specifies a particular one. While the entire Lamb is used for the offering, the *Spoutikon* is reserved for intinction in the chalice and is partaken of by the celebrant. The celebrant breaks the remainder of the body into small pieces for each of the communicants, who receive the Eucharist without shoes and with a small liturgical veil in their right hand.

Medieval canons prescribe a minimum of nine hours of abstinence from food and water before partaking of the Eucharistic Mystery. Conjugal continence and corporal purity are stipulated, although such prescriptions vary in duration and degree.

The Mystery of Repentance and Confession

St. Basil the Great once remarked, "In repentance is salvation, but folly is the death of repentance."[7] The mystery of Repentance and Confession is as ancient as the Church, yet often misunderstood. This mystery is not merely an act of contrition and regret, but the joyful, remedial, and salvific (cf. Heb 6:4–6) reorientation of mind (*metanoia*) and renewal of life in Christ. Far from a one-time event, repentance is a daily work with life-long commitment. It is not merely an individual or personal activity; it is an act of reconciliation and reintegration into the Body of Christ (cf. 1 Cor 12:26, Jam 5:16).

This mystery consists of several aspects: repentance before God, auricular confession of one's sins before an ordained priest, and the absolving of sins. The prayer of absolution is pronounced at the end of the confession, after which the penitent is granted permission to advance and partake of the Eucharist, given "for the remission of sins."

The priest announces absolution of sins as the minister or steward of God. This authority to loose and bind was planted by Christ (Matt 16:18–19, 18:18; Jn 20:22–23), rooted in apostolic practice (cf. Acts 19:18), and blossomed in the patristic tradition. Because the priest announces the absolution granted by God, the formula of pronouncing the absolution is precatory ("May God absolve you") and not indicative ("I absolve you"), as in the Roman Catholic tradition. God forgives sins not the priest. As St. Athanasius remarked, "He who confesses his sins, receives from the priest pardon for his fault, in virtue of the grace of Christ, just as he who is baptized" (*Fragment against the Novatians*).

A priest may withhold absolution or forbid reception of the Eucharist for a period of time. This period of penance, reflection, and abstinence from the mystery of the Eucharist is remedial and not punitive, with the intention to reconcile the sinner with God and the Church.

Though this mystery can be practiced at any time, and in various ways, some guidelines are germane to today's practice. Once of speaking age, the believer selects one priest as a father of confession, or confessor. Since one is advised to confess every four to six weeks, this confessor is typically the priest of the local parish. After a period of self-examination (Lk 15:17), the sinner repents before

God in prayer. A time is then arranged with his confessor to confess, without delay or hesitation. Ideally, the mystery is conducted in the nave of the church while the priest wears the stole (*sadra, epitrachelion*). After the penitent confesses, the priest places the cross on the head of the penitent and recites the Thanksgiving Prayer, Psalm 50 (51), the Litany of the Sick, and three absolution prayers. Due to the number of confessions today, these prayers are customarily truncated to the final absolution prayer. The confessor may prescribe spiritual exercises for spiritual growth and discipline.

The Mystery of Holy Matrimony, the Crowning Ceremony

The mystery of Holy Matrimony is more appropriately referred to as "the Crowning Ceremony," since the bride and bridegroom, children of the king of kings, are crowned as king and queen of the new kingdom and church in their home.

As with the other mysteries, the Crowning Ceremony originally preceded the Sunday celebration of the Divine Liturgy. Although this is no longer the case for most ceremonies, remnants of this liturgical celebration survive in its rubrics and well-suited lectionary (Eph 5:22–26:3; Pss 19:5–6, 128:3; Matt 19), which trumps the daily readings.

Throughout the service, the Holy Trinity is invoked to establish, bless, and protect the martial bond in unity and love. The service begins with a blessing of the rings three times, in the Name of the Father, the Son, and the Holy Spirit. After each blessing the presbyter ties a knot in a scarlet ribbon, symbolizing the union of the couple with the blood of Christ. Throughout the service, the priest appeals to God to bless the couple as He blessed Adam and Eve, Abraham and Sarah, Isaac and Rebecca, Jacob and Rachel, and Joseph and Asenath. Christ is entreated to bless the couple as He blessed the wedding at Cana of Galilee "by His gracious presence." The couple bow to receive the grace of the Holy Spirit, while a special hymn directed towards the Holy Spirit is chanted. The ceremony culminates when the priest places crowns on them and prays: "Crown them with glory, O Father. Bless them, O Only-Begotten Son. Sanctify them, O Holy Spirit!"

After a concluding ceremonial blessing, the couple is processed throughout the church. Traditionally, this procession continued to their new home and thus also served as the public announcement of their marital union. Marriage, much more than simply the consent of the couple, is an announcement before God, Church, and community.

The Mystery of the Holy Orders

The Coptic Orthodox Church retains seven holy orders, as mentioned in its liturgical petitions. Some ancient manuscripts define these seven as patriarch, bishop, priest, deacon, subdeacon, reader, and monastic;[8] others identify them as the bishop, hegomen (protopresbyter), priest, archdeacon, deacon, subdeacon, and reader. Special prayers also exist for consecrating a chanter (*psaltos*) or arch-chanter (*arch-psaltos*).

The minor orders (chanter, arch-chanter, reader, and subdeacon) are considered "blessings" or permissions; the deacon, priest, and bishop are "ordained"; and the archdeacon, hegomen, and metropolitan are "elevated" within the ranks of the diaconate, priesthood, and episcopate respectively. At the end of the service, the reader receives a book (sometimes a lectionary), the subdeacon and deacon receive the *patrachelion* (*orarion* or stole), while the priest and bishop receive their appropriate vestments.

Although Sunday is the preferred day for ordinations, the bishop may confer any of the orders from chanter to hegomen within a liturgy celebrated on any day of the week, after the Prayer of Reconciliation. Episcopal consecrations and elevations must be conferred within a Sunday liturgy, after the reading of Acts, as the bishop is to complete the work of the Apostles in the Church through the grace of the Holy Spirit.

The primary duty of the reader is to read the assigned readings during the Divine Liturgy, to recite the names of the reposed patriarchs during that service, to assist in the chanting of hymns, and to teach the faithful in word and in deed. His hair is cut with five crosses, denoting the five wounds of the Lord (Phil 3:10), and the mind of Christ (1 Cor 2:16, Phil 2:5).

The priest teaches his congregation in faithfulness (Mal 2:7), and pastors his children with compassion and humility. Parish pastors are married priests, yet monks may also be priests. During the final prayer of the Divine Liturgy in which he is ordained, the priest places his hands over the hands of the bishop, who holds the Holy Body, and repeats the final confession after the bishop, phrase by phrase. Before partaking of the mysteries, the bishop breathes on him the breath of the Holy Spirit, while saying, "Receive the Holy Spirit" (Jn 20:22), or "Open your mouth wide and I will fill it" (Ps 81:10). The newly-ordained priest responds, "With open mouth I pant" (Ps 119:131), or "I open my mouth and accept unto me the Spirit." He then spends 40 days in a monastery, where he fasts and receives liturgical instruction and pastoral advice. At the conclusion, a church delegation escorts him from the monastery to the church to a special Vespers, a rite of reception, officially marking the beginning of his pastoral service.

Since the service for a hegomen is not considered an ordination but an elevation, the candidate is already vested as a priest during the liturgical prayers. He fasts for one week, but is not required to go to a monastery.

Following ancient tradition, bishops were predominantly chosen and consecrated from among monastics, although exceptions have been made. If not already a priest, the monk is to be ordained as such before being consecrated as bishop. The Council of Nicaea (Canon 4) required the bishop to be consecrated by at least three bishops, and prevented the transfer of a bishop from one diocese to another (Canon 15)—a tradition still preserved today.

Perhaps the most ancient office is that of pope. Today, the official title includes pope, archbishop, and patriarch. In the third century, the Bishop of

Rome referred to Heraclas of Alexandria as "pope" (Gr. *papas*), approximately five centuries before this term was consistently applied to the Bishop of Rome. Epiphanius (*Haer.* 68) first speaks of Alexander (c. 320) as "archbishop" of Alexandria. Scholars speculate that prior to this the ancient Church of Alexandria was headed by a synod of 12 presbyters, one of which would be selected as the "high priest" or "archpriest." The title of "patriarch" was officially applied to the Archbishop of Alexandria by the middle of the seventh century. Throughout history, the patriarchs of Alexandria were nominated by at least nine means, including divine visions (Mark), direct appointments (Anianus), altar lots (ten patriarchs), and selections by the synod of presbyters (patriarchs 4–18). The majority were chosen by a consensus of bishops, priests, and lay leaders (Saad and Saad 2000).

The Mystery of the Holy Unction

Unction is also referred to as the "mystery of lamps," since one lamp was lit at the commencement of each of its seven prayers. Seven cotton wicks or oil vessels are used today, representing the seven spirits of God in Rev 3:1. In the related Armenian rite, a seven-branched candlestick is used.

Contrary to Western practice, the anointing of the sick is not a prayer of last rites for the terminally ill, but a mystery for physical and spiritual healing. Firmly rooted in Scripture (cf. Jam 5:14–15; Mk. 6:13) and early Christian writings (Origen, John Chrysostom, Cyril of Jerusalem, Nilus the Younger, and Victor of Antioch), this mystery may be conducted at any time of the year, except during Holy Week. In lieu of this proscription, a general unction service for the anointing of all the faithful is conducted on the last Friday of the Great Fast.

Much like Christ's healing of the sick and paralytics (Jn 5, Mt 9:2–6), this mystery is linked with repentance. Its prayers include appeals for physical sicknesses and spiritual maladies. Likewise, unction is administered after the sick person confesses his sins. If the illness allows, the sick person fasts before receiving the mystery.

Other Liturgical Services

As early as the seventh century ceremonial foot-washing prayers (*Laqqān* services) were conducted (Burmester 1932b: 235ff). Today, they are administered twice: on Great Thursday and on the Feast of the Apostles (5 Abib). Other blessings of water take place on the Feast of Theophany, which commemorates Christ's baptism, and on the Sunday of Palms. The latter is part of a general funeral service for anyone who may die during Holy Week, since no raising of incense or Eucharistic service is conducted from the eve of the Sunday of Palms until Great Thursday.

Another liturgical service is the consecration of male or female monastics. Since monasticism is understood as dying to the world, the consecration prayers mirror funeral prayers. The individual lies on the ground, before the altar, with his or her head facing east, as the funeral rite and other prayers are recited. The novice's hair, whether male or female, is then cut in the sign of the cross, as for a reader. The monastic is then dressed in a black robe, a hood (*qulunsuwa*), and the monastic belt.

A final liturgical prayer is the making of the Holy Chrism (*Mayrūn*). About 30 ingredients are combined with olive oil in a series of cookings over fire prepared by olive wood—precisely described in the medieval *Book of the Chrism (Mayrūn)* (Meinardus 1991). One of the ingredients is balsam from Maṭariyya, ancient Heliopolis, where it was believed the Holy Family spent some time during their flight to Egypt (Butler 1884: 2.331). This liturgical service takes several days and is accompanied by prayers, the recitation of the entire Psalter, and selected scriptural readings.[9] The consecration of the *Mayrūn* takes place in a solemn Divine Liturgy, which has traditionally been that of the Thursday of Holy Week (Burmester 1954). After its consecration, the *Mayrūn* is used in the consecration of the newly baptized in the Mystery of Chrismation. It is also used to consecrate altars, altar vessels, and icons during the Divine Liturgy with various prayers that predate Patriarch Gabriel V (1409–27).

Horologion or *Agpeya*

The highly penitential and contemplative character of the Coptic Orthodox *Horologion* stems from its robust monastic tradition, as John Cassian records (*Institutes* 2.11). Every Coptic Orthodox is required to keep the hours, but a spiritual guide will direct the number of psalms and hours suitable for each person. The modern Coptic Book of Hours (*Agpeya*) contains seven hours. These are the First Hour at 6:00 AM, the Third Hour at 9:00 AM, the Sixth Hour at 12:00 noon, the Ninth Hour at 3:00 PM, the Eleventh Hour at 5:00 PM, the Twelfth Hour at 6:00 PM, and the Midnight Hour with three services said from 9:00 PM until 3:00 AM. Monastics add the Prayer of the Veil before sleeping, when darkness veils or covers the earth.

The hours are also integrated into the liturgical prayers. The First Hour is prayed before the Morning Doxology and the Morning Offering of Incense (Matins, Orthros). The Third and Sixth Hours are prayed at the conclusion of the Morning Offering of Incense, before the Divine Liturgy. If it is a fasting day, the Ninth Hour is added, since the liturgy should conclude in the afternoon. If the liturgy is celebrated during the Great Fast, the congregation prays until the Twelfth Hour, as the liturgy would conclude near sunset. The Eleventh and Twelfth Hours are prayed before the Evening Offering of Incense, and the Ninth Hour is not prayed during the Divine Liturgy. The three watches of the Midnight Prayer precede the Midnight Psalmody. The Hours are not prayed during Holy Week and for the feasts of Nativity, Theophany and Resurrection, which include special offices.

Most unique to the Coptic *Horologion* is its selection of psalms for each hour. Every hour includes 12 psalms, except for the First (which includes seven

Table 10.2 Psalms in the Agpeya

Hour	*Psalms included in the Agpeya*	*Comments on psalms in boldface and italics*
First	1, 2, 3, 4, 5, 6, 8, 11, 12, 14, 15, 18 ***24, 26, 62, 66, 69, 112, 142***	Psalms of Ancient Morning Prayer
Third	19, 22, 23, 25, 28, 29, 33, 40, 42, 44, 45, 46	
Sixth	53, 56, 60, 62, 66, 69, 83, 84, 85, 86, 90, 92	
Ninth	95, 96, 97, 98, 99, 100, 109, 110, 111, 112, 114, 115	
Eleventh (Sunset)	116, 117, ***119, 120, 121, 122, 123, 124, 125, 126, 127, 128***	Psalms of Ascent
Twelfth (Compline)	***129***, 130, 131, 132, 133, 136, 137, ***140***, 141, 145, 146, 147	Psalms in Ancient Evening Prayer
Midnight: First Watch	***133***, 3, 6, 12, 69, 85, 90, 116, 117, 118(1–22)	Introduction to Midnight Psalmody
Midnight: Second Watch	119, 120, 121, 122, 123, 124, 125, 126, 127, 128	
Midnight: Third Watch	129, 130, 131, 132, 133, 136, 137, 140, 141, 145, 146, 147	Psalms 148–150 conclude Ancient Midnight Psalmody

additional psalms carried over from the ancient morning office) and the Midnight Hour, which includes three services. Each day contains a possible 111 psalms. These psalms were carefully selected in such a way that they progress approximately numerically from Psalm 1 in the First Hour to Psalm 147 in the 12th (see Table 10.2). The psalms are also most suitable for the themes of each hour, which are based on the economy of salvation: Resurrection (1st); Christ's Passion and Pentecost (3rd); Crucifixion (6th); Christ's death on the Cross (9th); taking Christ down from the Cross (11th), Burial (12th), and the Second Coming (Midnight). Moreover, the proportion of psalms written by each author (David, Solomon, Moses, etc.) correlates with the proportion of psalms selected within the Horologion.

When the *Horologion* is prayed within a liturgical service, the congregation recites the Introduction to Every Hour (Introduction, Thanksgiving Prayer, Psalm 50) in a low voice. Additional introductory prayers are added for the First and Midnight Hours. Psalms are distributed to each attendee (cf. 1 Cor 14:26), who prays that psalm in a low voice. The gospel of the hour is then prayed before the iconostasis, followed by short litanies (*Troparia, Theotokion*). *Kyrie eleison* is chanted 41 times, followed by the Holy, Holy, Holy, the Absolution (*Collect*), and the conclusion. Unlike the Byzantine and Latin rites, no incense is offered during these prayers.

Notes

1 The *Theotokia* and *Psali* are divided into two distinct melodies in modern usage: Sunday, Monday, and Tuesday follow the "Adam Tune" while the remaining days follow the

"Watos" tune. These designations come from the first word in the *Theotokion* for Sunday and Wednesday, respectively.

2 Cf. 1 Tim 3:16, 3:9; Rev 1:20, 10:7; Mk 4:11; Rom 11:25, 16:25; 1 Cor 15:51; Eph 1:9, 3:3, 3:9, 5:32; Col 1:26–27, 2:2, 4:3.

3 This phrase adopted from 1 Tim 3:16 is used in the Institution Narrative.

4 The anaphora attributed to St. Cyril preserves many elements of the ancient anaphora attributed to St. Mark the Evangelist. Although the original redaction is wanting, papyri manuscripts and other fragments date back to as early as the third century. Yet, the relationship between the Greek and Coptic versions is markedly labyrinthine. See Cuming 1990: xiii.

5 Many of the world's earliest surviving anaphoras are Egyptian: the Strasbourg Papyrus, the Euchologion of Sarapion, the Deir Balyzeh Papyrus, the British Museum Tablet, the Louvain Papyrus, and most probably the Barcelona Papyrus, to name a few. Cuming dates the Strasbourg Papyrus from 175–200, although it is debatable whether this is a complete anaphora or a portion of one. See Cuming 1984.

6 The Coptic (*ithbodikon*, *spoudikon*) and Arabic (*isbadiqun*) are adaptations from the Greek.

7 St. Basil the Great, *On Renunciation of the World*, 4 (PG 31:636B).

8 Butler (1884: 2: 301, n.4) cites the fourth-century manuscript from A. Georgius, *Fragmentum Evangelii S. Johannis* (Rome, 1789, 4to.), pp. 308–9, and the eleventh century copy by Joseph, the deacon of Abu Maqār.

9 Isa 61, Exo 30, 40; Heb 1:5–14, 1 Jn 2:21–29, Acts 8:14–40; Ps 88:19, Mk 14:3–9.

Selected Bibliography

Aquinas, T. and Sullivan, D.J. (1955) *The Summa theologica*, Chicago: Encyclopaedia Britannica.

Athanasius (Pseudo), *Fragments against Paul of Samosata, Macedonians, Novatians* (PG 26: 1293, 1313–1317).

Augustine (1995) *De Doctrina Christiana* ("On Christian Teaching"), trans. R.P.H. Green, Oxford/New York: Clarendon Press.

Basil of Caesarea (1950) "An Ascetical Discourse and Exhortation on the Renunciation of the World and Spiritual Perfection, " in *St. Basil: Ascetical Works,* trans. Sister M. Monica Wagner, C.S.C. Washington, DC: Catholic University of America Press.

Bates, W. H. (1981) "Thanksgiving and Intercession in the Liturgy of St. Mark," in B. Spinks (ed.) *The Sacrifice of Praise*, Rome: BEL Subsidia 19.

Burmester, O. H. E. (1932a) "The Canons of Christodoulos, Patriarch of Alexandria (A.D. 1047–77)," *Le Muséon*, 45: 51–84.

——(1932b) "Two Services of the Coptic Church Attributed to Peter, Bishop of Bahnasā," *Le Muséon*, 45: 235–54.

——(1936) "The Greek Kîrugmata, Versicles and Responses, and Hymns in the Coptic Liturgy," *Orientalia Christiana Periodica*, 2(3–4): 363–94.

——(1938) "The Turuhāt of the Saints," *Bulletin de la Société d'Archéologie Copte*, 4: 141–94.

——(1954) "A Coptic Tradition Concerning the Holy Myron (Chrism)," in *Publications de l'Institut d'études orientales de la Bibliothèque patriarcale d'Alexandrie*, 3: 52–58.

——(1963–64) "An Offeratory-Consecratory Prayer in the Greek and Coptic Liturgy of Saint Mark," *Bulletin de la Société d'Archéologie Copte*, 17: 23–33.

——(1967) *The Egyptian or Coptic Orthodox: A Detailed Description of Her Liturgical Services*, Cairo: Société d'Archéologie Copte.

Butler, A. J. (1884) *The Ancient Coptic Churches of Egypt*, 2 vols, Oxford: Clarendon Press.

Coquin, R. -G. (1969) "L'anaphore alexandrine de saint Marc," *Le Museón: revue d'études orientales*, 82 (1969): 307–56; reprinted in B. Botte (ed.) (1970), *Eucharisties d'Orient et d'Occident*, vol. II, Paris: Cerf.

Cuming, G. J. (1974) "Egyptian Elements in the Jerusalem Liturgy," *Journal of Theological Studies*, 25(1): 117–24.

——(1984) "Four Very Early Anaphoras," *Worship*, 58(2): 168–72.

——(1990) *The Liturgy of St. Mark*, Rome: Pontificum Institutum Orientalium.

——(1997) "The Liturgy of St. Mark: A Study of Development," in P. F. Bradshaw (ed.) *Essays on Early Eucharistic Prayers*, Collegeville: Liturgical Press.

Evdokimov, Paul (1965) "Nature," *Scottish Journal of Theology*, 18(1): 1–22.

Grillmeier, A. and Hainthaler, T. (1996) "On Christology in the Liturgical Prayer of the Coptic Orthodox," in A. Grillmeier (ed.) *Christ in the Christian Tradition, Vol. 2.4, The Church of Alexandria with Nubia and Ethiopia after 451*, trans. O. C. Dean, Jr., London: Continuum.

Hammerschmidt, E. (1967–68) "Some Remarks on the History of, and Present State of Investigation into the Coptic Liturgy," *Bulletin de la Société d'Archéologie Copte*, 19: 89–113.

Kosack, W. (2012) *Der koptische Heiligenkalender: Deutsch – Koptisch – Arabisch nach den besten Quellen neu bearbeitet und vollständig herausgegeben*. Berlin: Verlag Christoph Brunner.

Johnson, M. E. (1995) *Liturgy in Early Christian Egypt*, Cambridge: Grove.

Lantschoot, A. van (1932) "Le manuscrit Vatican Copte 44 et le Livre du Chême ms Paris arabe 100," *Le Muséon*, 45(3–4): 181–234.

Lodi, E. (2000) "Oriental Anaphoras," in A. J. Chupungo (ed.) *Handbook for Liturgical Studies*, vol. 3, Collegeville: Liturgical Press.

Malak, I. (1982) "The Eucharistic Liturgy According to the Rite of the Coptic Orthodox of Alexandria," in J. Madey (ed.) *The Eucharistic Liturgy in the Christian East*, Paderborn, West Germany: Eastern Churches Service/Kerala, India: Prakasam Publications.

Malaty, T. Y. (1993) *Introduction to the Coptic Church*, Alexandria: St. George's Coptic Orthodox Church.

Meinardus, O. (1991) "About the Coction and Consecration of the Holy Myron in the Coptic Church," *Coptic Church Review*, 12(3): 78–86.

Moftah, R., Robertson, M., Roy, M. and Tóth, M. (1991) "Music, Coptic: Description of the Corpus and Present Musical Practice," in A. Atiya (ed.) *Coptic Encyclopedia*, New York: Macmillan.

O'Leary, D. L. (1911) *The Daily Office and the Theotokia of the Coptic Church*, London: Simkin, Marshall, Kent.

Regnault, L. (1999) *The Day-to-Day Life of the Desert Fathers in Fourth-Century Egypt*, trans. É. Poirer, Jr. Petersham, MA: St. Bede's Publications.

Saad, S. M. and Saad, N. M (2000) "Electing Coptic Patriarchs: A Diversity of Traditions," *Bulletin of St. Shenouda the Archimandrite Coptic Society* (Los Angeles), 6: 20–32.

Takla, H. (1997–98) "Coptic Liturgy: Past, Present and Future." *St. Shenouda Annual Bulletin*, 4: 43–62.

Teres, G. (2000) *The Bible and Astronomy: The Magi and the Star in the Gospel*, Budapest: Springer Orvosi Kiado Kft.

Wassef, C. W. (1991) "Calendar, Months of Coptic," in A. S. Atiya (ed.) *Coptic Encyclopedia*, New York: Macmillan.

Zanetti, U. (2009) "Liturgy at Wadi al-Natroun," in M. S. A. Mikhail and M. Moussa (eds) *Christianity and Monasticism in Wadi al-Natroun*, Cairo/New York: The American University in Cairo Press.

Liturgical Books

Coptic Orthodox Diocese of the Southern United States (2007) *The Divine Liturgy: The Anaphoras of Saints Basil, Gregory and Cyril*, 2nd ed. Tallahassee, Florida.

Moftah, R. (1998) *The Coptic Orthodox Liturgy of St. Basil with Complete Musical Transcription*. Music transcription by M. Toth, M. Roy (ed.). Cairo: American University in Cairo Press.

St. Mary and St. Antonios Coptic Orthodox Church (1999) *The Holy Psalmody*, Ridgewood, NY: St. Mary's Coptic Orthodox Church.

Websites for Liturgical and Hymnological References

www.copticchurch.net
www.copticheritage.org
www.coptichymns.org
www.st-takla.org
www.tasbeha.org

11 Music

Performing Coptic Expressive Culture

Carolyn M. Ramzy

Introduction

From as early as the thirteenth century, the Coptic Orthodox community has fascinated explorers, missionaries, and scholars traveling to Egypt in search of ancient Egyptian ruins.[1] Besides the many murals, excavations, and other tangible artifacts they encountered, these scholars also stumbled upon an intangible living heritage: Coptic *alḥān* or the liturgical hymnody that the community performed in their church services. Drawing on both Jewish and Greek musical influences prevalent in Egypt in the first century AD, Coptic Orthodox *alḥān* also incorporated elements of Egyptian folk music as well as other musical survivals from their ancient Egyptian predecessors. *Alḥān* were performed in Coptic, the colloquial language of the people derived from the last stage of demotic, a simplified script of hieroglyphs dating back to 650 BC. Though Coptic Christians now speak the Arabic language, they continue to perform this Coptic genre in overflowing churches all over Egypt and in growing communities of the Coptic diaspora all around the world.

This chapter is a historical survey of the Coptic Orthodox musical heritage and the major figures that were seminal to its transmission and preservation. As early as the third and fourth century, unearthed Greek manuscripts testify to the transmission of an oral liturgical genre with the aid of an indigenous notation system. Arabic writings by Christian intellectuals such as Isḥāq al-Mu'taman Abū Ibn Al-'Assāl, and Shams al-Ri'āsah Abū al-Barakāt Ibn Kabar in the thirteenth and fourteenth centuries describe Coptic music as a central part of church ritual (see Graf 1948–49; Périer 1922; Villecourt 1923–25). The first western musical transcription, appearing close to 300 years later, became the first "sound clip" of Coptic chant as one Jesuit priest heard it in 1643. Besides scholarly attention the missionary presence in Egypt beginning in the nineteenth century also intensified interest in Coptic chant; as missionaries worked to convert Orthodox Christians to Catholicism or Protestant sects, they also preserved their liturgical genre so new converts could continue to perform their indigenous music during services. During this time, western musicologists also took a different interest in Coptic music; they believed that *alḥān* were not only directly rooted in ancient Egyptian chant, but they also shed light on the very beginnings of western art music. It was not until the late twentieth and early twenty-first century that Copts themselves took the initiative to preserve their own musical heritage. With a growing agitation for national independence from British colonial administration, and a resistance to growing missionary influences, Egyptian amateur collectors preserved and recorded Coptic *alḥān* themselves. This includes Ragheb Moftah, the Egyptian collector who is now known as the father of Coptic music studies in Egypt. Today, young cantors continue to organize digital sound archives on the Internet, while a growing number of Coptic Christian satellite channels broadcast educational music lessons on private television.

Coptic Music in its Cultural Context

An excerpt from *The Commemoration of the Saints*, The Coptic Liturgy of St. Basil reads:

> And we too, who are sojourners in
> this place, keep us in Your faith,
> and grant us Your peace unto the end.

To better understand the nuanced dynamics of Coptic music, one must first explore the underpinning of Coptic Orthodox culture. Coptic Christian beliefs and religious music are all largely defined by one reigning metaphor: Life on earth is a transient journey with the human spirit always longing to return to God. After death, one may rejoin God in heaven and spend eternity in a state of *tasbīḥ*, the Arabic term for musical praise. Musically then, Copts believe that the genres they perform during church services momentarily create a sense of heaven on earth and that musical worship and praise is integral to attaining a spiritual communion with God. Because of this, all major Coptic rites of passage, from infant baptism to weddings and funerals, are sung throughout. Outside of these formal church contexts, people also listen to and perform a variety of non-liturgical devotional genres in today's colloquial language, Arabic.

Alḥān

Coptic religious music is composed of three distinct genres: *alḥān, madā'ḥ*, and *tarafīl* or *taranīm*. *Alḥān* are best defined as the Coptic liturgical hymnody performed during formal church services and traditional rites. Exclusively a vocal genre, *alḥān* are characterized by their florid melismas and intricate ornamentation. They are also entirely monophonic, meaning that they are performed in one voice without any added harmony. During a liturgical service, *alḥān* are sung alternatingly by three parties: the clergy or the officiant of the service known in Arabic as *al-kāhin*, the choir of cantors and deacons known as *al-shammāmsa*, and the congregation known as *al-sha'b*. Just as the music helps believers achieve a spiritual union with God, heaven, and earth, performing together also binds all participants into a tight-knit church community that regularly shares in this musical union.

Scholars speculate that there are three sources that have strongly influenced the genre of *alḥān*: Jewish liturgical music, Greek imprints from the city of Alexandria, as well as survivals of ancient Egyptian music (Moftah et al. 1991: 1731–32). According to Church history, St. Mark the evangelist brought Christianity to Alexandria in AD 42, a bustling and cosmopolitan center of what was then the Greco-Roman Empire. There, newly converted Egyptian Christians drew on Jewish settings of religious texts and incorporated the Psalter as the oldest and most venerated song book in their church worship (ibid.). Early Coptic liturgical materials also relied heavily on the Greek language, as it was the language of the eastern empire. Hymn fragments found from as early as the third century containing Greek song texts testify to this phenomenon (Grenfell and Hunt 1898: papyrus 1786).

Ancient Egyptian musical survivals have garnered the most scholarly attention and become most venerated among today's Coptic community. German musicologist Hans Hickmann was prolific in his writings concerning these ancient Egyptian adaptations from temple to church worship.[2] He pointed out three distinct features: Firstly, the antiphonal singing, which still takes place today, in which two choirs of deacons, one standing at the north and the other at the south end of the church, sing in turn, lending a dynamic sound to the service. Second is the extensive ornamentation that takes place on vowels, filling each melodic line, as well as the accompaniment of a small pair of hand cymbals known as the *daff* (see below). Lastly, the continued use of blind cantors, known as *mu'allimīn*, has become a particular marker of the continued transmission of this genre from one generation to the next, from images of their performance on temple walls to their present position leading service at the front of the deacon choir (Ramzy 2009b).

Historically, the term *alḥān* (sing. *laḥn*) itself first appeared as early as the thirteenth century, though with a very different connotation and meanings than its contemporary use among today's Coptic Orthodox community. The Arabic Christian intellectual Shams al-Ri'āsah Abū al-Barakāt Ibn Kabar wrote in AD 1320 that the Arabic term *laḥn* actually meant a musical tone or scale with which each liturgical text would be performed according to its mood, season, or festivity (Villecourt 1923–25: 264). He goes on to say that there are eight Coptic tones, akin to the notion of Arabic mode or *maqam*, or the Greek Orthodox liturgical tones. Other writers, such as twelfth-century Abū Ishāq Ishāq al-Mu'taman Abū Ibn al-'Assāl, began to distinguish *alḥān* as solely church genre, different from other religious and devotional genres that Copts performed outside of church services, indicating the emerging variety and richness of early religious Coptic music (Graf 1948–49: 166).

Today, the Coptic community continues to regard *alḥān* as the most important and revered genre of musical praise or *tasbīḥ* to God. Drawing their

Figure 11.1 A pair of *sajjat*, a small pair of hand cymbals known as the *daff* together with a small metal triangle known as the *muthallath*, which helps to keep congregations in time with their cantor leaders [photograph by Lois M. Farag]

definitions from Biblical texts, the most frequently cited examples are from the Psalms of David, specifically Psalm 150, which is regularly performed during the Eucharist portion of the liturgy. While this psalm mentions musical instruments and dance as forms of *tasbīḥ*, the Coptic Orthodox Church highly frowns on both as they detract attention away from the text. Rather, the singing is entirely unaccompanied with the exception of a small pair of hand cymbals known as *al-daff* or *nāqūs* and a metal triangle known as *al-muthallath* or a *tri-anto*. When the *muthallath* and the *daff* are played together, not only do they keep time and ensure that the *kāhin*, *shammāmsa*, and the *sha'b* stay together, but they also produce intricate and interlocking rhythms with the embellished vocal lines they accompany.

Madā'ḥ

Besides *alḥān*, Copts also perform a wide variety of *madā'ḥ* (sing. *madīḥā*). *Madā'ḥ* are Arabic, Coptic, and Greek hymns praising various saints and apostles and the Virgin Mary, as well as patron saints of particular churches and sites of religious pilgrimage. Scholars do not know exactly when *madā'ḥ* were first introduced into the Coptic liturgical canon, but they estimate that they became an integral part of extra-liturgical worship beginning in the thirteenth century (Moftah et al. 1991: 1727).

Despite the church's ambivalent relationship to popular or secular music, *madā'ḥ* predominantly draw on contemporary Egyptian folk genres, borrowing from rural, devotional, and classical contexts. Long and strophic poems, *madā'ḥ* not only embed mnemonic devices to remind singers of the long strophes, but also hide the author's name in a verse at the end of the song. Additionally, *madā'ḥ* texts resemble the folk poetry of *mawwāl* songs with their frequent references to local fruits, seasons, and indigenous metaphors drawn from people's daily lives. An example of this can be found in a short translated excerpt from one of the most well known Christian *madīḥā* titled, "*Imadḥ fil Batūl*" or "Praise to the Virgin" dedicated to Mary, the Mother of God (El-Fares 2007: 96):

> Oh red dates, O yellow lemons
> Your love has captivated me
> O highest of ranks
> Moses saw you O Mary
> Wonder of wonders.

Here, the red dates and the yellow lemons refer not only to a particular seasonal harvest, but are also used as spiritual metaphors and pedagogical tools reminding Copts about their past. For Coptic Christians, the red dates represent their martyred forefathers who died for their faith. While their vibrant red skin symbolizes the sacrificed blood of Christ, their white sweetness and tough seed also represent their forefathers' purity and tenacity in maintaining their beliefs despite changing and at times aggressive political landscapes (see Ramzy 2009a: 100).

Lastly, *madā'ḥ* form an integral element of the *Psalmodia* services performed daily in Coptic monasteries and convents throughout Egypt. As the name indicates, the *Psalmodia* service is a collection of hymns drawing on Biblical psalms, prayers, and laudations to the saints. In more urban settings and now in immigrant communities outside of Egypt, *madā'ḥ* are customarily celebrated on the eve of a liturgical service, usually a Saturday evening. During the month of *Kiahk* prior to Christmas day, *madā'ḥ* hymns are transformed into Christmas carols preparing parishioners for the holiday festivities.

Taratīl *and* Taranīm

Apart from *alḥān* and *madā'ḥ, taratīl* (sing. *tartīla*) are the most widely performed genre of non-liturgical music. Also known as *taranīm* (sing. *tarnīma*), they are performed in the vernacular Arabic, which became the Egyptian mother tongue following the Arab conquest of Egypt in AD 641.[3] *Taratīl* and *taranīm* largely have their roots in the translated "spiritual songs" or *aghānī ruḥiya* that arrived with American Protestant missionaries in the mid-nineteenth century. While French Catholic missionaries, Jesuits, and British Protestants arrived as early as the sixteenth century, it was American Presbyterian missionaries who formed the largest and most active missionary enterprise in Egypt. Besides building schools, hospitals, and establishing the Evangelical Church of Egypt, they also transplanted many missionary hymns such as "Nearer my God to Thee" and "Jesus Loves Me," translated into Arabic (The American Presbyterian Missionaries in Egypt 1917). Soon, however, Coptic Orthodox Christians began publishing their own *tarafīl*, with texts based on their own theological beliefs and incorporating popular Egyptian melodies that everyone could recognize and sing. It is no surprise, then, to find a *tarfīla* called *"Ta'alla Īlayyi Īlayyi"* ["Come to Me"] based on one of the most popular songs, "*Ghanīlī Shiwayyi Shiwayyi*" ["Sing to Me"], performed by the Egyptian superstar Umm Kulthūm.

Orthodox *tarafīl* become quite popular during the Sunday School movement, a religious educational reform beginning in the 1920s that actively resisted American Protestant missionary efforts and challenged British colonial authority. Coptic middle-class laity organized classes that educated their youth about their religion, ancient language, and music, igniting an interest in preserving and performing Coptic expressive culture. The Sunday School reform was formally established by the noted Dean of the Coptic Clerical College, Ḥabīb Jirjis (1876–1951) who composed and published his own *tarafīl*. Unlike Protestant *aghānī ruḥiya*, Jirjis based the melodies of these Orthodox *tarafīl* largely on the church liturgical genre of *alḥān*. Drawing on American Presbyterian models, Jirjis published *tarafīl* pamphlets and encouraged his students to perform these songs during Bible meetings, community gatherings, performances, and even weddings.

Over the past century, this genre has slowly been transformed and has emerged outside of Sunday School classrooms to become the most prevalent popular devotional music that Copts listen to outside of church. As more and more community choirs began to form, more composers came on the scene to write new *tarafīl*, drawing on the latest musical trends from within and outside of Egypt. *Tarafīl* progressed from a previously unaccompanied genre to now being accompanied by musical instruments that range from Egyptian folk and classical instruments to the violin, piano, electric organ, and even the electric guitar. With the introduction of new media technologies such as the cassette player beginning in the 1970s, the Internet, and now the growth of Coptic Christian satellite channels, *tarafīl* have been transformed into a vibrant popular musical genre, complete with live concerts, music videos, and rising stars, such as the Better Life Choir, singer-song writer Maher Fayez, and even the venerated Lebanese singer Fairouz.[4]

In spite of the growing prevalence of *tarafīl* and *madā'ḥ* in Coptic life, media, and experiences outside of the church, it is Coptic *alḥān* that have garnered the most scholarly attention in the past few centuries. Due to early missionary and scholarly records as well as the efforts of the Coptic religious elite at the beginning of the twentieth century, the growing interest in and veneration of *alḥān* reveals a rich social commentary, firstly, as Copts grappled with their place in British colonial imagination, and secondly, as they negotiate an increasingly rocky political terrain after Egyptian independence in 1952. This chapter continues to explore the genre of *alḥān*, with special attention to how liturgical hymnody has emerged in the discipline of Coptic studies and been institutionalized within Coptic identity discourses in the past century.

Of Missionaries and Travelers: Coptic *Alḥān* and Colonial Imagination Before 1900

First Western Musical Transcription: Father Athanasius Kircher

Before the short-lived but influential French occupation of Egypt from 1798 to 1801, Egypt and its residents primarily lived in the imagination, popular literature, and writings of scholars, travelers, and missionaries for westerners. One particular missionary never even set foot in Egypt, but went on to become one of the most widely recognized scholars of ancient Egyptian antiquity of his time. His efforts began a long line of inquiry into the Coptic language, religion, culture, and finally, music. A German Jesuit priest, Father Athanasius Kircher (1602–80) is renowned as the father of Egyptology and is historically credited for being the first to correctly link the Coptic language to its roots in hieroglyphics. Though the Rosetta Stone was not found until more than a hundred years after his death, Kircher even asserted that he could read and translate the ancient script, a claim of which his colleagues were highly critical. A prodigious scholar of medicine, history, physics, astronomy, math and linguistics, Kircher expressed a keen and intersecting interest in Coptic language and church music. In one of his earliest and most influential lexicons of the Coptic language, *Lingua Aegyptiaca Restituta*, dated 1643, Kircher wrote down what he affirmed was a phrase of Coptic liturgical chant. He claimed it to be "the solemn intonation of the Mass with the musical notes just as I was able to extract it from the mouth of my Coptic scribe," likely one of the two Coptic cantors he reported to have visited Rome in the 1630s (Kircher 1643: 527).

Written in early western musical notation, contemporary musicologists and Coptic cantors quickly disregarded Kircher's transcription, pointing out the flawed Coptic language as well as a melodic line that today's Coptic cantors cannot place within the contemporary liturgical canon. Despite these musical and linguistic discrepancies, Kircher's work is significant for a myriad of other reasons. Firstly, this is the earliest known western transcription of Coptic music to date and illustrates the initial European fascination with the Coptic community as descendants of the ancient Egyptians. Kircher's Latin preface also provides a cultural context for this liturgical music tradition that had been absent from scholarly literature since the fourteenth century when Christian intellectuals Ibn Al-'Assāl, Ibn Sibā' and Ibn Kabar last left off.

The French Expedition: Guillaume-André Villoteau and the Description de l'Égypte

When Napoleon Bonaparte arrived on the shores of the Mediterranean city of Alexandria in 1798, he brought 167 scholars in tow and initiated the most comprehensive scientific expedition of Egypt of all time, transforming the mysterious Nile delta into a living laboratory. As part of the French Commission on the Sciences and the Arts, music scholar Guillaume-André Villoteau (1759–1839) would study Coptic liturgical music once again, providing the next insight into Coptic music studies and culture at the beginning of the nineteenth century. His intentions, as his writings would reveal, were quite different than Kircher's, however.

By the time Villoteau began his study, European exploration had moved into a new phase of colonial occupation and domination across the world at the turn of the nineteenth century. Cross-cultural studies in various disciplines became an imperialist method for legitimizing the expansion and establishment of empire, particularly of French and British powers. Music studies were not innocent of these underlying frameworks. Villoteau's transcriptions were a part of the *Description de l'Égypte*, a survey that prepared Egypt for French occupation after Napoleon Bonaparte's arrival. Like his colleagues, Villoteau conducted considerable fieldwork in Egypt, living in the country for two years and learning how to play the Egyptian musical instruments he was researching. While he held Arab classical music in high esteem, he did not hide his disdain for Coptic Orthodox liturgical chant, describing how it "lacerated his ears" and spread a "nauseating poison" that irritated his very soul and heart (Gillespie 1978: 227–45).[5] Perhaps infused with the growing ethnocentrism that found its way in early travelers' writings, Villoteau ranked Coptic *alḥān* as the least of African musical arts. Villoteau's tone did not come as a surprise however; as part of the colonial endeavor, many music scholars of his generation expressed similar sentiments about the new music they encountered and much of their criticism worked to justify imperial expansion.

Despite Villoteau's scathing musical review, his transcription and preface are still monumental for providing a wealth of information about Coptic liturgical chant. In his brief preface, he outlines early liturgical traditions and how Copts used to perform their religious services.[6] Besides this, Villoteau was also the first music scholar to invent new symbols to represent non-western music in western musical notation, illustrating the musical complexity of Egyptian music, including *alḥān. Alḥān* have highly florid and ornamented melodic lines as well as quarter-tones that do not fit neatly into western staff notation. Yet, in his study of Coptic chant, Villoteau notated a particularly florid excerpt of the "Alleluia" hymn using these new methods. Whenever the melismas or ornamentation he heard were too florid to notate or did not fit within the even temperament of the western scale, he indicated double dashes in the score, highlighting their complexity. Unlike Kircher, who attempted to write in Coptic, Villoteau transliterated the Coptic text, writing down phonetically the language as he heard it. Though this hymn as Villoteau rendered it does not exist in today's liturgical canon, it is likely related to the "Big Alleluia" that Coptic cantors perform during Psalmody services, midnight Advent services, Epiphany, Palm Sunday, as well as Easter (Coptic Orthodox Church n.d.).

Napoleon Bonaparte's expedition ended abruptly in 1801 when the Ottoman and British armies defeated his troops. Though his stay was particularly brief, the French expedition had long-lasting influences that extended beyond Coptic music studies alone. It formally introduced Egypt to the academic world. Scholars, missionaries, and collectors flocked to the country, determined to unearth the antiquities and glories of an ancient Egyptian past, and learn more about contemporary Coptic culture and its ties to the ancient Egyptian heritage. The schools, hospitals, museums, and churches that missionaries left behind substantially changed the way Copts have learned, preserved, and performed their oral heritage to this day.

A Missionary Perspective; the Works of Jesuit Fathers Jules Blin and Louis Badet

At the end of the nineteenth century, two French Jesuit priests arrived with the growing number of missionaries working in Egypt. Their work would prove particularly insightful to the growing community of Coptic Catholics who converted from Orthodox Christianity. Father Jules Blin (1853–1891) and Father Louis Badet (1873–1933) taught at one of the newly built schools in Cairo, the Collège de la Sainte Famille. As a seminary, it was formally established in 1879 with the explicit goal of educating newly converted clergy to lead their own congregations in worship. As Coptic Catholics could now maintain their Orthodox tradition, thanks to an edict by Pope Puis IX (r. 1846–78) (Sharkey 2008: 32), Fathers Blin and Badet worked to notate and standardize their traditional *alḥān* so they could continue performing them in their new services. Because it was an exclusively oral tradition, Fathers Blin and Badet believed that if Coptic music was not written down, it would disappear under the influences of contemporary Arabic and popular music in Egypt. They were in for a bit of a surprise. Long after their deaths, the genre continues to be widely performed in Orthodox and Catholic churches, though without the use of written notation.

Like Kircher's transcriptions, today's scholars have deemed Father Blin's work, soon followed by that of Father Badet, notably inaccurate. Yet their contributions are still noteworthy for the changes they inspired within western scholarship of Coptic music (Gillespie 1978: 231). Father Jules Blin was the first to move toward a culturally relativistic study of Coptic culture and expression. In other words, Father Blin defended *alḥān* against Villoteau's ethnocentric criticisms. He not only emphasized the beauty and sanctity of Coptic expression and worship, but he also identified *alḥān* as an indigenously Egyptian phenomenon. With its unique melismas, singing style, and role in Coptic worship, the genre was distinct from Egyptian popular music and something worthy of study, protection, and preservation.

Father Badet emphasized this culturally relativist stance declaring, "Anyone trying to compare Coptic music to modern European music would be making a grave error" (Badet 1899 [1936]: 5).[7] More precisely, he insisted that it was entirely ethnocentric to compare Coptic music to the European classical tradition and that the genre had to be understood within its own culturally specific context. With the hope of correcting many of Father Blin's inaccuracies, Father Badet not only reviewed his colleague's work, but also notated both of the most widely performed services, the liturgies of St. Basil and St. Gregory. Additionally, Father Badet also intended to educate Coptic Christians about western musical notation; the first twenty pages or so of his book are a review of elementary European music principles so that new Coptic clergy could read these western transcriptions themselves. Despite his good intentions, Father Badet's work was largely inaccurate. He left out many of the central melismas and ornaments that distinguish Coptic hymns. What did emerge from Father Badet's transcription, however, were the basic melodic structures with a strong resemblance to the actual sounds of today's *alḥān*.

Coptic Chant After 1900: Egyptians Preserving Their Own Traditions

A Coptic Folklorist: Mu'allim Takla

While European missionaries and scholars were researching and recording Coptic music in the late nineteenth century, Egyptians were also hard at work collecting and preserving their own heritage. Traditionally, *alḥān* have been orally transmitted through generations of blind teachers officially known as *mu'allimūn* (sing. *mu'allim*). Congregants and church authorities believe that because these teachers have lost their sight, their keener ears and memory make them perfect candidates to memorize and render *alḥān*. These cantors also depend on an ancient teaching method known as *chironomy* or the physical rendition of liturgical melodies using hand motions and gestures. Images of figures using these teaching methods are not only found on Pharaonic and ancient Egyptian wall reliefs, but can also be seen in contemporary church contexts where *mu'allimūn* continue to teach.[8]

Mu'allimūn, as they were known colloquially, emerged as gatekeepers of *alḥān* in the middle of the nineteenth century, under the tenure of the Coptic Pope Cyril IV (1853–61), otherwise known throughout Coptic history as "the Reformer." *Mu'allimūn* were a part of Pope Cyril's reform on education and the revival of Coptic liturgical music. Troubled by the errors made by uneducated cantors, the pope sought out *mu'allim* Takla at one of his newly established Coptic schools and officially assigned him the duty of collecting and revitalizing the correct rendition of the Coptic hymnody. Like a contemporary folklorist, *mu'allim* Takla traveled between Upper and Lower Egypt, gathering and memorizing these hymns. Upon his return to Cairo, he published the very first edition of *The Service of the Deacons* in 1859. This book did not include any musical notation. Instead, it presented the texts of all *alḥān* performed during the liturgical services and church rites and became a canonical publication with editions still in use. While *mu'allimūn* continued to depend on oral transmission, they now had the texts of all the hymns in one place. *Mu'allim* Takla went on to teach *mu'allim* Mikha'īl Jirgis al-Batanūnī, the most well-known teacher of all time. He was nicknamed "*mu'allim* Mikha'īl the Great," for his involvement with one of the most comprehensive projects in Coptic music, the work of Egyptian collector Ragheb Moftah. While Moftah has been credited with being the first Egyptian to transcribe Coptic *alḥān* into western musical notation, it was actually Kamīl Ibrahīm Ghubriyāl who made this first attempt close to eighty years earlier.

Egyptians Transcribing Coptic Music: Kamīl Ibrahīm Ghubriyāl

Coptic *alḥān* have been traditionally transmitted though countless generations of *mu'allimīn* and an indigenous notation system known as *hazzāt*. An Arabic term, *hazzāt* literally means "motion" or "movement" and comprises a series of neumes (dots and dashes) placed above Coptic hymn texts to indicate the melodic direction of *alḥān*. Though scholars have not confirmed it to be the same notation found in Greek manuscripts discovered in Egypt as early as the third century,[9] this notation system shares a similar mnemonic function, to help singers distinguish between hymns. Despite this indigenous system and the long tradition of *mu'allimīn* teaching in churches, a few Copts, including Kamīl Ibrahīm Ghubriyāl, still insisted on notating Coptic music in western musical notation.

Fueled by growing Egyptian nationalism, the desire for independence from British occupation, and an increasing agitation against missionary influence, Ghubriyāl notated Coptic hymns into western musical notation in a rather timely publication. Two years later, in 1918, an Egyptian *wafd* delegation traveled to Paris to petition for Egypt's independence. When they were outrightly refused, this incited the 1919 revolution that eventually ousted a majority of the English. This nationalism was not lost on the Copts. In his introduction, Ghubriyāl not only urged Copts to return to their indigenous traditions, but he explicitly targeted Coptic youth, particularly girls and young women in Coptic schools. This is fairly surprising considering the fact that the Coptic liturgical genre is predominantly performed and transmitted by men, even to this day. To compete with secular musical forms, such as the imported piano parlor songs that accompanied the arrival of pianos in middle-class Egyptian homes, Ghubriyāl was determined to make Coptic chants more attractive by adding rhythmic accompaniment played at the octave. Though he does not include any other harmony, he altered some notes and traditional rhythms to accommodate his newly introduced duple meter.

In the face of rapid modernization, British and American missionary schooling, and increased contact with the west, Ghubriyāl feared that traditional Coptic culture, deeply vested in church life, would disintegrate due to the community's apathy and ignorance of their own heritage. Ghubriyāl, however, did not think that scholarship was enough. Believing that the negative influences of secular music would ultimately harm the larger social fabric of what he specifically called the Coptic nation, Ghubriyāl was hoping that modified Coptic chant would replace the performance of non-religious music performed in Coptic schools, at social gatherings and weddings, and in community organizations. Ghubriyāl proposed modernizing Coptic music and liturgical services by adding an organ to all the churches in Cairo. He even offered to help finance such an endeavor, though church officials and other religious elite opposed his proposition.

Ragheb Moftah, the Father of Coptic Music Studies

Many scholars consider Ragheb Moftah (1898–2001) the father of Coptic music studies. Coming from an upper middle-class family, he was motivated by similar concerns to Ḥabīb Jirjis about missionary encroachment on Coptic culture and was eager to safeguard Coptic heritage against outside influence. He rejected outright Ghubriyāl's proposal to modernize Coptic hymns by adding piano accompaniment, convinced that this would adulterate their ancient Egyptian roots. Instead, he investigated how to collect and notate them for the purpose of standardizing and teaching them to future generations. He would dedicate seventy-five years of his life to this endeavor beginning with his meeting with British violinist and composer, Ernest Newlandsmith (1875–after 1951), in 1926.

Between 1926 and 1936, Moftah and Newlandsmith worked together to produce sixteen folios of Coptic liturgical music notation, fourteen of which are now at the heart of the Ragheb Moftah Collection at the Library of Congress. In what proved to be the most comprehensive undertaking on Coptic music of its time, Newlandsmith notated the complete liturgy of St. Basil as well as twenty-five major seasonal hymns. He notated what the great cantor, Mikha'īl Jirgis al-Batanūnī sang to him when the two met on Moftah's houseboat. Newlandsmith's transcriptions, particularly his drafts, reveal this live-performance dynamic and how he struggled to find the best key in order to avoid adding unnecessary accidentals that would add to the complexity of *alḥān.* They also reflect his repeated attempts to capture the same hymn. In contrast to Kircher, Villoteau, and Fathers Blin and Badet, Newlandsmith admits to leaving out ornamentation and embellishments on purpose, describing them as the "appalling debris of Arabic ornamentation."[10] In fact, after auditioning several singers, both Moftah and Newlandsmith agreed to work with Batanūnī because of his clear rendition of Coptic hymns, devoid of an overtly embellished style. Working with Moftah to standardize the Coptic hymnody for easier transmission, Newlandsmith's transcriptions are largely prescriptive, meaning that they only capture the basic melodic structure of the hymns. Most of them are outlined in duple meter, with simplified rhythms.

Perhaps what was most interesting about Newlandsmith's work, however, was his preoccupation with finding what he considered the most authentic elements of ancient Egyptian sound in Coptic chant. Newlandsmith believed western classical music had its roots in ancient Egyptian music rather than Greek, which was the widely accepted notion. During one of his lecture tours across England, Newlandsmith declared, "After a careful study of these very simple themes, we cannot but feel that much of the music of western civilization must have its source in the Orient" (Newlandsmith 1931: 9). His argument is not surprising, considering the rising fascination that England had with its newest prosperous colony, Egypt, beginning in 1882. Though Newlandsmith's audiences were not necessarily convinced, his talks served to spark further interest in Coptic music, with American researchers John Gillespie and Marian Robertson-Wilson, as well as Hungarian musicologists Ilona Borsai and Margit Tóth, all of whom traveled to Egypt to work with Moftah.

It was Margit Tóth's transcriptions that were particularly significant to Moftah's preservation project. Using the recordings that Moftah made, she notated the entire liturgy of St. Basil as sung by two soloists, including *Mu'allim* Sādiq 'Attallah, and a male choir at the newly opened Higher Institute of Coptic Studies in 1954. What is unique about her transcriptions is that, unlike Ernest Newlandsmith, she was the first to notate extensively the melodic ornaments that make Coptic hymns so distinctive. She notated every nuanced embellishment, turn, and vibrato that *Mu'allim* Sādiq chanted on these recordings to showcase the melodic complexity of Coptic chant.

Close to thirty years in the making, Tóth's transcriptions were finally published in *The Coptic Orthodox Liturgy of St. Basil with Complete Transcription* in 1998. With the help of Martha Roy, a retired educator and missionary who translated and transliterated the Coptic into English, and Ragheb Moftah, who supplied the recordings, this became the culmination of Moftah's lifetime of work collecting and preserving Coptic chant. However, due to the technical complexity of Margit Tóth's transcriptions, and the fact that most of the Coptic community do not read western musical notation, it was Moftah's recordings, rather than these notations, that were embraced as a teaching tool by cantors and deacons. Today, many young cantors continue in Ragheb Moftah's footsteps by organizing digital sound archives on the Internet and forming choirs specifically to learn and perform Coptic *alḥān* outside of liturgical contexts.

A Living Heritage: Coptic Liturgical Chant Today

The Coptic Orthodox community continues to be the largest Christian minority in the Middle East.[11] There is also a growing diaspora all over the world, with communities in the United States, Canada, Australia, South America, sub-Saharan Africa, as well as many parts of Europe. Coptic immigrant communities are now performing in various languages, translating Coptic *alḥān, tarafīl*, and *madā'ḥ*. They also openly borrow devotional songs from other Christian denominations while composing their own spiritual songs. Yet, wherever they are, whenever they walk into a Coptic Orthodox Christian Church, they know they have come home.[12] In the interwoven mix of *alḥān, tarafīl*, and *madā'ḥ*, they are bound to one another and to the memory of their forefathers through worship and song.

Figure 11.2 Psaltos chant at St. Mark's Coptic Orthodox Church in Fairfax, Virginia [photograph by Carolyn M. Ramzy]

Notes

1 This chapter is based largely on my work as curator of the *Coptic Orthodox Liturgical Chant and Hymnody: The Ragheb Moftah Collection at the Library of Congress*. Manuscript excerpts cited here are courtesy of the Library of Congress Music Division and can be found at the *Performing Arts Encyclopedia* Special Presentations at http://lcweb2.loc.gov/diglib/ihas/html/coptic/coptic-home.html (accessed September 19, 2011).

2 A complete bibliography is listed in "Hans R.H. Hickmann, 1908–68." Ethnomusicology 1969 vol. 13, no. 2, 316–19.

3 With the Arab conquest of Egypt, the official language of the state and its dealings became Arabic. Copts, however, still continued to use the Coptic language as their vernacular tongue well into the eleventh century. See Moftah et al. 1991: 1734; and Moawad and Takla in this volume.

4 It is important to note the role of women in Coptic Christian music culture. Traditionally, it is male cantors, clergy, and deacons who perform and lead *alḥān* and *madā'ḥ* in liturgical church worship. Women are not silent in these contexts however, but are active participants as part of the congregations. In non-liturgical contexts, women are increasingly performing, composing, and recording *tarānīl* performances, as well as leading community choirs, orchestras, and other musical dramas.

5 Maryvonne Mavroukaksis provides a complete translation of Villoteau's introduction on the Library of Congress Coptic music web presentation at http://lcweb2.loc.gov/diglib/ihas/loc.natlib.ihas.200155950/default.html.

6 In one of his footnotes, Villoteau mentions the presence of a *'ekāz* or a double-crossed staff that congregants used to lean on during their long services. Unlike contemporary

Coptic churches today, these early churches did not have pews and worshippers used the *'ekāz* for momentary rest.

7 Maryvonne Mavroukaksis has kindly translated this introduction on the Library of Congress website at http://memory.loc.gov/diglib/ihas/loc.natlib.ihas.200155814/default.html (accessed December 12, 2010).

8 For more on representations of music making on ancient Egyptian wall reliefs, please see Hickmann 1961.

9 Three of these papyri were edited by Jourdan-Hemmerdinger (1979: 81–111). *Hazzāt* are also informally known as "*kharāyit*," an Arabic term meaning "maps." This notation does not supply the cantors with pitches or specific rhythms, but rather reminds singers of the length of melismas, placement of words, transitions, the motion of extended melodies, and the upward or downward direction of embellishments. In other words, they are "maps" on how to maneuver through a particular melody of a chant. As part of an exclusively oral tradition, *hazzāt* are primarily a tool of education and hymn transmission, and are rarely ever used during performance, though deacons have been known to use them during seasonal hymns that are rarely performed throughout the year.

10 Newlandsmith mentions this a few times, such as in his lecture at the Oxford University Church entitled, "The Ancient Music of the Coptic Church," on May 21, 1931. Also see his three-part article, "Music of the Orient: Recent Discoveries in Egypt," in *The Musical Standard* 37, May, June, and July 1932, pp.146, 161–62, 184–85.

11 While there is no accurate consensus of their size in Egypt, numerous accounts place them between 8 to 12 percent of Egypt's rapidly growing current population of about 80 million. According to the 2008 census undertaken by the Egyptian State Information service, as of May 1, 2008, Egypt's population reached 78.7 million. Copts however, have been routinely discounted in these national surveys and the Coptic Orthodox Church has traditionally contested the numbers projected by the Egyptian state.

12 For more on nostalgia and music among Coptic immigrant communities see Carolyn Ramzy, "*Tarafil*: Songs of Praise and the Musical Discourse of Nostalgia Among Coptic Immigrants in Toronto, Canada." Master's Thesis, Tallahassee, Florida: The Florida State University, 2007.

Selected Bibliography

The American Presbyterian Missionaries in Egypt (1917) *Bahgat al-Dhamīr fi Nazm al-Mazamir* [The Joys of the Spirit in the Psalter], Cairo: The English-American Publishing House.

Badet, L. (1899) *Chants Liturgiques des Coptes, notés et mis en ordre par Le Père Louis Badet, S.J. [Première] Partie Office de la Sainte Messe, Chants du Peuple et du Diacre*, Cairo: Collège de la Sainte-Famille, Petit Séminaire Copte; reprinted (1936) Rome: La Filografica. Introduction trans. M. Mavroukaksis. Online. http://memory.loc.gov/diglib/ihas/loc.natlib.ihas.200155814/default.html (accessed December 12, 2010).

Blin, J. (1988) *Chants liturgiques des Coptes. Notés et mis en ordre par le Père Jules Blin de la Compagnie de Jésus missionnaire en Egypte. 1 Partie chantée par le peuple et le diacre.* Cairo: Imprimerie nationale.

Coptic Orthodox Church (n.d.) *The Three Liturgies of Saint Basil, Gregory, and Cyril*, Asyut: Egypt, Al-Muhharaq Monastery.

El-Fares, R. (2007) *Fi al-fulklūr al-Qibfi* [*In Coptic Folklore*], Cairo: al-Hay'a al-Ama li-Qusur al-Thaqafa.

Ethnomusicology "Hans R.H. Hickmann, 1908–68" (1969) Memorial biography, 13(2): 316–19.

Gillespie, J. (1978) "A Survey of Past Research and a Projection for the Future," in R. Mcl. Wilson (ed.), *The Future of Coptic Studies*, Leiden: E.J. Brill.

Graf, G. (1948–49) "Der kirchliche Gesang nach Abū Ishāq Ishāq al-Mu'taman Abū ibn al-'Assāl (fl.1230–60)" [Extracts from *The Foundation of Religion* by Ibn al Assāl], *Bulletin de la Société d'archéologie copte*, 13: 161–78.
Grenfell, B. and Hunt, A. (eds) (1898) *The Oxyrhynchus Papyri*, London: Egypt Exploration Fund, 1898.
Hamilton, A. (2006) *The Copts and the West, 1439–1822: The European Discovery of the Egyptian Church*, Oxford: Oxford University Press.
Hickmann, H. (1961) *Musikgeschichte in Bildern. Ägypten*, vol. 2: *Musik des Altertums*, Leipzig: VEB Deutscher Verlag für Musik.
Jourdan-Hemmerdinger, D. (1979) "Nouveaux fragments musicaux sur papyrus (une notation antique par points)," *Studies in Eastern Chant*, 4: 81–111.
Kircher, A. (1643) *Lingua Aegyptiaca restituta*, Rome: Apud Ludovicum Grignanum.
Moftah, R. (ed.) (1998) *The Coptic Orthodox Liturgy of St. Basil with Complete Musical Transcription*, Cairo: The American University in Cairo Press.
Moftah, R., Robertson, M., Roy, M. and Toth, M. (1991) "Music, Coptic," in A.S. Atiya (ed.) *The Coptic Encyclopedia*. New York: Macmillan.
Newlandsmith, E. (1931) "The Ancient Music of the Coptic Church," lecture at the Oxford University Church on May 21, 1931.
——(1932) "Music of the Orient: Recent Discoveries in Egypt," *The Musical Standard*, 37: 146, 161–62, 184–85.
Périer, J. (ed.) (1922) *La Perle précieuse: traitant des sciences ecclésiastiques (chapitres I–LVI)* [*al-Jawarah al-Nafisah* by Yuhānnā ibn Abī Zakāriyyā ibn Sība'], *Patrologia Orientalis*, 16, fasc. 4: [593]–760, Paris: Firmin Didot, reprinted (1973) Turnhout, Belgium: Editions Brepols.
Ramzy, C. (2007) "*Tarafīl*: Songs of Praise and the Musical Discourse of Nostalgia Among Coptic Immigrants in Toronto, Canada," unpublished master's thesis, Tallahassee, Florida: The Florida State University.
——(2009a) "'Colors that Sing': Marguerite Nakhla's Folk Paintings and Non-Liturgical Folk Songs," in H. Moussa (ed.) *Marguerite Nakhla; A Legacy to Modern Egyptian Art*, Toronto: St. Mark's Coptic Museum.
——(2009b) "A Musical Inheritance: Coptic Cantors and an Orally Transmitted Tradition," in Library of Congress, Music Division, Performing Arts Encyclopedia. Online. http://lcweb2.loc.gov/diglib/ihas/loc.natlib.ihas.200155645/default.html (accessed December 28, 2012).
Sharkey, H. (2008) *American Evangelicals in Egypt; Missionary Encounters in an Age of Empire*, Princeton N.J.: Princeton University Press.
Villecourt, L. (1923–25) "Les Observances liturgiques et la discipline du jeûne dans l'église copte," (Chapters XVI–XIX from *Misbah al Zulmah* by Abū al-Barakāt ibn Kabar) *Le Muséon: revue d'études orientales* 36 (1923): 249–92, 37 (1924): 201–80, 38 (1925): 261–320.
Villoteau, G.-A. (1809) "De la Musique des Qobtes," in *Description de l'Égypte, ou, Recueil des observations et des recherches qui ont été faites en Égypte pendant l'éxpédition de l'armée française, publié par les ordres de Sa Majesté l'empereur Napoléon le Grand*, vol. 2, Paris: Imprimerie impériale.

Additional Web Resources

Coptic Orthodox Liturgical Chant & Hymnody; The Ragheb Moftah Collection at the Library of Congress [Special Presentation in the Library of Congress *Performing Arts Encyclopedia*]

http://lcweb2.loc.gov/diglib/ihas/html/coptic/coptic-home.html
Coptic Hymns: http://www.coptichymns.net
Coptic Orthodox Diocese of the Southern U.S.A.: http://suscopts.org
Coptic Orthodox Electronic Publishing Australia: http://www.coepaonline.org
Tasbeha.org: http://tasbeha.org
The Heritage of the Coptic Orthodox Church: http://www.copticheritage.org

Part III

Coptic Literary Culture

12 The Coptic Language

The Link to Ancient Egyptian

Hany N. Takla

Introduction

Coptic is the last written stage of the Egyptian family of languages. It guaranteed written Egyptian a continuous existence of over six millennia. It differed from the traditional Egyptian scripts of Hieroglyphic, Hieratic, and Demotic in two important aspects: an exclusively phonetic-based character system and the inclusion of vowels. Its fully developed alphabet system utilized elements from the two scripts that were used in administering Egypt during the first century AD: Greek and Demotic. This new and last version of Egyptian continued to develop over time, slowly gaining literary dominance over Greek until the Arab conquest of Egypt and then slowly fading away to a mere liturgical relic by the fourteenth century. This chapter will discuss Coptic's early Egyptian roots, origin in Christian and Pagan circles, dialects, historical development, the history of its study, and its future.

Early Egyptian Roots

Being the last written stage of the Egyptian languages, Coptic shared a great deal with its predecessors. The geography of Egypt placed most of the habitable land along the banks of the great Nile River. It is understandable that members of the multiple yet separate and stable agricultural communities there would eventually have had need of a standard written system with which to communicate. Such a system would probably have used pictograms of items familiar to the region in which these communities lived. Each pictogram initially represented a word. The development of the two kingdoms, Lower Egypt and Upper Egypt, and their subsequent union reinforced such a system and further developed it into what is observed in the Pyramid texts: a system in which pictograms developed into phonemes related to the sound value of whatever they originally represented. This new and comprehensive writing system is now referred to as *Old Egyptian*. It has survived primarily, if not exclusively, in wall inscriptions rather than written papyri. One cannot help but wonder why the country that gave the ancient world papyri writing material would not yield any Old Egyptian text on papyrus. The only clue I can present at this time is the biblical record of the great flood in the time of Noah. According to the chronology preserved in Genesis, the time of this cataclysmic event would have coincided with the end of the Old Kingdom and the ensuing First Intermediate period circa 2600 BC. This may explain why such written material from this period did not survive.[1]

After the reunification of Egypt in the Middle Kingdom, a new Egyptian language developed, known as *Middle Egyptian*. The surviving texts reveal a variety of literary genres beyond the almost exclusively religious ones of the Old Kingdom. This is the standard introductory Ancient Egyptian language taught in academia. It differed not only in its textual variety but also in its use of fewer hieroglyphic signs than its predecessor. Gardiner's *Egyptian Grammar* (Gardiner 1957: 438–548) provides a list of about 750 hieroglyphs as opposed to the 1,000 or so found in *Old Egyptian*. It survived up to the middle of the 18th Dynasty in the New Kingdom. It then became the language exclusively of worship in the temples.

Possibly following the end of the era of Akhnaton, the last of the Egyptian languages emerged, commonly referred to as *Late Egyptian*. This more vernacular-based language displayed significant grammatical changes from Middle Egyptian as well as hieroglyphic orthography. This orthography is called "Ramesside Orthography" and is observed in documents from 1310–1195 BC. More hieroglyphic signs were used in this new language. Scholars have identified over 4,000 hieroglyphs by the Ptolemaic and the early Roman periods.[2] This is considered the last language change in Egyptian. Further changes were primarily in script and vocabulary.

The collapse of the New Kingdom weakened support for such a beautiful but complex writing system. By the seventh century BC a new popular Late Egyptian script emerged, *Demotic*. It recorded the Late Egyptian grammar in a script with fewer symbols, about 500, but with less appealing orthography. Literature as well as administrative texts was recorded in this script, while Middle Egyptian continued its reign in Egyptian religion. This new orthographic shape of Egyptian continued for over a millennium until the fifth century AD, well into the Christian period. In Greco-Roman Egypt its use represented Egyptian defiance, albeit exclusively pagan, of the ruling Greek culture of the land.

Origin of Coptic in Pagan and Christian Circles

The Greek language during the Greco-Roman period became the lingua franca of educated and affluent Egyptians. This posed a problem for Egyptian temples still using the Egyptian language in its Middle Egyptian form. Their main product for sale to the populace, written magical spells, would have suffered greatly as a result of educated Egyptians preferring Greek over their native language. The solution devised by these enterprising religious institutions was to develop a writing system to transmit a transliteration of these spells in a script familiar to their targeted audience. Though the method of recording Egyptian in Greek characters arose much earlier, as can be seen in mummy labels found in the cemeteries of ancient Fayyum (Krause 1991), the new practice of the Egyptian temples gave birth to the oldest form of literary Coptic by the end of the first century AD. The surviving literature is commonly referred to as *Old Coptic* (Satzinger 1991). This type of Coptic utilized more characters from Demotic than have survived in classical Coptic. This was due to their emphasis on the pronunciation needed for such texts.

Christianity was officially introduced in Egypt in the mid-first century by St. Mark. Nearly a century and a half later the mostly Hellenized Christians of Alexandria developed a new script primarily to record the Egyptian language for their own missionary use, to introduce Christianity to Egypt's majority peasant population. In the late second century AD the motivation for such a venture can be found in the arrival of the famous Christian missionary Pantaenus to head the catechetical school of Alexandria and the election of Demetrius the Vinedresser as Bishop of Alexandria. It is logical to assume that the Christian message would be recorded in writing. The missionaries carrying out this task would doubtless have been bilingual Egyptians who needed a new script to meet such requirements. This resulted in a script much like that developed a century earlier by the pagans. This script, however, included almost no characters from the rather unfamiliar Demotic. Eventually, the experience of the returning missionaries made the addition of some of these Demotic characters a necessity to compensate for the lack of some necessary Egyptian sounds in Greek. The early literary production of this movement was the translation of selected parts of the Old and New Testaments.

As seen above, Coptic had two independent origins. They both shared the religiously motivated goal of bridging the gap between Greek and Egyptian to benefit their respective sides. However each approached it from a different side. Pagans approached it from the Egyptian side while Christians approached it from the Greek side. The targeted audience was also different. Pagans were targeting more educated and affluent Egyptians while Christians were targeting, in particular, illiterate and poor Egyptians. The rapid spread of Christianity in the fourth and fifth centuries AD influenced how and in what form Coptic was transmitted. Christians drew closer to the pagan linguistic approach by adding more Demotic characters to the original set of Greek characters that they had exclusively used. They diverged from the pagans' one-standard-language approach, however, by reviving many of the local dialects as literary ones. This was due to the Christians' target audience. Eventually, all these local literary dialects disappeared in the following centuries and were again limited to oral communications.

Dialects

As seen above, the Christians in their missionary approach made literary dialects out of the local vernaculars. They primarily served as vehicles for transmitting Scripture. They were distinguished by their unique orthography and geographical location. Although many dialects and subdialects have been identified by scholars, especially Rodolphe Kasser, there are six major ones that have yielded significant literary manuscripts:

- *Sahidic*: This is considered a neutral language/dialect, used throughout Egypt. Its Upper Egyptian designation is due to the provenance of its manuscripts.[3] It uses only six modified Demotic characters plus those of the Greek alphabet. Early Coptic scholars used the term Thebaic or Thebaine to refer to it.
- *Bohairic*: This is now considered a language rather than a regional dialect (Kasser 1991: 145). It originated in Lower Egypt, especially around modern-day Cairo. It was first called Coptic then scholars adopted the term Bohairic.[4] After the Coptic Orthodox patriarchate moved from Alexandria to Cairo in the eleventh century, it steadily replaced Sahidic to become the lone dialect of Coptic after the fourteenth century. It is still used now, but primarily as an ecclesiastical language. It is characterized by having seven Demotic characters plus those derived from Greek. In early publications the term Memphitic was also used to reference this dialect (Horner 1898–1905).
- *Fayyumic*: This dialect was confined to the Fayyum area, southwest of modern Cairo. It survived longer than any of the other regional dialects except for Bohairic. The area's economical vibrancy and its thriving monastic communities added to its longevity. It continued until the twelfth century but its surviving manuscripts are mostly fragmentary due to extended use. Some of these manuscripts traveled as far south as Sohag.[5] Classical Fayyumic has the unique characteristic of substituting l for r. It uses the same character set as Sahidic while adopting some features from Bohairic. In early publications it was referred to as "Middle Egyptian", or "Moyen Egyptien" (Crum 1905: 237; Vaschalde 1933). The term "Bashmuric" or "dialecte Baschmourique" was also used in earlier works (Quatremère 1808: ix).
- *Akhmimic*: This was confined to the region of Akhmim and Sohag. It is distinguished by the use of the Demotic character ⳉ, corresponding to the Bohairic ϧ. According to Frank Hallock, most of its manuscripts have come from the St. Shenouda monastery (Hallock 1933: 334–35). It was the vernacular dialect of those living around that monastery, as is reflected at times in St. Shenouda's sermons (Shisha-Halevy 1976). It survived until the eighth century, though it must have been eclipsed in the fifth century by the abbot's Sahidic writings, which dominated the region's literature.
- *Lycopolitan*: This dialect was probably confined to the modern-day Asyūṭ area in Middle Egypt. It uses the same character set as Sahidic. This area was a hotbed of heterodoxy or at least anti-Alexandrian-Church sentiments. The survival of translated Gnostic and Manichean texts in this dialect or bearing its influence suggests that such communities found a safe haven there, where I believe these texts were translated from Greek into Coptic. This also was identified as the dialect of a Manichean community in the Kellis area or the Dakhla Oasis (Gardiner et al. 1999: 90–91). This association with

heterodoxy undoubtedly contributed to its early disappearance as a literary dialect by the fifth century. It was referred to by Maurice Chaine as "siutic" or "Assioutique", i.e. "Asyutic" (Chaine 1933, 1934). Walter E. Crum referred to it in his dictionary as Subachmimic and used Chaine's siglum of "A^2" (Crum 1939: vii).

- *Mesokemic*: This is the last of the major dialects to be identified. Proper identification is attributed to Kahle (1954: Vol. 1, 220–27). It was probably native to the area around modern-day Banī Suef and the al-Bahnasā region in Middle Egypt. Similar to Lycopolitan, it is distinguished by word-spelling rather than uniqueness of character set. It was referred to as Middle Egyptian or Oxyrhnchite before Mesokemic was adopted. Like Lycopolitan it had disappeared as a literary dialect by the fifth century.
- *Others*: Many more minor, though distinct, dialects and subdialects were identified by Kasser. It should be pointed out that such classification was made possible by the presence of literary evidence, preserving a unique diction and/or grammar.

History of Development of the Language

From its first- and second-century roots, Coptic developed over the years. Its earlier pagan use does not seem to have gone beyond religious and astrological purposes, as far as the surviving literature attests. Later Christian use of the language grew faster and became dominant as the Christian population dramatically grew during the fourth century AD (Bagnall 1993: 280–81). The following discussion will be limited to the development of the language within Christian circles.

The history of Christianity in Egypt has played the most important role in this development. The surviving literary tradition shows that certain events in this history were landmarks in the language's development. In the past half century scholars have tried to chronicle these developments in the context of its literature. Kasser and Tito Orlandi are the most notable of these scholars. Kasser pioneered the most comprehensive historical scheme for the development of the Coptic Bible, while Orlandi has devised the most comprehensive system to date for the evolution of the literature in general. Though there is no similar scheme in linguistic terms, Kasser's and Orlandi's systems together with the history of the Church of Alexandria can provide a rough chronology of the development of the language. A true history of linguistic development still awaits more advanced dating techniques of manuscripts as well as their proper cataloging and publication. In the meantime one can observe seven distinct stages that have shaped this development from the standpoint of literary usage.

The Early Stage (Late Second–Third Centuries AD)

Egypt experienced the steady growth of its native Christian population. The language was primarily a translation tool for Christian literature originally written in Greek such as the Scriptures. In the later decades of this stage the language was used to preserve the heterodox literature of Gnostic and Manichean communities as they were being chased southward by the Orthodox authorities in Alexandria.[6] Grammatical syntax closely followed the Greek it was translated from. Greek also influenced the choice of vocabulary used. Biblical translators apparently shied away from using Egyptian words with theological significance in the Egyptian religion. This could be due to the conservative practice of the early translators or possibly to a cultural disconnect with pagan practices. Orthodox literature, such as the Scriptures, showed a wider circle of distribution in multiple dialects.

The Golden Age (Early Fourth Century to AD 451)

Following the Great Persecutions of the early fourth century, two dramatic changes occurred: the accelerated conversion of the Egyptian countryside and the rapid growth of monasticism. These changes helped to elevate and expand the role of the Coptic language from a translation tool to a fully literary language. In particular, we see in the case of the rise of coenobitic monasticism that the ability to read was required of all monks. The lives of saints, martyrs, and monks became required reading material for these monks. Their substantial numbers also necessitated the written codification of monastic rules to preserve order within these new communities. Sahidic was the dialect of choice as far as is known. The literary height of Coptic, however, did not occur until the middle of this stage with the writings of St. Shenouda the Archimandrite. His eloquent writing style and the variety of topics he discussed made him the Shakespeare of the Coptic language. He wrote in Sahidic but his style of writing is just now being studied to shed light on the linguistic depth he brought to it.[7] Unfortunately out of his seventeen volumes of works only about 12 percent have survived and been identified (Emmel 2004a). Writings in other dialects reached their zenith, but they were virtually all translations from Sahidic. Keep in mind that in the ecclesiastical circles of the metropolitan areas, Greek was still the language of choice.

The Isolation Stage (AD 451–641)

Following the Council of Chalcedon (AD 451), the Coptic Orthodox Church entered an age of nearly two centuries of isolation from the rest of the eastern churches as well as those of the west. The influence of monasticism grew more and more as it became the backbone of the oft-oppressed anti-Chalcedonian Church of Alexandria. A new genre of Coptic literature, Plephorics, emerged in response to the change in the ecclesiastical landscape. It was designed to demonstrate to the faithful the Lord's protection of the church against those who wanted to force the Chalcedonian Definition of the Faith upon them. Many of the martyrologies took their present shape in the latter part of this period. Sahidic became more dominant and most of the other dialects were in rapid decline, except for Bohairic and Fayyumic. Greek was still in use, but more liturgical and biblical texts began to appear in bilingual form with Coptic and Greek on facing pages.

The Coping Stage (AD 642–Tenth Century)

When the Arab conquest of Egypt was completed in AD 642, a new era started to unfold. By the end of that century the Arab governor decreed Arabic as the language of the administration. This may not have been crucial except for the fact that affluent Copts who occupied government positions did not want to lose them. So they learned Arabic and also taught their children in order to keep such lucrative jobs in the family. As a result, they gradually neglected educating their children in Coptic in favor of Arabic. The language, however, continued to be strong among the less affluent sectors of society as well as in the church. For them Coptic was what distinguished the non-Chalcedonian Egyptian Christians from the Greek-speaking Chalcedonians and the Arabic-speaking Moslems. This worked as long as non-Chalcedonian Christians had the majority. This majority soon became a minority following the crushing of the Bashmuric Revolt in the mid ninth century. Sahidic was still dominant throughout Egypt and it began to adopt some Arabic terms (Worrell 1934: 3). Arabic did not yet invade the literary domain of the church.

The Struggling Stage (Eleventh–Fourteenth Centuries AD)

The loss of majority status and centuries of Arabic education for the children of affluent Copts manifested itself in the famous work of Bishop Severus of al-Ashmūnayn. He lamented at the beginning of this stage in the first theological composition in Arabic among the Copts: "The reason for the suppression of this mystery (the Trinity) in this era from the faithful is their mixing with the Ḥunafā' (i.e the Muslims) and their state of having lost from among them their Coptic language that from it they used to know the truth of their belief."[8] Arabic slowly became the lingua franca of literary composition among the educated Copts of the time. Consequently, Coptic literature became restricted to hagiographic and liturgical compositions. Even hagiographic works were primarily produced for liturgical use. Sahidic became secondary to Bohairic in ecclesiastical use after the relocation of the Patriarchate from Alexandria to Cairo in the eleventh century. Fayyumic also died a slow death brought about by al-Hakim bi Amr Allah's destruction of the scriptoria of al-Fayyum in the eleventh century, which also ended the dominance of this area in the production of parchment codices in Sahidic (Depuydt 1993: cxv–cxvi). Sahidic retreated to its stronghold in the Monastery of St. Shenouda in Akhmim.[9]

During this period also Arabic made inroads in liturgical texts. This was done in two different ways: as a reference-column translation, following the example of Pope Ghubrīāl Ibn-Turayk, in the Coptic Paschal Lectionary, and as separate Arabic books especially for other lectionaries (Takla 2004a). The dominance of

Bohairic slowly regressed from translating the rich literary corpus of Sahidic to strictly simpler liturgical texts and praises. This was due in great part to the infiltration of Arabic. As a result of this decline scholars from among the Copts began to document the language's grammar and vocabulary to preserve it. By the end of this period it is safe to conclude that literary Coptic was in advanced decline but was still strong among the peasants, especially in Upper Egypt, as a means of communication. Those working in the government and in commerce tended to lose the language as a form of speech as a result of their social and work interactions.

The Dormant Stage (Fifteenth–Eighteenth Centuries AD)

Coptic survives only in Bohairic in this stage. Manuscripts in Coptic or Copto-Arabic were reproduced whenever old ones were no longer fit for use. By the early 1600s manuscripts of the most common liturgical manual, the Horologion, were produced only in Arabic. Other liturgical books continued their development with the addition of hymns and prayers based on earlier compositions and not as new or innovative compositions in Coptic. The strongholds of Coptic, the monasteries, began to weaken in quantity and quality. The Coptic language as a form of speech was rapidly declining, more in the north than in the south. But even in the south it was only a matter of time. The only saving grace was its continued use in churches. Though its individual educational value was declining among the clergy, they are to be lauded for their tenacious adherence to the language of their fathers. The age of isolation and quasi self-governance practiced in the Ottoman period in fact helped to stem the language's decay, though it was far from being described as vibrant.

The Revival Stage (Nineteenth Century AD to Present)

Pope Cyril IV's mid-nineteenth-century reform is credited with a revival in the language. Its seeds were sown earlier, however, as can be observed in the early efforts of the Church of England in the first half of the nineteenth century. These included efforts by Henry Tattam and J. Lieder in publishing Scripture texts in Coptic and establishing a school to teach young men to be priests (Takla 2004b; also Okilo 2008). The essence of this reform was to make this traditional language a modern one like any other European language. In 1858 a new Neo-Bohairic movement was launched by 'Iryān Mūftāḥ, who tried to modernize the pronunciation based on the modern Greek of his time (Maher 1985: 7). This created a documented system representing some sounds not familiar to Egyptians.[10] The short duration of Pope Cyril IV's busy patriarchate, 1854–61, did not allow him to realize this particular vision. Meanwhile, later in the century, Iqlādyūs Labīb and others published new liturgical manuals in Coptic from manuscripts, providing easier access for people to learn and use the language. The Neo-Bohairic movement continued unchallenged until the early 1970s when a young Coptic doctor, Emile Maher Eshaq,[11] challenged it with a rival one based on Coptic transliterated in Arabic characters as found in manuscripts and scholarly editions from the mid-seventeenth century. His system, referred to now as Old Bohairic, represented a seemingly radical change from Neo-Bohairic. It became popular because it sounded more Egyptian. These two rival systems are in conflict with each other with no possible reconciliation. Neo-Bohairic is currently the dominant system in most influential ecclesiastical circles. Ironically, both are applied to the exact same written words!

History of the Study of Coptic

Lexical works on Coptic span almost eight centuries. The study of Coptic began with Copts trying to protect the language of their heritage and church and later was dominated by western scholarship for a variety of reasons. The evolution of the study of the language can be divided into eight major stages as follows:

Medieval Coptic Lexical Works (Thirteenth–Fourteenth Century AD)

Copts were the obvious pioneers in writing lexical works about their own language. They were motivated by the observed decline of its knowledge as a result of the factors discussed above. Such works are referred to as *Muqaddimah* or Grammar and *Sullam* or Vocabulary lists. The first author was bishop Yūḥannā al-Sammanūdi, consecrated bishop of Sammanūd in the Western Delta in 1235. His work became the basis for more improved ones later that century by al-Wajīh Yūḥannā al-Qalyūbī, al-As'ad ibn al-'Assāl, Abū Shākir ibn al-Rāhib, and Ibn Kātib Qayṣar. These works were originally done in Bohairic as their authors were from Lower Egypt. They were translated by others into Sahidic at a later date. The last of them was composed by the Upper Egyptian Athanasius, bishop of Qūṣ, either late in that century or early in the next. His work, *al-Qiladat al-Taḥrīr fi 'ilm al-Tafsīr*, was the most comprehensive and complete and was in both dialects (Bauer 1972). It is also notable for being the first and only one to mention the existence of three dialects of Coptic based on their region. The common denominator of all these works is their reliance on Arabic grammar and dictionaries in their methodology. The vocabulary lists were either based on subject matters or biblical books. The order of words was either by their occurrences in a text or arranged by last letter in the word. They neglected the original roots of these words, primarily because of the continuous script found in Coptic manuscripts. Nonetheless, they provided valuable tools for the western scholars who pursued the study of the language in the following stages.

The Polyglot Stage (Fifteenth–mid Seventeenth Century AD)

Coptic manuscripts began to appear in Europe following the Council of Florence in 1439. With the advent of the Renaissance in Europe, scholars gave attention to Greek and subsequently biblical versions translated from it to enhance the study of the Bible. Thus the age of Polyglots was inaugurated and the learning of Oriental languages became popular. The study of those with challenging non-Latin scripts, like Syriac, Ethiopian, and Arabic, flourished first due to the arrival of native speakers in the west. Coptic did not have native speakers to bring its knowledge across the Mediterranean. But this was not as fatal as it might seem. The affinity of its script to Greek and its antiquity were enough to lure some scholars to its study during this stage. A small number of scholars in Italy, France, and Holland made rudimentary attempts, resembling stabs in the dark (cf. Emmel 2004b: 1: 1–11; also Hamilton 2006: 195–99). More success was made in bringing Coptic manuscripts to the West, including copies of the lexical works mentioned above (Hamilton 2006: 199–203). This paved the way for the more significant work of Athanasius Kircher later in the seventeenth century.

Athanasius Kircher (AD 1636–80)

A devout German Catholic, Kircher approached Coptic from a religious perspective. While in Rome he connected with a rich Roman, Pietro Della Valle, who collected Coptic manuscripts in his journeys to Egypt. Kircher was a man hungry for learning and much interested in the Egyptian script. His recognition that Coptic is the modern form of Ancient Egyptian fed his desire to study it and write about it. From 1636 to 1654 he published three major works in Rome in five volumes (Kircher 1636, 1643, 1652–54). In 1643 he published four of the lexical works of thirteenth-century Copts from a Vatican manuscript that Della Valle brought from Egypt. In this over 700-page work, he included an impressive display of languages, though there were many inaccuracies born out of his imperfect knowledge of Arabic and Coptic, the quality of the manuscripts, and his eagerness to prove his theories at the expense of sound methodology. Despite such shortcomings, what he produced fueled the interest in Coptic that followed. Keep in mind that in a European academic library his works would have been more readily available than those of his critics. It is worthy of mention that he only dealt with Bohairic, which was the recognized representative of Coptic in the West until Sahidic manuscripts appeared in quantity there.

After Kircher (AD 1680–1777)

Kircher's publications awakened scholars throughout Europe. The glaring mistakes found in them along with his far-fetched conclusions provided enough fodder for the discriminating scholarly minds of the time. Criticism came from Protestant as well as Catholic scholars. But criticism of Kircher's publications would not detract from their impact for many years to come. In Hamilton's words, "For many years one scholar after another appealed exclusively to Kircher when discussing Coptic" (Hamilton 2006: 217). The positive outcome from such criticism was a closer look at Coptic by a wider circle of more competent specialists. This stage's most significant work was by Guillaume Bonjour (1670–1714). It was his unpublished Bohairic grammar, *Elementa linguae copticicae seu aegypticae*, composed in 1698.[12] The first published Coptic grammar in this stage was made in Leipzig in 1716 by Christian Gotthilf Blumberg. His work, entitled *Fundamenta linguae copticae*, was better than Kircher's work but not as good as Bonjour's. It was later criticized by Veyssiere de La Croze, Paul Ernst Jablonski, and Christian Scholtz. By the early eighteenth century three unpublished Bohairic dictionaries were independently produced by Bonjour, La Croze, and Thomas Edwards. The inability to recognize proper word roots plagued these authors much as it did the thirteenth-century Coptic authors. Bohairic was still the sole representative of Coptic though more and more Sahidic manuscripts began appearing in Europe.

The Early Sahidic Stage (AD 1778–1822)

Recognition of Sahidic made earlier grammars out of date as well as incomplete. As new manuscripts coming from the library of the St. Shenouda monastery began to be studied at the end of the previous stage, two important new published grammars appeared in 1778, one by Rūfā'īl al-Ṭūkhy in Rome and the second posthumously by Christian Scholtz, abridged and edited by his famous student Karl Gottfried Woide (Scholtz 1778). The first was in Arabic with some Latin and was directed ultimately to those involved in Egyptian missionary work, while the second was done in the scholarly language of the time, Latin. Both treated Bohairic and Sahidic side by side, citing many scriptural examples. Scholtz's was obviously of greater scholarly value and had a higher degree of accuracy. Interestingly enough, it assumed that Sahidic was a dialect of Bohairic. At the beginning of the nineteenth century Quatremère translated, though did not publish, al-Ṭūkhy's work into French despite his criticism of its numerous inaccuracies. During this stage much debate and speculation centered on the identification of the three dialects mentioned by Athanasius of Qūṣ a few centuries earlier. Georgius Zoega's catalog of Coptic manuscripts of the Borgia collection, published posthumously in 1810, was the first to include texts from all three dialects: Bohairic, Sahidic, and Bashmuric. The last was finally identified as Fayyumic. By 1822, Jean-François Champollion, drawing from his extensive knowledge of Coptic, received from Kircher and others, published his first translation of the Rosetta Stone. In doing so, he established the science of Egyptology and inaugurated a different age in the study of Coptic, which was actually first attempted by Kircher!

The Pre-Modern Stage (AD 1823–79)

The study of Coptic expanded from an ecclesiastical perspective to become also a key to enter the new mystical world of Egyptian hieroglyphs. The earliest publications were by Henry Tattam in the form of a Grammar of Bohairic and Sahidic with notes on Bashmuric in 1830, which was followed by a Coptic–Latin dictionary in 1836. Better lexical tools appeared shortly thereafter in the form of a dictionary in 1835 and a grammar in 1841 by Amedio Peyron of Turin. His dictionary was the first one arranged by radicals and has been imitated by all other Coptic dictionaries published since. This was followed in 1850 by Moritz Gotthilf Schwartz's grammar published in Berlin. In 1853 Maximilian A. Uhlemann in Leipzig followed with a shorter grammatical work. Emphasis during this stage shifted to Sahidic as the main dialect of Coptic though most of the period's published texts were still in Bohairic. Late in this stage some elementary Bohairic grammar books appeared in Egypt as a part of the revival of the language.

The Golden Stage (AD 1880–1950)

Ludwig Stern's *Koptische Grammatik* of 1880 inaugurated this stage of more academic treatment of Coptic written in modern European languages. It was the first exclusively Sahidic grammar published and the most scientific to date. With more publications of Coptic texts in multiple dialects, the language became academically available in many places in the West, prompting more lexical publications. In 1893 Georg Steindorff published a grammar similar to Stern's but more abridged, also dealing with Sahidic in German. Alexis Mallon published a French grammar of Bohairic in 1904, which is still in use. In 1911 Margret Murray published a simple Sahidic grammar in English, which was followed by a similar one in Italian by Ignazio Guidi in 1924. In 1928 Walter C. Till published a grammar of Akhmimic and Lycopolitan followed by a simplified textbook dealing with all five known dialects of his time. In 1933–34, Chaine published two works in French in Paris, also dealing with the grammar of these dialects (Chaine 1933, 1934). The first American publication on Coptic grammar was by William Worrell in 1934. It dealt with Coptic pronunciation, including the documentation of newly discovered native Coptic speakers in Upper Egypt. The most advanced work of the period was done in 1944 by the German Hans Jakob Polotsky on Coptic syntax (Polotsky 1944). In 1948 J. Martin Plumley published a better Sahidic grammar in English to replace Murray's work. The most significant dictionaries were one published by Wilhelm Spiegelberg in 1921, in German, and the best Coptic dictionary in any European language by Crum in 1939.[13] Copts in Egypt also published grammars and dictionaries in Arabic during this stage. The most notable was a two-part grammar textbook in 1894 by Labīb followed by his five-part dictionary in 1895–1915, which was in Bohairic but included some Greek and Sahidic words. In 1925 Georgi Sobhy published a more extensive Bohairic grammar in Cairo.

The Modern Stage (1950–Present)

The discovery of the Nag Hammadi Coptic codices made Coptic a household word in academia. Scholars and students from nearly all branches of the humanities flocked to study them. It became necessary to publish new grammars and abridged and more up-to-date dictionaries. In grammars we encounter published works in German by Till, in French by Josef Vergote, and in English by C. C. Walters and Thomas O. Lambdin (Lambdin 1983). The latter is still favored among university instructors because of its systematic and progressive treatment of the language. There were also multiple grammatical works on Coptic in Russian. Dictionaries were published by Wolfhart Westendorf in German, Werner Vycichl in French, and Jarolslav Cerny and Richard Smith in English. In 1954 Kahle identified the last major literary dialect of Coptic, now known as Mesokemic. There were also several works published dealing with specific aspects of Sahidic grammar. Such publications included one on the nominal sentence by Chaine in 1955, on future tenses by Marvin Wilson in 1970, on the nominal sentence in Egyptian and Coptic by John B. Callender in 1984, and on the present of habitude by Michael Green in 1987. The most significant contributions were by Polotsky on the Sahidic verbal conjugation system, followed in 1987–90 by his larger work on sentence syntax (Polotsky 1960, 1987, 1990).

Along with Nag Hammadi texts, work on newly acquired Coptic texts of the Swiss Bodmer collection propelled Kasser to publish an impressive number of works on Coptic dialects and their associated sub-dialects. The English-speaking world was not totally deprived of his exclusively French works when volume 8 of the *Coptic Encyclopedia* appeared in 1991.[14] He also attempted a new edition of the Coptic dictionary, adding all new words he discovered in the new dialects and texts he studied. Unfortunately he stopped after the first two letters, leaving Crum's dictionary as the best dictionary for serious students of Coptic. Shisha-Halevy, a devout student of Polotsky, published several important grammatical works. Two in particular were entirely devoted to St. Shenouda's works (Shisha-Halevy 1986, 1988). Later, in 2007, he published the first linguistic work on Bohairic on the basis of a Paris manuscript of the Pentateuch (Shisha-Halevy 2007). In 2004 Bentley Layton published his comprehensive grammar of Sahidic followed by a shorter textbook in 2007 (Layton 2004, 2007).[15] In the 1990s scholars at Leiden University began to devise a different linguistic approach to Coptic from that of Polotsky. Chris Reintges published a new grammar of Sahidic in 2004, reflecting this approach (Reintges 2004). The reception of this approach was hostile or lukewarm by many. Several other textbooks and dictionaries have also been published in the past decade. Still, the works of Polotsky and Crum hold prominence in the field to date.

Publications of grammatical works by Copts in Egypt were plentiful in quantity but not significant in quality. They were designed to teach laypeople and not to add to scholarship in the field. They did however reflect a growing interest in learning the language. The Copts in the Diaspora also contributed. In 1990, Nabil Mattar in Los Angeles published a large Bohairic textbook in English, adopted from Lambdin's Sahidic textbook (Mattar 1990). In 2004, Boulos Ayad Ayad published the first English translation of Mallon's Bohairic grammar (Mallon 2004). In 2005, Sameh Younan published a new and simplified textbook for Bohairic in Sydney, Australia (Younan 2005). On the Internet, a simplified Bohairic Coptic course was posted as early as 1995 by the St. Shenouda the Archimandrite Coptic Society in Los Angeles.[16] Many other Bohairic lessons have been posted since that time.[17]

The Future of Coptic

The growing number of young people desiring to study the language and revive it makes the future bright. The constant tension between the Neo-Bohairic and Old Bohairic schools, however, is literally stifling the movement at present. What is needed is a revised and more modern standard vocabulary, generated on the basis of clear and sound methodology. So far new vocabulary is being produced on an individual basis and unsatisfactorily. Also, a better understanding of grammar is required to spur new literary production instead of the inferior products being generated now. Though Coptic has long been recognized as the language of the Church of Egypt, the future of its growth will be in its promotion as the language of the Egyptians and not only of just a religious minority in society. This would require development of a more secular form of the language acceptable to multiple segments of the society. Some in Egypt are already advocating such an approach, but still without a new form acceptable to a wider audience.

Notes

1 This, I may conjecture, may also explain why the reason for stopping the building of massive pyramids after the Old Kingdom was not just economics but rather that the technology behind their building perished with those who died as a result of the deluge.
2 Egypt was governed by the descendants of one of Alexander the Great's generals, Ptolemy, who ruled Egypt from 313–30 BC.
3 Paul E. Kahle, Jr. asserted that it was the language of the North or the Delta (Kahle 1954, Vol. 1, 247).
4 The first occurrence of the term in European scholarly work is found in Ludwig Stern's work (Stern 1880: 12), where he coined the term "boheirisch."
5 The Monastery of St. Shenouda. Takla 2008; in particular see the discussion of the three biblical Fayyumic manuscripts that were preserved among the contents of the monastery library.
6 The Lycopolitan dialect is well attested in the Gnostic Corpus of Nag Hammadi and that of the Manicheans. Early Fayyumic fragments of biblical translations have been found along with a unique Proto-Sahidic or Dialect p manuscript of Proverbs.
7 The importance of the works of St. Shenouda to the study of Sahidic Coptic is clearly laid out in two important works by Ariel Shisha-Halevy (Shisha-Halevy 1986, 1988).
8 Manuscript ML.MS.42, f.2r. Part of the collection of the St. Shenouda the Archimandrite Coptic Society in Los Angeles.
9 The presence of multiple Fayyumic manuscripts in the Library of the Monastery of St. Shenouda along with the unexplained absence of certain popular biblical books from the collection found in the Fayyum Hamuli collection leads to speculation that such manuscripts were relocated from the Fayyum in the aftermath of al-Hakim bi Amr Allah's action.

10 One sound in particular is the Theta, which now has the phonetic value of the Arabic "dh" or "th." Such a sound is absent from colloquial Egyptian and is only used in Sahidic as a ligature letter for the aspirated T.
11 Now Fr. Shenouda Maher, serving the Coptic Community in Rochester, New York.
12 Ariel Shisha-Halevy, one of the noted Coptic grammarians of our time, in his preface to the 2005 publication of this work has lauded it as a work "of extraordinary importance." (Aufrère and Bosson 2005: vii).
13 See note 17.
14 It is worthy of mention that Kasser was not happy with the English translation of his scores of entries in the *Coptic Encyclopedia*. During the Washington, DC, Coptic Congress in 1992, he gave a paper about this and distributed a booklet that included all his contributions in their original French.
15 Two more editions were done by him including an expanded one in 2011.
16 www.stshenouda.org/coptlang.htm. Last updated March 24, 2009.
17 www.remenkimi.com/. Last updated July 21, 2010.

Selected Bibliography

For further reference: Crum (1939), Lambdin (1983), Layton (2011), Mallon (2004), Mattar (1990).

Aufrère, S. H. and Bosson, N. (2005) *Guillaume Bonjour: Elementa Linguae Copticae. Grammaire Inédite du XVIIe Siècle*, Geneva: Patrick Cramer Éditeur.

Bagnall, R. (1993) *Egypt in Late Antiquity*, New Jersey: Princeton University Press.

Bauer, G. (1972) *Athanasius Von Qus. Qiladat at-Tahrir fi 'ilm at-Tafsir. Eine Koptische Grammatik in Arabischer Sprache aus dem 13/14 Jahrhundert*, Freiburg im Breisgau: Klaus Schwarz Verlag.

Chaine, M. (1933) *Elements de Grammaire Dialectale Copte*, Paris: Geuthner.

——(1934) *Les Dialectes Coptes Assioutiques A2*, Paris: Geuthner.

Crum, W. E. (1905) *Catalogue of the Coptic Manuscripts in the British Library*, London: British Museum.

——(1939) *A Coptic Dictionary*, Oxford: Clarendon Press.

Depuydt, L. (1993) *Catalogue of Coptic Manuscripts in the Pierpont Morgan Library*, Louvain: Peeters.

Emmel, S. L. (2004a) *Shenoute's Literary Corpus*. Louvain: Peeters (= *Corpus Scriptorum Christianorum Orientalium* v. 599–600, *Subsidia* 111–12).

——(2004b) "Coptic Studies before Kircher," in M. Immerzeel and J. Van der Vliet (eds) *Coptic Studies on the Threshold of a New Millennium*, 2 vols, Louvain: Peeters.

Gardiner, A. (1957) *Egyptian Grammar*, 3rd edn, Oxford: Griffith Institute.

Gardiner, I., Alcock, A. and Funk, W.-F. (eds) (1999) *Coptic Documentary Texts from Kellis*, vol. 1, Oxford: Oxbow.

Hallock, F. H. (1933) "The Coptic Old Testament," *The American Journal of Semitic Languages and Literatures*, 49(4): 325–35.

Hamilton, A. (2006) *The Copts and the West 1439–1822. The European Discovery of the Egyptian Church*, Oxford: Oxford University Press.

Horner, G. (1898–1905) *The Coptic Version of the New Testament in the Northern Dialect, Otherwise Called Memphitic and Bohairic*, 4 vols, Oxford: Clarendon Press.

Kahle, P. E., Jr (1954) *Bala'izah: Coptic Texts from Deir el-Bala'izah in Upper Egypt*, 2 vols, Oxford: Griffith Institute.

Kasser, R. (1991) "Language(s), Coptic," in A. S. Atiya (ed.) *Coptic Encyclopedia*, 8 vols, New York: Macmillan.

Kircher, A. (1636) *Prodromus Coptus sive Aegyptiacus*, Rome: typis S. Congregationis de propaganda fide.

——(1643) *Lingua Egyptiaca Restituta*, Rome: Scheus.

——(1652–54) *Oedipus Aegyptiacus*, 3 vols, Rome: ex Typographia Vitalis Mascardi.

Krause, M. (1991) "Mummy Labels," in A. S. Atiya (ed.) *Coptic Encyclopedia*, 8 vols, New York: Macmillan.

Lambdin, T. O. (1983) *Introduction to Sahidic Coptic*, Macon: Mercer University Press.

Layton, B. (2004) *A Coptic Grammar*, Wiesbaden: Harrassowitz.

——(2007) *Coptic in 20 Lessons: An Introduction to Sahidic Coptic with Exercises and Vocabularies*. Leuven-Paris-Dudley: Peeters.

Maher, E. (1985) *Saji Neman*, Vol. II 3rd edn, Cairo: Youssef Kamal Printing House.

Mallon, A. (2004) *Coptic Grammar (Grammaire Copte)*, trans. B. Ayad Ayad, Cairo: Youssef Kamal Printing House.

Mattar, N. (1990) *A Study in Bohairic Coptic*, Pasadena: Hope Publishing House.

Okilo, I. (2008) "Contributions of the Church of England to the Copts: Rev. Henry Tattam and the Coptic Scriptures, 1826–52," *St. Shenouda Coptic Quarterly*, 4(3–4): 46–56.

Polotsky, H. J. (1944) *Études de Syntaxe Copte*, Cairo: Société d'Archéologie Copte.

——(1960) "The Coptic Conjugation System," *Orientalia*, 29(4): 392–422.

——(1987) *Grundlagen Des Koptischen Satzbaus*, Decatur: Scholars Press.

——(1990) *Grundlagen Des Koptischen Satzbaus Zweite Halfte*, Atlanta: Scholars Press.

Quatremère, E. (1808) *Recherches Critiques et Historiques sur la Langue et la Litterature de l'Égypte*, Paris: Imprimerie Impériale.

Reintges, C. H. (2004) *Coptic Egyptian (Sahidic Dialect): A Learner's Grammar*, Köln: Rüdiger Köppe Verlag.

Satzinger, H. (1991) "Old Coptic," in A. S. Atiya (ed.) *Coptic Encyclopedia*, 8 vols, New York: Macmillan.

Scholtz, C. (1778) *Grammatica Aegyptiaca Utriusque Dialecti*, Oxford: E Typographeo Clarendoniano.

Shisha-Halevy, A. (1976) "Akhmimoid Features in Sheoute's Idiolect," *Le Muséon*, 89(3–4): 353–66.

——(1986) *Coptic Grammatical Categories*, Rome: Pontificium Institutum Biblicum.

——(1988) *Coptic Grammatical Chrestomathy*, Louvain: Peeters.

——(2007) *Topics in Coptic Syntax: Structural Studies in the Bohairic Dialect*, Louvain: Peeters.

Stern, L. (1880) *Koptische Grammatik*, Leipzig: Weigel.

Takla, H. N. (2004a) "Copto (Bohairic)-Arabic Manuscripts: Their Role in the Tradition of the Coptic Church," in M. Immerzeel and J. Van der Vliet (eds) *Coptic Studies on the Threshold of a New Millennium*, 2 vols, Louvain: Peeters.

——(2004b) "Relations between the Church of England and the Coptic Church (1836–48)," *St. Shenouda Coptic Newsletter*, 10(N.S.7)(2): 9–14.

——(2008) "Biblical Manuscripts of the Monastery of St. Shenoute," In G. Gabra and H. N. Takla (eds) *Christianity and Monasticism in Upper Egypt*. vol. 1. *Akhmim and Sohag*, Cairo: AUC Press.

Vaschalde, A. (1933) "Ce qui a été publié des versions coptes de la Bible. Troisieme Groupe. Textes en Moyen Egyptien. Quatrieme Groupe. Textes Akhmimiques," *Le Muséon*, 46: 299–313.

Worrell, W. (1934) *Coptic Sounds*, Ann Arbor: University of Michigan Press.

Younan, S. (2005) *So you want to learn COPTIC?* Kirawee: St. Mary, St. Bakhomius, and St. Shenouda Coptic Orthodox Church.

13 The Greek Literature of the Copts

Innovative and Formative Era

Lois M. Farag

The first era of Greek Christian literature is epitomized by the Gospels, New Testament epistles, and the post-Apostolic literature of the Apostolic Fathers. This chapter discusses the following era of literary compositions beginning in the middle of the second century in Alexandria, Egypt, the birthplace of experimentation with new Greek Christian literary genres. The focus of this chapter is on Christian literature written by Greek-speaking Egyptians whose writings expressed a distinctive Coptic/Alexandrian cultural and theological character. This Alexandrian literature is foundational to Coptic heritage and should equally be called Copto-Greek Literature since it is preliminary to the Coptic and Copto-Arabic literature. The literary production discussed in this chapter set the theological trajectory of the Coptic Orthodox Church and determined many aspects of the history of Christianity in Egypt. The chapter follows the shifts in literary development. The first period is characterized by texts that are groundbreaking in genre, literary style, and topic choice. The second period sifts through the ideas articulated in the first and lays foundations for the theological principles that will set the trajectory of Alexandrian/Coptic theology. This period concludes with the literary production that upholds the distinctive Alexandrian theological thought against attempts to dismantle it. Monastic literature is another Egyptian literary genre characteristic of the second period; it is addressed in the last section together with liturgical texts. The chapter will introduce major literary figures chronologically and present aspects of their literary production. Antiochene, Cappadocian, and Byzantine Christian Greek literature will not be included.

The Innovative Period: From Clement to Peter I

Early Christian Greek writings emerged within the tutelage of the Greek educational system (*paideia*) which left an indelible mark on early Christian literary production. Early Christian writers adopted Greek rhetorical tools and methods of approaching texts. Alexandria was an important cultural center where mathematics, medicine, and natural sciences flourished and developed within the cultural institution of the museum. Poetry and philology were among the literary interests pursued in Alexandria, as were textual criticism, the publication of texts, and the allegorical exegesis or interpretation of Homer "in order to justify the anthropomorphism and immoral behavior of the Homeric gods" (Moreschini and Norelli 2005: 248). This allegorical exegesis was adopted by Philo of Alexandria (d. c. 40), a Jewish philosopher, to produce an allegorical interpretation of the Pentateuch, the first five books of the Old Testament. Philo also employed the philosophy of Middle Platonism to explain Judaism. Alexandria, as a seaport and commercial center, was a place where many ideas interacted, such as Gnosticism, Manichaeism, and many others. The city was famous as a center not only of Greek culture but also of Christian culture. It is within this highly intellectual climate that early Christian writers emerged and were shaped. Eusebius refers to a catechetical school in Alexandria (*Hist. eccl.* 6.3), the oldest we know of, which provided Christian education in theology as well as philosophy. Famous teachers and theologians such as Pantaenus, Clement, Origen, Dionysius, Pierius, Peter, and Didymus were connected with this school. Of these theologians, writings survive from Clement, Origen, Dionysius, Peter, and Didymus.

Clement of Alexandria (c. 150–c. 215) is considered a pioneer of what we might call "Christian Literature." He is the first Christian writer to use rhetorical tools to write a Christian literary text which uses Scripture as the foundational text, interacts with Greek philosophical ideas, especially Platonism, and responds to challenging ideas like Gnosticism. His most famous writings are *Exhortation to the Greeks*, *Christ the Educator*, *Miscellanies*, and *Salvation of the Rich*. *Exhortation* is a critique of pagan religion but also claims that Greek philosophers, especially Plato, were inspired by the Truth, that is, the Logos, to reveal some truth about God. In the *Educator*, Clement instructs the faithful how to live the Christian life in conformity with Christian teachings. In *Salvation of the Rich* he asserts that the rich do not need to give away all their wealth to be saved, but if they use their wealth to provide for the poor they will be saved. Clement "alludes to the Old Testament in 1500 passages and to the New in 2000. He is also well versed in the classics, from which he quotes no fewer than 360 passages" (Quasten 1950–60: Vol. II, 6).

Origen (c. 185–c. 253), another member of the Alexandrian school, was pioneering in his attempt to write Christian commentary on all the books of the Bible, systematically expounding the Bible verse by verse. He commented on most of the Biblical books through commentaries, homilies, and *scholia* (interpretations of individual Biblical passages). These Biblical commentaries were the basis of many of his theological formulations. Biblically based theology would be adopted by most Egyptian Christian writers, including the most famous, Cyril of Alexandria, who wrote commentaries on most of the Biblical books, which became the basis of his theological treatises. Origen also set the foundation of the method of Biblical interpretation, which considered all Scripture inspired by God. His method was outlined in the fourth book of his famous *On First Principles*. Origen argued that, just as a person consists of body, soul, and spirit, there are three levels of Scriptural meaning. The first level of understanding Scripture is the simple, obvious sense, while the perfect ascend to the highest level of interpretation, which is according to the spirit. This three-fold manner of interpreting Scripture came to be known as allegorical interpretation. Origen explained that Paul himself interpreted Scripture beyond the obvious sense; in Gal 4:24 Paul interpreted Hagar and Sarah allegorically as representing two covenants. Similarly, Paul interpreted the crossing of the Red Sea as baptism (1 Cor 10: 2). Origen adds that not all Scripture can be interpreted according to the simple, obvious sense; tearing our eyes out and cutting our hands off for every sin (Matthew 5:29–30) cannot be interpreted literally. Origen did not ignore the literal meaning of Scripture. He was aware of the variants in the Septuagint manuscripts and collated six translations of Scripture in six adjacent columns to be able to know the original text of the Old Testament. This pioneering project came to be called the Hexapla. This project was important to Origen, since the literal interpretation serves as the preliminary step towards an allegorical interpretation.

Origen also wrote treatises *On Prayer*, *On Martyrdom*, and *On the Pascha*. In *On First Principles*, Origen was the first Christian writer to write a systematic theological exposition of the Christian faith, addressing theological difficulties with great boldness and speculation. He discussed, for example, the origin of the created world, free will, moral issues, and Scripture and its interpretation. In discussing such topics, Origen did not claim that such speculations were final, but rather encouraged others to investigate the truth on their own. Because of some of these speculations, however, he was condemned by Theophilus of Alexandria in the year 400, a century and a half after his death. Examples of condemned speculations include the eternity of creation, the pre-existence of the soul, the salvation of the devil, and the universal restoration of things to their original spiritual state (the *apokatastasis*). Condemnations of Origen's writings led to the loss of many of his texts; some of them we know only through their Latin translations. Through these translations Origen's writings were influential not only in the Greek-speaking East but also in the Latin-speaking West. Victorinus, bishop of Pattau on the frontier of present-day Austria, who died during the persecution of Diocletian (probably in 304), composed Biblical commentaries following Origen's method of Biblical interpretation (Moreschini and Norelli 2005: 396–97). Origen also influenced Hilary of Poitiers and Ambrose of Milan, whose exposition of Scriptures was one of the influences in the conversion of Augustine of Hippo. Origen's writings influenced those who agreed as well as those who disagreed with him. For centuries, Origen's writings were at the center of many ecclesial debates and discussions and his influence has not faded even in the twenty-first century.

Dionysius was bishop of Alexandria (247–64) and head of the Alexandrian school. His writings are preserved in fragments or through other sources (Feltoe 1904). They exhibit philosophical training and deep Biblical thought. Though he was one of Origen's students, he denounced the pre-existence of the soul. *On Promises* is in response to Nepos, an Egyptian bishop who advanced the idea of millenarianism. Dionysius refuted millenarianism based on a critical study of the Apocalypse of John. Interestingly enough, in this critical study Dionysius proved that the author of the Apocalypse is different than the writer of the Johannine Gospel, based on language, style, and Greek syntax, though there is no reason to doubt that the writer was also called John. His literary criticism of the text was unparalleled till modern times, and his argument about the authorship of the Apocalypse remains valid to the present day. Dionysius defended the three hypostases of the Godhead in his *Refutation and Defense* and asserted the eternity of both the Father and the Son. His letters indicate that he was involved in many of the theological discussions of his time. Dionysius was the first Coptic pope to send a Festal Letter announcing the date for celebrating the Feast of the Resurrection, a tradition held by Coptic popes for at least seven more centuries.

Theognostus succeeded Dionysius as head of the Alexandrian school and wrote seven books with the title *Hypotyposes* which are now lost. *Hypotyposes*' description indicates that it was dogmatic in content. Pierius followed him as the head of the Alexandrian school and wrote homilies *On the Prophet Hosea* and *On the Gospel of Luke*, and also wrote *On the Mother of God* and *On the Life of St. Pamphilius*, who was a martyr and Pierius' disciple. Few fragments survive of his writings. Both writers followed Origen's scholarly methods. Peter of Alexandria, bishop of Alexandria, was most probably also the head of the Alexandrian school. He died as a martyr in 311; the Coptic Church calls him "the Seal of the Martyrs" because his martyrdom marked the end of the era of persecution. Peter was known for his anti-Origenist opinions and wrote a treatise *On the Soul* against the pre-existence of souls, arguing that Origen's premises were based on Greek philosophy rather than Scripture. Peter wrote *On Penance*, in which he discussed the canons against the lapsed—those who recanted their faith during persecution—and a letter warning the faithful against Meletius, a schismatic bishop. He also wrote *On the Deity*, *On the Resurrection*, and *On Easter*. The rest of Peter's writings survive only in Coptic fragments because, unfortunately, the Greek original was lost. Peter wrote several letters: one about *Persecution and the Celebration of the Eucharist*, another during the persecution, a third to Emperor Diocletian, another as a reprimand to Bishop Apollonius, most probably for his apostasy, one concerning heretics, and the last one concerning his visit to Oxyrhynchus (Vivian 1988: 53–57). There is an encomium written by his successor, Alexander of Alexandria, which survives in a Coptic translation (ibid. 78–86).

This period is critical to understanding the rise and development of early Christian literature. Pioneers like Clement and Origen created the genres of Christian literature by using the tools of Greek rhetoric and philosophy to express Christian ideas based on Scripture. The venture was most successful in defining and creating Christian literature, but it also had its downfalls. They and their disciples, who successively led the Alexandrian school, established the genres of Biblical commentary, treatises, hagiography, letters, and Festal Letters. They also composed treatises in defense of the Christian faith, that is, apologetic literature. Their influence went beyond the Egyptian Church, beyond even the Greek-speaking churches of the East, extending to the Latin West.

They courageously asked theological questions that led to the formulations of dogmas, such as the three hypostases of the Godhead and the coeternity of the Father and Son. Their excessive reliance on Greek philosophy and speculation created criticism. By the time of Peter of Alexandria, treatises began to be composed in response to Origen, some attacking his theological views and others opposing the excessively allegorical bent of his Biblical commentaries. This marks the beginning of the following era of Christian Greek literature in Egypt.

The Formative Period: From Alexander to Timothy

When Alexander of Alexandria took the lead of the Coptic Church in 312, the socio-political environment of Egypt, and the rest of the Roman world, had shifted dramatically. The Christian population was no longer a minority required to explain its religion or to defend its faith. By the time Athanasius of Alexandria (326–73), the successor of Alexander, wrote his apologetic treatise *Against the Heathens*, it was already a literary genre that had begun to be abandoned. With the Christianization of the empire, the Christians faced the threat of heresies from within the Church, not from outside. This socio-political shift was accompanied by a literary shift. The literary audience became the Christians who needed instruction in the Christian faith and awareness of the heretical teachings that were emerging within the Church. Alexander of Alexandria faced a major heresy that rocked the Church of Alexandria and eventually the rest of the Christian Churches, the Arian heresy. Arius, a priest in Alexandria influenced by Neo-Platonic categories, preached that Christ, the Son of God, was not divine but a created being. Alexander, from whom only two letters are extant, responded by informing the rest of the bishops about the new teaching. Discussing theological matters in a letter marked a literary development in the role and content of letter writing.

Athanasius, Alexander's successor as bishop, took the lead in opposing Arianism. He developed letter writing even further, to include full theological treatises. Examples of these momentous letters are the *Letters to Serapion of Thmuis Concerning the Holy Spirit*, in which Athanasius asserts the divinity of the Holy Spirit long before the Council of Constantinople in 381. The divinity of the Spirit was connected to the Arian controversy; asserting the divinity of the Holy Spirit is closely connected to the divinity of the Son and the Christian understanding of the Trinity. The *Letter to Epictetus*, the bishop of Corinth, addresses the Docetic views of some Arian and Apollinarian groups who struggled with the nature of the body of the Incarnate Son, questioning whether the crucified Christ had a fully human body like ours or a transformed body. This was an influential letter during the Nestorian and Chalcedonian debates, becoming part of the canonical texts consulted by the Council of Chalcedon. Athanasius' *Tome to the People of Antioch* on behalf of the Synod of Alexandria of 362 discussed important theological terms such as "hypostasis" and "substance" and what was required to accept those who wanted to return to the Church after renouncing the Arian heresy. The *Letter to the Monks* and the *Letter to the Bishops of Africa* warn the recipients of the Arian views; though these letters are dogmatic in content, they reveal Athanasius' pastoral responsibilities at work. His letter *On the Councils* inaugurates the tradition of letters sent to inform synodical deliberations. Unfortunately, only a portion of the large correspondence of Athanasius survives. Apart from personal and synodical letters, Athanasius wrote *Festal Letters* that announced the dates of celebrating the Resurrection, keeping with the tradition of the bishops of Alexandria that started with Dionysius of Alexandria. He regularly sent these *Festal Letters* in spite of his exiles, but only thirty-five survive. Three of them are worthy of mention. Athanasius mentions in his first Festal Letter six days of fast, starting on the Monday before celebrating the Feast of the Resurrection. The following Festal Letter instructs the recipients about the six weeks' of fasting, thus marking the development of the observance of the Great Lent in the Coptic Church. Athanasius' monumental *Letter 39* lists the books of the Bible considered canonical and became the most influential document in the establishment of the Biblical canon.

Athanasius' dogmatic and apologetic writings are foundational for the theology of the Coptic Orthodox Church, if not for Christian theology in general. The most two influential theological treatises that Athanasius wrote are *Against the Heathens/On the Incarnation* and *Discourses Against the Arians*. The former is a single work in two parts. His focus in the first part, *Against the Heathens*, is the condition of fallen humanity and the state of humanity before the fall. The only way for humanity to overcome its fallen status is through the Incarnation, which is the focus of the second part, *On the Incarnation*. Through the Incarnation God granted humanity salvation, which restored all that humanity had lost: the image of the Father, incorruption and victory over death, knowledge of God, and the ability to contemplate God. This understanding of the Incarnation influenced Coptic theology, liturgy, and spirituality.

There are no extant Biblical commentaries by Athanasius. We have some references and fragments to commentaries on Genesis, Job, the Psalms, Ecclesiastes, the Songs of Songs, Matthew, Luke, and First Corinthians. His *Letter to Marcellinus on the Interpretation of the Psalms* is more about the content and the devotional use of the Psalms than a commentary. It is one of the examples of Athanasius' integration of Scripture and spirituality (Gregg 1980: 101–29). Nevertheless, Athanasius' dogmatic writings comprise a series of Biblical interpretations and stem from a close reading and interpretation of Scripture. For example, in his *Discourses Against the Arians* he refutes the Arian teachings on the basis of Scripture, interpreting a series of Old and New Testament texts that affirm the divinity of the Son against the Arians' denial, which was based on Neo-Platonic philosophical thought. In the course of his discussion he establishes the foundational theological premises of Biblical interpretation, which will have far reaching implications. All of Athanasius' writings are comprised of strings of Biblical verses, references, or allusions. His whole thought and writings are Biblically based. In his interpretation, Athanasius never used the term allegory.

The Life of Antony is one of the most famous and popular writings of Athanasius. With Antony's hagiography he created a new type of biography, which provided the model of a Christian hero and sage, and a literary genre that became a classic for later Greek and Latin hagiographies. Athanasius wrote the *Life of Antony* as an example to emulate and as an excellent model of the ascetic life (*Life of Antony*: preface 2). Historically, it fulfilled its goal by becoming the example of the Christian monastic life *par excellence*. The *Life* was also successful in raising interest in the desert fathers and mothers and Egyptian monasticism in general.

Athanasius' literary production set the literary, theological, and spiritual trajectory for Alexandrian Greek literature. He redefined some of the Christian Greek literary genres of Egypt and created others. He did not abandon the rhetorical literary tools of Greek writing; he did, however, abandon philosophical categories and the allegorical interpretation of Scriptures. His dogmatic arguments were primarily Biblically based to avoid the pitfalls of Origen and Arius. He thus set the foundation of Biblically based theology that would be followed by Cyril of Alexandria and his successors. He redefined the genre of "letter" to give it the form of a theological treatise. His hagiography of Antony established the model of Christian hagiography and the principles of desert spirituality. His theological writings set the foundation for the Coptic understanding of salvation, the Trinity, the nature of Christ, Biblical interpretation, and spirituality. It should be noted that the *Athanasian Creed* used in western churches was composed in Latin, not Greek, and is falsely attributed to Athanasius. Serapion of Thmuis, a contemporary of Athanasius who received several letters from him, left one known treatise, *Against the Manichaens*, which has been reconstructed from other writings.

Didymus of Alexandria (313–98) is one of the last names associated with the School of Alexandria. He lived an ascetical life and visited Antony when he came to Alexandria. He became blind at the age of four and this makes his erudition more remarkable. Didymus wrote many Biblical commentaries and treatises. He defended Origen's *On First Principles* and was accused of Origenism, an accusation that caused the loss of most of his works. The treatise *On the Holy Spirit* was the only work of Didymus available until 1941, when papyri were discovered in Ṭurah, Egypt. These papyri yielded his commentaries on Zachariah, Job, Ecclesiastes, and the Gospel of John, and the treatise *On the Trinity*, together with other fragments of various commentaries and treatises. His treatise *On the Holy Spirit* starts with an introduction on the nature and activity of the Holy Spirit followed by an analysis of some passages of Scripture and a conclusion. In this treatise he asserts the divinity of the Holy Spirit based on Biblical exegesis and does not use philosophical categories in his analysis. This is very much in conformity with the newly emerging Alexandrian exegetical method used by Athanasius. The treatise *On the Trinity* also defends the divinity of the Holy Spirit and the Godhead through an analysis of various Biblical passages relevant to the topic. There is still much work to be done on the writings of Didymus and further examination of his exegetical method.

Theophilus of Alexandria (385–412) wrote twenty-seven Festal Letters in addition to many homilies, letters of correspondence, canons and a table on the dates of Easter. He did not, however, write any dogmatic treatises or Biblical commentaries (Russell 2007: 45). Theophilus' theology is not speculative like that of Origen but based on Biblical exegesis following Athanasius' principle of Biblical interpretation. Theophilus did not oppose allegory but rather arbitrary readings (ibid. 35). By the fifth century, the Nicene faith became the standard of Orthodoxy. It affirmed the divinity of Father, Son, and Holy Spirit as distinct from created beings. This understanding conflicted with pre-Nicene Origenist ideas, especially the understanding of the descent and return of the soul (ibid. 26). Theophilus condemned the Origenist ideas in a synod held in Egypt around the year 400, some 150 years after Origen's death. The Origenist controversy became the topic of seven of Theophilus' letters, two of which were synodical and three Festal (ibid. 89–174). Theophilus left a few homilies, in which he did not use allegory but rather typology (ibid. 50). Typology interprets the Old Testament in light of the New, immersing the reader in the deeper, spiritual, and theological meaning of the text, thus transforming the type into the truth of Christ.

Cyril (378–444) succeeded Theophilus as Bishop of Alexandria. He was a theologian, a Biblical interpreter, a gifted homilist, and a prolific writer. His writings are so important to the Church that many of them were translated even during his lifetime. Cyril's writings occupy ten volumes of the Migne collection, seven of which are Biblical interpretations. Though he is known more for his theology, it was his work in Biblical exegesis that formed his theology. Both *Glaphyra* (*Elegant Comments*) and *De Adoratione*, which complements it, interpret specific passages from the Pentateuch. He also wrote a *Commentary on Isaiah* (Hill 2008) and another *Commentary on the Minor Prophets* (Hill 2007–2012). Other commentaries on the Old Testament were lost, though many fragments remain. As for the New Testament, his *Commentary on the Gospel of John* interprets the gospel verse by verse in what he calls "dogmatic exegesis," an interpretation that is primarily focused on the theological meaning of the verses. Cyril interprets the gospel typologically, applying his understanding of rhetoric to attend to the literal meaning of the text while intertwining his spiritual interpretation. This commentary gives an excellent illustration of Cyril's theology of the Trinity and his method of interpretation. The *Commentary on the Gospel of St. Luke* consists of 156 homilies; the Greek text is lost but it is fortunately preserved in Syriac translation (Cyril of Alexandria 1983). Very few fragments remain of his *Commentary on the Gospel of Matthew* as well as commentaries of the Book of Acts and some Epistles.

Most of Cyril's treatises are in response to the Nestorian controversy, though the *Thesaurus* and *De Sancta et consubstantiali Trinitate* are polemical work against the Arians. The *Thesaurus* is very dependent on Athanasius' *Discourses Against the Arians* mentioned above, which is an indication of Athanasius' influence on Cyril's thought and represents the beginning of the transmission of Athanasian theology as foundational to Coptic theology. Cyril wrote *Five Tomes against*

Nestorius in which he refutes Nestorius' idea of the duality of the person of Christ and rejection of the term *Theotokos*. He also sent three different letters refuting the Nestorian claims with the title *On the True Faith*, the first addressed to Emperor Theodosius II, the second to his younger sisters Arcadia and Marina, and the third to Theodosius' elder sister Pulcheria and his wife Eudocia. Cyril wrote another important treatise *On the Oneness of Christ*, sometimes translated as "On the Unity of Christ," in which he refutes the duality of Nestorius; it was highly regarded in antiquity as the mature expression of Cyril's thought (Cyril of Alexandria 1995). Other treatises defend against false accusations and assert his theological point of view against Nestorius.

Cyril wrote numerous letters, eighty-eight of which are extant. Some of these letters, such as the *Second* and *Third Letters to Nestorius*, became important theological documents of almost canonical standing because they were used in ecumenical councils. The full correspondence of Cyril, including what he received, totals 110 letters. They became historical records witnessing to the interaction of episcopal sees with each other and the state, and the development of theological debates (McEnerney 1987, a and b). In addition, twenty-nine of his Festal Letters are preserved, though the third letter is missing. In the Festal Letters Cyril usually includes a spiritual message on the occasion of Lent that encourages fasting, prayer, and almsgiving, a theological interpretation of one or two Biblical passages, and the announcement of the date to celebrate the Feast of the Resurrection. Festal letters also inform us of Cyril's pastoral sensitivities (Amidon 2009).

Cyril has only twenty-two extant sermons, other than the homilies on the Gospel of Luke. Some of Cyril's sermons are famous, especially the eight delivered in Ephesus on the theme of the *Theotokos*. Four other homilies deal with the theme of the Incarnation. Because these two themes were crucial in the theological debate of Cyril's time, these homilies earned their place in history.

Cyril uses Greek rhetorical tools in his writings but avoids Greek philosophy in his arguments because of his focus on Scripture as the main source of his theological discourse. Though his style of writing is verbose, he captures the essence of his ideas in catchy phrases or terms. A few examples will suffice. "Newness of life" came to represent one of the main aspects of the Resurrection as well as salvation. "All things are from the Father through the Son in the Holy Spirit" came to expresses the oneness of activity of the Trinity while demonstrating an understanding of each person within the Trinity; this phrase encapsulates the main framework within which Cyril elaborates his theological understanding of the Godhead. Equally famous is the often quoted "One nature of God the Word Incarnate," a phrase that summarizes Cyril's understanding of the nature of the Incarnate Son, which is closely connected with the previous Trinitarian phrase. This style of writing was also practiced by Athanasius, whose oft-quoted phrase, "God assumed humanity so that we might become God" (*On the Incarnation* 54) might seem audacious, but when read within its context reflects his understanding of the renewal of the image of God within humanity achieved by the Incarnation. Cyril's phrases, too, are often misinterpreted because they are taken out of the context of his writings. This literary style reflects the clear thinking of authors who, though most of the time verbose, were able to articulate their theological thought in succinct phrases that would endure through history.

Isidore of Pelusium (c. 360–c. 435) was born in Alexandria and was a contemporary of Cyril of Alexandria. According to Severus of Antioch he was a priest of Pelusium and an ascetic who had good knowledge of Scripture. His writings reveal his excellent training in rhetoric and knowledge of Demosthenes, Plato, Aristotle, and Homer. His discourses *Against the Greeks* and *On the Non-existence of Fate* are not what earned him literary renown; it was rather the elegant literary style demonstrated in his epistolography, which amounts to more than 2,000 letters. The topics of his letters are primarily exegetical in nature, many of them on the Pauline epistles, but he also wrote letters on moral and ascetical topics. In his theological letters he insisted on adhering closely to the teachings of the Council of Nicea. He also corresponded with state and ecclesial figures, the most famous of whom was Cyril of Alexandria. Isidore followed the Alexandrian tradition that redefined the letters to function as theological as well as exegetical treatises. Another little known late fifth century figure, Ammonius of Alexandria, wrote exegetical works on the Old and New Testament of which only fragments have survived.

This era laid down the foundational theological tenets not only of the Coptic Orthodox Church but also of the universal church. The events of the Council of Chalcedon forced a shift in the literary production of the Church of Alexandria with respect to subject matter. Theological treatises became apologetic in nature. For example, Timothy of Alexandria (458–80), known in historical references as Timothy Aelurus, wrote a refutation of the Council of Chalcedon. In addition, he wrote letters in defense of the faith addressed to the citizens of the cities of Constantinople and Alexandria, to Egypt, and to specific persons such as Faustinus the Deacon and Claudianus the Priest (Ebied and Wickham 1970; Ebied 1985). The writings of Dioscorus of Alexandria as well as his successor Timothy survive only in translation, and the writings of Peter III of Alexandria, referred to as Peter Mongus (the Stammerer), the successor of Timothy, are lost.

Liturgical and Monastic Texts

The formative era also produced liturgical and monastic texts that shaped the prayer and spiritual life of the Coptic Orthodox Church. The liturgical prayers attributed to Serapion of Thmuis consist of thirty prayers that are certainly of Egyptian origin and date to the middle of the fourth century. The text contains eighteen Eucharistic prayers, seven of baptism and confirmation, three for ordination, and two for the blessing of the oil and funerals (Wordsworth 1923; Johnson 1995). Findings from Dayr al-Balāīzah include a papyrus with part of a Coptic liturgy that represents fourth-century Egyptian liturgical practices (Stewart 2010). Another fourth-century papyrus contains fragments that represent an early, if not the original, text of St. Mark's liturgy. The recension of St. Mark's liturgy presently used in Coptic Orthodox churches is known as the Liturgy of St. Cyril.

The formative era also produced monastic literature including hagiographies, monastic rules, sayings, letters, ascetic treatises, sermons, and history. Monastic literature emerged among Coptic monastics in response to their needs as oral tradition in the vernacular. But since the fame of the Coptic monastics attracted men and women from all over the world, early on their literature was written and translated into Greek and Latin for a global audience. The most famous hagiography is *The Life of Antony* by Athanasius, mentioned above, which was composed in Greek for foreign readers. There are at least six versions of the *Life of Pachomius*, the founder of the communal monastic system; the most important is the Coptic, according to Lefort, though other scholars consider the Greek redaction better (Lefort 1953; Veilleux 1980); soon, a Latin translation followed. The literary genre of monastic rules emerged with the Pachomian Koinonia (Veilleux 1981). The rules are simple and primarily concerned with work regulations and moral and monastic conduct; they also insist that all monks have to learn reading and writing before admittance to the monastery. The text was composed in Coptic because of its importance; it was translated with adaptations into Greek and served as a source of Basil's monastic rule, which became the foundation of Byzantine monasticism. It was later adapted further into Latin to form, together with Basil's rule, the foundation of Latin monasticism. The Latin represents the short recension adapted for Italian monasteries.

The monastic writings include letters that explore various topics. Pachomian literature includes eleven letters to various monastic leaders and monks. It also includes two letters from Theodore and four from Horsiesios, the successors of Pachomius, together with various instructions (Veilleux 1982). Ammonas, the disciple of St. Antony, has seven extant Greek letters which are primarily mystical but also provide valuable information about the history of early monastic practices (Chitty 1985). Similarly, the *Letter of Ammon* provides important information about Pachomian monasteries (Goehring 1986). Barsanuphius, a sixth-century Egyptian Chalcedonian monk, wrote 396 letters addressed primarily to monks but which also include responses to questions from bishops, priests, and laypersons (Chryssavgis 2006–7). The oldest and most important letters are those of Antony, which were composed in Coptic but translated into Greek; only a fragment of the Greek translation survives, but it is attested to by the Latin translation (Rubenson 1995).

The sayings of the desert fathers and mothers are preserved in discourses and sayings; some sayings were even taken from the discourses. Two examples of discourses can be mentioned, those of Abba Isaiah of Scetis and Amma Syncletica. Sayings were extracted from them and included in what came to be known as the *Sayings of the Desert Fathers*. Isaiah of Scetis, a disciple of Macarius the Great of Egypt, fled to Gaza, most probably after the devastation of Scetis in 434. He left twenty-nine ascetic discourses that are exemplary of Egyptian monastic spirituality (Chryssavgis 2002). Syncletica was born in Alexandria and left some discourses and sayings preserved in *The Life of Blessed Syncletica*. The *Life* provides a very short biographical description; the main part of the text preserves her teachings and ascetic practices (Bongie 1995).

The most celebrated of the monastic writings are the *Sayings* (*Apophthegmata Patrum*). Monastic spiritual guidance was transmitted sometimes through discourses, like those just mentioned, sometimes through a response to a personal question about a disciple's struggles in the spiritual journey, and sometimes in response to a general request, such as, "Tell me a word to live by." The response could be in the form of a pithy statement, a parable or story, or a short discourse. The response could be specifically tailored to the questioner or general, and both types of answers were collected because they were deemed suitable for edification. As the leading elders of the desert began to age, and after the devastation of Scetis, one of the main monastic centers, their disciples began gathering their sayings in written form. This produced two collections, a systematic collection that presents the sayings topically and an alphabetical collection that presents the sayings of certain monastic figures (Ward 2003, 1984, 1986). Though the sayings were pronounced in Coptic, the collections were written in both Coptic and Greek, for the benefit of the local as well as a wider audience, and were soon translated into Latin. These sayings were instrumental in spreading the monastic ideals throughout the world and had a far reaching impact. Many foreign travelers came to visit the Egyptian deserts and documented their journey in texts such as the *Lausiac History* and the *Lives of the Desert Fathers*.

The Greek writings of the early Church of Alexandria are an indispensable source for understanding Coptic theology, spirituality, and history. The Coptic Greek literary production is huge. Many texts, even by some of the most famous writers, have not been edited or translated into any modern language. On the other hand, many of the translated texts are available on the web and are easily accessible through a title or author search.

Selected Bibliography

For handbooks in Patrology:

Di Berardino, A., Walford, A. and Quasten, J. (2006) *Patrology: The Eastern Fathers from the Council of Chalcedon (451) to John of Damascus (†750)*, Cambridge: James Clarke.

Kannengiesser, C. (2006) *Handbook of Patristic Exegesis*, Leiden: Brill.

Moreschini, C. and Norelli, E. (2005) *Early Christian Greek and Latin Literature*, 2 vols, Peabody, MA: Hendrickson.

Quasten, J. (1950–60) *Patrology*, 3 vols, Westminster, Md.: Newman.

For Early Church Fathers' writings in English translation the following series are a good start:

Ancient Christian Writings Series published by Paulist Press and Newman Press.

The Ante-Nicene and Post-Nicene Nicene Fathers series published by Hendrickson (also available on www.ccel.org/fathers.html).

The Early Church Fathers series published by Routledge.
The Fathers of the Church Series published by the Catholic University of America.

Other websites also provide writings of the Fathers, for example:

www.ccel.org/ccel/pearse/morefathers/files/morefathers.html
www.earlychristianwritings.com/churchfathers.html
www.newadvent.org/fathers

Examples of websites dedicated to individual ancient Christian writers:

For Clement of Alexandria: www.earlychristianwritings.com/clement.html
For Origen of Alexandria: www.john-uebersax.com/plato/origen2.htm

Amidon, P. R. (trans.) (2009) *St. Cyril of Alexandria, Festal Letters 1–12*, Washington, DC: The Catholic University of America Press.

Athanasius of Alexandria (2008) *On the Incarnation*, New York: St. Vladimir Orthodox Theological Seminary.

Bongie, E. B. (1995) *The Life & Regimen of the Blessed & Holy Teacher, Syncletica*, Toronto: Peregrina.

Chitty, D. (ed. and trans.) (1985) *The Letters of Ammonas, Successor of Saint Antony*, Oxford: SLG Press.

Chryssavgis, J. (trans.) (2002) *Abba Isaiah of Scetis, Ascetic Discourses*, Kalamazoo, Michigan: Cistercian Publications.

——(trans.) (2006–7) *Barsanuphius and John, Letters*, 2 vols, Washington, DC: Catholic University of America Press.

Cyril of Alexandria (1983) *Commentary on the Gospel of St. Luke*, R. P. Smith (trans.) Long Island, NY: Studion.

——(1995) *On the Unity of Christ*, McGuckin, J. (trans.) New York: St. Vladimir's Seminary Press.

Ebied, R. Y. (1985) "Timothy Aelurus: Against the Definition of the Council of Chalcedon," in C. Laga, J. A. Munitiz, and L. Van Rompay (eds) *After Chalcedon: Studies in Theology and Church History*, Orientalia Lovaniensia Analecta 18, Louvain: Peeters.

Ebied, R. Y. and Wickham, L. R. (1970) "A Collection of Unpublished Syriac Letters of Timothy Aelurus," *The Journal of Theological Studies* 21(2): 321–69.

Eusebius *Ecclesiastical History*. (Historia ecclesiastica [*Hist. eccl.*]).

Feltoe, C. L. (ed.) (1904) *Dionysiou Leipsana. The Letters and Other Remains of Dionysius of Alexandria*, Cambridge: Cambridge University Press.

——(trans.) (1918) *St. Dionysius of Alexandria. Letters and Treatises*, London: SPCK.

Goehring, J. (1986) *The Letter of Ammon and Pachomian Monasticism*, Berlin: Walter de Gruyter.

Gregg, R. C. (1980) *Athanasius, The Life of Antony and the Letter to Marcellinus*, New York: Paulist Press.

Hill, R. C. (trans.) (2007–2012) *St. Cyril of Alexandria: Commentary on the Twelve Prophets*, 3 vols. Washington DC: The Catholic University of America Press.

——(trans.) (2008) *Cyril of Alexandria, Commentary on Isaiah*, 3 vols, Brookline, MA: Holy Cross Orthodox Press.

Johnson, M. E. (1995) *The Prayers of Serapion of Thmuis: a literary, liturgical, and theological analysis*. Roma: Pontificio instituto orientale.

Lefort, L. T. (1953 reprint) *Sancti Pachomii Vita Bohairice scripta*, CSCO 89 and 107. Louvain: L. Durbecq.

Maxwell, E. J. (1995) *Prayers of Sarapion of Thmuis*, Rome: Pontificio istituto orientale.
McEnerney, J. (trans.) (1987a) *St. Cyril of Alexandria, Letters 1–50*, Washington, DC: The Catholic University of America Press.
——(1987b) *St. Cyril of Alexandria, Letters 51–110*, Washington, DC: The Catholic University of America Press.
Pearson, B. and Vivian, T. (1993) *Two Coptic Homilies attributed to Saint Peter of Alexandria on Riches, on the Epiphany*, Rome: CIM.
Rubenson, S. (1995) *The Letters of St. Antony*, Minneapolis: Fortress Press.
Russell, N. (2007) *Theophilus of Alexandria*, London: Routledge.
Stewart, A. (2010) *Two Early Egyptian Liturgical Papyri: The Deir Balyzeh Papyrus and the Barcelona Papyrus: with Appendices Containing Comparative Material.* Norwich, UK: Hymns Ancient and Modern.
Veilleux, A. (ed. and trans.) (1980) *Pachomian Koinonia, The Life of Saint Pachomius and His Disciples*, vol. 1, Kalamazoo, Michigan: Cistercian Publications.
——(ed. and trans.) (1981) *Pachomian Koinonia, Pachomian Chronicles and Rules*, vol. 2, Kalamazoo, Michigan: Cistercian Publications.
——(ed. and trans.) (1982) *Pachomian Koinonia, Instructions, Letters, and Other Writings of Saint Pachomius and His Disciples*, vol. 3, Kalamazoo, Michigan: Cistercian Publications.
Vivian, T. (1988) *St. Peter of Alexandria, Bishop and Martyr*, Philadelphia: Fortress Press.
Ward, B. (1984) *The Sayings of the Desert Fathers: The Alphabetical Collection*, Kalamazoo, Michigan: Cistercian Publications.
——(1986) *The Wisdom of the Desert Fathers: Systematic Sayings from the Anonymous Series of the* Apophthegmata Patrum, Oxford: SLG Press.
——(2003) *The Desert Fathers: Sayings of the Early Christian Monks*, London: Penguin.
Wordsworth, J. (1923) *Bishop Sarapion's Prayer-Book, An Egyptian Sacramentary Dated Probably about A.D. 350–356*, London: SPCK.

14 Coptic Literature

Copts Writing in their Own Tongue

Hany N. Takla

Introduction

Coptic literature in the proper sense of the term originated in Egypt as a result of Christian missionary work there by the Church of Alexandria. It began as a way to satisfy the need for preaching the Gospel to native Egyptians. Its wide spread, however, was the result of the monastic movement that the Copts gave birth to in the fourth century AD. In particular, coenobitic monasticism required of its new recruits the ability to read the Scriptures. So it would not be surprising to see that early literature in Coptic was either biblical or monastic. As the number of Christians increased in Egypt, Coptic literature slowly began to gain prominence in relation to Greek, which was the lingua franca of both literature and administration in Egypt. The steady oppression that the Copts faced in post-Chalcedonian Egypt greatly affected the type of Coptic literature circulating among the Copts. It became a way of uplifting their spirits in the face of adversity.[1] It declined in quantity and quality, however, as the number of Coptic-speaking Christians steadily began to decline after the late ninth century. It was being replaced by Arabic, which already had more than a two-century head start as it functioned as the official language of the country's administration.

Definition and Scope

In this chapter Coptic literature is defined as literature written in Coptic and circulating among the inhabitants of Egypt or elsewhere. It includes both texts composed in Coptic and translations from Greek.[2] It is part of the family of Christian literature that scholars call Oriental, which also includes Syriac, Armenian, Georgian, Nubian, and Arabic. It is predominantly related to non-Chalcedonian Egyptian Christians, though some of the surviving literature is heterodox or even pagan.

Coptic literature can best be described as biblical or biblically influenced and monastically influenced, if the minor pagan compositions are excluded.[3] Its time frame begins as early as the second half of the second century and goes up to the present day. Anything written after 1400, however, is liturgical and not of high quality. The most significant portion of surviving literature is found in Sahidic and Bohairic, though important texts, especially biblical translations, have survived in six major known dialects. Works in those other dialects are translations from Sahidic or Bohairic, except for the heterodox literature. The audience for Coptic Orthodox literature was in general a monastic one. Monasteries seem to have had the highest concentration of Copts who were literate in the Coptic language as it was mandatory in the coenobitic system for the monk to be literate in order to read the Scriptures.[4]

Contents

Based on the literature that survived one can classify Coptic literature into eleven distinct categories as follows.

Biblical Texts

This category began as translations of selections from the Bible made primarily for preaching Christianity to the Egyptian population who did not know Greek. They were initially done to standardize the dissemination of these texts. Literate and affluent Copts began to use such literature, but its usage in monastic circles must have accelerated its production and inspired the translation of the entire biblical canon by the fourth century, at least into Sahidic. Certain books were translated into regional dialects in accordance with local need. It is worthy of mention here that Copts, like most Orthodox Christians, consider the Old and New Testament as one entity in their Bible canon and include the Deuterocanonical books from the Septuagint in the Old Testament. This canon of scriptures distinguished the Orthodox from the followers of heretical teachings in the first few centuries of Christianity. This is evident from the way that the early fathers referred to biblical texts and the way the manuscripts were produced. Two early Coptic Sahidic manuscripts combine books from both the Old and New Testaments in the same codex. They are both dated by their respective editors to the third or fourth century. The first is British Library Or. 7594, edited by Wallis Budge in 1912, which contains the text of Deuteronomy, Jonah, and Acts (Budge 1912). The second, the Crosby-Schøyen Ms. 193 edited by James E. Goehring and others in 1990, contains 2 Maccabees, 1 Peter, and Jonah (Goehring 1990).

Seven major dialects yielded biblical texts. Sahidic and Bohairic are the ones which have substantial surviving portions translated from two distinct Greek Recensions. Texts found in all other dialects, with the possible exception of some Fayyūmic texts, were translations from Sahidic, though their manuscripts may be older than what has survived in Sahidic. The text of the New Testament is complete in both Bohairic and Sahidic with some fragments of individual books surviving in other dialects. The picture in the Old Testament is much different. Neither of the two main dialects has a complete text of the entire Old Testament. More of the text is preserved in Sahidic, but in a more fragmentary way in several places. Books surviving in Bohairic tend to be more complete. However, the historical books in Bohairic are nearly all lost. What has survived in the other dialects has also survived in either Bohairic or Sahidic, or both. There are books that did not survive at all in any known dialect, such as Ezra, Nehemiah, and 1 Maccabees. When all verses of the Old Testament surviving in either Bohairic or Sahidic are combined, only 82 percent are found. Seventy percent of the verses survive in Sahidic alone, while only 60 percent survive in Bohairic. It is worthy of mention that Bohairic texts that have survived are mostly from the twelfth century and later, while other dialects yield manuscripts from as early as the fourth century.[5] Nearly all surviving texts have been published or are available in facsimile format for scholars and students to consult.[6]

Gnostic/Manichaean Literature

Heterodox texts in Coptic came about as a result of efforts by their followers to conceal the texts' identity from the eyes of the Orthodox Church in Alexandria, which actively sought to confiscate them. In the case of the Gnostic literature, the groups took their texts south into Upper Egypt and in the process the texts were translated into Coptic in the early fourth century, most likely in Lycopolis, modern-day Asyūṭ.[7] Most likely due to the pressure that St. Shenouda applied in the fifth century, these groups had to flee further south as their numbers undoubtedly diminished dramatically.[8] The trail of their literature leads to Akhmīm, the backyard of St. Shenouda. There only one text was found, in a cemetery, in a format suited for private use rather than a community library like the one we will speak about next. This trail of Gnostic literature continues south along the Nile to what is known now as Nag Hammadi, where the books of a community library known as the Nag Hammadi Corpus were found. The Gnostics settled near or at a Pachomian monastery, judging by copies of Pachomian letters found in the texts' binding.[9] There the texts were eventually buried in jars and hidden from view as the remnants of the community died out. They remained buried until they were unearthed by two brothers digging for fertilizer in 1945.[10]

The core literature of the Gnostic community survived in thirteen codices, containing over one hundred works translated from lost Greek originals into Coptic.[11] The library is not uniform in character as it contains, according to Orlandi's survey, eight different categories (Orlandi 2006: 507–25). The topics range in heterodoxy from the extreme texts of the Valentinian Gnostics to the more neutral *Gospel of Thomas*. The latter has been the subject of much debate and study among scholars of Early Christianity and the New Testament as the text exhibits evidence that it may contain the Q-Text, which the writers of the Synoptic Gospels presumably drew upon in the writing of their gospels. According to Orlandi's assessment, no general agreement has been reached as to its origin or even its relationship to either the canonical gospels or the Gnostic ones (ibid. 517). Most interestingly, the corpus includes texts not really

Gnostic in nature but apparently read by the community. This includes a treatise of Zostrianos along with a host of other moral and philosophical texts. The theology of these texts is a strange mixture of Jewish, Christian, Greek, and ancient Egyptian, cloaked in a secret-society type mold. The complex nature of this theology would not have won it many converts outside the sophisticated Alexandria, except in Lycopolis, which in the fourth century was a haven for everyone with a gripe against the central Church in Alexandria! The variety of the texts excavated or discovered preserve a rich vocabulary that cannot be found elsewhere in Coptic literature. In other words, though from an Orthodox perspective the texts are theologically heterodox, they are a linguistic treasure that can aid in the revival of the Coptic language.

The other members of this heterodox family of literature are Manichaean texts. This community adhered to the teaching of Mani, who was killed in Persia in the third century. His brand of heterodoxy can be best described as "Gnostic Lite." Their theology is simpler than that found in Gnostic texts. This widened their appeal beyond the closed circle of intellectuals that Gnosticism seems to have attracted. The surviving texts show evidence of Lycopolitan influence, indicating that this group also spent time in Lycopolis. Sometime in the fifth century they were made unwelcome and left the area, though their escape route was to the north to modern day Fayyūm. In 1929–30, a total of seven manuscripts were discovered, though in much worse condition than the Gnostic ones. They were eventually sold to libraries in Berlin and Dublin. There were three distinct genres found in these manuscripts: Manichaean Psalms, Kephalia, and Manichaean Homilies. The majority of these texts are published, though in older editions, which need revision. There is a new four-volume facsimile edition for what is kept in Dublin, but not of those preserved in Berlin. The importance of these texts lies in their survival in other languages like Chinese, where Manichaeism was practiced as late as the seventeenth century.

Homilies

This category is the main source for patristic texts in Coptic. There are essentially two main groups: texts composed in one of the Coptic dialects, and texts translated from Greek. For some of the texts attributed to Greek authors, however, no known original Greek version has survived. Scholars tend to label them as productions probably composed in Coptic but attributed to recognized patristic names to insure their acceptability to the reader. Criteria for determining what was originally written in Coptic versus what is a translation from Greek have not developed enough to allow scholars to make definitive conclusions on the issue. Texts in this category can be in the form of a treatise or a homily. In the case of a delivered homily, it can be in the form of a Panegyric (Eulogy) or simply a sermon. In many cases there is a hagiographic background or an ecclesiastical occasion for such sermons. Tito Orlandi enumerated in his index of the *Clavis Patrum Copticorum* one hundred writers whose work survives in Coptic (Orlandi 2004).

In the case of translated works, their value is in their content, the original text, and choice of text by Copts. They were translated as early as there was a need by the new Coptic-speaking converts, sometimes in the third century. The earliest witness we find is Melito of Sardis *On Passions*.[12] The most popular Greek father with works translated into Coptic was St. John Chrysostom, due mainly to the less complex nature of his writings and their biblical subject matter. Other fathers included the Apostolic Fathers,[13] St. Basil of Caesarea, St. Gregory the Theologian, St. Gregory of Nyssa, and St. Severus of Antioch. Surprisingly the main corpus of the Great Alexandrian fathers St. Athanasius and St. Cyril I was not translated. This meant that they only circulated in Greek. What has survived of the Coptic Athanasian corpus were probably works that monks read, like the Festal Letters and some other select works. It has been conjectured that some of the works of both fathers were actually written only to be translated and distributed in Coptic through a monastic source. An example is found in a letter from Pope Dioscorus to St. Shenouda the Archimandrite preserved in the St. Shenouda Monastery in Sohag (Thompson 1922).[14] Other patriarchs who left literary works in Coptic that may have been translated from Greek are Theophilus in the fourth–fifth century, Dioscorus and Timothy Aelurus in the fifth century, Theodosius and Damianus in the sixth century, and Benjamin in the seventh century.

Literature composed in Coptic comprises the larger share of this category, though it may not be as well known. According to Epiphanius of Salamis the first to write in his native language of Coptic was Hieracas of Leontopolis, probably in the late third century.[15] The more substantial literature that followed is the Pachomian corpus. This includes the fourth-century rules, epistles, and teachings of St. Pachomius and his disciples Theodore and Horsiesi. These texts are the earliest preserved literary texts in Coptic. They are a reflection of both the biblically based life that coenobitic monasticism called for and the emphasis on literacy among the monks. The Pachomian texts are simple and unsophisticated because they were intended as instructions. They can best be described as the foundation upon which this Upper Egyptian monastic system was based.

Later on, in the fourth century and into the first half of the fifth, a new monastic abbot arose just to the north of the center of Pachomian monasticism in Fāw al-Qiblī. This new abbot was St. Shenouda the Archimandrite. His life span of over a century was a pivotal period in native Coptic literature.[16] It would not be an exaggeration to label his works the crown jewels of Coptic literature. Though he was a monk, his literature went beyond the monastic audience. Due to his charismatic and strong personality he became a shepherd of monks, a champion of the oppressed people, a moral guide to the rich and poor, the Upper Egyptian ambassador to the Orthodox Church of Alexandria, and the interpreter of its theology to his wide audience. Though we do not know what education he received, his literary production indicates it was an exceptional one. His writings are as sophisticated as needed for the audiences he addressed. These audiences included his own monastic community,[17] the peasants that flocked to his monastery from far and near, and government and military officials.[18] Scholars are still unraveling his sophisticated literary style. His writings display the most complex grammatical structures that students learn when studying Sahidic Coptic, the language he perfected. His writings were collected, probably after his repose, in seventeen volumes of a few hundred pages each.[19] Nine volumes were devoted to works addressed to his monastic community and eight included his discourses. In addition there is a collection of his letters. Of 122 of his works at least the titles or incipits are known. At least twenty-six more works are attributed to him but their headings have not survived. Of the seventeen volumes only a relatively small fraction have survived and/or been identified so far, though they are preserved in over one hundred manuscripts. Yet what survives is probably more substantial than the corpus of any other writer who composed in Coptic or had his work translated into it.

St. Shenouda's contribution to Coptic literature extended beyond its volume, variety of audience and themes, and advanced grammar. He exhibits three important features: prolific use of the Bible, respect for those who came before him, and transmission of the teachings of the Church of Alexandria. With respect to the Bible, he quoted long biblical passages in both his writings and sermons. He also employed a style of weaving his message within the structure of biblical quotations, especially when using the words of the prophet Jeremiah. Apa Besa, his disciple, also employed this literary style in his large corpus of surviving sermons. St. Shenouda's reverence for Antony and Pachomius is evident in his writings (Vivian 2005). His allegiance to the teachings of the Alexandrian church is phenomenal considering the home of heterodoxy in his time was not too far to his north.

During St. Shenouda's lifetime, a dispute arose among the monks in the Nitrian desert about Patriarch Theophilus' shift away from the anti-anthropomorphic view of God attributed to Origen. The writings of Origen were the real victims in this dispute. The opposing response from the Pachomian monks has survived in Coptic in a group of texts attributed to Bishop Agathonicus of Tarsus, though Orlandi doubts his authorship as well as his historicity, attributing these texts to one or more unknown authors. No Greek version of these texts has survived, probably because the texts were intended for monks rather than to be sent to Patriarch Theophilus. To no one's surprise St. Shenouda's writings on the subject take the patriarch's views.

Following the golden age of St. Shenouda and before the Arab Conquest of Egypt in the mid-seventh century, we find five authors of whom at least some works have survived: Constantine of Asyūṭ, Bishop John of Shmun, Bishop Pisentius of Qift or Coptos, Rufus of Shotep, and Mena of Nikiou. They also lived in Middle or Upper Egypt and wrote in the late sixth to the beginning of the seventh centuries. Their writings are usually hagiographic, related to important saints in the Church, with the exception of Rufus of Shotep, who wrote homilies as exposition of or commentary on the Gospels. Following the Arab Conquest there are only two known Coptic writers whose works have survived: Zakharia of Sakha in the eighth century and Mark, Patriarch of Alexandria, in the ninth century.

The language of the texts surveyed above is primarily Sahidic with occasional translations in other minor dialects. In the library of St. Macarius Monastery, however, are several texts from John Chrysostom, Zakharia of Sakha, and Mark of Alexandria preserved in Bohairic, which are in a better state of preservation than the Sahidic ones.

Monastic Literature

This category is not very distinctive, since most of the works discussed in this chapter were written for a monastic audience. Aside from the early Pachomian works and the canons of St. Shenouda one encounters many sayings of the desert fathers arranged in different collections either by author or subject. These are commonly referred to as the "Apophthegmata Patrum." They are extant in several ancient languages, wherever monks lived around the world. Émile Amélineau argued that Coptic was the original language of these texts but most scholars have opted for a Greek original from which the Coptic was translated. In Bohairic we have very important texts of the sayings of St. Macarius. Most of what has survived, however, is in Sahidic.

Hagiographic Texts

Sermons and hagiographic texts dominated Coptic literature until shortly after the Arab conquest of Egypt. The majority of hagiographic texts are either about martyrs from the Diocletian era or the lives of monastic figures. Much of the martyr literature was in an abbreviated form as brief records of what happened just before the saints were martyred. Two examples have been identified and published from the Oxyrhynchus and Duke University collections (Alcock 1982; van Minnen 1995). The first mentions a certain John of Alexandria during the persecution of Septimus Severus in the early third century, and the second is a record of the martyrdom of Stephen of Alexandria during the Diocletian persecution. Hagiography generally includes martyrologies, miracles, or lives (*vitae*) mostly of monastic figures. Some were composed in Greek and then translated into Coptic, some were translated from Greek and then survived in a later, expanded Coptic version, and some were composed in Coptic. Important texts are extant in Sahidic as well as Bohairic. According to Orlandi's proposed historical periodization of Coptic literature, these texts were compiled in the seventh and eighth centuries in related groups which he labeled "cycles," in each of which there is a central figure (Orlandi 1991b: Vol. 5, 1450–60). The most extensive and important collections are those of Basilides and Julius of Aqfahṣ. Later, such literature began to serve a liturgical function, which Orlandi labeled the "Synaxarial" arrangement, by being assigned for reading on certain days of the Coptic calendar. Such theories have led some scholars to claim that all these texts are fabricated fables with no historical value. This view was later revised by other scholars as important historical information was discovered when studying the Fayyūm's Ḥamuli collection. More recently, scholarship views the value of cycles in the social history they transmit rather than in the chronological history of the person depicted. Modern scholarship, however, has found that these texts also provide important history of the times they discuss (Reymond and Barns 1973: 1–21).

There is no comprehensive list of all the hagiographic texts in Coptic. However, by using the most complete list, published in 1910 by Paulus Peeters, one can get a good idea of the scope of what has survived or has been published so far (Peeters 1910). Of the list that he compiled of all hagiographic texts in the different Oriental languages about 12 percent are in Coptic. The majority of the texts have survived in Sahidic (S), though most of the complete texts are found only in Bohairic (B). Very little is found in the other dialects. The texts mostly cover the martyrs of the Diocletian era (fourth century), monastic figures (fourth–seventh century), and acts of the apostles (first century). The exceptions would be a few texts about personalities from the second, third, twelfth, and fourteenth centuries.

The most important and complete texts are those of the martyrs and the monastic fathers. Among the major martyrdoms surviving are those of St. Claudius of Antioch (S), St. Coluthus (S), St. Menas (S), St. Mercurius (S), St. Peter of Alexandria (B), Piroou and Athom (B), St. Theodore Strateletes (B), and St. Victor (S), to name a few. Among the important lives of monastic fathers are those of St. Antony the Great (S), St. Daniel of Scetis (B), St. John Colobos (B, S), the Three Macarii (B), St. Pachomius (B, S), St. Pisentius (B), and St Shenouda (B, S). Almost all the Bohairic hagiographic texts come from what remained from the library of the St. Macarius Monastery in Wādī al-Naṭrūn. The Sahidic texts survive from the remains of the library of St. Shenouda Monastery in Sohag, Archangel Michael Monastery in Ḥamuli, Fayyūm, and Archangel Michael Monastery in Edfu.

Historical Literature

Purely historical or chronological works are rather scarce in Coptic, at least as far as what has survived. There is a fragmentary ecclesiastical history in Sahidic that probably served as the base text for the Arabic *History of the Patriarchs of the Coptic Church*. In monastic history we have fragments of the *Historia Monachorum*. There are also several biographies of patriarchs like those of St. Athanasius, St. Dioscorus, and St. Isaac of Alexandria. From the library of the St. Shenouda Monastery the *Acts* of the Councils of Nicaea and Ephesus have survived in Sahidic. The very important seventh-century *Chronicles* of John of Nikiou may have been written in Coptic but no fragments of the Coptic have been identified yet. It has survived complete in Ethiopic.

Plerophoriae (Anti-Chalcedonian Polemics)

Between AD 451 and the Arab conquest of Egypt, the Church was in constant struggle with the imperial-backed Melkite Church. This struggle inspired several works available in Sahidic Coptic. These are primarily lives of Pachomian monks who resisted the Chalcedonian faith as foreign to the Church. Even though they are hagiographic, they tend to be dogmatic also (Orlandi 2006: 562–66). Sometimes they try to demonstrate the righteousness of the Orthodox faith by recounting the miracles performed by God through these heroic monastic figures. The most representative texts from this type are the lives of Apollo, Abraham of Farshūṭ, Matthew the Poor, Moses the Archimandrite, Zenobius the Archimandrite, John of Lycopolis, Daniel of Scetis, Pambo of Scetis, Manassas the Archimandrite, and the monks Phib and Longinus.

Canon Law

Coptic literature has yielded the oldest translations of canon laws. Although these texts are more complete in Arabic, there are still a significant number of texts that have survived in this category in both Sahidic and, to a lesser extent, in Bohairic. These include the Apostolic Canons (S, B), the Didache (S), the Ecclesiastical Canons (S, B), and the canons of St. Athanasius (S).

Liturgical Texts

Liturgical texts that have survived are scarce and mostly in the form of prayers and bilingual Sahidic–Greek lectionaries. Apparently, Greek was the predominant language in the Church of Alexandria's liturgy at least till the tenth century. From the ninth and tenth centuries, however, we have an important Sahidic lectionary, a *psalmodia* (a book of texts for a sung service of the same name), and an antiphonary from the Fayyūm as well as an important manuscript of anaphoras (Eucharistic prayers) from St. Shenouda Monastery (Lanne 1956). The liturgical reform of Patriarch Gabriel II in the early twelfth century yielded a new manual for reading during Holy Week, known as the Pascha Book, as well as a restriction of the anaphora texts used to those of St. Basil, St. Gregory, and St. Cyril. From that time up to the early fifteenth century, new Coptic literature was mostly if not exclusively confined to liturgical compositions. This included revisions of and new services in such works as the lectionaries (annual, Lenten, Paschaltide), *psalmodias* (annual, Kiahk), anaphoras, offices (baptism, matrimony, unction, funerals, Abū Ṭarbū), and others. The majority of these texts are in Bohairic and probably have their roots in monastic circles. There is also an important Pascha Book in Sahidic that has survived from the fourteenth century. In the early fifteenth century Patriarch Gabriel V instituted another liturgical reform, apparently to regulate the scope of the diverse and new liturgical services that appeared during this period. Since that time Coptic composition diminished greatly and was confined to additions to the lectionary readings, hymns related to the liturgical year, and the *psalmodia*.

Apocrypha

This category of literature may be assumed by some scholars to be spurious and of dubious value, but for the Copts such compositions were edifying and useful, as can be seen in the way they were used and quoted. They are very valuable for the study of early Christianity as well as later periods. They are exclusively translations, from Greek and possibly Syriac, and they are independent of the Gnostic texts even if they share common names. The surviving texts have been preserved mainly in three dialects: Akhmimic and Sahidic from St. Shenouda Monastery in Sohag, and Bohairic from St. Macarius Monastery in Wādī al-Naṭrūn. Examples of apocryphal texts with Old Testament themes are 4 Ezra, the 14th Vision of Daniel, an unknown text of Adam, the Apocryphon of Enoch, the Ascension of Isaiah, the Apocryphon of Jeremiah, the Apocalypse of Elijah, the Apocalypse of Moses, the Testament of Abraham, Isaac, and Jacob, the Testament of Zephaniah, etc. Texts on New Testament themes include texts related to the Virgin Mary,[20] Joseph the Carpenter, John the Baptist, and the other texts relevant to the apostles. We also have other important texts, such as the Gospel of Nicodemus and the Acts of Pilate.

Poetry

Not much was produced or has survived in this category outside the biblical and liturgical works mentioned previously. It should be noted that the Manichaean Psalms are highly regarded for their poetic composition. Other than that there is a long bilingual poem in Sahidic and Arabic from the fourteenth century, which survived, though incomplete, from the Monastery of St. Shenouda (Lemm 1903). It has been regarded by scholars as a last attempt to write in Coptic. The clear purpose of its author was to exalt the Coptic language and its heritage (Kuhn 1991: Vol. 6, 1985–86).

History of Academic Research

Interest in Coptic literature began as early as the late sixteenth century in Europe. Almost all the work in the field was dominated by editions of texts and the study of biblical or apocryphal texts up until the late nineteenth century.[21] In Germany, Paul de Largarde published non-biblical works during the nineteenth century. But the French Egyptologists were the most prolific publishers of Coptic literary texts, especially Amélineau, who published nearly everything known in Bohairic and Sahidic in his time up into the early twentieth century. Other scholars began to publish Coptic texts but only the ones found in their country of origin: E. A. Wallis Budge in England, Oscar von Lemm in Russia, Francesco Rossi in Italy, Carl Wessely in Austria. Toward the beginning of the twentieth century a new crop of scholars began to publish in Coptic Studies on a wider scale, like Walter E. Crum, Johannes Leipoldt, Henri Hyvernat, and

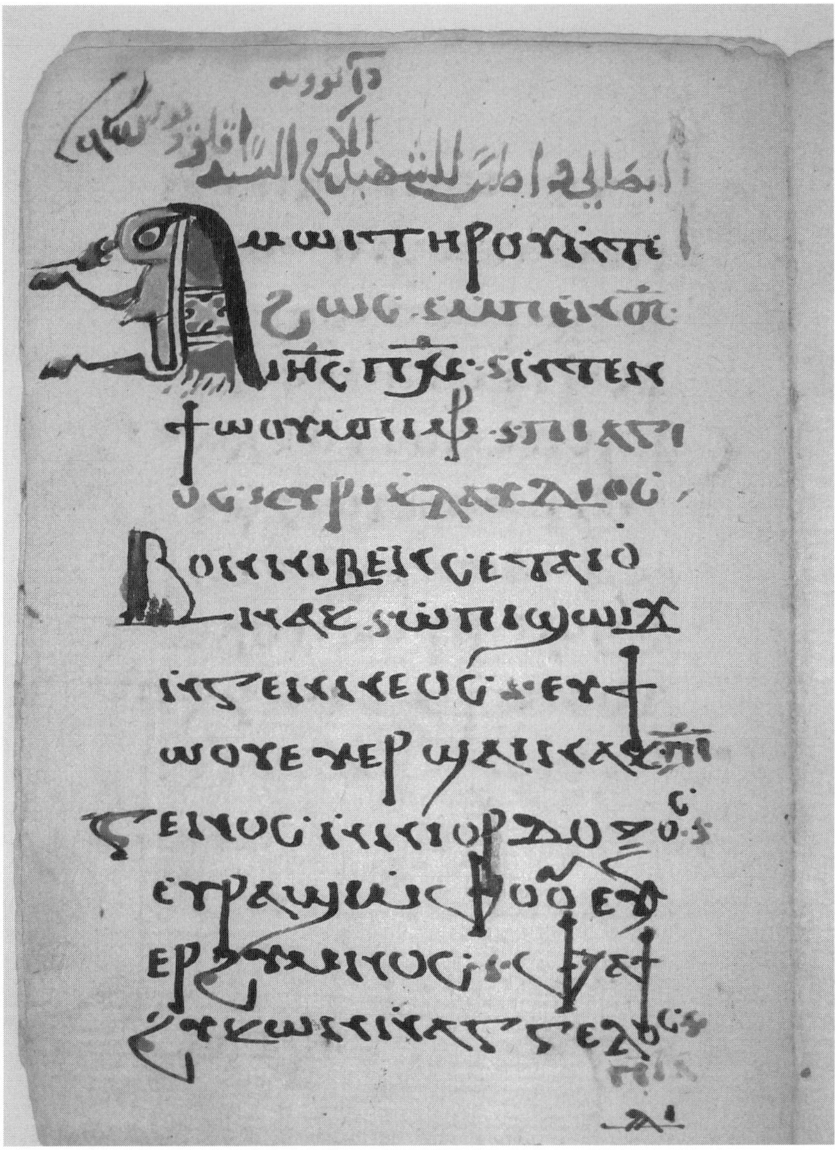

Figure 14.1 A fragment of a Bohairic Manuscript of Psalis for the Saints, paper, undated. Collection of the St. Shenouda the Archimandrite Coptic Society in Los Angeles, Ms. No. 9. Courtesy of Hany N. Takla

Carl Schmidt. Their works included critical editions accompanied by analytical studies. In the following generation one encounters the works of Jakob Polotsky, L. Th. Lefort, Walter C. Till, and William Worrell. Beginning in the late 1960s Coptic literature received a boost from the efforts of James

M. Robinson and his team working on the Gnostic corpus of Nag Hammadi; Rodolphe Kasser, on the biblical corpus from Dishna; and Tito Orlandi, on the dismembered and scattered library of the St. Shenouda Monastery.

Orlandi published, gathered, and cataloged manuscript collections of the Sahidic material in Europe. In addition, he developed the most comprehensive history of Coptic literature to date, arranging the development of this literature into eleven historical periods as follows:

1. Formation of the biblical corpus
2. Formation of the Gnostic corpus
3. Formation of the Manichaean corpus
4. The Origenist controversy (IV–V century)
5. Shenoute (V century)
6. Translations from Greek (V–VI century)
7. After Chalcedon: the Plerophories (V–VI century)
8. The period of Damianus (VI–VII century)
9. Early Islamic occupation (VII century)
10. Formation of the Cycles (VII–VIII century)
11. Synaxarial arrangement (VIII–IX century)

This periodization system is founded on Orlandi's study of the contents of the major libraries discovered so far: Nag Hammadi, Madinat Madi, St. Michael Monastery in Ḥamuli, and St. Shenouda Monastery in Sohag. Notably absent is the Late Liturgical Age (XI–XIV century). Liturgical texts have a legitimate place in this chronology as they became the last attempt by the Copts to write in Coptic. In essence, these texts are primarily an anthology of biblical and patristic texts arranged to musical melodies and recorded in multiple service manuals. Further, it is worthy of mention that the Coptic Church has many reservations about the tenth period above, i.e. the Cycles. The reason stems from the assertion that these so-called cycles assume an extreme lack of authenticity in these martyrologies. Such an assumption was rejected by the Coptic Church.

In 1993 a new boost of energy was injected into the study of Coptic literature in the form of Stephen Emmel's seminal work on the recovery of the literary corpus of St. Shenouda (Emmel 2004). Since then, many scholars have found a map to navigate this difficult branch of Coptic literature. As a result much work has been produced and more announced in publishing the remains of this important corpus. It is headed of course by Emmel himself and coordinated from the birthplace of the discipline of Coptology, the University of Münster in Germany.

This new revival in Shenoutian study was preceded and accompanied by other important works in the field by such scholars as Anne Boud'hors, Nathalie Bosson, Martin Krause, Nashaat Mekhael, Hans Quecke, Tim Vivian, Youhanna N. Youssef, and Ugo Zanetti, to name just a few.

Challenges

The study of Coptic literature is a growing field with much still to be discovered, properly analyzed, and placed in proper context. The following are some of the questions and challenges facing researchers:

- Was the Jewish community in Alexandria the first to translate the Greek Septuagint into Coptic? Such a conjecture has been advanced or contemplated by some prominent scholars such as Josef Vergote and Leo Depuydt. Seeing that the translation of biblical texts was primarily for the purpose of preaching, there was no incentive for the Jewish community to be, or evidence that it was, involved in such a practice at such an early date or at any time at all.
- The fragmentary state of preservation of many of these literary works often poses a significant challenge.
- The question of authorship or the authentication of the given author has been problematic, especially in the case of literature translated from Greek.
- The dating of the manuscripts for the proper historical placement of these texts also poses a challenge due to the lack of comprehensive manuals of paleography.

Overall, much has been achieved but much is still needed, such as better editions of texts as well as better translations.

Notes

1. This type of literature is most exemplified in the lives of the monks who struggled to defend the non-Chalcedonian faith against the pressure applied on them from the followers of the Chalcedonian camp. It is also visible in the hagiographic literature that flourished in Egypt since the sixth century.
2. Other languages that may have texts translated into Coptic would be possibly Syriac and even Arabic, but they would be limited to later liturgical texts.
3. Liturgical texts generally have a wider audience but their Coptic version was most likely influenced by monastic use.
4. Rule No. 139 of the Rules of Pachomius reads: "Whoever enters the monastery uninstructed shall be taught first what he must observe; and when, so taught, he has consented to it all, they shall give him twenty psalms or two of the Apostle's epistles, or some other part of the Scriptures. And if he is illiterate, he shall go at the first, third, and sixth hours to someone who can teach and has been appointed for him. He shall stand before him and learn studiously with all gratitude. Then the fundamentals of the syllable, the verbs, and nouns shall be written for him, and even if he does not want to, he shall be compelled to read." Veilleux 1981: 166.
5. For a fuller discussion of the Coptic Old Testament consult Takla 2007. For an assessment of both Old and New Testament consult Takla (forthcoming).
6. For a list of all these editions consult the references in the previous note.
7. The language of two of the thirteen codices found is the dialect of the area, Lycopolitan, and the rest of the texts are in Sahidic but exhibit influence from the same dialect.
8. Tito Orlandi speaks of some kind of anti-heretical campaign circa 445, which St. Shenouda would have participated in, as evidenced by his famous treatise Contra Origenistas (Orlandi 2006: 542). This crusade may have helped to drive away the Gnostics from their Lycopolis stronghold.

9 For discussion and edition of the contents of these cartonnage fragments, consult Barns et al. 1981.
10 For the investigative story of their discovery, consult Robinson 1981.
11 Fragments from the Gospel of Thomas were found among the Oxyrhynchus manuscripts over a century ago. They were never fully identified, however, until the Coptic translation of the book was studied and published.
12 This text with an English translation is published in Goehring 1990: 12–79. According to James Robinson this was part of a library of an ancient Pachomian monastery in Dishna in Upper Egypt. It probably was donated by one of the more affluent literate monks who lived there. Cf. Robinson 2011.
13 From what has survived we see texts related to Ignatius of Antioch, Pseudo-Clement, the Shepherd of Hermas, etc. (Lefort 1952). The Coptic version of the first letter of Clement of Rome was published by Carl Schmidt in 1908.
14 The letter pertains to a priest named Helias, condemned and excommunicated for heresy.
15 For more information about Hieracas and what may have survived from his writings cf. Guillaumont 1991: Vol. 4, 1128–29.
16 For discussion of the history and the age of St. Shenouda consult Emmel 2004: 1, 6–14
17 In his Arabic vita, it is mentioned that there were 2,200 monks and 1,800 nuns.
18 For discussion of the visitors to St. Shenouda in his monastery, consult Behlmer 1998.
19 For a summary discussion of the structure of these volumes consult Young 2005.
20 e.g. On the life of the Virgin, on the death of Mary
21 For more detailed history on work done on the Coptic Bible in general and the Coptic Old Testament in particular consult Takla 2007: 15–49.

Selected Bibliography

Recommended for further reading: Burmester (1967), Coquin (1991), Depyudt (2010), Emmel (2007), Kuhn (1991), Orlandi (2006), Richter (2005), Takla (2007).

Alcock, A. (1982) "Persecution Under Septimius Severus," *Enchoria*, 11: 1–5.

Barns, J. W. B., Browne, G. M., and Shelton, J. C. (1981) *Nag Hammadi Codices: Greek and Coptic Papyri from the Cartonnage of the Covers*, Leiden: Brill.

Behlmer, H. (1998) "Visitors to Shenoute's Monastery," in D. Frankfurter (ed.) *Pilgrimage & Holy Space in Late Antique Egypt*, Leiden: Brill.

Budge, W. (1912) *Coptic Biblical Texts in the Dialect of Upper Egypt*, London: British Museum.

Burmester, O. H. E. Khs. (1967) *The Egyptian or Coptic Church: A Detailed Description of Her Liturgical Services and the Rites and Ceremonies Observed in the Administration of Her Sacraments*, Cairo: Société d'Archéologie Copte.

Coquin, R-G. (1991) "Canon Law," in A. S. Atiya (ed.) *The Coptic Encyclopedia*, 8 vols, New York: Macmillan.

Depyudt, L. (2010) "Coptic and Coptic Literature," in A. B. Lloyd (ed.) *A Companion to Ancient Egypt*, 2 vols, West Sussex: Wiley-Blackwell.

Emmel, S. L. (2004) *Shenoute's Literary Corpus* (*Corpus Scriptorum Christianorum Orientalium (CSCO)*, 599–600, *Subsidia*, 111–12), Louvain: Peeters.

——(2007) "Coptic Literature in the Byzantine and Early Islamic World," in R. S. Bagnall, *Egypt in the Byzantine World 300–700*, Cambridge: Cambridge University Press.

Goehring, James E. (ed.) (1990) *The Crosby-Schøyen Codex Ms 193 in the Schøyen Collection* (*CSCO*, 521, *Subsidia*, 85), Louvain: Peeters.

Guillaumont, A. (1991) "Hieracas of Leontopolis," in A. S. Atiya (ed.) *The Coptic Encyclopedia*, 8 vols, New York: Macmillan.

Kuhn, K. H. (1991) "Poetry," in A. S. Atiya (ed.) *The Coptic Encyclopedia*, 8 vols, New York: Macmillan.

Lanne, E. (1956) *Le Grand Euchologe du Monastère Blanc* (*Patrologia Orientalis* T. 28, F. 2. No. 135), Paris: Firmin Didot.

Lefort, L. T. (1952) *Les Pères apostoliques en Copte* (*CSCO*, 135, *Scriptores Coptici*, 17), Louvain: Peeters.

Lemm, O. von (1903) *Das Triadon: Ein Sahidisches Gedicht mit Arabischer Ubersetzung*, St. Petersbourge: Akademie Imperiale des Sciences.

Orlandi, T. (1986) "Coptic Literature," in B. A. Pearson and J. E. Goehring (eds) *The Roots of Egyptian Christianity*, Philadelphia: Fortress Press.

——(1991a) "Hagiography, Coptic," in A. S. Atiya (ed.) *The Coptic Encyclopedia*, 8 vols, New York: Macmillan.

——(1991b) "Literature, Coptic," in A. S. Atiya (ed.) *The Coptic Encyclopedia*, 8 vols, New York: Macmillan.

——(2004) "Clavis Patrum Copticorum," in *CMCL – Corpus dei Manoscritti Copti Letterari*. Online. http://rmcisadu.let.uniroma1.it/cgi-bin/cmcl/entrata.cgi (accessed October 14, 2011).

——(2006) "Patristic Texts in Coptic," in A. di Berardino *Patrology: The Eastern Fathers from the Council of Chalcedon (451) to John of Damascus (750)*, trans. A. Walford, Cambridge: James Clark.

Peeters, P. (1910) *Bibliotheca Hagiographica Orientalis*, (Subsidia Hagiographica, 10), Bruxelles: Apud Editores.

Reymond, E. A. E. and Barns, J. W. B. (1973) *Four Martyrdoms from the Pierpont Morgan Coptic Codices*, Oxford: Oxford University Press.

Richter, S. (2005) "The Coptic Manichaean Library from Madinat Habu," in G. Gabra (ed.) *Christianity and Monasticism in the Fayoum Oasis*, Cairo: AUC Press.

Robinson, J. (1981) "From the Cliff to Cairo: The Story of the Discoverers and the Middlemen of the Nag Hammadi Codices," in B. Barc (ed.) *Colloque international sur les textes de Nag Hammadi (Québec, 22–25 août 1978)*, Quebec and Louvain: Les Presses de l'Université Laval and Éditions Peeters.

——(2011) *The Story of the Bodmer Papyri*, Eugene: Wipf & Stock Publishers.

Takla, H. N. (2007) *Introduction to the Coptic Old Testament* (*Coptica*, 6) Los Angeles: St. Shenouda the Archimandrite Coptic Society.

——(forthcoming) "The Coptic Bible," in G. Gabra (ed.) *Coptic Civilization*, Cairo: AUC Press.

Thompson, H. (1922) "Dioscorus and Shenoute," *École pratique des hautes études. Bibliotheque*, 234: 367–76.

van Minnen, P. (1995) "The Earliest Account of a Martyrdom in Coptic," *Analecta Bollandiana*, 113(1–2): 13–38.

Veilleux, A. (1981) *Pachomian Koinonia*, vol. 2, *Pachomian Chronicles and Rules*, Kalamazoo: Cistercian Publications.

Vivian, T. (2005) "'Those whom God made Famous throughout the World': Holy Men from Middle and Lower Egypt in the Writings of Saint Shenoute the Great," *Coptica*, 4: 75–85.

Young, D. W. (2005) "Literary Corpus of Shenoute," *Coptica*, 4: 86–104.

15 Coptic Arabic Literature

When Arabic Became the Language of Saints

Samuel Moawad

Copto-Arabic literature is rich and diverse, just like its authors: popes, bishops, monks, and most notably, intellectual laymen. It is a subject, of course, that cannot be covered in such a short essay, which aims mainly to give an overview and to focus on some important examples.

The Arab conquest of Egypt in AD 641 was a turning point in the history of Egypt in general and the Coptic Orthodox Church in particular. The new conquerors brought with them not only a new political and military hierarchy, but also a new religion and a new language. In contrast to previous invaders of Egypt, such as the Persians in AD 619, the Romans in 30 BC and the Greeks in 332 BC, the Arabs aimed not only to expand the area of their nascent empire and guarantee new financial sources, but also to spread their new religion. This fact was reflected clearly in Coptic literature under Islamic rule; it motivated the Christian natives of Egypt to generate literature written in Arabic to save their own identity and existence.

From Coptic to Arabic

Language is an important feature of any culture and hence any identity. Coptic literature peaked from the fourth to the seventh centuries, while Coptic was the language of the daily life of the majority of Egyptians at least until the tenth century. One can call the period from the fourth to the ninth century "the Coptic period" (Mikhail 2004).

As is to be expected, the conquerors and new sovereigns of Egypt, the Arabs, sought to enforce Arabic among their subjects. The decision of the Umayyad caliph 'Abd al-Malik ibn Marwān (685–705) to impose Arabic as the official language of administration marked the border between two periods and two cultures in the history of Egypt. However, it took over two centuries from this date to see the first fruits of the Copto-Arabic literature by the well-known Sawīrus ibn al-Muqaffa', bishop of al-Ashmūnīn in Upper Egypt in the tenth century. The transitional period from Coptic to Arabic is marked by three features:

1 The retreat of literature written in Coptic in the eighth and ninth centuries. In each century only one famous writer is known, Bishop Zakariyyā of Sakhā (d. 725) in the eighth and Pope Mark II (799–819) in the ninth.

2 The copying of older Coptic manuscripts. It is well known that in periods of literary deterioration one considers older literary works ideal and exemplary literary accomplishments that were achieved in the golden age. Two of the richest collections of Coptic manuscripts were copied in the period from the ninth to the eleventh century in the libraries of two famous Coptic monasteries: the so called White Monastery in Sohag (Sūhāj) and the Monastery of the Archangel Michael in al-Ḥāmūlī in Fayyūm. Both collections are copies of older Coptic writings offering monks spiritual literature in a period where very little contemporary literature in Coptic language was produced.
3 Writing Arabic with Coptic letters. Arabic is a Semitic language that differs entirely from Coptic. As a temporary compromise, the Copts transliterated Arabic texts with Coptic letters to make them readable. Some manuscript fragments remain as witness to this phenomenon. It is interesting that the present-day Copts, who for the most part cannot understand or read Coptic any more, transliterate Coptic texts with Arabic letters, their mother tongue. Most of the Coptic liturgical books that are regularly used in the Coptic Church have three columns: Coptic, Arabic translation, and Coptic written with Arabic letters.

With the passage of time and some delay, in comparison to Syria and Palestine, Arabic replaced or displaced Coptic in daily life as well as in literature. In the Kitāb al-īḍāḥ by pseudo-Sawīrus ibn al-Muqaffa‘ there are some passages in which the author complains about the retreat of Coptic in favour of Arabic. He complains that not one Copt remains who knows what is read to him in church in the Coptic language. The Copts have become those who hear but do not understand (Davis 2008b: 201–2). This fact led Coptic intellectuals in the thirteenth and fourteenth centuries to write books explaining Coptic grammar known as *muqaddimāt* (introductions) and Coptic-Arabic lexica known as *salālim* (ladders). These philological works helped in the translation movement from Coptic into Arabic, which began in the tenth century but flourished from the eleventh to the thirteenth centuries (Rubenson 1996). We have a chain of authors who produced great achievements in this field, like al-Wajīh al-Qalyūbī, Yūḥannā al-Samannūdī, al-As‘ad ibn al-‘Assāl, Abū Shākir ibn al-Rāhib, Ibn al-Duhayrī, Abū al-Barakāt ibn Kabar, and Athanasius al-Qūṣī (Graf 1944–53: Vol. II, 371–80, 404–5, 407–9, 432, 443–44; Atiya 1991: Vol. VIII, 166–69, 204–7; Sidarus 1997, 2001; Gabra 2008: 17–18, 25–26, 42, 152–54, 269–70, 279–80, 286–87, 293–94; al-Maqārī 2011: 45–51, 422–40, 537–40, 634–35, 750–61).

Over time knowledge of Coptic by patriarchs and clerics became a special quality proudly emphasized by Coptic historians. On the other hand, non-literary sources from the tenth and eleventh centuries prove that Egypt at that time was still bilingual. From this period we have letters written in good Sahidic Coptic as well as Arabic. Some of these Coptic documents were even written by Muslims (MacCoull 1989: 37–39; Zaborowski 2008: 33–34). In the twelfth century it became clear that Coptic could no longer be the only liturgical language because the faithful in church could not understand it. This fact motivated Pope Gabriel II ibn Turayk (1131–45), who was fluent in Arabic and a good copyist of Coptic and Arabic manuscripts, to encourage his priests to teach their children the Arabic language and to instruct the Christian people in the language which they knew (Gabra 2008: 111, 284–85; Swanson 2010: 71–74).

Coptic Theology in Arabic

It is well known that Bishop Sawīrus ibn al-Muqaffaʿ (tenth century) is the first Coptic theologian who wrote his works in Arabic, which he mastered as a professional scribe before becoming a monk (Gabra 2008: 233–34, 292; Thomas 2009–12: Vol. II, 491–509). It seems he was convinced that a clever writer should write in a language the reader understood, which was by that time the Arabic language. By analysing the preserved works of Sawīrus, it becomes clear that he had another reason to write in Arabic. Most of the works of Sawīrus have an apologetic tendency. His main purpose was to explain the Christian faith to the Copts, but also to defend it against Melkites, Muslims, and Jews (Davis 2008b: 217–20). The theological literary production of the Copts under Islamic rule focuses on three main topics: refutation of the distortion of the Bible, explaining the Trinity as consistent with the oneness of God, and the incarnation of the Son of God. In this field, Sawīrus was a pioneer. He had to translate the patristic sources written in Coptic and Greek into Arabic and coined new terms (ibid. 205–36).

Within a few centuries after the Arab conquest in 641 the Copts had been heavily influenced by Islam and were ignorant of their own faith: "It has come to be the case that they do not hear any mention of 'the Trinity' among themselves except rarely; nor do they hear any mention of 'the Son of God' except in a metaphorical sense. Instead, most of what they hear is that God is 'unique' (fard), 'everlasting' (ṣamad) and the rest of the language that the ḥunafāʾ use. The believers have become accustomed to this, and have been brought up with it, so that the mention of 'the Son of God' has come to be difficult for them; they do not know any interpretation or meaning for it" (quoted in Swanson 2010: 73). In his book Miṣbāḥ al-ʿAql (The Lamp of the Intellect) Sawīrus presents the Christian faith in detail, from the Trinity and the Incarnation to prayer, fasting, and marriage. This work, as was usual in that time, responds to the request of a friend who had asked Sawīrus to define the Christian dogmas for "the opponents" of the Christian religion. This friend had not found any book by previous authors containing a description of the doctrines of the Christians in the form of an expository summary that was able to remove their doubts and explain the things that were difficult for them. These "opponents," to whom this treatise is addressed, are the Muslims. But it was without doubt very useful for those Coptic Christians who were ignorant of their own faith.

Although no works of Sawīrus have come down to us that are explicitly against the Islamic faith, he occasionally refutes Islamic allegations against Christianity. After Sawīrus explains the circumstances of the Council of Nicaea

(325) and its creed in his work *Tafsīr al-amāna* (*The Explanation of the Creed*), he begins to refute what the opponents have said against it. He does not mention them by name, but his arguments do not let us hesitate to believe that he means the Muslims. In the same work he refers to his previous (now lost) work *al-Majālis* (*Sittings* or *Conferences*) in which he mentions his discussions with Muslims. In another book, *al-Majāmi'* (*The Councils*), Sawīrus requests that his addressee not show this work to the opponents of the [Christian] religion but to use it only to prepare for questions they pose.

In the above mentioned works and others, Sawīrus refutes the dogmas of Melkites and Nestorians, discuses the history of the most famous heresies, and rebuts their allegations. It is also interesting to observe how the Coptic bishop Sawīrus was influenced by the Islamic culture and literature of his time. He uses Islamic diction and Koranic expressions (Farag 1979; Davis 2008b: 211–13).

In the thirteenth century, known as "the Coptic renaissance," we meet another great theologian, al-Mu'taman ibn al-'Assāl. He belonged to a wealthy and influential family. Two of his brothers, al-As'ad and al-Ṣafī, were also famous Coptic scholars (Graf 1944–53: Vol. II, 387–88; Wadi 1985; Gabra 2008: 44–45, 280). In addition to his philological and biblical competence, al-Mu'taman wrote a theological encyclopedia called *Majmū' uṣūl al-dīn* (*The Compilation of the Fundamentals of Religion*) (Graf 1944–53: Vol. II, 407–14; Gabra 2008: 23, 291; Thomas 2009–12: Vol. IV, 530–37). The reason he wrote this encyclopedia, as he states elsewhere, was that people who did not belong to the Christian religion posed questions to befuddle Christians who were ignorant of the principles of Christianity. Al-Mu'taman decided to offer a brief explanation of the Christian fundamentals and principles to help his co-religionists refute their opponents. He promised to deal with this theme in detail in another work, his encyclopedia. When we peruse his theological encyclopedia, we realize how rich, intercultural, and interconfessional al-Mu'taman's knowledge was. He quotes not only Coptic authors, but also Church Fathers as well as Syrian, Melkite, Nestorian, and even Muslim authors. Al-Mu'taman divides his work into five parts. Every part consists of an introduction and several chapters with subtitles. In the first part he mentions his literary sources (bibliography) and gives a philosophical introduction. In the same part he asserts the correctness of Christianity and the Bible and lists the various Christian confessions. The second part focuses on the oneness of God and the Trinity. The third part discusses Christological topics, in particular the union of the two natures in Christ according to Coptic Orthodox theology (*miaphysis*). The fourth part deals with various themes, such as the veneration of the Holy Virgin, prophets, angels, repentance, and death. The last part is dedicated to eschatological subjects according to the Bible, the Church Fathers, and even apocryphal writings.

Biblical Translations and Commentaries

The Bible as a text and the revelation of God has its place in Copto-Arabic literature. The translation of some parts of the Bible from Coptic into Arabic belongs to the earliest attempts at translating Coptic literature in the tenth century. Liturgical needs, to help the congregation follow the liturgy, had priority in this translation process. The Copts benefited from earlier Arabic translations of the Bible made by Melkites (from Greek), Syrians (from Syriac), and Egyptian Jews (from Hebrew) (Graf 1944–53: Vol. I, 103–4, 155–63; Rubenson 1996: 6–7; Kashouh 2012).

The most important work in this field is the Arabic translation of the four gospels by al-As'ad ibn al-'Assāl. This unpublished critical translation was made from Bohairic Coptic in 1253. For this task he used, in addition to the Coptic text, older Arabic translations from Greek and Syriac. From all these versions he created a critical apparatus and marginal notes. In an appendix he mentions all of the abbreviations he uses and their meaning (*sigla*). Moreover, he added to his translation a general introduction as well as an introduction to every gospel. It is in every respect a masterful work, even according to our modern scientific measures. However, it seems that the work of al-As'ad was too complicated to spread among the Copts. Most of the transmitted manuscripts of this translation are without the critical apparatus and contain only the translation or even just the introductions. Moreover, the translation of al-As'ad has never been adopted by the Coptic Church in its lectionaries or other liturgical books (Graf 1944–53: Vol. I, 162–63; Wadi 1991, 2006; Samir 1994; Kashouh 2012: 258–74).

From old sources we know of lost biblical commentaries written by Copts in Arabic, like the commentary of Sawīrus ibn al-Muqaffa' on the gospels and the commentary of Būlus al-Būshī (d. 1250) on the Epistle to the Hebrews. Other biblical commentaries are available but still unpublished, like the introduction of Sim'ān ibn Kalil (d. 1206) to the Psalms and the Gospel of Matthew, and the commentary of Yūḥannā al-Qalyūbī (thirteenth century) on the Epistle of Paul to the Romans. Among the well-known biblical commentaries, two are on the Apocalypse of John, by Būlus al-Būshī and Ibn Kātib Qayṣar (d. after 1260), who also wrote commentaries on the Acts of the Apostles, and the Pauline and the Catholic Epistles. The commentary of al-Būshī, Bishop of Miṣr (Old Cairo) from 1240, was the first commentary on this biblical book written in Arabic. It is concise and uses typology. Al-Būshī interprets the visions and symbols as the church and the angels as its bishops. In some cases, he offers various possible interpretations (Gabra 2008: 51, 280; Davis 2008b: 238–39; Thomas 2009–12: Vol. IV, 453–56; al-Maqārī 2011: 377–80).

In contrast to al-Būshī's commentary, Ibn Kātib Qayṣar's commentary on the Apocalypse, written in 1266/67, is extensive, detailed, and systematic. He arranged and systematized his large work in such a way that the reader can follow his point of view easily and without any confusion. Ibn Kātib Qayṣar draws great attention to the philology of the text since he was also a Coptic grammarian and, as is clear from his commentary, he understood some Greek, Syriac, and Hebrew. In his commentary he takes the historical context into consideration. Moreover, he quotes older and contemporary authors, not only Coptic, but also Melkites, Nestorians, and Jews. He discusses their interpretations and in some cases criticizes and rejects them (Graf 1944–53: Vol. II, 379–84; Davis 2008a: 77–84; Gabra 2008: 154, 287; al-Maqārī 2011: 456–71).

Before I move to the next topic I would like to refer to a commentary by Marqus ibn Qunbur (d. 1208) on Genesis, Exodus, and Leviticus, erroneously attributed to Ephrem the Syrian in its published form, and an introduction to the Pauline Epistles by al-Mu'taman ibn al-'Assāl called *Ablagh al-wasā'il fi 'ilm al-rasā'il*. This introduction gives a brief account of the life of Paul up to his death, then comments on important verses in every chapter in the Pauline Epistles, including the one to the Hebrews. He offers an index of Paul's quotations from the Old Testament and studies twelve topics based on the Pauline Epistles, e.g., the Christian faith according to the Nicene Creed, encouragement for believers to do good deeds, and what sins they should avoid. The work ends with an index of the obscure words in the epistles and their meaning (Graf 1944–53: Vol. II, 327–32, 412–13; al-Maqārī 2011: 248–64, 573–75).

Historical Works

From Late Antiquity we have few Christian historical writings in the narrow sense. Copts wrote history using various frameworks, such as martyrdoms, hagiographies, encomiums, and even miracle narratives. Some Coptic historians compiled secular histories in Arabic with minimal interest in ecclesiastical matters. However, due to the religious environment that dominated Egyptian society, Copts were more interested in church history.

The only historical work in the Coptic language from Byzantine Egypt (324–641) is a fragmentary church history with the title "The Histories of the Holy Church" by an anonymous author. The first chapters of this church history are lost, but it probably began with the first-century evangelization of Mark the Apostle in Alexandria. The work concludes with the return of Pope Timothy II from exile in AD 475. The whole work can be divided into two parts. The first part consists of seven books and is dependent on the well-known church history of Eusebius of Caesarea. The second part consists of the remaining five books and reports on the Coptic Orthodox Church from Pope Peter I (300–311) to Timothy II (457–77) and is independent from Eusebius' church history (Orlandi 2007; Moawad 2010: 242–49).

Although the rest of the Sahidic text is not extant, it is evident that other Coptic authors continued this work in the Coptic language until the patriarchate of Shenoute II (1032–46). In 1088 the Alexandrian deacon Mawhūb ibn Manṣūr ibn Mufarrij gathered the Coptic texts related to the "Histories of the Church" and translated them into Arabic. Mawhūb himself continued this history and included the biographies of Popes Christodolus (1047–77) and Cyril II (1078–92) in Arabic, which became the original language of this historical encyclopaedia known as The History of the Patriarchs. After Mawhūb, other authors, some known and some anonymous, continued the biographies of the successive Coptic patriarchs up to the patriarchate of Cyril V (1874–1927).

From the editorial remarks in the Arabic *History of the Patriarchs*, we can follow the progression of the composition of this work in its Coptic as well as in its Arabic phases and gather the names of some of its authors. As we mentioned above, the part from Apostle Mark to Pope Timothy II (d. 477) was written in Coptic by one or more historians including a monk named George (Jurja or Mirka) from the Monastery of St. Macarius (in 715) and possibly another person named Mina. The Coptic Sahidic text was continued by John the Deacon (after 767), John the Writer (after 866), and Bishop Michael of Tanis (in 1051). After Mawhūb had translated the earlier biographies from Coptic into Arabic, he composed the biographies of his contemporary patriarchs in 1088 as mentioned above. The biographies of Pope Michael IV (1092–1102) and his successor Macarius II (1102–28) were written in Arabic by Yūḥannā (John) ibn Ṣā'id al-Qulzumī. Pope Mark III (Marqus) ibn Zur'a is the author of the biographies of his predecessors Gabriel II ibn Turaik (1131–45), Michael V (1145–46), and John V (1147–67). Unfortunately, the author of the biographies of Marqus ibn Zur'a (1167–89) and John VI (1189–1216) is anonymous. The biography of the controversial Pope Cyril III ibn Laqlaq (1235–43) is by far the longest biography of a Coptic patriarch. Its author is Yūḥannā (John) ibn Wahb who had personal contact with the patriarch. The biographies of the following popes are very brief and mostly mention only the name of the pope, the monastery in which he became a monk, the dates of his consecration, election to the papacy, and death, as well as the length of his papacy. However, the biography of Pope Mattā al-Miskīn or Matthew the Poor (1378–1409), which was written by his contemporary bishop of al-Khandaq, is an exception in its length. The biographies of Popes Buṭrus (Peter) VII (1809–52), Kirillus (Cyril) IV (1854–61), and Demetrius II (1862–70) were written down by Tadrus al-Mishriqī in the year 1868 (Den Heijer 1989, 1996: 69–77; Gabra 2008: 139, 286; Moawad 2010: 251–57).

History of the Patriarchs is the most important source for our information about the Coptic Orthodox Church, in particular under Islamic rule. Moreover, some biographies, such as those of John V and Cyril III, are sources for the social and political life in Egypt. Most of the authors of this work were contemporary to the events or even eyewitnesses.

Sometime between 1676 and 1718 an anonymous author composed a historical work with the title "The History of the Fathers, the Patriarchs" attributed by modern scholars to Yūsāb, bishop of Fuwwa in the thirteenth century (Den Heijer 1996: 81–83). However, actual studies demonstrate that this work is in fact a compilation by an anonymous author contemporary to Pope John XVI (1676–1718), the last patriarch mentioned in this work (Moawad 2006; Thomas 2009–12: Vol. IV, 486–90). This work reports on the Coptic popes of Alexandria from the Apostle Mark to John XVI. It offers information that we also find in the Arabic *History of the Patriarchs*, sometimes even word for word. On the other hand, however, it offers additional information from older and partly unknown or lost sources, which makes this history valuable. Although it is published, it still needs a study of its sources and, first of all, a new critical edition.

In addition to these two historical sources it is worth mentioning another work that is unique in its genre in the Copto-Arabic literature and therefore became an important historical work, even if its authors did not intend to make it so. It is the *History of the Churches and Monasteries of Egypt* (*Tārīkh al-kanā'is wa-l-adyura*) preserved in only one incomplete manuscript divided between Paris and Munich. It describes the churches and monasteries of Upper and Lower Egypt, in addition to some places in Abyssinia, Palestine, and Rome. At the same time it gives valuable information about their history and the historical events and persons connected with them. Although this work aimed to give topographical accounts of the Christian holy places in Egypt, it went beyond this aim and became an important historical source as well. For the compilation of this work many Coptic, Melkite, and Islamic sources have been used. Like *History of the Patriarchs*, the *History of the Churches and Monasteries* cannot be attributed to only one author, as was once suggested. In fact, its composition was carried out in four stages between 1160 and 1349 by more than one author, including Abū al-Makārim and Abū Ṣāliḥ the Armenian, whose contributions are hard to identify (Den Heijer 1996: 77–81; Gabra 2008: 138–39, 285–86; Moawad 2010: 261–62; Thomas 2009–12: Vol. IV, 983–88).

Other Coptic historians were more interested in secular and political history than ecclesiastical. Two works of this type are preserved. The first one is known by the title *al-Majmū' al-mubārak* (*The Blessed Collection*). This work was compiled by al-Makīn Jirjis ibn al-'Amīd (the elder) sometime after 1277 and covers, in two parts, the period from Creation to the beginning of the reign of al-Ẓāhir Baybars in 1260. It is, for the most part, a compilation and abridgement of older sources and lacks a certain degree of originality (Thomas 2009–12: Vol. IV, 566–71). In his work, Ibn al-'Amīd tends to mention historical events briefly and without any of his own comment or analysis. He wrote his historical work neither as a Christian nor as an Egyptian, but merely as a historian within the Islamic state. His work is not a history of Egypt but of the Islamic caliphate in general. This work enjoyed popularity among Muslim historians who quoted and used it as a source, predominantly in matters concerning the pre-Islamic period or specifically Christian events.

The second work is nothing but a continuation of al-Majmū' al-Mubārak by the Coptic historian al-Mufaḍḍal ibn Abī al-Faḍā'il who might have been the nephew of Ibn al-'Amīd. He compiled his work sometime after 1358 and called it *al-Nahj al-sadīd*. This historical work deals with the history of Egypt and Syria in the period from the sultanate of al-Ẓāhir Baybars beginning in 1260 to the death of al-Malik al-Nāṣir in 1341, with some additional events up to 1348. In contrast to al-Majmū' al-Mubārak, although al-Mufaḍḍal's work is more informative and detailed than Ibn al-'Amīd's work, it did not find any consideration by later historians and is preserved in a unique manuscript. The Copt al-Mufaḍḍal followed Ibn al-'Amīd in the way in which he reported historical events. Both of them wrote works of secular history with minimal interest in Christian matters, despite their Coptic confession. Both of them depended mainly on Muslim historians and shared an interest in wonders and supernatural events (Den Heijer 1996: 88–95; Gabra 2008: 23–24, 291).

Liturgical Encyclopedias

Liturgical manuscripts from Egypt before the seventh century are scarce. This fact makes the documentation of the history of Coptic liturgy a hard task. However, this is not the case in the medieval period thanks to two Coptic scholars, Ibn Kabar and Ibn Sabbāʿ, who compiled two major works describing the Coptic liturgy and rites in their time. Both encyclopedic works are, therefore, invaluable sources for the shape of the Coptic Orthodox liturgy in the thirteenth and fourteenth centuries and above all for studying the development of the Coptic liturgy in general.

Shams al-Riyāsa Abū al-Barakāt ibn Kabar served as scribe to the Mamluk Amīr Baybars al-Manṣūrī. In 1300 Ibn Kabar was ordained priest with the name of Barsūm or Barṣūmā and served at the famous al-Muʿallaqa church in Old Cairo until his death in 1324. He compiled his liturgical encyclopedia *Miṣbāḥ al-ẓulma wa-iḍāḥ al-khidma* (*The Lamp of the Darkness and the Illumination of Service*) when he noticed that some Coptic priests and particularly many deacons were ignorant of the liturgical rites and lacked the necessary theological knowledge to understand and practice the ecclesiastical rituals. The first seven chapters of his work, however, have nothing to do with liturgy but focus on dogmatic as well as canonical matters and include a list of many famous Christian writers and some of their works. This puzzle can be clarified if we read the words of Ibn Kabar himself in his preface, where he says that a deacon should have insight into his tasks in the church and the purposes of divine laws, and be familiar with ecclesiastical customs and rules. This cannot be achieved without a theological education and knowing the patristic sources upon which the liturgical rituals are based. The remaining seventeen chapters deal with the building of a church and its consecration, the ceremony of ordination of the various ranks of clergy, from patriarch to deacons and monks, the celebration of the sacraments like Eucharist, baptism, and marriage, and other matters like fasting, Holy Week, and lectionaries (Graf 1944–53: Vol. II, 438–42; Atiya 1991: Vol. IV, 1267–68; Gabra 2008: 153–54, 286–87; al-Maqārī 2011: 730–47).

The other liturgical encyclopedia is *al-Jawhara al-nafīsa fī ʿulūm al-kanīsa* (*The Precious Jewel in the Ecclesiastical Sciences*) by Yūḥannā ibn Abī Zakariyya ibn Sabbāʿ (thirteenth–fourteenth century) about whom we do not know anything and of whom we do not possess any other writings. Ibn Sabbāʿ dedicates the first twenty-six chapters of his work to theological, biblical, and apologetic matters that help to follow the principles of offering, oblation, church, and salvation in the Old Testament. The other eighty-seven chapters are dedicated to the liturgy, ordinations, sacraments (baptism, Eucharist, marriage, priesthood), and liturgical ceremonies throughout the Coptic year. Ibn Sabbāʿ tends toward the spiritual interpretation of liturgical instruments and gestures. The whole work is a compilation based on older sources that Ibn Sabbāʿ unfortunately does not mention. However, al-Jawhara al-nafīsa remains an important source for our knowledge concerning the Coptic ecclesiastical life in the fourteenth century (Graf 1944–53: II, 448–49; Atiya 1991: IV, 1272; Gabra 2008: 270, 295; al-Maqārī 2011: 769–74).

Church Laws (Nomocanon)

After the Arab conquest of Egypt and the retreat of Coptic there was a need to translate old canons into Arabic and enact new ecclesiastical laws to arrange the affairs of the Church and dissuade the clergy and believers from bad habits that resulted from ignorance of Christian principles and association with non-Christians.

There is evidence that Copts began to translate ecclesiastical canons from Coptic into Arabic at least from the early eleventh century (Graf 1944–53: Vol. I, 556–621). In the same period they began to compile such canons in Arabic. Before the end of the fourteenth century there were more than ten collections of canons, which were gathered in fifty-four books (chapters) by a monk named Maqāra (Macarius) from the Monastery of St. John the Little (Yiḥnis al-Qaṣīr) in the same century (Graf 1944–53: Vol. II, 437; Atiya 1991: Vol. V, 1490–91; Gabra 2008: 172–73, 288–89: al-Maqārī 2011: 728–30). The first known Coptic author of Church laws in Arabic is a certain Abū Ṣāliḥ (Ṣulḥ) Yū'annis ibn 'Abd Allah, known as Sadīd ibn Yānā, sometime before 1028. He summarized some Church laws from the Coptic original in forty-eight paragraphs (Graf 1944–53: Vol. II, 320–21; al-Maqārī 2011: 202–4). The most important Church laws in Arabic, however, were compiled by Coptic patriarchs: Christodoulus (1047–77), Cyril II (1078–92), Gabriel ibn Turayk (1131–45), and Cyril III (1235–43). Additional canons were written or compiled by bishops, like Michael of Damietta in 1188 and Michael of Atrīb and Malīj (al-Ṭibb al-ruḥānī) in the thirteenth century, or by notable Copts, like al-Ṣafī ibn al-'Assāl (al-Majmū' al-ṣafawī) in 1236–38, Ibn al-Rāhib (Kitāb al-burhān) in 1270/1 and Farag Allah al-Akhmīmī in the fourteenth century. Only three of these collections of laws can be called nomocanons, however, those of Pope Gabriel, Bishop Michael of Damietta, and al-Ṣafī ibn al-'Assāl (Graf 1944–53: Vol. II, 321, 323–28, 360–65, 389–403; al-Maqārī 2009, 2011: 205–8, 218–21, 228–34, 265–68, 386–91, 511–31, 604–18; Thomas 2009–12: Vol. IV, 109–14).

Apocalypses

It took the Copts a long time to realize the consequences of the Arab conquest and to perceive the difference between it and any other occupations they had experienced; most recently, the Persian occupation (619–29). With the passage of time the desire for freedom and the yearning for the past and their own identity developed and expressed itself in literary writings, the so-called apocalypses, in Coptic, but more frequently in Arabic (Lent 1998; Suermann 2004). The Copto-Arabic literature preserves some interesting examples of such apocalypses by anonymous authors who preferred to attribute their writings to

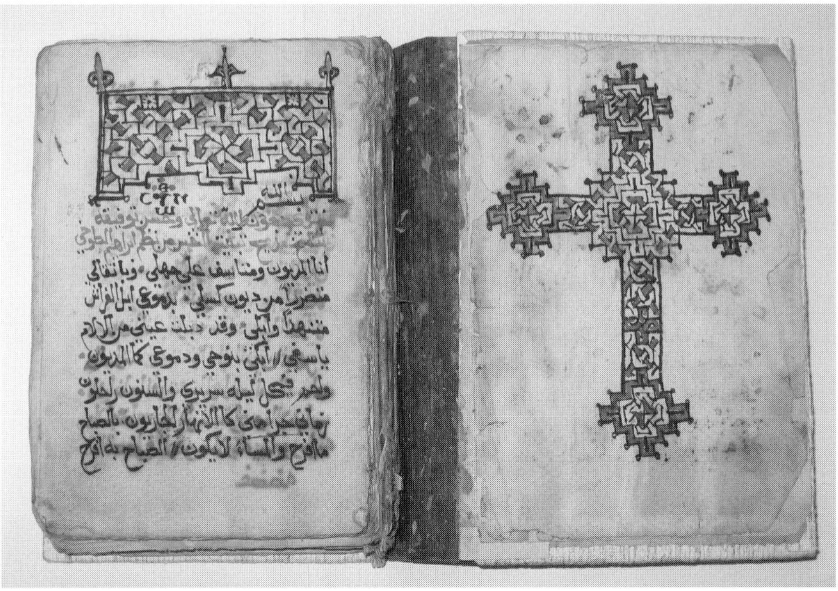

Figure 15.1 A Cross miniature from an Arabic Manuscript of Hymns, paper, undated. Collection of the St. Shenouda the Archimandrite Coptic Society in Los Angeles, Ms. No. 78. Courtesy of Hany N. Takla

famous Coptic saints, such as Athanasius (328–73), Shenoute of Atripe (d. 465), Pisentius of Coptos or Qifṭ (d. 632), and Samuel of Qalamūn (d. 695), to let their writings win credibility among the Coptic readers and to protect themselves from any punishment by the rulers. These apocalypses were a Coptic attempt to evaluate Islamic rule in Egypt and to rewrite their own history (the past), describe the present time, and express their wishes for the future.

The main topic in the Apocalypse ascribed to Samuel of Qalamūn is the retreat of the Coptic language and the sorrow for not using it even in the liturgy within the sanctuary. This apocalypse, which claims to be a prophecy of what will happen in the future, is nothing but a description of the actual circumstances of the time in which it was written. Also interesting is a passage in a letter attributed to Bishop Pisentius in which the anonymous author prophesies or rather wishes the return of Byzantine rule to Egypt and the union between the two Christian kings, the Byzantine and the Ethiopian.

Selected Bibliography

al-Maqārī, Athanasius (2009) *Qawānīn baṭārikat al-kanīsa al-qibṭiyya fī al-'uṣūr al-wusṭā*, Cairo.

——(2011) *Fihris kitābāt ābā' kanīsat al-iskandariyya: al-kitābāt al-'arabiyya*, 2 vols, Cairo.

Atiya, A. S. (ed.) (1991) *The Coptic Encyclopedia*, 8 vols, New York and Toronto: Macmillan.

Coquin, R.-G. (1993) "Langue et littérature arabes chrétiennes," in M. Albert (ed.) *Christianismes orientaux. Introduction à l'étude des langues et des littératures*, Paris: Éditions du Cerf, 35–106.

Davis, S. J. (2008a) "Introducing an Arabic Commentary on the Apocalypse: Ibn Kātib Qayṣar on Revelation," *Harvard Theological Review*, 101(1): 77–96.

——(2008b) *Coptic Christology in Practice. Incarnation and Divine Participation in Late Antique and Medieval Egypt*, Oxford: Oxford University Press.

Den Heijer, J. (1989) *Mawhub ibn Mansur ibn Mufarrig et l'historiographie copto-arabe. Etude sur la composition de l'Histoire des Patriarches d'Alexandrie* (Corpus Scriptorum Christianorum Orientalium 513, subsidia 83), Leuven: Peeters.

——(1996) "Coptic Historiography in the Fatimid, Ayyubid and Early Mamluk Periods," *Medieval Encounters*, 2(1): 67–98.

Farag, F. R. (1979) "The Usage of the Early Islamic Terminology as a Constituent of the Literary Form of a Tenth-Century Christian Arab Writer: Severus ibn Al-Muqaff," *Journal of the American Oriental Society*, 99(1): 49–57.

Gabra, G. (ed.) (2008) *Historical Dictionary of the Coptic Church*, Cairo: The American University in Cairo Press.

Graf, G. (1944–53) *Geschichte der christlichen arabischen Literatur*, 5 vols (Studi e testi, 118, 133, 146, 147, 172), Vatican City: Biblioteca Apostolica Vaticana.

Kashouh, H. (2012) *The Arabic Versions of the Gospels* (Arbeiten zur Neutestamentlichen Textforschung 42), Berlin and Boston: De Gruyter.

Lent, J. van (1998) "Les Apocalypses Coptes de l'époque Arabe: Quelques réflexions," in M. Rassart-Debergh (ed.) *Sixième journées d'études*, Limoges 18–20 juin 1993 et septième journée d'études. Neuchâtel 18–20 mai 1995 (Études coptes, 5; Cahiers de la Bibliothèque Copte, 10), Paris and Leuven: Peeters.

MacCoull, L. S. B. (1989) "The Strange Death of Coptic Culture," *Coptic Church Review*, 10 (2): 35–43.

Mikhail, M. (2004) "An Historical Definition for the 'Coptic Period,'" in M. Immerzeel and J. van der Vliet (eds) *Coptic Studies on the Threshold of a New Millennium. Proceedings of the Seventh International Congress of Coptic Studies, Leiden, 27 August–2 September 2000*, 2 vols (Orientalia Lovaniensia Analecta 132–33), Leuven and Paris: Peeters.

Moawad, S. (2006) "Zur Originalität der Yūsāb von Fuwah zugeschriebenen Patriarchengeschichte," *Le Muséon*, 119(3–4): 255–70.

——(2010) *Untersuchungen zum Panegyrikos auf Makarios von Tkōou und zu seiner Überlieferung* (Sprachen und Kulturen des christlichen Orients 18), Wiesbaden: L. Reichert.

Orlandi, T. (2007) "The Coptic Ecclesiastical History: A Survey," in J. E. Goehring and J. A. Timbie (eds) *The World of Early Egyptian Christianity: Language, Literature, and Social Context. Essays in Honor of David W. Johnson*, Washington DC: The Catholic University of America Press, 2007.

Rubenson, S. (1996) "Translating the Tradition. Some Remarks on the Arabization of the Patristic Heritage in Egypt," *Medieval Encounters*, 2(1): 4–14.

Samir, S. Kh. (1994) "La Version arabe des Évangiles d'al-As'ad Ibn al-'Assāl," *Parole de l'Orient*, 19: 441–551.

Sidarus, A. Y. (1997) "Sullam," in *Encyclopedia of Islam*, vol. 9, Leiden: Brill.

——(2001) "Medieval Coptic Grammars in Arabic. The Coptic Muqaddimāt," *Journal of Coptic Studies*, 3: 63–79.

Suermann, H. (2004) "Koptische Arabische Apokalypsen," in R. Ebied and H. Teule (eds) *Studies on the Christian Arabic Heritage in Honour of Father Prof. Dr. Samir Khalil Samir S.I. at the Occasion of his Sixty-Fifth Birthday* (Eastern Christian Studies, 5). Louvain: Peeters.

Swanson, M. N. (2010) *The Coptic Papacy in Islamic Egypt (641–1517)*, Cairo and New York: The American University in Cairo Press.
Thomas, D. (ed.) (2009–12) *Christian–Muslim Relations. A Bibliographical History*, 4 vols. (History of Christian–Muslim Relations, 11, 14, 15, 17). Leiden and Boston: Brill.
Wadi, A. (1985) "Bibliografia sugli Aulād al-'Assāl, tre fratelli scrittori copti del sec. XIII," *Studia Orientalia Christiana Collectanea*, 18: 31–79.
——(1991) "La traduction des Quatre Evangiles de al-As'ad Ibn al-'Assāl (XIIIe s.)," *Studia Orientalia Christiana Collectanea*, 24: 217–24.
——(1996–97) "Introduzione alla letteratura arabo-cristiana dei Copti," *Studia Orientalia Christiana Collectanea*, 29–30: 441–92.
——(2006) "Al-As'ad Ibn al-'Assāl: Introduzioni alla traduzione dei quattro Vangeli," *Studia Orientalia Christiana Collectanea*, 39: 47–120.
Zaborowski, J. R. (2008) "From Coptic to Arabic in Medieval Egypt," *Medieval Encounters*, 14 (1): 15–40.

Part IV

Coptic Material Culture

16 Coptic Art

A Multifaceted Artistic Heritage

Gawdat Gabra[1]

As space does not permit a detailed presentation of Coptic art, this chapter aims to introduce briefly the main sources, iconography, techniques and characteristics of Coptic art along with the necessary references in English for a bibliography for further study.

Introduction

Coptic art is the richest among the arts of the Christian communities of the Middle East. Coptic churches—ancient, medieval, and modern, built within monasteries, villages or towns—are remarkably decorated. In the late nineteenth century and the first decades of the last century beautiful wall paintings, stone architectural sculptures, and carved wood were discovered through archaeological excavations, and illegal diggings as well, in a number of ancient monastic churches. A considerable portion of these monuments, which restorers could preserve, are exhibited in the Coptic Museum in Cairo and other museums all over the world. In the past two decades many mural paintings from different periods layered on top of each other were uncovered in a few existing churches, and more wall paintings are expected to be found in the years to come. The majority of the scenes are from the Old and New Testaments. Representations of saints are also very popular. Coptic churches are richly decorated with icons that are highly venerated. These churches preserve magnificent wooden doors, altars, ciboria, and screens. Many elaborate metal objects, such as censers, lamps, chandeliers, and Bible caskets, as well as illuminated manuscripts, which have found their way to museums, libraries, and other collections, also originated from monasteries and churches. Moreover, Egypt yielded a huge quantity of objects from daily life manufactured from metal, wood, leather, ivory, bone, terracotta, and glass. Many of them are beautiful artifacts that belong to late-antique and medieval times. (For a general survey of Coptic art see Badawy 1978; Bourguet 1991a; Immerzeel 1997; Török 2005.)

Although Coptic art began to appear in the fourth century, some of its symbols, such as the looped cross (Figure 16.1), betray their pharaonic origins (Bourguet 1991b; Török 2005: 17–19; Gabra and Eaton-Krauss 2007: 41–51). The scene of "Maria lactans," in which the Virgin Mary is depicted nursing the

Figure 16.1 Tombstone with the looped cross, limestone, H: 43 cm, W: 88 cm, sixth/seventh century, Coptic Museum, Inv. No. 4302

Christ child, tempts scholars to search for an ancient Egyptian connection. It is generally accepted that the prototype of such a scene could well be the image of the goddess Isis nursing her son Horus. A number of beautiful paintings rendering this scene have been discovered in the Monastery of the Syrians in Wādī al-Naṭrūn (Scetes) and the Monastery of St. Pshai (known as the Red Monastery) as well as in the two abandoned monasteries of St. Jeremiah at Saqqara and St. Apollo at Bāwīṭ. They date from the seventh or eighth century. On the other hand their style betrays Byzantine influences (Figure 16.2) (see also Gabra and Loon 2007: 282–83). The exterior architecture of the Monastery of St. Shenoute at Sohag (known as the White Monastery) that was built in the fifth century shows the unmistakable influence of ancient Egyptian temple architecture. But its interior architectural sculptures derive from Hellenistic and Roman sources (Török 2005: 153–64).

The main difficulty in the study of Coptic art is the lack of precise dating of significant wall paintings and artifacts. As a matter of fact, most of the "excavations" in important sites like Antinoë and Akhmim were carried out in the nineteenth and early twentieth centuries as treasure hunts rather than scientific undertakings. Two of the largest Coptic monastic complexes, the Monastery of St. Jeremiah at Saqqara and the Monastery of St. Apollo at Bāwīṭ, were excavated at the beginning of the twentieth century when excavation techniques were very limited. Moreover, the Copts have reused many architectural elements of older buildings in their monasteries and churches, which makes any exact dating of a considerable part of Coptic monuments difficult.

Coptic monuments have begun to enjoy serious attention and care as well as modern methods of documentation only in the last few decades. At the same time, the general public began to be aware of Coptic art when several magnificent exhibitions took place in major European cities, such as Vienna (March

Figure 16.2 The Virgin nursing the Christ child, eighth century, Monastery of the Syrians, Wādī al-Naṭrūn. Courtesy of Karel Innemée

11–May 3, 1964), Zurich (mid-November 1963–mid-January, 1964), Geneva (October 12, 1989–January 7, 1990), Paris (May 15–September 3, 2000), and Budapest (March 18–May 18, 2005). To enhance the benefits of those magnificent exhibitions, catalogs were provided that included attractive color illustrations and detailed catalog entries, as well as accounts of Coptic history and culture. The last forty years also witnessed carefully recorded excavations in many Coptic sites, especially at Abu Mina, Kellia, Wādī al-Naṭrūn, Naqlūn, Antinoë, Bāwīṭ, the Monastery of St. Shenoute near Sohag, and Esna. Further remarkable progress is represented by many new discoveries of Coptic wall paintings in the Monastery of the Syrians and the Monastery of al-Baramus at Wādī al-Naṭrūn (Scetis), the Monastery of the Archangel Gabriel at Naqlūn near al-Fayyūm, the Monastery of St Pshai (the Red Monastery) near Sohag, and the two monasteries of St Antony and St Paul at the Red Sea.

Coptic art is different from ancient Egyptian art and from both Greek and Roman art. In contrast to the imposing ancient Egyptian art and elegant productions of Egypt's Greek and Roman art, Coptic art lacks the grandeur of ancient Egyptian art and the elegance of Hellenic art with its beautiful proportions. However, even if it looks inferior in quality, it is a very impressive and individual art. This is not surprising for Coptic art has never enjoyed the patronage of rulers. The state treasury was not expended on that art in any period. It is perhaps best characterized as folk art. Evidently, Coptic art has been influenced in its beginnings by Greco-Roman art. Some mythological scenes and decorative elements, such as vine scrolls and interlaced patterns, derive from pagan art. Moreover, the iconography of many Christian themes goes back to early Christian and Byzantine traditions. But Byzantine styles and fashions were adapted with originality and individuality. One of the most striking features of "classical" Coptic art from the sixth to the eighth centuries is that the figures are depicted frontally. Sometimes the faces are shown in a three-quarter pose while the upper part of the body is depicted frontally and the lower part is represented from the side. The eyes are rounded or oval with large pupils. They are represented under relatively thick eyebrows. Garments are frequently depicted with details of the folds. Christianity and Egyptian monasticism have undoubtedly influenced Egypt's Christian art for many centuries. While Coptic art and architecture have influenced early Islamic art and architecture in Egypt (Figure 16.3), Coptic ornamentation began to assume an Islamic flavor by the tenth century.

Symbolism

Symbolism is a distinguishing characteristic of Coptic art. Coptic art utilized not only Christian symbols but also symbols from pagan cultures. The cross is undoubtedly the most significant symbol of Christianity. The cross supported by two victories (figures similar to angels) or angels is one of the central elements of Coptic art (Figure 16.4, 16.5). Also significant to Coptic symbols is the conch shell; it is associated with Aphrodite and thus symbolizes new birth. Christians appropriated the shell from Greco-Roman iconography and sometimes added to it the cross. The shell appears often as an architectural ornament in Coptic churches and on tombstones. Alpha and Omega are among the popular symbols in Coptic art that are widely used in the funerary stelae (upright slabs usually showing inscriptions and sculptures). The dolphin, a symbol of salvation, is also among the sea creatures that are often represented in Egypt's Christian art, especially on tombstones. The eagle, which appeared often in Roman times as an emblem of power and victory, became a popular motif in Coptic art. It was interpreted as a symbol of Christ. It decorates some of the chapels in the Monastery of St. Apollo at Bāwīṭ and many tombstones (Francia et al. 1991).

Subjects of Coptic Art

Coptic art is characterized by the richness of its themes. The majority represent religious scenes, especially the life of Christ. Old Testament scenes appear as early as the fourth century in the paintings of the Chapel of the Exodus in the Bagawat necropolis. Some of them represent Adam and Eve, Noah's Ark, the

Figure 16.3 Pulpit from the monastery of St. Jeremiah at Saqqara, limestone, H: 213 cm, sixth/seventh century, Coptic Museum, Inv. No. 7988. The design of pulpits found in mosques (minbars) is derived from Coptic pulpits

Figure 16.4 Two victories displaying a cross, limestone, H: 32 cm, W: 105.5 cm, late fourth/ early fifth century, Coptic Museum, Inv. No. 7030

Figure 16.5 Two superimposed foliate friezes from the monastery of St. Apollo, limestone, the upper one dates approximately to the fifth century and the lower to the seventh century, Coptic Museum, Inv. No. 7121

Sacrifice of Abraham, the Exodus, the Three Hebrews in the Fiery Furnace, Daniel in the Lions' Den, and Jonah and the Whale. The story of Joseph, son of Jacob is illustrated in around fifty Coptic textiles (for Old Testament scenes in Coptic art, see Loon 1999). New Testament scenes are more common and they show episodes of the life cycle of Christ, such as the Nativity, Baptism, and the Entry into Jerusalem. Christ and the Virgin accompanied by angels and apostles, the four apocalyptic Creatures, and the Twenty-four Elders, are depicted in the churches of many monasteries (for New Testament scenes, see Kupelian 2010). Saints appear often in mural painting. However, Coptic art does not lack scenes taken from everyday life, such as dancing, fishing, and fowling in the marshes (Figure 16.6), hunting wild animals, and the grape harvest (Figure 16.7). The Nile played an extremely significant role in the life of the Egyptians. Both pagans and Christians celebrated the Nile's inundation. Some themes are taken from the Nilotic landscapes that were familiar throughout the Hellenistic Mediterranean world. Scenes featuring fish and aquatic plants are employed decoratively in various media, especially in wood carving. Some of the daily life scenes of Coptic art remind us of similar works in ancient Egyptian art (Figure 16.6).

Figure 16.6 Part of an archivolt decorated with a fishing scene, limestone, H: 48 cm, W: 33 cm, fifth century, Coptic Museum, Inv. No. 8002

Figure 16.7 A frieze fragment featuring a grape harvest scene, limestone, H: 22 cm, W: 66 cm, fourth/fifth century, Coptic Museum, Inv. No. 7961

Sculpture

Egypt is rich in the kinds of stone that were widely used in ancient Egypt and in both the Roman and Byzantine periods, such as granite, porphyry, basalt, sandstone, and limestone. Almost all the marble imported by Egypt in Late Antiquity was from Proconnesos near Constantinople. However, the vast majority of Coptic stone sculptures are executed in limestone. There are a huge number of stone sculptures whose provenance is not known, but an important part of Coptic architectural sculpture has been preserved in the monasteries of St. Shenoute and St. Pshai near Sohag as well as in the Monastery of St. Apollo at Bāwīṭ and the Monastery of St. Jeremiah at Saqqara. The early Christian sculpture in Egypt had been influenced by pagan sculpture. By the late fourth century, sculptors of Heracleopolis Magna (Ahnas in Middle Egypt) were executing architectural carvings based on Greek mythology for the decoration of elite tomb chapels and at the same time working for Christians, as exemplified by two broken pediments: One features the Greek musician Orpheus and his wife Eurydice (Figure 16.8), while the other shows two erotes (little nude boys) with triangular faces, stylized hair and disproportionate lower limbs holding a wreathed cross (Figure 16.4). It is clear that the Christians of Egypt followed pagan traditions in their sculpture (Török 2005: 208). The majority of Coptic stone sculptures are represented by column capitals, lintels, door jambs, consoles, friezes, and niche heads. Unfortunately, many of them have reached us separated from their archaeological context because of the lack of modern methods of documentation. Moreover, pieces taken from late Roman sepulchral buildings, presumably mausolea, were often reused and blended with other specially made carvings to decorate churches.

The architectural sculpture of the church of the Monastery of St. Shenoute is of great importance. A considerable amount of the limestone architectural

Figure 16.8 A broken pediment showing Orpheus and Eurydice, limestone, H: 58 cm, W: 132 cm, fourth century, Coptic Museum, Inv. No. 7004

sculpture was commissioned specially for the church about the middle to late fifth century. The church's sculptures comprise seventy-seven wall niches of at least four different variations. They comprise half-columns or pilasters, capitals, bases and gables, entablatures and cornices of high-quality workmanship (Hodak 2008). But many of the column capitals that were found in the church represent *spolia* (reused pieces). Thus the architectural sculpture of this imposing church is the result of several repairs and the insertion of foreign material into the original decoration.

The magnificent painted architectural decoration of the church of the Monastery of St. Pshai shows that a considerable part of the church architectural sculpture in Egypt was once painted. The church's sculpture, which dates most probably to around 525, is of great significance not only for Egypt's Christian art but also for Late Antique art. The attractive architectural decoration of the sanctuary is uniquely preserved. Its walls are adorned with two rows of niches embellished with columns, pilasters, and pediments. (For the art in the Monastery of St. Pshai, see Bolman 2008.)

The greater part of the beautiful sculptures of the Monastery of St. Jeremiah at Saqqara are displayed in the Coptic Museum, Cairo. Two sixth-century pieces bear witness to the splendid churches that once existed in Egypt. The first, a limestone column capital (Figure 16.9), features acanthus leaves in two

Figure 16.9 Column capital with acanthus foliage, limestone, H: 43 cm, sixth century, Coptic Museum, Inv. No. 7978

Figure 16.10 Relief depicting a Greek cross in the center flanked by branches of acanthus, limestone, H: 38 cm, W: 100 cm, sixth century, Coptic Museum, Inv. No. 8251

rows twisting as if they are shaken by the wind. The top is decorated with a cross in a wreath of foliage. The other piece reflects the evident tendency towards the floral decoration of the sculpture (Figure 16.10). Its relief represents a Greek cross in the center flanked by branches of acanthus that cover the remaining space of the plaque.

Various types of stone sculpture carving techniques are attested in Bāwīṭ, especially in frieze ornamentation. The great variety of techniques and styles in the Bāwīṭ sculptures is undoubtedly due to the reuse of architectural sculptures from different sources along with the mural sculptures that were commissioned for new buildings (Figure 16.5). A sixth-century column capital carved with stylized acanthus branches still bears its dark green coloring. The capital's base resembles a shallow platter carved with meander patterns, rosettes, and quatrefoils. The acanthus branches that spring from the base form groups. The lower group retains a natural appearance as the tips curl downwards (Figure 16.11). (For a representative choice of the Saqqara and Bāwīṭ sculptures with bibliography, see Gabra and Eaton-Krauss 2007: 63–93.)

Coptic carpenters skillfully used indigenous woods, such as acacia, sycamore, and tamarisk, as well as imported kinds such as ebony, pine, and liquidambar. Many ancient and medieval churches were once adorned with elaborate wooden sculpture. The Coptic Museum possesses treasures of wooden sculptures; among them three pieces are of special importance (Gabra and Eaton-Krauss 2007: 194–95, 206–10, 215–17). The first is a fifth-century small elegant altar executed in pine wood (Figure 16.12). It originates from the church of St. Sergius and Bacchus in Old Cairo. The altar's design imitates an arcade supported by torsaded columns with modified Corinthian capitals, surmounted by panels showing a shell with a centered cross. The second piece, which originates from al-Mo'allaqa, "the Hanging Church," is a magnificent large lintel of sycamore wood carved in raised relief featuring the Entry into Jerusalem and the Ascension (Figures 16.13a, 16.13b). A part of its Greek inscription, a hymn

Figure 16.11 Column capital decorated with acanthus leaves, limestone, H: 65 cm, sixth century, Coptic Museum, Inv. No. 7179

Figure 16.12 Altar, pine, H: 100 cm, W: 120 cm, D: 75 cm, fifth century, Coptic Museum, Inv. No. 1172

Figure 16.13a Lintel showing the Entry into Jerusalem and the Ascension, sycamore, H: 36, L: 274 cm, AD 735, Coptic Museum, Inv. No. 753

Figure 16.13b Detail of Figure 16.13a: Entry into Jerusalem

to Christ, reads: "Holy, Holy, Holy are you, O Lord: heaven and earth are full of your holy glory, because they are full of your greatness." The date mentioned in the Greek text is not complete and should be Pachon 12, indiction 3, year of Diocletian 451 (May 7, AD 735). The masterfully carved sculpture of the lintel shows that Hellenism continued in Egypt long after the Arab conquest of Egypt in 641. The third piece is a double-leaved door of sycamore and pine wood. It was discovered during restoration work in the earlier twentieth century in the church of St. Barbara at Old Cairo (Figures 16.14a, 16.14b). It is the most significant of the few existing doors from the Roman and Byzantine periods in Egypt. Its upper panels feature the bust of Christ within a ribboned wreath carried by two angels and flanked by two men, probably Evangelists. Christ, St. Mark, Christ in a mandorla, the Virgin Mary and the twelve apostles appear on other panels. The panels on the back of the door are executed in higher relief with vine scrolls, which show an unmistakable stylistic connection to the early sixth-century court art of Constantinople (Figure 16.14c).

The church of the Holy Virgin Mary in the Monastery of the Syrians at Wādī al-Naṭrūn (Scetis) boasts tenth-century wooden doors. The decoration of

Figure 16.14a Door with two leaves, sycamore and pine, sixth century

Figure 16.14b

Figure 16.14c Detail of Figure 16.14b

their ivory inlays combines elaborate geometric design with the figures of Christ and the Virgin Mary accompanied by saints. The decorative stucco-work in the sanctuary of this church and in the chapel of the Forty Martyrs at the same monastery also dates to the tenth century. It reflects the influence of the Islamic stucco style from Iran and Mesopotamia that appears in the mosque of Ahmed Ibn Tulun in Cairo (Immerzeel 2009: 254–56). Unlike stone sculptures, wooden sculptures continued to decorate churches in medieval times as well as in modern times. A wooden sanctuary screen of the church of St. Barbara, now displayed in the Coptic Museum, and another in one of the chapels of Persian St. James, known as Ya'qub al-Muqatta', at the church of St. Mercurius (Abū Sayfayn) in Old Cairo, feature panels that are elaborately carved in fine relief showing human figures, riders on galloping horses, animals and birds within foliage ornament. They date from the Fatimid period (tenth–twelfth century) and bear witness to interaction between the Coptic and Islamic art of that time. Many churches of later periods, especially those of the monasteries of Wādī al-Naṭrūn and Old Cairo, preserve splendid wooden sanctuary screens carved in segments showing fine geometric designs and crosses. Some of the wooden carvings manifest the insistence of artists and craftsmen on creating Eastern Christian art, which has been influenced by Byzantine art (Gabra and Loon 2007: 114–15). However, the influence of Islamic decorative designs is also unmistakable despite the crosses and the Christian images.

Wall Paintings

Most of the Coptic wall paintings belong to monasteries (Loon in Gabra and Loon 2007: 30–37; Bolman 2002, 2007, 2008; Innemée 2001; Innemée and Rompay 2002; Zibawi 2003). Wonderful monastic paintings come from monasteries that were abandoned in the ninth, tenth, and eleventh centuries. They were discovered in Kellia, Saqqara, and Bāwīṭ. The discovery of significant monastic paintings during a number of restoration campaigns beginning in the 1980s greatly increased our knowledge of Coptic painting. The technique used for the vast majority of Coptic paintings is tempera; encaustic (hot wax) was rarely used. A considerable number of the paintings were found in oratories (prayer cells). The murals were applied on mud brick walls that had been plastered and whitewashed. Unfortunately, many of the mural paintings, which were discovered before the application of modern preservation technology, were lost as they crumbled and became like sand. The walls of churches usually consist of two levels: the lower part is painted with floral and geometric designs that sometimes imitate painted stones. The upper part of the nave is occupied by figurative scenes: Virgin and Child, angels, saints, martyrs, including equestrian saints, monks, especially those who founded monasteries, as well as scenes from the Old and New Testaments.

The murals of the Kellia hermitages represent a valuable contribution to the Coptic paintings for the period from the fifth to the eighth century. The earliest paintings of the fifth century show simple crosses. Beginning in the sixth century, many of the eastern walls of the oratories feature beautiful paintings, often imitating architectural sculptures, that depict fluted columns with modified capitals or a shell-shaped apse. Crosses are depicted in many locations in the Kellia hermitages, but the cross is the essential element of the eastern walls of the oratories, and it is drawn with a special care and embellishment. Christ, the apostles, saints, and monks also appear in the Kellia wall paintings. Boats, animals, such as gazelles, horses, sheep, lions, crocodiles and hippopotami, and birds, such as parrots, partridges, peacocks and doves, are depicted with attractive spontaneity.

The murals of the Monastery of St. Apollo at Bāwīṭ represent a most important source for the history of Coptic art. In the early twentieth century a large number of paintings were discovered. The surviving murals, together with those known only from photographs and watercolors made at the time of discovery, represent indispensable material for the study of Coptic wall paintings. More excavations were carried out at the site in 1976 by the Egyptian Antiquities Organization, and since 2003, by the Louvre Museum and the French Archaeological Institute in Cairo. Modern methods of topographical survey, excavation, and documentation enhance our knowledge of Bāwīṭ. Scenes depicting the Virgin Mary and the life of Christ including the Annunciation, Visitation, Nativity, the Massacre of the Innocents, the Baptism, and some of Christ's miracles are very common in Bāwīṭ. The oratory niches include great variety, though most of them show Christ in Majesty and

Figure 16.15 A prayer niche featuring Christ in Majesty and the Virgin holding the infant Christ flanked by apostles and two local saints, tempera, H: 220 cm, W: 170 cm, sixth/seventh century, Coptic Museum, Inv. No. 7118

the Virgin with the Christ child, often depicted together in the two-zone composition. Christ in Majesty is depicted seated on a throne within a mandorla surrounded by the four incorporeal beings (the eagle, ox, lion, and a man) and carried by flaming chariot wheels (Figure 16.15) inspired by the apocalyptic visions of Ezekiel, Isaiah, and the book of Revelation (Ezekiel 1, Isaiah 6, Revelation 4). Old Testament scenes, such as the Three Hebrews in the Furnace, also appear at Bāwīṭ. A hunting scene (Figure 16.16), in which a lion is depicted with stylized oversized paws and his head already pierced with an arrow, may allude to the Biblical story of David and Goliath (I Samuel 17: 37). It is interesting to note that episodes of David's life (I Samuel 17) have survived in Coptic art only at Bāwīṭ. A unique painting depicts three mice suing for peace in front of a fat cat. One of them carries a banner, another holds a scroll, while the third mouse has a vial in one paw and a funnel in the other (Figure 16.17). Satirical scenes have a long history in ancient Egypt.

Unlike the Monastery of St Apollo at Bāwīṭ, little remains of the murals of the Monastery of St. Jeremiah at Saqqara. The greater part of the wall paintings came from the east side niches of the prayer cells. They represent the customary depiction of the enthroned Christ, either alone or above the Virgin

Figure 16.16 A hunting scene (watercolor). *Le monastère et la nécropole de Baouit*, MIFAO 12: 1. Cairo, 1904, pl. 37

Figure 16.17 A satirical scene of mice suing for peace, tempera, H: 45.3 cm, W: 80 cm, seventh/eighth century, Coptic Museum, Inv. No. 8441

Mary flanked by archangels and sometimes by St. Jeremiah and Enoch as well. A significant fragmentary wall painting of the Sacrifice of Abraham, which was depicted on the north wall of the refectory, has been preserved. One of the most interesting scenes representing monastic saints is that of the four saints and a supplicant. It shows the famous monks Macarius, Apollo, and Pamun in addition to the anchorite Onuphrius with his extraordinary long hair and beard (Figure 16.18). The vast majority of the wall paintings of Bāwīṭ and Saqqara have disappeared. Most of the murals that have been saved can be seen in the Coptic Museum in Cairo and the Louvre Museum. No firm chronology has been established for these wall paintings. The reason lies mainly in the absence

Figure 16.18 Saints and a supplicant, tempera, H: 110 cm, W: 145 cm, sixth/seventh century, Coptic Museum, Inv. No. 7951

of modern methods of archaeological investigation during the early clearances. However, the vast majority of the murals of Bāwīṭ and Saqqara are generally dated from the sixth to the eighth century.

Numerous campaigns using modern techniques of conservation led to the discovery of invaluable paintings in several monastic churches belonging to the Monastery of the Syrians in Wādī al-Naṭrūn, the Monastery of St. Pshai near Sohag, and the Monastery of St. Antony at the Red Sea. One of the most interesting discoveries in the church of the Holy Virgin Mary in the Monastery of the Syrians is an eighth-century Annunciation scene painted on the half-dome of the western apse showing the Virgin Mary and the Archangel Gabriel accompanied by four prophets, Moses, Isaiah, Ezekiel, and Daniel, who carry the text of their prophecies, written in Coptic, on an opened scroll (Figure 16.19). A unique eighth-century scene of the Virgin enthroned with Child flanked by Magi and shepherds occupies the northern half-dome of the *Khurus* (a transverse space in front of the sanctuary). One of the scenes on the eastern wall of the *Khurus* shows the Dormition. The Virgin lies on a bed surrounded by six virgins, three on each side, swinging censers. This tenth-century scene is unique in the world's Orthodox churches (Figure 16.20). The three half-domes of the sanctuary of the church of the Monastery of St. Pshai had been painted four times within a relatively short period of time of perhaps one century. The fourth layer dates to the late seventh or the eighth century. The

Figure 16.19 Annunciation, eighth century, Monastery of the Syrians, Wādī al-Naṭrūn. Courtesy of Karel Innemée

Figure 16.20 The Holy Virgin surrounded by six virgins swinging censers, tenth century, Monastery of the Syrians, Wādī al-Naṭrūn. Courtesy of Karel Innemée

eastern semi-dome features the customary scene of the enthroned Christ on the chariot of fire surrounded by the four apocalyptic creatures. A fantastic scene of the Virgin nursing the Child Christ flanked by four Old Testament prophets, angels, Joseph and Salome, and the midwife, occupies the northern half-dome (Gabra and Loon 2007: 282–83). The facing southern half-dome is decorated with the enthroned Christ flanked by the four Evangelists. Thus, both Old Testament prophets and New Testament Evangelists are represented in the sanctuary. Significant patriarchs of the Coptic Church, such as Athanasius, Cyril, and Theophilus, are beautifully illustrated in this church. It is to be noted that the encaustic technique has been used in the wall paintings of the Monastery of St. Pshai and some of the murals of the Monastery of the Syrians.

The wall paintings of the church of the Monastery of the Archangel Gabriel in Fayyūm feature Christ and the apostles, the enthroned Virgin flanked by the Archangels Michael and Gabriel, and equestrian saints, as well as other saints. The Coptic foundation text accompanying the paintings shows that the church was renovated during the patriarchate of Zacharias (1004–32) and thus its decoration belongs to the rare number of precisely dated Coptic paintings. During the twelfth and the thirteenth centuries huge Coptic wall paintings were executed in the monasteries of Wādī al-Naṭrūn and the monasteries of St. Antony and St. Paul, and in some churches of Old Cairo. The old church of the Monastery of St. Antony boasts the most complete program of wall paintings that has been preserved in Egypt. The Coptic inscriptions demonstrate that the painter Theodore worked there in 1332/33. The church's murals represent the last important, sizable artistic achievements of the Copts before the waves of persecution under Mamluk rule (1250–1517). The distribution of the scenes reflects the function of each of the parts of the church; for example, scenes from the Old Testament, such as Abraham's sacrifice and his meeting with Melchizedek, the sacrifice of Jephthah, and the Seraph cleansing Isaiah's lips with a glowing coal, decorate the sanctuary because of their reference to the Eucharist. Above these scenes the Twenty-Four Priests are represented, and on the dome of the sanctuary Christ Pantocrator surrounded by alternating angels and cherubim is depicted. The main apse is decorated with the usual two-zoned composition of Christ in Majesty above and Virgin and Child below. Thus, the Coptic liturgy influenced church decoration. While the walls of the western part of the nave, presumably where visitors were allowed to pray, are dedicated to equestrian saints and other martyrs, the walls of the eastern nave are decorated with portraits of Virgin and Child and of famous monks. The art of wall painting ceased for a few centuries. It appeared again in the eighteenth century in the Monastery of St. Paul. At the same time icon painting flourished and continued all over Egypt and, beginning in the 1960s, in the Diaspora.

Icons

Icons are considered among the most important decorations of Coptic monasteries and churches. Coptic icons are made of panels of wood painted mostly in tempera. In a relatively few icons encaustic was also used. The panels may be covered with a layer of gesso. Most of the Coptic icons that have come down to us date from the eighteenth and nineteenth centuries. In the late 1980s and through the 1990s important medieval icons of the thirteenth and fourteenth centuries were professionally conserved in a number of churches, especially in Old Cairo, as well as in the Coptic Museum (Skalova and Gabra 2003). In the 1950s Isaac Fanous founded the School of Contemporary Coptic Art, which provided the churches in Egypt and in the immigrant lands with icons. The majority of scholars agree that pagan mummy portraits, which date from the first to the fourth century and are collectively known as the Fayyūm portraits, represent the forerunners of the Coptic icons (Rutschowscaya 2005).

The oldest Christian portraits are of saints. They were discovered in Antinoë and could be dated to the fifth or sixth century. A unique double-sided icon of St. Theodore the General and the Archangel Gabriel, which was found in the Monastery of St. Apollo in Bāwīṭ, dates from the sixth century (Skalova and Gabra 2003: 165, 168–67). Bishop John of Ephesus (c. 516–85) informs us that portraits of new bishops were hung in their churches. Unfortunately, only one such portrait of a Coptic bishop survives. This icon depicts Bishop Abraham and belongs to the very few Coptic icons that belong to the period from the late sixth to the eighth century in Egypt (Fluck 2008). A second famous icon that could be dated from the same period represents Christ the Savior and St. Menas standing together, while the right hand of Christ rests on the shoulder of the saint (Rutschowscaya 1991: 250–51). The figures in these icons are represented frontally, the eyes are wide, and the outlines are clear.

There is no convincing justification for the absence of icons in Egypt from the ninth to the twelfth century. Coptic icons were not affected by iconoclasm (the destruction of icons), a movement that was initiated by Emperor Leo III (717–41), who issued the first edict against the use of images in 726. While Christian art greatly suffered within the Byzantine Empire from 731 to 843, Coptic icons suffered the many waves of persecutions in medieval times when Muslim mobs attacked the churches and plundered them. Medieval icons of the thirteen and fourteenth centuries show the influence of painters of several other Middle Eastern Christian communities such as Syrians and Armenians. Coptic patrons entrusted them to decorate their churches with icons according to Coptic theological concepts (Figure 16.21) (Skalova and Gabra 2003: 180–81). Although local wood was used for the panels, and the icons were inscribed in Coptic or Greek and Arabic, icons from that period betray a Byzantine influence. A number of sixteenth- and seventeenth-century icons are preserved in churches of Old Cairo as well as in the Coptic Museum (ibid. 132–33, 220–27). By the second half of the seventeenth century there began a movement for the protection and restoration of the Coptic heritage. Influential Coptic laymen or archons, "*Arakhinah*," were instrumental in that movement (Guirgis 2008: 39–60). Icon painting flourished in the eighteenth and nineteenth centuries (Figure 16.22). Famous icon painters of that period enriched the Coptic churches

Figure 16.21 Part of an icon showing the patriarchs Peter Last Martyr (right), Athanasius the Great (middle) and Cyril of Alexandria (left), thirteenth century, Church of St. Mercurius, Old Cairo. Courtesy of the Church of St. Mercurius in Old Cairo

Figure 16.22 Icon featuring the visit of St. Antony to St. Paul of Thebes, painted wood, H: 55 cm, W: 56.5 cm, AD 1777, Coptic Museum, Inv. No. 8418

with hundreds of icons. Known by name are Ibrahim al-Nāsikh, Yuḥanna al-Armanī (the Armenian), and Anasṭāsī al-Rumī (the Greek) (Moorsel et al. 1994: 16–18, 52–53).

The vast majority of icons feature portraits of Christ, the Holy Virgin Mary, apostles and saints, while narrative icons depicting events in their lives are less frequent. Many Coptic churches dedicate shrines to icons, where candles are lit beside them. Two significant icons flank the Royal Door, or the door of the principal sanctuary, to the right an icon of Christ, to the left an icon of the Virgin Mary with the Infant Christ. Icons of the twelve apostles, which usually flank the scene of the Last Supper, surmount the wooden sanctuary screen. Some icons have been famous for their miracles. Icons are usually consecrated by a bishop by anointing with Holy Chrism (holy oil). Icons are carried in processions during pilgrimages and on festival days such as the feasts of Easter, Ascension, and Pentecost. The most celebrated feasts are those which occur at sites associated with the Holy Virgin Mary, where thousands of Copts venerate an icon of the Virgin by singing songs of praise.

The School of Contemporary Coptic Art, or Neo-Coptic Art, was founded by Isaac Fanous, who established the Art section of the Coptic Patriarchate's Higher Institute of Coptic Studies in 1956. His school attempts to provide a conscious fusion of ancient Egyptian and Coptic conventions with contemporary ideas. Fanous and his pupils have left a great artistic legacy in many of the Coptic churches in Egypt, and in most of the churches which the Coptic emigrants established in the United States, Canada, Australia, and Europe. The most common conventions of this school are the significance of the full-face, the use of outlines to depict the figures, and the non-realistic proportions of the facial features. Light radiates from Christ, the Holy Virgin Mary and the saints who appear in harmony with the other elements of the scene and the background (Figure 16.23). One of the most popular scenes, especially in the immigrant lands, is the Flight of the Holy Family into Egypt. The landscapes of Egypt, such as the River Nile and the pyramids or obelisks, remind the Copts in the Diaspora of their mother land (Figure 16.24) (Sadek and Sadek 2000).

Textiles

Textiles are a distinctive, characteristic product of Coptic art. The term "Coptic textiles" is used to designate a huge number of textiles found in Egypt dating from the Roman and Byzantine periods as well as from the first few centuries of Islamic rule (Bourguet 1991c; Rutschowscaya 1991; Wipszycka 1991; Schrenk 1998; Gabra and Eaton-Krauss 2007: 169–77). Thanks to Egypt's dry soil, a great amount of textiles have been preserved. The great majority have been found in Coptic burials; some estimates suggest a number of 100,000 pieces and fragments. However, only shrouds for the corpse were specifically made for funerary purposes. The vast majority of pieces represent articles from

Figure 16.23 Nativity, H: 220 cm, W: 350 cm, Church of the Holy Virgin Mary, Los Angeles. Courtesy of the Church of the Holy Virgin Mary, Los Angeles

daily life such as tunics, wall hangings, pillows, and towels. Thus, textiles are not merely beautifully colored and attractive objects but also an invaluable source of information about social classes, everyday life, practices and beliefs. The nineteenth- and early twentieth-century excavations in Antinoë and Akhmim were not carried out as systematic scientific undertakings. Moreover, thousands of textile pieces were brought to the antiquities market without information about the circumstances of their discovery. But the past three decades have witnessed carefully recorded excavations at many important sites including the Fayyūm, Antinoë, the oasis of Kharga, and Dakhla. The use of modern methods of excavation and dye radiocarbon analyses have greatly increased our knowledge about textiles in Egypt.

Linen and wool were the principal fibers used for manufacturing textiles. Weavers employed linen for the warp (threads running lengthwise). Wool was used to execute the colored designs in the weft (threads running crosswise). Silk, mostly imported, was known in Egypt as early as the fourth century. Cotton was occasionally used, but it was first cultivated after the Arab conquest. Dyes were developed from plant, animal, and mineral sources. Weavers excelled in a variety of techniques. The most famous textiles were the tapestry-woven bands, known as *clavi*, roundles (*orbiculae*), and rectangular pieces (*tabulae*), that decorated garments, especially tunics, and wall hangings. The "flying shuttle" was used independently of the warp and weft to add threads creating fine details. The loop-pile technique was also used to create

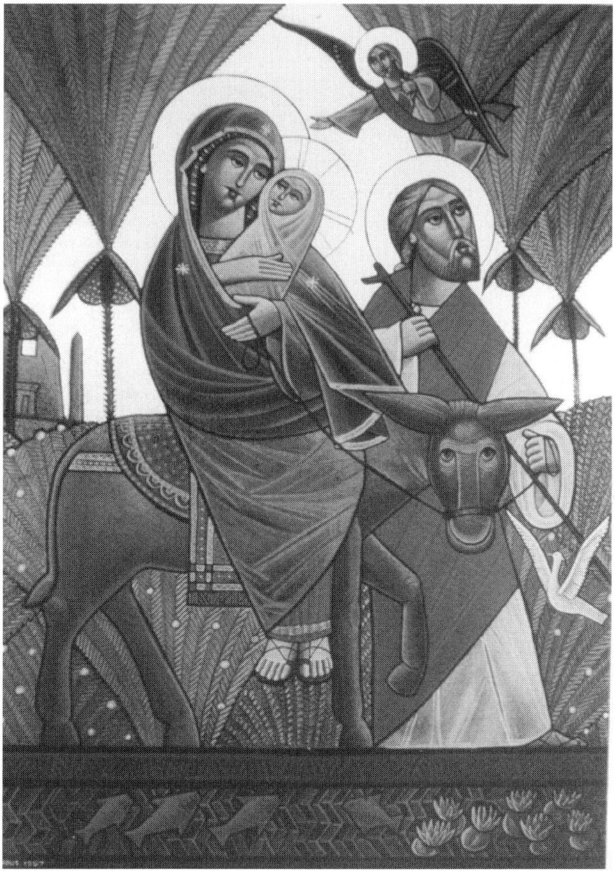

Figure 16.24 The Flight into Egypt, H: 120 cm, W: 80 cm, Church of Saints Peter and Paul, Santa Monica, California. Courtesy of the Church of Saints Peter and Paul, Santa Monica, California

decorative effect. Written sources indicate that textiles were manufactured throughout Egypt (Wipszycka 1991). Important centers were in Antinoë, Akhmim, the Fayyūm, and Oxyrhynchos (al-Bahnasā). Copts continued to produce the beautifully-colored textiles that were exported to the whole Islamic world.

Among the most famous textile pieces of the Coptic Museum is a fourth- or fifth-century linen and wool tapestry hanging that shows a well-proportioned dark skinned piper wearing a red kilt with black dots and a green garment with yellow dots over his left shoulder (Figure 16.25). Warriors and dancers, riders and roses occupy the decorative border that runs down to the left of the piper. The weaver used a flying shuttle to execute the details of the figures and the outlines in general. The hanging is an excellent example of the high quality of workmanship of Coptic textiles. Another treasure of the same museum is a fifth- or sixth-century multicolored tapestry (Figure 16.26)

Figure 16.25 Tapestry hanging with a piper, H: 142 cm, W: 103 cm, fourth/fifth century, Coptic Museum, Inv. No. 7948

that features a series of torsaded columns supporting three arches. Beneath the two lateral arches is a red looped cross decorated with yellow and green squares imitating metal encrusted with cabochons (polished gemstones). The loop of crosses encloses a christogram (a symbol combining the first two letters of the Greek word for Christ). A significant symbol must have been represented in the middle arch as the peacocks and doves, which perch above the arches, look towards it. The Christian motif of the tapestry suggests that it belonged to a church or a monastery (Gabra and Eaton-Krauss 2007: 46, 174–75).

Objects From Daily Life

Many beautiful objects from daily life are represented in several media, such as pottery, wood, and metals. The following three pieces from the Coptic

Figure 16.26 Tapestry featuring looped crosses and birds, H: 76 cm, W: 136 cm, fifth/sixth century, Coptic Museum, Inv. No. 2023

Museum show that craftsmen were skilled in decorative techniques using different materials. A seventh-century storage pottery jar from the Monastery of St. Jeremiah at Saqqara is decorated with floral motifs and a fish (Figure 16.27). The fish is sketched with lines in black and with red filling. Animals, birds, and fish are the common motifs of Coptic pottery decoration. The second piece, a fine sixth- or seventh-century panel with extraordinary, vivid relief (Figure 16.28), once decorated the front of a wooden box made of panels held together with wooden pegs. It depicts a lion hunting an antelope while an elegant plant fills the empty spaces within the frame. Although the lion's mane and the legs of the two animals are stylized, the scene is extremely attractive and does not lack harmony. The handle of a sixth- or seventh-century bronze lamp features a cross set in a crescent (Figure 16.29). The base of its fantastic stand is composed of three graceful unicorns, the tails of which undulate down. Their forelegs support a trefoil of three stylized leaves. Metal lamps with baluster-shaped stands are among the common types in Egypt. Many of them are elaborately executed (Gabra and Eaton-Krauss 2007: 144, 152–53, 160–61).

Comparatively little Coptic art has survived because many Coptic churches and monasteries were demolished and the majority suffered many waves of destruction in medieval times, especially in the Mamluk period (1250–1517). It suffices to mention that on one day in 1321 fanatic Muslims sacked and burned over sixty of the main churches and monasteries throughout Egypt (Megally 1991). Indeed, many of the Copts' beautiful and original murals, woodwork pieces, icons, and valuable liturgical objects were destroyed or plundered by mobs under Muslim rulers. Nevertheless, what remains of their artistic heritage is beyond estimation.

Figure 16.27 Storage jar, pottery, H: 78 cm, D of rim: 26.6 cm, D of base: 18.8 cm, seventh century, Coptic Museum, Inv. No. 9065

Figure 16.28 Lion hunting an antelope, wood, H: 35.2 cm, W: 26.3 cm, sixth/seventh century, Coptic Museum, Inv. No. 10519

Figure 16.29 Bronze lamp with a cross set in a crescent, H of stand: 36.5, H of Lamp: 14.5 cm, L of lamp: 18.4 cm, sixth/seventh century, Coptic Museum, Inv. No. 5185

Note

1 I would like to thank Dr. Zahi Hawass for his kind permission to use the images of the pieces from the Coptic Museum, and Dr. Karel Innemée for providing the images from the monastery of the Syrians in Wādī al-Naṭrūn.

Selected Bibliography

Badawy, A. (1978) *Coptic Art and Archaeology. The Arts of the Christian Egyptians from the Late Antique to the Middle Ages*, Cambridge, MA: MIT Press.

Bolman, E. (ed.) (2002) *Monastic Visions: Wall Paintings in the Monastery of St. Antony at the Red Sea*, New Haven, CN: Yale University Press.

——(2007) "Depicting the Kingdom of Heaven: Painting and Monastic Practice in Early Byzantine Egypt", in R. S. Bagnall (ed.) *Egypt in the Byzantine World, 300–700*, Cambridge: Cambridge University Press.

——(2008) "The Red Monastery Conservation Project, 2006 and 2007 Campaigns: Contributing to the Corpus of Late Antique Art," in G. Gabra and H. Takla (eds) *Christianity and Monasticism in Upper Egypt: Volume I: Akhmim and Sohag*, Cairo and New York: American University in Cairo Press.

Bourguet, P. du (1991a) "Art and Architecture, Coptic," in A. S. Atiya (ed.) *The Coptic Encyclopedia*, New York: Macmillan.

——(1991b) "Art Survival from Ancient Egypt," in A. S. Atiya (ed.) *The Coptic Encyclopedia*, New York: Macmillan.

——(1991c) "Textiles, Coptic: Iconography of Woven Textiles; Iconography of Resist-Dyed Textiles," in A. S. Atiya (ed.) *The Coptic Encyclopedia*, New York: Macmillan.

Fluck, C. (2008) "The Portrait of Apa Abraham of Hermonthis," in G. Gabra and H. Takla (eds) *Christianity and Monasticism in Upper Egypt: Volume I: Akhmim and Sohag*, Cairo and New York: American University in Cairo Press.

Francia, L. del, Bourguet, P. du, Bénazeth, D., Luccehsi-Palli, E. and Kiss, Z. (1991) "Symbols in Coptic Art," in A. S. Atiya (ed.) *The Coptic Encyclopedia*, New York: Macmillan.

Gabra, G. (with T. Vivian) (2002) *Coptic Monasteries: Egypt's Monastic Art and Architecture*, Cairo: American University in Cairo Press.

Gabra, G. and Eaton-Krauss, M. (2007) *The Treasures of Coptic Art in the Coptic Museum and Churches of Old Cairo*, Cairo: American University in Cairo Press.

Gabra, G. and Loon, G. M. J. van (with D. L. Brooks Hedstrom) (2007) *The Churches of Egypt*, Cairo: American University in Cairo Press.

Guirgis, M. (2008) *An Armenian Artist in Ottoman Egypt. Yuhanna al-Armani and His Coptic Icons*, Cairo: American University Press.

Hodak, S. (2008) "Snapshots on the Sculptural Heritage of the White Monastery at Sohag: The Wall Niches," in G. Gabra and H. Takla (eds) *Christianity and Monasticism in Upper Egypt: Volume I: Akhmim and Sohag*, Cairo and New York: American University in Cairo Press.

Hunt, L. A. (1998) *Byzantium, Eastern Christendom and Islam: Art at the Crossroads of the Medieval Mediterranean*, 2 vols, London: Pindar.

Immerzeel, M. (1997) "Coptic Art," in N. van Doorn-Harder and K. Vogt (eds) *Between Desert and City: The Coptic Orthodox Church Today*, Oslo: The Institute for Comparative Research in Human Culture, Novus forlag.

——(2009) "A Play of Light and Shadow: The Stuccoes of Dayr al-Suryan and their Historical Context," in M. S. A. Mikhail and M. Moussa (eds) *Christianity and Monasticism in Wadi al-Natrun*, Cairo: American University in Cairo Press.

Innemée, K. C. (2001) "Deir al-Surian (Egypt): Conservation work of Autumn 2000," *Hugoye: Journal of Syriac Studies* 4. Online. http://syrcom.cua.edu/hugoye, accessed December 21, 2012.

——(2011) "A newly discovered painting of the Epiphany in Deir al-Surian," *Hugoye, Journal of Syriac Studies* 14 Online. http://syrcom.cua.edu/hugoye, accessed December 21, 2012.

Innemée, K. C. and Rompay, L. Van (2002) "Deir al-Surian (Egypt): New Discoveries of 2001–2," *Hugoye: Journal of Syriac Studies* 5. Online. http://syrcom.cua.edu/hugoye, accessed December 21, 2012.

Kupelian, M. M. (2010) "A Comparative Study of the New Testament Scenes in Coptic Monastic Churches," unpublished dissertation, Cairo: Helwan University.

Loon, G. J. M. van (1999) *The Gate of Heaven: Wall Paintings with Old Testament Scenes in the Altar Room and the Hurus of Coptic Churches*, Uitgaven van het Nederlands Historisch-Archaologisch Instituut te Istanbul 85, Leiden: Nederlands Instituur voor het Nabije Oosten.

Louvre (n.d.) *Nouvelles fouilles sur le site copte de Baouit*, Online. http://www.louvre.fr/media/repository/ressources/sources/pdf/src_document_51210_v2_m56577569831215283.pdf, accessed December 21, 2012.

Lyster, W. (ed.) (2008) *The Cave Church of Paul the Hermit at the Monastery of St. Paul in the Eastern Desert of Egypt*, New Haven,CN: Yale University Press.

Megally, M. (1991) "Waq'at al-Kana'is," in A. S. Atiya (ed.) *The Coptic Encyclopedia*, New York: Macmillan.

Moorsel, P. van, Immerzeel, M. and Langen, L. with the collaboration of A. Serafeem (1994) *The Icons: Catalogue général du Musée Copte*, Cairo: Supreme Council of Antiquities Press.

Rutschowscaya, M.-H. (1991) "Textiles, Coptic: Types of Fiber; Manufacturing Techniques," in A. S. Atiya (ed.) *The Coptic Encyclopedia*, New York: Macmillan.

——(2005) "Fayoum Portraits and Their Influence on the First Coptic Icons," in G. Gabra (ed.) *Christianity and Monasticism in the Fayoum Oasis. Essays from the 2004 International Symposium of the Saint Mark Foundation and the Saint Shenouda the Archimandrite Coptic Society in Honor of Martin Krause*, Cairo and New York: American University in Cairo Press.

Sadek, A. and Sadek, B. (2000) *L'incarnation de la lumière. Le renouveau iconographique copte à travers l'œuvre de Isaac Fanous*, Le Monde Copte 29–31, Limoges: Le Monde Copte.

Schrenk, S. (1998) "Spätrömisch-frühislamische Textilien aus Ägypten," in M. Krause (ed.) *Ägypten in spätantik-christlicher Zeit. Einführung in die koptische Kultur*, Wiesbaden: Reichert Verlag.

Skalova, Z. and Gabra, G. (2003) *Icons of the Nile Valley*, Cairo: Longman.

Thomas, T. K. (2000) *Late Antique Egyptian Funerary Sculpture: Images for This World and the Next*, Princeton, NJ: Princeton University Press.

Török, L. (2005) *Transfigurations of Hellenism. Aspects of Late Antique Art in Egypt AD 250–700*, Probleme der Ägyptologie 23, Leiden and Boston: Brill.

Wipszycka, E. (1991) "Textiles, Coptic: Organization of Production," in A. S. Atiya (ed.) *The Coptic Encyclopedia*, New York: Macmillan.

Zibawi, M. (2003) *Images de l'Égypte chrétienne. Iconologie copte*, Paris: Picard.

Index